Mediating the Uprising

The Politics of Marriage and Gender:
Global Issues in Local Contexts

Series Editor: Péter Berta

The Politics of Marriage and Gender: Global Issues in Local Contexts series from Rutgers University Press fills a gap in research by examining the politics of marriage and related practices, ideologies, and interpretations, and addresses the key question of how the politics of marriage has affected social, cultural, and political processes, relations, and boundaries. The series looks at the complex relationships between the politics of marriage and gender, ethnic, national, religious, racial, and class identities, and analyzes how these relationships contribute to the development and management of social and political differences, inequalities, and conflicts.

Joanne Payton, *Honor and the Political Economy of Marriage: Violence against Women in the Kurdistan Region of Iraq*

Rama Srinivasan, *Courting Desire: Litigating for Love in North India*

Hui Liu, Corinne Reczek, and Lindsey Wilkinson, eds., *Marriage and Health: The Well-Being of Same-Sex Couples*

Sara Smith, *Intimate Geopolitics: Love, Territory, and the Future on India's Northern Threshold*

Rebecca Joubin, *Mediating the Uprising: Narratives of Gender and Marriage in Syrian Television Drama*

Mediating the Uprising

Narratives of Gender and Marriage in Syrian Television Drama

REBECCA JOUBIN

RUTGERS UNIVERSITY PRESS

NEW BRUNSWICK, CAMDEN, AND NEWARK, NEW JERSEY, AND LONDON

LCCN: 2019030611

A British Cataloging-in-Publication record for this book is
available from the British Library.

Copyright © 2020 by Rebecca Joubin

♾ The paper used in this publication meets the requirements of the American
National Standard for Information Sciences—Permanence of Paper for
Printed Library Materials, ANSI Z39.48-1992.

www.rutgersuniversitypress.org

Manufactured in the United States of America

For my daughter, Jana

CONTENTS

SERIES FOREWORD

The politics of marriage (and divorce) is an often-used strategic tool in various social, cultural, economic, and political identity projects as well as in symbolic conflicts between ethnic, national, or religious communities. Despite having multiple strategic applicabilities, pervasiveness in everyday life, and huge significance in performing and managing identities, the politics of marriage is surprisingly underrepresented both in the international book publishing market and in the social sciences.

The Politics of Marriage and Gender: Global Issues in Local Contexts is a series from Rutgers University Press examining the politics of marriage as a phenomenon embedded in and intensely interacting with much broader social, cultural, economic, and political processes and practices such as globalization; transnationalization; international migration; human trafficking; vertical social mobility; the creation of symbolic boundaries between ethnic populations, nations, religious denominations, or classes; family formation; and struggles for women's and children's rights. The series primarily aims to analyze practices, ideologies, and interpretations related to the politics of marriage and to outline the dynamics and diversity of relatedness—interplay and interdependence, for instance—between the politics of marriage and the broader processes and practices mentioned above. In other words, most books in the series devote special attention to how the politics of marriage and these processes and practices mutually shape and explain each other.

The series concentrates on, among other things, the complex relationships between the politics of marriage and gender, ethnic, national, religious, racial, and class identities globally, and examines how these relationships contribute to the development and management of social, cultural, and political differences, inequalities, and conflicts.

The series seeks to publish single-authored books and edited volumes that develop a gap-filling and thought-provoking critical perspective, that are well-balanced between a high degree of theoretical sophistication and empirical richness, and that cross or rethink disciplinary, methodological, or theoretical boundaries. The thematic scope of the series is intentionally left broad to encourage creative submissions that fit within the perspectives outlined above.

Among the potential topics closely connected with the problem sensitivity of the series are "honor"-based violence; arranged (forced, child, etc.) marriage; transnational marriage markets, migration, and brokerage; intersections of marriage and religion/class/race; the politics of agency and power within marriage; reconfiguration of family: same-sex marriage/union; the politics of love, intimacy, and desire; marriage and multicultural families; the (religious, legal, etc.) politics of divorce; the causes, forms, and consequences of polygamy in contemporary societies; sport marriage; refusing marriage; and so forth.

MEDIATING THE UPRISING IS A UNIQUE, insightful, and thought-provoking summary of why and how metaphors of marriage and gender are used strategically in postrevolutionary Syrian television drama. The chapters brilliantly outline how (the subculture of) post-uprising television miniseries can mediate—through staging and framing the themes of love, sexuality, and marriage—political critique of the state and current power relations; social critique of the ethics of sociability amid war and bloodshed; and, finally, a cultural critique of certain gender and marital roles and identities. *Mediating the Uprising* offers an excellent insight not only into the dynamics of (narrative, value-based) conflicts between the political regime and the opposition, but also into how the politics of nostalgia, fatherhood, and masculinity work; how various (often contesting) interpretations and visions of the nation's past and future are negotiated; and how cultural forms and mechanisms of everyday resistance against oppression are deployed in contemporary Syrian society. Using the lens of marriage and gender, the ultimate aim of Joubin's nuanced and impressive monograph is to demonstrate and analyze continuities and discontinuities in Syrian television drama, politics, and society—convincingly highlighting (via investigating, among other things, seven seasons of drama, press releases, anecdotes, and interviews) how art and the drama creators themselves are involved in shaping the ongoing public debate on the meanings and consequences of the 2011 Syrian revolution.

PÉTER BERTA
University College London
School of Slavonic and
East European Studies

ABBREVIATIONS

Da'ish   al-Dawla al-Islamiyya fi al-'Iraq wa-l-Sham
FSA   Free Syrian Army
GCC   Gulf Cooperation Council
SANA   Syrian Arab News Agency
SAPI   Sama al-Fann al-Dawliyya li-l-Intaj; Suriyya al-Dawliyya li-l-Intaj
          al-Fanni (Syrian Art Production International)
SNC   Syrian National Council
SOHR   Syrian Observatory for Human Rights

NOTE ON TRANSLITERATION

Arabic words, names, and reference material have been translated according to the system used by the *International Journal of Middle East Studies*. I have omitted diacritical marks, but have maintained the constant *ayn* (') and the *hamza* glottal stop ('). Commonly known Arabic words have not been italicized. Many Syrian writers, directors, and actors transliterate their names on their Facebook pages and websites in a simplified manner. In order to avoid irregularity and confusion in my book, however, I have spelled the majority of names according to the *IJMES* system. To preserve the Syrian ambiance, I have translated titles of miniseries as they are pronounced in colloquial. Furthermore, expressions quoted by drama creators have been transliterated in colloquial. In these cases, the *ta'-marbuta* is pronounced "eh" rather than "a," as in Modern Standard Arabic. However, I have transliterated Arabic bibliography and endnote material according to Modern Standard Arabic. For reasons of clarity, in my transliterations I have kept the letter *qaf* as in standard Arabic. Unless otherwise indicated, all transliterations of dialogue from the *musalsalat* from Arabic into English are my own.

CHRONOLOGY OF THE SYRIAN UPRISING

2011

January 31 — Asad tells the *Wall Street Journal* that Syria is more stable than Tunisia and he sees no danger of political upheaval.

February 1 — *Vogue*'s profile of Asma al-Asad describes her as "glamorous, young, and chic" and marvels that her husband won a "startling 97% of the vote."

February 17 — The interior minister visits a protest expressing solidarity with a store owner in Hariqa who was struck by police.

February 23 — A small vigil in front of Libyan embassy in Damascus supports recent protests.

March 1 — *Vogue* removes the profile of Asma al-Asad.

March 6 — Twelve school children are arrested and tortured for graffiti that says "the people want the regime to fall" and "your turn is coming, doctor."

March 15 — Day of Rage protest occurs. Widely considered to be the date of the start of the Syrian uprising, it initiates a practice of naming Friday protests. On the Day of Rage, hundreds of staged protests in Damascus and Aleppo are dispersed. Protests are also reported in al-Hasakah, Dar'a, Deir ez-Zor, and Hama.

March 16 — Approximately 100 people protest at Marjeh Square in Damascus. In Damascus, BBC's Lina Sinjab says that the silence that dominated the country has been broken.

March 18 — The first large-scale protest in Syria takes place in four cities. On Facebook it is called the Day of Dignity. Protests break out in cities such as Baniyas, al-Hassake, Dar'a, Deir ez-Zor, and Hama. In Dar'a, demonstrators march from al-Omari Mosque chanting, "God, Syria, and freedom only." Police open fire and kill six in Dar'a. In Damascus, a crowd protests outside the Umayyad mosque; 30 are arrested, while more are beaten.

March 19	In Dar'a, more than 20,000 people march at funerals. Security forces use tear gas and shoot live ammunition at the mourners. Unnamed protests take place in other cities.
March 20	Asad sends delegation of high-ranking officials to offer condolences to the families of those killed in Dar'a. Hundreds gather around the al-'Omari Mosque in Dar'a, chanting for the release of political prisoners and prosecutions for those who shot and killed protesters, as well as for freedom, an end to corruption, and the abolition of emergency law. Protesters tear down a billboard-size photo of President Bashar al-Asad. Police retaliate. Protesters in Dar'a burn the local Ba'th Party headquarters.
March 21	In Dar'a, 300 young men climb on a statue of Hafez al-Asad, shouting anti-regime chants.
March 22	On the fifth day of protests, hundreds of people march in Dar'a and Nawa demanding freedom.
March 25	In Latakia, progovernment forces kill two protesters.
March 26	The Syrian Observatory for Human Rights reports that more than 200 inmates, mostly Islamists, are freed from Damascus's Saidnaya prison.
March 29	The Syrian government, headed by Prime Minister Najib Ottari, resigns. Asad promises new reforms, including lifting the state of emergency. Award-winning Syrian actor Bassam Kousa speaks on SHAM-FM regarding the position of artists on the current Syrian political conflict. He says that it "is the humanistic and nationalist obligation of all citizens to bring peace to Syria and bar any path that will lead to further destruction."
March 30	In the People's Assembly, Asad addresses the nation for the first time since protests began. He blames the turmoil on prodemocracy demonstrators plotting to destroy the nation.
April 3	Asad appoints 'Adel Safar as the new prime minister, then dismisses his cabinet and tells Safar to form a new government.
April 6	To appease Sunnis, Asad closes down the first and only casino. Stateless Kurds are now granted citizenship. Asad also reverses the ban on school teachers wearing *niqab*.

April 13	In the coastal town of Baniyas, women and children march in protest, calling for the release of arrested men.
April 15	Protesters in Douma march to the square. *Mukhabarat* attack them with pistols and tear gas. Protests erupt in the Barzeh district of Damascus.
April 16	In total, there are more than 200 deaths from police brutality toward protesters so far. Asad briefs his cabinet in a televised speech and promises to give "greater political and social rights," to allow regulated demonstrations, to lift emergency law by the following week, and to open more room for political parties and the press.
April 18	The regime shoots at thousands of demonstrators who have occupied al-Saa'a Square in Homs.
April 19	After swearing in the new cabinet, Asad gives a televised address for the second time since protests began. He pledges further reforms, such as lifting the emergency law.
April 22	Security forces fire tear gas and live ammunition to disperse crowds of demonstrators in Damascus and at least 20 other cities after noon prayer on Friday. At least 81 people are killed, according to *New York Times*; the *Christian Science Monitor* reports 75 deaths. This is considered the bloodiest day yet.
April 25	The siege of Dar'a begins. Syria's information minister, 'Adnan Hassan Mahmoud, tells reporters that a national dialogue with the opposition will begin in days.
April 29	Thirteen-year-old Hamza al-Khatib is arrested while attending a protest with his family in Saida. Screenwriter Reema Fleihan launches the Milk Petition on her Facebook page. The petition calls on the government to lift the siege of Dar'a so that food can be delivered to children.
April 30	Security forces arrest 11 women who participate in a peaceful women-only silent protest in Arnous, near the center of Damascus.
May 5	Three hundred Syrian artists and intellectuals sign the Milk Petition, which calls for humanitarian assistance for the besieged Dar'a. Shortly afterward, 21 production companies with links to the regime call for the blacklisting of all who signed the Milk Petition.
May 6	Friday of Challenge, Day of Defiance.

May 7	The siege of Baniyas begins. The U.S. Treasury Department announces the imposition of sanctions on Asad and six top aides for human rights abuses.
May 10	The EU presses sanctions on 13 government members, including Maher al-Asad, who has been under U.S. sanctions since 2008.
May 11	Syria withdraws from UN Human Rights Council.
May 13	Friday of Free Women. Secretary of State Hillary Rodham Clinton says that Asad's government will be held accountable for "brutal reprisals" against protesters and that sanctions might tighten but does not suggest that Asad should step down. According to the *Guardian*, women-only protests erupt in towns throughout the country.
May 18	President Obama signs Executive Order 13573, which accuses Asad and five other regime officials of violence. Obama calls for Asad to either embrace political change in Syria or give up power.
May 20	Friday of Azadi.
May 24	The Syrian death toll reaches over 1,100, according to Syrian human rights groups. Hamza al-Khatib's body is returned to his family and shows that he was severely tortured.
May 31	Asad announces via the state-run SANA the formation of a committee to coordinate a national dialogue. Hundreds of political prisoners are released, including members of the Muslim Brotherhood.
June 1	Pro- and anti-Syrian-government factions clash in Tripoli, Lebanon.
June 3	Friday of Children Protests. The largest protests to date take place in Hama with more than 50,000 participants. The government disconnects internet access throughout much of the city.
June 10	Friday of Tribes and siege of Jisr al-Shughour.
June 13	More than 1,300 protesters have been killed since the start of the uprising. Syrian actress May Skaf, screenwriter Reema Fleihan, and other artists are arrested at a demonstration of intellectuals at the Midan.
June 14	The Arab League condemns the crackdown for the first time. More than 8,000 Syrian refugees have relocated to Turkey.
June 17	Friday of Saleh al-'Ali. In Lebanon, Tripoli becomes a war zone.

June 19	Opposition activists announce the formation of the National Council to resist Asad.
June 20	Asad gives a speech at Damascus University where he says, "Conspiracies are like germs, after all, multiplying every moment everywhere."
June 24	Friday of Lost Legitimacy. An estimated 20,000 people demonstrate in Hama. People in Damascus begin protesting. Activists say the death toll has reached 1,400 people. More than 11,700 refugees have crossed into Turkey.
June 30	Demonstrations take place across Aleppo.
July 1	Friday of Departure. Hundreds are reportedly killed in Hama in direct response to protests around Assi Square (renamed Freedom Square by protestors).
July 4	Ibrahim Qashoush, known for music that mocks Asad and the ruling Ba'th Party, including the protest anthem "Yalla Erhal Ya Bashar" ("Come On, Bashar, Time to Leave"), is found dead in the Orontes River, his throat cut and his vocal cords ripped out.
July 8	Friday of No Dialogue. Tens of thousands of Syrians, many carrying roses and olive branches, stage a demonstration in Hama.
July 12	"From our perspective, Asad has lost legitimacy," Secretary of State Clinton states.
July 15	Friday of Freedom for the Hostages. In Damascus, intellectuals gather alongside protesters at the Hassan Mosque in Midan after morning prayer. Brothers Muhammad and Ahmad Malas, both involved in theater, are among those arrested.
July 17	Syrian National Salvation Opposition meets in Istanbul.
July 22	Friday of Khalid ibn al-Walid Grandsons. Mass demonstrations in Deir ez-Zor, in Hama, and across the country.
July 29	Friday of Your Silence Is Killing Us. Twenty protesters are killed, mainly in Deir ez-Zor. A video is released on the internet of a uniformed group of dissenters from the Syrian military, including Colonel Riad al-Asaad, calling members of the Syrian army to defect and join them. They announce the formation of the Free Syrian Army (FSA).
July 31	Ramadan and the 2011 television drama season begin. *Al-Jazeera* reports that 136 people are killed in anti-protest crackdowns in Hama, Deir ez-Zor, Harak, and Abu Kamal.

Forces attempt to stifle protests before Ramadan. President Obama issues an official White House statement: "I am appalled by the Syrian government's use of violence and brutality against its own people. The reports out of Hama are horrifying and demonstrate the true character of the Syrian regime." In July, protests peak, with perhaps a million people turning out in just Hama and Deir ez-Zor on the last Friday of the month.

August 1	FSA leader Colonel Riad al-Asaad announces that the FSA will work with demonstrators to topple the regime. The Syrian National Council is formed in Istanbul.
August 5	Friday of God Is with Us.
August 8	Saudi Arabia, Bahrain, and Kuwait recall ambassadors from Damascus.
August 18	Syrian ambassador to the UN, Bashar Ja'afari, accuses U.S. and Western critics of a plot to encourage "terrorist armed groups." Obama issues his first explicit call for Asad to resign. Secretary of State Clinton makes a statement about sanctions against Syria. Viewers throughout the Arab world call for a boycott of Syrian satellite channels.
August 25	Pro-regime forces beat up 'Ali Ferzat, a famed political cartoonist, shortly after a cartoon depicting Asad hitching a ride with outgoing Libyan leader Muammar al-Gaddafi begins circulating in Syria. At least 2,200 people have been killed since mid-March, says the UN.
August 27	French president François Hollande says that there is a possibility of foreign intervention in Syria if the regime uses chemical weapons on its citizens.
August 30	Ramadan and the 2011 television drama season end.
September 2	The European Union bans imports of Syrian oil.
September 9	Friday of International Protection.
September 16	Friday of Continuing Until We Bring Down the Regime. Based on UN estimates, 2,600 civilians have been killed.
September 23	Friday of Unification Against the Regime. Protests erupt in Hama, Damascus, Aleppo, Dar'a, and Homs.
September 30	Friday of Victory for the Levant and Yemen.
October 4	The United Nations Security Council fails to pass a draft resolution condemning Asad's crackdown because of Chinese and Russian veto power.

October 21	Friday of the Martyrs of the Arab Deadline.
October 28	Friday of No-Fly Zone.
October 29	In his first interview with a Western journalist, Asad tells the *Sunday Telegraph*, "We've been fighting the Muslim brotherhood since the 1950s and we are still fighting them."
November 4	Friday of God Is Greatest.
November 11	Friday of Freezing Syria's Arab League Membership.
November 18	Friday of Expulsion of the Ambassadors.
November 25	Friday of the Free Syrian Army Is Protecting Me.
November 27	Second and third episodes of *Top Goon,* Season 1.
November 29	Secretary of State Clinton meets with Syrian National Council.
December 1	The Ba'th regime sets up a fake Syrian Brotherhood website purporting to claim responsibility for the terrorist attacks that strike Damascus a few weeks later. Civil war is declared. UN officials report over 4,000 people dead and an increasing number of soldiers defecting from the army to fight Asad.
December 2	Friday of the Syrian Buffer Zone.
December 7	ABC News airs an interview with Bashar al-Asad. Asad tells veteran journalist Barbara Walters he does not feel guilty or remorseful over Syria's violence because he is trying to "protect the Syrian people."
December 9	Friday of the Dignity Strike.
December 16	Friday of the Arab League Is Killing Us.
December 22	Arab League monitors arrive in Syria. Syrian actor Jalal al-Taweel, who considers art a strong weapon against the regime's unjust rule, is severely beaten by Syrian police and members of the military for taking part in a demonstration in Damascus calling for Asad's resignation. A photo of al-Taweel covered in blood circulates on social media.
December 23	Friday of the Protocol of Death.
December 30	UN estimates more than 5,000 deaths in Syria.

2012

January 6	A suicide bomber attacks an area of Damascus, killing 26 people. This is the first attack for which Jabhat al-Nusra claimed responsibility.

January 15	Security forces raid Aleppo University's campus following a student protest against the regime.
January 21	Rebels seize parts of Douma.
January 23	Abu Mohammad al-Julani, an Iraq war veteran, rejuvenates al-Qaeda's brand and announces the formation of Jabhat al-Nusra.
January 28	The Arab League suspends its monitoring mission in Syria. In Damascus, insurgents launch two bombs, one in the parking garage of the Palace of Justice and the other at a police station.
February 3	The FSA attacks Syrian army checkpoints, killing 10 soldiers.
February 4	The Homs offensive begins with an artillery bombardment by the Syrian army. Russia and China veto a UN Security Council resolution backing an Arab League peace plan.
February 6	The United States closes its embassy in Damascus. Abu Mus'ab al-Suri, a former jihadist of the Fighting Vanguard, is released from custody.
February 12	Al-Qaeda's Ayman al-Zawahri issues a video calling on militants across the region to join the fight against Asad.
February 23	Former UN Secretary-General Kofi Annan is appointed Joint UN-Arab League special envoy for the Syria crisis.
February 26	Syrian screenwriter Adnan Zira'i is arrested and imprisoned. His sketches such as the "spray can man" are seen as having ignited the revolution.
February 29	Regime forces raid the Baba 'Amru neighborhood once again. Since early February, the regime has directed the harshest siege on Baba 'Amru, since it is viewed as a hub for opposition soldiers.
March 16	The six member states of the Gulf Cooperation Council (GCC) shut down their embassies in Syria.
March 19	Asma al-Asad is added to the EU sanctions list.
March 21	The Security Council agrees to back Kofi Annan's plan calling on the Syrian government to do the following: allow for an inclusive political transition process, cease violence and withdraw security forces, allow access for humanitarian assistance, release prisoners, enable freedom of movement for journalists, and allow Syrians to demonstrate freely.
March 27	Bashar al-Asad visits Baba 'Amru in order to assure everyone that the neighborhood is under control and that life is

continuing as usual. This is his first visit outside of Damascus since the commencement of the uprising.

May 3	Four Aleppo University students die in a government crackdown.
May 7	Syria holds parliamentary elections amid boycotts by opposition.
May 10	Suicide bomb attacks kill more than 50 people near a police base in Damascus.
May 17	In the presence of UN monitors, hundreds of students protest at Aleppo University.
May 25	Houla Massacre: the regime is alleged to have killed 108 people in the opposition town of Taldou in the Houla region.
May 28	Regime forces kill Basel Shehadeh, a well-known Syrian film producer.
May 30	The United States, Britain, France, and at least five other major nations expel senior Syrian diplomats in response to the Houla Massacre.
June 1	Activists say as many as 13,000 people have died in Asad's crackdown against the antigovernment uprising.
June 6	Al-Qubair Massacre: Asad forces are accused of committing a second massacre of innocent people in the village of al-Qubair in Hama. The number of victims is contested, and the regime alleges that terrorists are responsible.
June 12	For the first time the UN states that Syria is involved in a civil war.
June 22	Daret Azzeh Massacre: Syrian rebels are accused of killing 25 people in a small village in Aleppo province. The FSA states that they were pro-regime militiamen.
July 6	Brigadier General Manaf Tlass defects.
July 18	The Daughters of al-Walid, a group of women from Homs, announces on YouTube that they arm and train women to defend themselves.
July 19	Ramadan and the 2012 television drama season begin. In the deadliest assault on government officials since violence broke out, the FSA bombs the National Security Building and kills three of Asad's inner circle, including his brother-in-law, Assef Shawqat, and Defense Minister General Rajha. Hisham Bekhtay, head of national security, is among those seriously

wounded. This attack marks the commencement of war between the Free Syrian Army and government forces in Aleppo. With the nationwide death toll rising daily, July is one of the bloodiest months of the uprising up to date.

July 28	In Jordan the UNHCR's Za'atari refugee camp opens.
August 1	Syrian combat aircraft and artillery pound Aleppo. Refugee status: up to 18,000 people have been forced to leave their homes in Aleppo.
August 2	Kofi Annan announces his plan to step down as UN–Arab League mediator in Syria on August 31.
August 6	Syrian prime minister Riad Hijab defects to Jordan.
August 11	Syrian actor Zaki Cordello is arrested at his apartment in Doumar along with his son, cousin, and friend.
August 15	Actress Kinda 'Aloosh, addressing a televised message to Asma al-Asad, beseeches her to listen to her maternal instinct and empathize with the mothers of the martyrs.
August 17	The UN names Lakhdar Brahimi, a veteran Algerian diplomat and current envoy in Afghanistan and Iraq, to replace former secretary-general Kofi Annan as peace envoy to Syria.
August 18	Ramadan and the 2012 television drama season end.
August 20	President Obama establishes the "red line" in the Syrian civil war: the use of chemical weapons would compel the United States to intervene.
August 30	Government forces bomb bread lines in Aleppo.
September 16	Iran confirms that its Revolutionary Guards are helping Asad.
October 1	Aleppo's historic souk is destroyed. Over the weekend, at least 1,500 shops are lost in a fire in the souk after rebel and government clashes.
October 26	Violence erupts hours before the government announces a cease-fire for Eid al-Adha that has been proposed by UN envoy Brahimi.
October 31	Secretary of State Clinton calls for the overthrow of SNC.
November 5	Mohammed Rafeh, actor from the popular series *Bab al-Hara* and a notable supporter of Bashar al-Asad, is brutally murdered in Damascus, sparking debate over whether the murder is related to Rafeh's pro-regime opinions. The actor's killing comes one day after an online video showed rebel gunmen shooting captured soldiers.

November 22   John Cantlie is kidnapped in Syria, along with American
               freelance journalist James Foley.

December 5   Dubai removes three Syrian films from official selection.

December 14   A video posted online shows Sunni Muslim rebels burning a
               Shi'i Husseiniya mosque and Shi'i flags in the town of Jisr
               al-Shughur. According to Reuters 40,000 people have been
               killed since March alone.

2013

January 15   Bombings at Aleppo University kill at least 82 people, includ-
               ing students and children.

February 24   Yassin Bakoush (1938–2013), a famous Syrian actor, is killed by
               a rocket.

March 10   Rebel groups including the jihadist al-Nusra Front set up a
               religious council to administer affairs in eastern Syria.

March 21   Leading pro-Asad Sheikh Muhammad Sa'id Ramadan al-Buti
               is reportedly killed in a bomb explosion in Damascus.

March 23   The government allegedly carries out a chemical weapons
               attack on Khan al-Assal (on the outskirts of Aleppo).

April 7   The Syrian army launches an offensive in Eastern Ghouta.

April 9   A massive blast kills at least 15 people in Damascus.

April 11   Al-Baghdadi moves from Iraq to Syria and announces that his
               Islamic State of Iraq and the al-Nusra Front in Syria will merge
               to become the Islamic State in Iraq and the Levant.

April 19   Screenwriter 'Adnan Zira'i has been imprisoned since the early
               days of the uprising. No one knows what has become of him.
               On Facebook, discussions appear about his wife's arrest as she
               is out walking with her friend, sister, and son. Facebook
               reports that Zira'i's son, now without his mother and father, is
               unable to eat or sleep.

April 24   The 1,000-year-old minaret of Aleppo's Umayyad Mosque
               collapses due to clashes between rebels and loyalists.

April 25   White House states that U.S. intelligence has learned that
               Asad used chemical weapons twice.

May 3   Syrian screenwriter Fu'ad Humayra writes on his Facebook
               page, "To hell with the secular individuals who are defending
               the regime's genocide."

May 26	The UN says at least 100,000 have been killed since the protests began.
May 28	SOHR reports a death toll of more than 200 civilians, including women and children, in the Baniyas Massacre.
June 4	Putin denies criticism of Russian arms sales to Damascus.
June 13	U.S. officials conclude that Asad used chemical weapons; they plan to send weapons to Syrian rebels.
June 29	The regime launches an offensive on Homs.
July 8	Ramadan and the 2013 television drama season commences. The prime minister of the Syria opposition government, Ghassan Hitto, resigns.
August 7	Ramadan and the 2013 television drama season end.
August 21	The government launches a chemical attack on East Ghouta that kills 1,429 people.
August 27	U.K. prime minister Dave Cameron calls for a military response but is blocked in a parliamentary vote.
September 2	Asad tells *Le Figaro* that he blames rebels for the chemical weapon deaths. He claims it would be irrational for the Syrian army to use weapons of mass destruction on its own troops.
September 4	Obama emphasizes the worldwide consensus on setting a "red line" against using chemical weapon in Syria prior to a congressional vote on the U.S. response to recent chemical attacks.
September 28	Sixteen-year-old Rawan Qaddah testifies on Syrian state television that her jihadist father who fought in the Free Syrian Army forced her to sleep with his comrades in arms as a form of *jihad al-nikah*—sexual jihad. Many believed that she was kidnapped by regime thugs and that this forced testimony was the price she had to pay for her freedom.
November 15	Battle of Qalamoun.
December 6	Al-Nasra Front and Jaysh al-Islam massacre 32 civilians in 'Adra.
December 11	Syrian actress Leila 'Awad is arrested at the Syrian-Lebanese border when returning home from Germany to see her son.
December 13	Human Rights activist Razan Zaitouneh, her husband, and two colleagues are kidnapped.
December 30	Da'ish takes control of Fallujah and parts of Ramadi in Iraq.

2014

January 7	Syria delivers the first load of chemical weapons to Latakia to be sailed into international waters. China and Russia provide protection to the ship, which is to be transferred for dumping.
January 16	The examining magistrate of Syria's counterterrorism court issues a decision to imprison Laila 'Awad and Samr Koksh, who has been detained by the regime since the end of 2013.
February 1–5	Barrel bombs reportedly dropped by security forces kill at least 246 civilians in Aleppo.
February 3	Al-Qaeda officially cuts ties with Da'ish.
February 10	A second round of Geneva II talks is held. Government and opposition representatives fail to agree on the agenda.
February 15	The Geneva Council is interrupted.
April 3	According to the UN, the number of Syrian refugees in Lebanon passes one million.
April 11	In the Hama governorate, reports of a chlorine gas attack emerge in the rebel-controlled village of Kafr Zita.
May 13	Lakhdar Brahimi announces that he will step down as special envoy to Syria.
June 3	Syrians in government-controlled areas vote in presidential elections.
	Secretary of State John Kerry denounces the vote as "meaningless."
June 9	Syrian state television reports that Asad has issued a decree granting "a general amnesty" for all crimes except "acts of terrorism."
June 10	In Iraq, Da'ish takes over Mosul.
June 11	Da'ish seizes Tikrit.
June 12	Iran deploys forces to fight Da'ish in Iraq, helping Iraqi troops regain control of most of Tikrit.
June 18	Iraq asks the United States to conduct airstrikes against Da'ish.
June 21	Da'ish seizes the border between Deir ez-Zor province and Iraq.
June 26	Actress Suzanne Salman, known for her role in the popular television miniseries *Bab al-Hara*, is killed in a shelling of residential areas in Damascus.

June 28   Ramadan and the 2014 television drama season begin.

June 29   Da'ish announces the establishment of a caliphate in Iraq and Syria.

July 3   Da'ish takes control of al-Omar, Syria's largest oil field.

July 25   Da'ish seizes a Syrian 17th Division base outside of Raqqa, beheads several soldiers, and displays their heads in Raqqa.

July 28   Ramadan and the 2014 television drama season end.

August 4   Da'ish takes over Mosul Dam.

August 19   Da'ish releases a video depicting the beheading of prominent American journalist James Foley.

August 24   Da'ish militants seize the Taqba airbase in Raqqa, Syria.

September 2   Da'ish releases a video depicting the beheading of journalist Steven Sotloff.

September 23   The U.S.-led coalition launches its first air strikes against Da'ish in Syria.

December 16   A gunman allegedly aligned with Da'ish abducts 17 hostages in a café in Sydney.

December 30   The United Nations says around 200,000 people have been killed since 2011.

Da'ish takes responsibility for a suicide attack during a funeral north of Baghdad that kills 16 and injures 34 people.

2015

January 7   Saïd and Chérif Kouachi open fire in the offices of *Charlie Hebdo* in Paris, killing 12 people and injuring 11 more.

January 28   Militants allied with Da'ish claim responsibility for an armed assault on a luxury hotel in Tripoli that kills eight.

March 7   Da'ish begins to destroy two of northern Iraq's most prized ancient cities, Nimrud and al-Hadr, as well as parts of Dur Sharrakin, a 2,800-year-old Assyrian site.

March 18   Da'ish claims responsibility for an attack on the Bardo museum in Tunis that leaves 22 people dead.

March 19   *Al-Jazeera* interviews four Syrian artists (Wissam al-Jazairy, Souad al-Jundi, Tammam 'Azzam, and 'Amr Fahed) in Syria.

March 20   Da'ish-allied militants bomb two mosques in Sanaa, Yemen, killing 137 people.

April 5	Da'ish militants seize the Yarmouk Palestinian refugee camp in Damascus.
April 8	Da'ish releases more than 200 captive Yazidis, many of whom had been held captive since mid-2014.
May 17	Da'ish takes over Ramadi, Iraq.
May 20	In Syria, Da'ish seizes the ancient city of Palmyra.
June 17	Ramadan and the 2015 season of television drama commence. A Ramadan Rating show is broadcast for the first time and will continue for 30 days through the end of Ramadan.
June 22	Kurdish forces take full control of 'Ain 'Issa military base from Da'ish.
June 26	Da'ish launch a string of terrorist attacks in Tunisia, France, and Kuwait and warn that Ramadan will be a month of disaster. Da'ish launches terrorist attacks in Saint-Quentin-Fallavier, near Lyon, France; a suicide bombing at a Shi'i mosque in Kuwait; and a terrorist attack on Tunisian resort in Sousse, where 38 people are killed—mainly tourists.
July 17	Ramadan and the 2015 season of television drama end.
July 20	In Turkey a suicide bomber with links to Da'ish strikes a cultural center in Suruc, killing 30 people.
August 6	Da'ish claims a suicide bombing on a Saudi mosque in the Asir province, killing 15 people, including 12 Saudi police officers.
August 16	Douma Massacre: The Syrian Air Force launches strikes on the rebel-held town of Douma, killing at least 200 people.
August 18	Da'ish publicly beheads 81-year-old archeologist Khaled al-Asaad, keeper of Palmyra's ancient ruins.
August 25	Da'ish blows up the 2,000-year-old ruins of the Baal Shamin temple in the ancient Roman city of Palmyra after capturing the city from Asad's forces in May.
September 3	Da'ish's Yemeni affiliate kills 20 people in two bombings in Sanaa.
September 25	Three-year-old Alan Kurdi drowns in the Mediterranean Sea as his family flees Syria.
September 30	Russia begins air campaigns in Syria targeting Da'ish. U.S. officials allege that many strikes target civilians and Western-backed militia groups.
October 5	Da'ish blows up the Arch of Triumph in Palmyra.

October 6	In Yemen, Da'ish kills at least 25 people in a series of car bombings in Aden and Sanaa.
October 9	Da'ish makes gains in northwestern Syria.
November 12	Da'ish claims a suicide attack in Beirut that kills 40 people.
November 13	Da'ish-coordinated attacks in Paris kill 130 people.
December 2	In California, a married couple allegedly inspired by Da'ish kills 14 people in San Bernardino.
December 27	Iraqi military forces take Ramadi from Da'ish.

2016

January 12	A suicide bomber linked to Da'ish kills 10 people and injures 15 others, mostly German tourists, in Istanbul's Sultanahmet Square.
January 14	In Indonesia, Da'ish claims responsibility for an attack in Jakarta that kills at least two people and injures 19 others.
January 31	Da'ish claims responsibility for a bombing attack in Damascus near the Sayyida Zainab shrine that kills 45 people and wounds over 100.
February 24	Nabil al-Maleh, known as the father of Syrian cinema, dies in Dubai at the age of 79.
March 15	Putin announces the partial withdrawal of Russian forces from Syria.
March 18	Salah Abdesalam, the most wanted suspect in the Paris attacks, is arrested in Brussels.
March 22	Da'ish launches three terrorist attacks in Brussels—one at a metro station and two at the airport in Zaventem—that claim 32 lives.
May 5	Da'ish captures the Shaer gas field near Palmyra.
May 12	Da'ish claims a series of bombings in Baghdad that kills more than 100 people.
May 24	Kurdish forces backed by U.S. airstrikes launch an offensive on territory north of Raqqa.
June 5	Ramadan and the 2016 television season start.
June 12	A gunman named Omar Mateen who pledged allegiance to Da'ish attacks a gay nightclub in Orlando, killing a dozen people and injuring at least 53.
June 26	The Iraqi army recaptures Fallujah from Da'ish.

June 28	Three suicide bombers kill at least 40 people at Istanbul Ataturk Airport. The Turkish government suspects Da'ish, but the group does not formally claim responsibility.
July 1	In Bangladesh, five Da'ish-aligned militants kill more than 20 people, many of whom are foreigners, at a Dhaka restaurant.
July 3	Da'ish carries out suicide bombings that kill more than 200 people on a busy shopping street in Baghdad. The bombing is Da'ish's deadliest attack on civilians to date.
July 4	Suicide bombers attack three locations across Saudi Arabia, including the Prophet's Mosque in Medina, a Shi'i mosque in Qatif, and an area near the U.S. consulate in Jeddah.
July 6	Ramadan ends.
July 14	A Tunisian man drives a truck through a crowd in Nice, killing 84 people. Da'ish claims credit.
July 18	An Afghan teen, inspired by Da'ish, carries an axe onto a German commuter train and injures five people.
August 17	Five-year-old Omran Daqneesh is wounded in an alleged Russian Air Force attack on a rebel-controlled neighborhood of Aleppo. The image of the injured boy ignites international condemnation.
August 31	The United States admits 10,000 Syrian refugees this year. Since the war began, the United States has accepted a total of 12,000 Syrian refugees.
September 20	Donald Trump Jr. shares a tweet comparing Syrian refugees to a bowl of Skittles, a few of which "would kill you."
November 15	Regime forces begin Operation Dawn of Victory to retake Aleppo from rebels.
November 27	As violence escalates in Syria, the United Nations reports that the number of children trapped in besieged areas has doubled in less than a year.
December 19	In Germany, 12 people die and 56 are injured after Anis 'Amri, a Tunisian who was refused asylum, drives a stolen truck into a crowd at a Berlin Christmas market. Amri has reportedly pledged allegiance to Da'ish.
December 22	The Syrian government retakes Eastern Aleppo.
December 23	According to SOHR, at least 21 children are killed in the air raids on the northern town of al-Bab.
December 30	A truce agreement is brokered by Russia, Turkey, and Iran.

2017

January 20	Da'ish destroys part of the Roman Theatre in Palmyra.
January 23	More than 300,000 people have been killed and 11 million others displaced since the uprising began in March 2011.
January 25	Trump is expected to sign executive orders including a temporary ban on most refugees and a suspension of visas for citizens of Syria, Iraq, Iran, Libya, Somalia, Sudan, and Yemen.
February 23	Most of Mosul Airport is retaken by Iraqi forces in a push against Da'ish. The 2017 Geneva peace conference officially begins.
February 25	Suicide bombers for Hay'at Tahrir al-Sham kill at least 32 people in Homs.
March 3	The Geneva IV talks conclude without achieving any breakthroughs.
May 22	In the United Kingdom, 22 die and more than 500 are injured in a suicide bombing at the Manchester arena. British-born 22-year-old Salman 'Abedi is arrested. Da'ish claims responsibility.
May 26	Ramadan and the 2017 television drama season begin.
May 28	The Iraqi army launches an offensive to recapture Da'ish's remaining enclaves across the country.
May 30	A terrorist attack in a popular ice cream shop in southern Baghdad kills at least 17 people and wounds 32. Shortly afterward, another bomb goes off in Baghdad outside an office where people collect government pensions. Da'ish claims responsibility.
June 4	Seven people die and 48 are injured in a terror attack at London Bridge. Da'ish takes credit for the attack.
June 6	In Paris, an Algerian student attacks an officer with a hammer outside Notre Dame Cathedral, saying, "This is for Syria!"
June 7	Da'ish attacks the Iranian parliament and Ayatollah Khomeini's mausoleum.
June 24	Ramadan and the 2017 drama season end.
August 17	'Alawi actress, Fadwa Suleiman, an outspoken critic of the Asad regime, dies of cancer at the age of 47 in France, where she has been residing since 2012.
September 5	The Syrian Army, supported by Iranian militias, ends Da'ish's three-year siege of Deir ez-Zor.

November 1	Representatives of the Syrian opposition reject a new round of Russia-sponsored peace talks scheduled for November 18 in Sochi.
November 19	The Syrian army and its allies retake the village of Albu Kamal, Da'ish's last urban stronghold in Syria.
November 27	Jordan's al-Za'tari refugee camp now enjoys solar power, thanks to an $18 million German-government-funded project.
December 6	Trump announces that the United States recognizes Jerusalem as the undisputed capital of Israel.
December 9	Iraqi prime minister Haider al-'Abadi announces that Iraqi forces have achieved military victory over Da'ish.
December 26	Russia establishes a permanent military presence at its naval and air bases in Syria.

2018

January 4	Russian airstrikes have killed 25 civilians in Eastern Ghouta.
February 19	Heavy fighting occurs in Aleppo and Idlib between Tahrir al-Sham and the Syrian Liberation Front.
February 24	UN Security Council calls for immediate 30-day cease-fire.
February 26	The Syrian regime ignores the cease-fire and persists in bombing Eastern Ghouta.
March 29	Trump announces that the United States will withdraw from Syria "very soon."
April 14	Britain and France join U.S.-led airstrikes targeting chemical weapons sites in Syria.
May 16	Ramadan begins.
June 15	Ramadan ends.
June 29	The Syrian government bombs Dar'a.
July 21	On her Facebook page, 49-year-old Syrian actress-activist Mai Skaf posts from her current residence in Paris: "I will not lose hope, never lose hope. It is Great Syria, not Assad's Syria."
July 23	Mai Skaf dies in Paris of a severe brain hemorrhage. Friends and family say that circumstances surrounding her death are mysterious.
September 2	Director Soudade Kaadan's film *The Day I Lost My Shadow* debuts at the Venice Film Festival. She goes on to win the Lion of the Future award for best debut film. French foreign

minister Jean-Yves Le Drian states, "Asad won the war, we have to say this. But he hasn't won the peace."

September 7   Putin refuses call for truce in Idlib. In Tehran, no agreement is reached on the Idlib cease-fire during the summit on the Syrian war.

September 17   Russia and Turkey declare a demilitarized zone in Idlib.

October 4   The UN cautions that the one million children in Idlib could be injured if the fragile truce collapses and the regime carries out its offensive.

October 15   The Jaber-Nassib border between Syria and Jordan reopens.

November 10   Director Joud Sa'id's *Musaferu al-Harb* (Travelers of War) wins best film in the Carthage Film Festival.

November 23   Opposition activist Ra'ed Fares, who was considered a symbol of the Syrian civil movement, is assassinated by gunmen in Idlib.

December 19   Trump announces that since Da'ish has been vanquished, the United States will withdraw about 2,000 to 2,500 troops from Syria.

December 21   Turkey delays assault on northern Syria.

2019

January 17   French president Emmanuel Macron states that since Da'ish has not yet been conquered, French troops will remain in Syria.

February 18   Two deadly explosions in Idlib.

March 21   Trump declares that he will acknowledge and honor Israel's legitimate control of the Golan Heights.

March 23   The Islamic State loses its final remaining territory in Syria.

March 25   Trump signs a declaration stating that the United States honors Israel's claim to possess the Golan Heights.

April 7   Fighting between rebel and government forces erupts in the Idlib-Hama region.

April 29   Abu Bakr al-Baghdadi appears in a video. (This is his first appearance since 2014.)

May 6   The 2019 Ramadan season begins.

June 4   The 2019 Ramadan season ends.

August 1   The Syrian regime concedes to a ceasefire in Idlib.

Mediating the Uprising

Introduction

New Directions in Television Drama amid an Uprising

*T*he thirteenth season of the popular Syrian sketch comedy Buq'at Daw' (Spotlight)
aired during Ramadan 2017. Viewers tuned into an episode titled Mu'arrikh Azmeh
(A Historian of the Crisis),[1] where they were introduced to Nasser Adib, a beleaguered,
low-key historian with white stubble on his face who is being interviewed on television.
Wearing white glasses and a white suit, he explains that it is his duty to record the
events of the azmeh (crisis). When the interviewer asks if he is writing about a politically heated topic, Adib assures him that his historical account has nothing to do with
politics. He promises that in his writing he will record events realistically and beams
as he announces that his book will be translated into Russian, French, and Spanish.
The camera then shows an anxious high-ranking government official making a frantic
phone call to ask if the person on the other end is watching the interview. Adib returns
home to a stranger in a black suit waiting in front of his house. The stranger escorts
Adib to the office of the same high-ranking official; he tells Adib that writing the history of the azmeh is a nationalist project and that "they" would like to help publicize
his work. The man then provides documents that evidence his own nationalist efforts
against terrorists. Adib leaves the man's office with a pile of black binders.

When Adib returns home, he finds another stranger in a black suit waiting at his
door. Adib barely has a chance to drop his binders off before being hurried to see a
second high-ranking government official. This official is hysterical and loudly insists
that Adib must write about the danger of the Syrian azmeh. He quickly adds that Adib
must, of course, remain true to his conscience. The official gives Adib stacks of red and
blue binders that direct him to a particular historical framework.

Next, a businessman named Nabil summons Adib to his art-filled office. He presents Adib with a fancy cigar and instructs him to discuss the azmeh's devastating
impact on the businessmen who have sacrificed to remain in Syria when so many others
have abandoned their country. He then hands Adib a green folder and offers him "a

super deluxe" apartment where he can write. Finally, the daughter of a deceased surgeon tells Adib about the work she is doing in her late father's hospital, how she is unfairly criticized for monopolizing certain medications and not letting others access them, and how she is addressing the country's needs during the "crisis." She asks him to meet her on the seventh floor of the hospital. When he asks her what is happening on the seventh floor, she hands him a stack of folders.

In the following scene, a ragged Adib wearing mismatched slippers sells knickknacks on the streets of the bustling Salihiyya commercial district in Damascus. Soliciting customers for his goods seems far simpler than compiling a history of the time period.

MU'ARRIKH AZMEH EXPOSES THE DIFFICULTY of writing on the azmeh, a term first propagated by the regime to delegitimize the uprising. It comments, as well, on the human tendency to manipulate facts to fit specific historical and political perspectives. Creating a collective memory is thorny work, as most individuals possess hidden agendas that complicate the work of recording history. The job of the true historian of the azmeh is virtually impossible in a country that is engulfed in a civil war and constantly confronting the question of what to remember and what to forget. Adding to the challenge is the fact that the available narratives actively contradict and resist each other. As Donatella Della Ratta has poignantly written in *Shooting a Revolution: Visual Media and Warfare in Syria* (2018), "Never before has the seemingly endless multiplication of media and its makers in the networked environment matched so astonishingly with the explosion and consequent disruption of subjects and meanings on the ground: a hyper-fragmentation of digital 'me' versions of national belonging and identity that mixes up and confounds with the raw materiality of the armed conflict."[2] Della Ratta's new study focuses on the process of recording visual culture that can transform into a "device to perform violence, and the quintessential tool to resist it."[3] Rather than linking the filming process inextricably with violence, *Mediating the Uprising* portrays drama creators' more prosaic engagement with the quotidian details of life during war, along with their visions of an imagined and at times idealized society. I argue that, seen through the lens of gender and marriage, their dramatic projects serve to construct a collective memory of postuprising Syria for future generations.

Indeed, drama creators are keenly attuned to the high stakes of narratives, as well as their own investment in the project of remembering. As seen in the above sketch, they seek to self-consciously reflect on this contested archivebuilding aspect of *musalsalat* (miniseries). Yet for Syrian drama creators, debates about the role of art, history, and collective memory construction are not theoretical exercises. These divergent forms of remembering and forgetting occur in a violent historical context in which representations of the past and present are highly polarized and the writing of *musalsalat* is influenced by the surrounding bloodshed. In her recent book *No Turning Back: Life, Loss, and Hope in Wartime*

Syria (2018), Rania Abouzeid writes, "Syria has ceased to exist as a unified state except in memories and on maps. In its place are many Syrians. The war has become a conflict where the dead are not merely nameless, reduced to figures. They are not even numbers." She continues on to say that although the United Nations stopped trying to track Syrian casualties in mid-2013, according to some estimates the current death toll is over half a million people.[4]

The story of the Syrian uprising turned civil war is recounted widely and variably. Indeed, even the term to describe Syria's current reality is contested, since some individuals use "azmeh" to mitigate the implications of the uprising turned civil war. As is well known, after security forces arrested and tortured twelve schoolchildren on March 6, 2011, for writing graffiti that demanded Bashar al-Asad's downfall, protests and demonstrations swept the country. The regime responded by offering limited economic concessions and a "military solution" that radicalized and divided the opposition. Not long after, during the summer of 2011, army defectors and other locally armed groups began to defend the protesters. By the summer of 2012, the number, nature, and objectives of armed opposition groups had diversified. Subsequently, the rise in regime violence, the internal struggles of the local opposition movements, and the flow of arms and funding from external powers transformed the uprising into a war. The year 2013 saw the formation of Da'ish (al-Dawla al-Islamiyya fi al-'Iraq wa-l-Sham). Capturing large swaths of territory in Syria, the group specialized in guerrilla warfare and flaunted political assassinations, public floggings, rapes, random kidnappings, and the murder of religious minorities. Furthermore, it set loose a morality police that monitored rigid gender laws and norms of behavior. As Da'ish's violence and religious extremism spread, the nation descended into further devastation.[5]

As I completed the writing of this book during the winter of 2018, experts estimated that out of a population of twenty-two million Syrians, six million were internally displaced and five million refugees live outside Syria.[6] Yet the initial intensity of the critical mass media attention on Syria, involving a constant stream of images of desperation and death, caused many in the international community to grow numb to the magnitude of human loss. Since then, Syria has incrementally shifted into the background as new stories have taken center stage. Indeed, as of now, Bashar al-Asad has gained the upper hand and all but squashed the uprising. Idlib, in northern Syria, held together by a fragile truce, remains the sole oppositional zone currently not under regime control. Indeed, Idlib's three million inhabitants survive precariously among pockets of religious extremists and the continual threat of regime reprisal. This reprisal could lead to the forced exit of many Syrians to Turkey and Europe and the exacerbation of an already-acute refugee crisis.[7] Indeed, on August 5, 2019, Syrian regime forces, with the support of Russia, broke a subsequent ceasefire and attacked the region of Idlib under the pretext of targeting terrorists. According to the United Nations, this military offensive had already caused the evacuation of four hundred and forty thousand people.[8]

A Metaphorical Roundtable of Voices of Drama Creators amid Production Pressures

As readers begin to turn the pages of this book, they are invited into the world of Syrian drama creators who aspire to keep the relevance of art alive against a landscape of ongoing catastrophe. By sharing their thought processes, they offer a rare glimpse into Syrian life during the various stages of the uprising and war. Some share their perspectives on the sociopolitical roots of the uprising and engage in critique through the lens of gender and marriage, thus providing a vision of the human side of war often lost in media representation. Others use gender and marriage metaphors to conjure imaginary worlds beyond Syria, luring viewers away from the bitterness of their reality and into new realms of understanding. Some recall oppression, and some choose to forget. I intend for the reader to engage with this introduction as if sitting around the café table during the month of Ramadan, as Syrian drama creators debate the relevance of this popular art form and the role of art more generally in a time of "crisis" and war. This roundtable of opinions is gleaned from café table conversations, magazine interviews, and media outlets through various Ramadan seasons. It offers readers a sense of the various representative voices and points of view on the role and relevance of *musalsalat,* as well as on the process of remembering and misremembering in war-torn Syria.

But first, a brief description of *musalsalat* during the Ramadan season is in order. Since the advent of Syrian television drama in the 1960s, *musalsalat* have been highly didactic in nature and offered sharp criticism of official political discourse.[9] After the Ba'thists banned political parties in the 1960s, many activists became writers and journalists. Due to its transformative power and ability to reach the masses, television attracted highly talented, politically conscious writers. During the pre-Ramadan months in the boom years, Damascus was transformed into a lively set. Productions were shot in every corner of the country, while large sums were spent scouting locations for even the smallest scenes. The viewing of *musalsalat* during Ramadan grew into a national pastime, drawing millions of viewers each day.[10] Christa Salamandra has shown how with the spread of satellite technologies, Syria developed a drama industry that aimed to surpass that of Egypt, which traditionally dominated Arab media production.[11]

From 2000 to 2010, Syria experienced an outpouring of drama termed *fawra dramiyyeh.* Each year during Ramadan, channels aired thirty-five to forty Syrian miniseries, which emerged as a leading purveyor of drama in the Arab world.[12] During this time, each miniseries was composed of approximately thirty episodes, each about forty to fifty minutes in length. Syrian productions were distinguished in areas such as screenwriting, directing, acting, music, and mise-en-scène.[13] In 2011, however, the number of miniseries dropped to twenty-six amid increased violence, poor access to historical sites, and the exodus of important figures from Syrian drama. The number rose slightly to twenty-seven in 2012, but then there were roadblocks and bombings in Damascus and beyond. Filming for the 2013 season was confined to calmer areas like Tartous and Suwayda or relocated outside Syria, primarily in Lebanon, creating the phenomenon of Syrian-Lebanese coproduction.[14] This shift was a frequent topic of conversation in both the industry and the press.[15] At the same time, some production crews preferred to take the risk of filming in Syria. This dedication—and willingness to try out new, lesser-known talent—boosted the 2013 crop to twenty-nine *musalsalat*.[16]

In *The Politics of Love* (2013), I examined Syrian drama from the 1960s onward, touching on debates among drama creators from 2011 through 2013 on the alleged Majlis al-Ta'awun al-Khaleeji (Gulf Cooperation Council, or GCC) embargo, issues of government censorship, and the relevance of their art form during a time of war and bloodshed.[17] Through their voices, I showed the complicated political stances of these intellectuals as well as the reasons some chose silence and their fundamental philosophical divisions. I also observed that as of 2013, despite the regime's efforts to clamp down on oppositional drama, the quality and frequency of Syrian drama had not eroded.[18]

My analysis of Syrian drama from 2014 onward has shown not only the survival but the flourishing of this art form. The 2014 season situated six of the miniseries during the civil war and at times probed the war's roots. Many established actors, such as 'Abd al-Mon'em 'Amayri, Amal 'Arafeh, and Ayman Zeidan, whose departure in the early years of the uprising left a cultural void, returned to Damascus for the 2014 season. Syrian miniseries were slated to appear on channels such as MBC, MTV, al-Sumaria, Abu Dhabi, and al-Jadid. By this time, some miniseries commented directly on politics—whether pro- or anti-regime—rather than relying on gender and marriage metaphors to engage in subtle political critique. And so, while pre-uprising miniseries dealt directly with the corruption of government employees (without implicating the president), by 2014 stories such as *Qalam Humra* (Lipstick) and *al-Qurban* (Sacrifice) took politics to another level as they directly addressed political arrests. Miniseries like *al-Hubb Kullu* (All the Love) contained nationalistic messages that lamented war's destructive powers and expressed nostalgia for the stability of the past. At the same time, sensationalist stories of marital betrayal that were popular in post-uprising drama dominated the scene and elicited self-critique by those in the industry. On July 31, 2014, Ayman Zeidan posted to Facebook, "Drama portrays our society to only be governed by betrayal. Is there this much betrayal in our society? More than twenty miniseries were produced—but such an embarrassment. Did the 'azmeh' cause us to create such silly stories?"

Yet compared to previous seasons, production slowed in 2014; only twenty-two miniseries were broadcast. Several of these miniseries were filmed in the same location, and seven located their storylines directly within the current upheaval in Syria. Texts were not always complete and often relied on actors' improvisation. This season also witnessed adaptations of foreign films and serials to escape the "crisis." Other miniseries, such as *New Look*, *Suber Family 2*, and *Zunud al-Sitt*, avoided the war altogether. There were also seven Old Damascus tales that many perceived as historically inaccurate. Some shows were broadcast during the spring of 2014 before the Ramadan season in order to attract more viewers, since the World Cup took place that upcoming summer and would distract the public. In advance of the formal Ramadan season, *Nisa' min Hadha al-Zaman* (Women of the Time) was broadcast on MBC 1, *al-Ikhweh* (The Brothers) on Abu Dhabi, *Sarkhat al-Ruh* (Scream of the Soul) on Orbit, and *Khuwatam* (Rings) on Orbit. Additionally, more Syrian actors appeared in Egyptian *musalsalat* during this time. Indeed, Syrians played leading roles in the strongest Egyptian miniseries of the season.[19]

Having established the context, we now arrive at a metaphorical roundtable of voices of drama creators. Here, they debate the topic of whether or not didactic messages should prevail amid a tendency to engage in escapist storylines from the 2014 Ramadan season onward. During my fieldwork, prior to the 2014 Ramadan season, Syrian drama creators based in Beirut had much to say. Director Inas Haqqi expressed concern that filming was occurring in Damascus where bombing occurred and worried that directors were neglecting actors' safety. She also bemoaned the market-driven decline in Syrian political drama in exchange for escapist dramas. As evidence of this, Haqqi cited two miniseries produced by the well-known Syrian production company Clacket that addressed the current upheaval in Syria: *al-Wilada min al-Khasira* (Born from the Loins, 2011, 2012, 2013) and also *Sa-Na'ud Ba'da Qalil* (We'll Return Soon, 2013). While *al-Wilada min al-Khasira* succeeded, *Sa-Na'ud Ba'da Qalil* aired only three times. On the other hand, *al-Ikhweh*, produced one year later in 2014, was less political, as its Clacket producer, a Syrian now working outside the country, did not want to stir trouble and had decided that it was best to avoid the revolution in his stories as much as possible from that time onward. According to Haqqi, Clacket's miniseries depicting upheaval in Syria often caused difficulty with the regime. For example, she cited how the president's office contacted the Clacket producer to object to the casting of Kinda 'Aloosh, an actress in the opposition, in *Sa-Na'ud Ba'da Qalil*. In defense, the producer emphasized his selection of pro-regime actor Durayd Lahham for a starring role in the series also. In the end, though the producer allowed 'Aloosh to continue, Haqqi believes the role was diminished in response to governmental pressure.[20]

According to Haqqi, the government returns about 30 percent of the cost to the producer for filming in Abu Dhabi, in exchange for the publicity. In addition, restaurant and other businesses charges are covered. Yet actors are expensive. Haqqi contrasted Syrian drama mechanisms with Egypt's, pointing out that Egypt has about seventy-five channels, so even if there is an embargo against their country, many options remain. But because Syria does not have many channels, they depend on the GCC, which prefers shallow stories like *al-Ikhweh* or religiously motivated ones like *Bab al-Hara* (The Neighborhood Gate). Furthermore, as Haqqi made clear, the GCC was not accepting miniseries from a civil, secular perspective during this time of upheaval. Screenwriter Inas Haqqi and her husband, Ghassan Zakariyya, continued filming episodes for a new miniseries in Beirut with minimum resources. However, the actors were not professional and refused to listen, so she chose not to broadcast. Instead, she launched an internet show called *Under 35*, which brands her as the first online Syrian production company. *Under 35* aired on YouTube and aimed to give young people an uncensored platform for expression.[21]

For others, too, capturing the reality of war was essential despite marketing pressures. In a June 27, 2014, interview in Beirut, Rafi Wahbi said,

> I was critiqued by some for the way *Halawat al-Ruh* [Beauty of the Soul] transferred viewers right into the middle of bloodshed they have already had enough of. . . . I looked at this as a way to document the intimacies of war. I imagined a group of young individuals who loved their country, who had all broken off from all different groups and were bonded together in their desire to protect national treasures, which are a symbol of our history and ancient civilization. I watched YouTube to see how people live in Syria throughout the war and knew that showing the beauty of music and art amid the destruction would relay a powerful message. . . . Toward the end of the story, Sara sees an old man saying: "Wahed, Wahed, al-Sh'ab al-Suri Wahed" (One. One. One. The Syrian people are one). This is based on my memories in Beirut. Once I saw an elderly man who was drunk and mumbling this phrase to himself. I remembered that this was what people were saying at the beginning of uprising; it was the core message that the masses were trying to relay to the regime and the outside world. When I saw him murmuring this after death and destruction had taken over the uprising, I asked myself, how far have we moved from our initial impulses? I wanted to remind viewers that we were once one even though we are now in the midst of so much destruction.[22]

The above discussions about whether or not to portray the current reality in storylines were happening amid heated debates among actors about the nation's politics. Those who were pro-regime advocated standing by their nation.[23] Many pro-regime actors and actresses continue to live in the midst of danger, as leaving felt like a betrayal of Syria. Actress Suzanne Nejm al-Din believed that war "created bodies without souls," but even amid the turmoil, many actors remained committed to Syrian drama. Selma al-Mesri asserted her unwillingness to leave Syria during a time of "crisis," when one must stand with one's country.[24] Actor Jamal Suleiman thought it was a shame that many actors had been blacklisted. Nejm al-Din, on the other hand, accused opposition actors of selling out their country, complaining that Arabs did not understand the meaning of the freedom for which they were fighting and lambasting anyone who criticized Syria.[25] Actress Sulafa Me'mar believed there was a third world war taking place on Syrian soil and refused to divide Syrians into anti- and pro-regime stances.[26]

Inevitable debates flared up during Da'ish's escalating levels of violence in 2015. Despite mounting uncertainty, Syrian screenwriters diligently prepared for the new Ramadan season. Many considered Ramadan 2015 a comeback year when twenty-nine miniseries were aired (though several others were delayed or canceled). According to screenwriter Reem Hanna, some viewers needed to watch shows based on the uprising, while others preferred to escape this reality. Accordingly, drama creators offered a mix of shows that catered to different interests.[27] As drama creators wrote stories, Syrian intellectuals engaged in heated debates about the role of the arts during crisis. In light of new forms of opposition since the uprising, some scholars have critiqued Syrian drama creators for what they perceive as years of government co-optation and have questioned the relevance of the previous generation of drama creators.

The phenomena of Lebanese-Syrian and pan-Arab productions dominated discussion during the transitional 2015 Ramadan season. Adaptations of escapist foreign novels sprinkled the viewing landscape. On the other hand, certain Old Damascus tales indirectly captured the rhetoric of the uprising in scenes that appeared detached from current events, and a greater number of contemporary miniseries, broadcast both within and beyond Syria, covered the uprising than in previous years. With the exception of shows like Haitham Haqqi's *Wujuh wa Amaken* (Faces and Places, 2015), which emphasized the revolution's roots in a peaceful opposition movement, most shows focused on events taking place five years after the uprising, during a time of increased, Da'ish-generated violence. In fact, Da'ish became a major character and continued to be the subject of jokes whether indirectly (through a historical lens in Old Damascus tales) or directly (in contemporary tales portraying the current uprising).

By 2016, criticism of the direction Syrian drama had taken was proliferating. Of the twenty-six miniseries this year, ten dealt with the uprising, though the treatment was superficial at times. Drama creators continued to debate the role of drama amid an uprising turned civil war. Actor Mo'tasam al-Nahar contended that people need drama that is not didactic; the goal of Syrian drama should not be to rehearse daily problems in dramatic form. From al-Nahar's point of view, it is not just the content or the message but the approach that matters. Al-Nahar continued, "The 'crisis' has affected all of us. This makes me want to present my characters in the most credible form that respects the intelligence of the viewer."[28]

While al-Nahar was apprehensive that didactic messages were prevailing over realistic and complex characters with authentic, empathy-inducing lives, screenwriter Reem Hanna expressed concern that Syrian drama no longer conveyed a clear message or lesson. Hanna, who had been making escapist adaptations of Hollywood films during the early part of the uprising, shifted to a historical miniseries on the life of the nationalist feminist Nazik Khanum to ground Syrians in their own history. She also hoped to explore issues of gender and sexual orientation in the historical storyline while eliding contemporary events. She expounded on the predicament faced by screenwriters during the marketing pressures of war: "In contemporary storylines, our fans criticize us whether or not we talk of the war." Furthermore, Hanna contended that in general, production companies prefer pan-Arab miniseries to their Syrian counterparts. She explained that she had written a five-episode story for *Ahl al-Qaram*, but the miniseries was delayed until 2017, since only Syrians acted in it. She continued,

> We need to find a solution to the current predicament of Syrian drama. I wrote adaptations at first since I felt disillusioned. None of the writing we had done over the years had made any difference. Also, I felt it was too early to analyze what was going on. For this reason, I've decided to create a miniseries based on the life of Nazik Khanum. I'm adapting the miniseries from an Arab novel. I feel this is a way to use our own history rather than basing our storylines on Hollywood films. . . . While Egyptian drama is improving, Syrian drama this season is weak. It isn't even clear what direction we are heading in. Samer al-Barqawi, Laith Hajjo, and Hatim 'Ali are the only directors producing good work during this uprising. Unfortunately, drama has become commercial and is not offering important messages.[29]

As we have sat at a metaphorical roundtable of opinions of this book's protagonists (writers, directors, actors, producers) through Ramadan seasons, we have gained a sense of what these debates sound like within a broader range of views related to the relevance of the creative writing process during the instability of war. Also up for debate is the allure of escapism versus the necessity of documenting the current reality despite marketing difficulties. Furthermore, these drama creators' questions propel us to this book's central issue, namely, the desire among writers, producers, and artists to contribute to collective memory. In the following section, which examines 2014 onward, a time in which Da'ish intensified its acts of terrorism, we will continue this metaphorical roundtable as we observe drama creators' investment in this project of remembering and, for some, forgetting. This section overlaps chronologically and intersects with the discussion featured above, highlighting their concurrent concerns. This continuation of the metaphorical roundtable will lead us to an examination of the use of gender and marriage metaphors to capture various visions.

Post-Uprising Syrian Television Drama and Collective Memory Construction

In *After Image: Film, Trauma, and the Holocaust*, Joshua Hirsch delineates how, despite the murder of millions during the Holocaust, only two minutes of motion picture footage of this violence exists. Taken by Reinhard Wiener, the film captures firing squads shooting Jews after they were forced to jump into a pit. Wiener's film proclaimed cinema's role as both a conveyer of historical trauma and a form of posttraumatic historical memory. At the same time, it opened debates among survivors about whether the traumatic past could ever actually be remembered and represented.[30] In contrast, the Syrian civil war, known as one of the twenty-first century's greatest humanitarian disasters,[31] has been characterized by a continual bombardment of film footage and information that makes it impossible to interpret or make sense of events. Screenwriter Rafi Wahbi, whose miniseries *Halawat al-Ruh* was a hit during the summer of 2014, elaborates,

> It goes without saying that currently Syrian television screenwriters face numerous challenges. First, we are writing and trying to impart a modicum of wisdom during a time when events are still taking place and the outcome is unclear. These days, media outlets have as their goal the quick relaying of information, and thus, they bombard the population with constant, contradictory information. All sides of the internal conflict, as well as all external players, take part in this information war. There are many different viewpoints, and it is nearly impossible to sift through truths and lies. Despite all this information, the majority of the population is confused and has no idea what is really happening. In this context, television drama has the potential of falling into danger. For years, Syrian drama was famous for the fact that it portrayed the details of daily life in a realistic way. Indeed, that was what has distinguished Syrian drama from its inception. Now drama creators are in a difficult position. We are asked to take a position and play a role in the uprising while, at the same time, our audience is looking for miniseries that either tell their own perspective or allow them to completely escape reality.[32]

Seeing his screenwriting process as contributing to the historical archives of the period for future generations, Wahbi insisted on a neutral portrayal of all sides in the war.[33] Wahbi's use of the term "historical archive" is intentional and diverges from previous studies of history and memory that have been critical of the role of archives in transmitting the past. In *The Politics of Loss and Trauma in Contemporary Israeli Cinema* (2011), for instance, Raz Yosef examines French historian Pierre Nora's analysis of the collapse of memory and "acceleration of history," which nevertheless posits that "memory is absolute, while history is always relative." Nora explains how the duty to remember compels individuals to construct archives, "places of memory," which aspire to preserve fragments of the past but ironically make the distance from the past even greater and allow the archives to break from history. Basing his analysis on Jacques Derrida, Yosef expands on the notion that the archive is not a site of neutral safeguarding of the past but is, rather, marked by an unreliable selection process. In deciding what will be remembered, the archive also determines what will pass into oblivion.[34] Yet in creating *Halawat al-Ruh*, Wahbi designates a twofold process in the construction of a historical archive for future generations. Even as Wahbi seeks to document a dying time, the story centers on Sara and Isma'il, who travel to Syria to record the efforts of a group fighting to save ancient historical artifacts. In a conversation several months later, Wahbi specified the role that drama plays as a transmitter of cultural and historical memory for future generations: "While I realize that viewership is down, I believe that *Halawat al-Ruh* forms part of the historical archives of this period of war and destruction to which later generations will turn for understanding. I'm interested in how drama may influence people not today, but ten years down the road."[35]

Christa Salamandra has shown that prior to the uprising, drama creators insisted confidently that miniseries served as a potent form of media due to their transformative nature and ability to reach the masses.[36] After the uprising, accompanying a heightened critique of drama creators viewed as having abandoned the revolution, a shift in consciousness occurred. Drama creators now questioned the relevance of their art form amid the trauma of war. Wahbi's insistence on drama as a historical archive is part of a wartime effort to establish the importance of miniseries as cultural memory, transmitting the trauma of war to future generations. For Wahbi, memory, history, and archives are interchangeable. They are also integral considerations within the work of drama. In *Surviving Images: Cinema, War, and Cultural Memory in the Middle East* (2015), Kamran Rastegar affectingly analyzes cinema's role in constructing memories of social conflicts and historical trauma. His research documents filmmakers' contributions to and opposition of hegemonic paradigms as they vie for narrative space and create cultural memories of war for future generations.[37] The research presented in this book occurs in conversation with Rastegar's formidable contribution to film. I wish to add another dimension of visual culture to this conversation by portraying how Syrian drama creators strive to ensure their art form's survival and relevance in the midst of war.

Renowned director Haitham Haqqi withdrew from Syrian drama during the initial years of the uprising, instead writing political pieces in Paris for the

Arabic-speaking press. In 2014, however, he had begun preparing a new miniseries, *Wujuh wa Amaken*, which would be filmed in Turkey and would archive early memories of the revolution.[38] Despite production pressures, Haqqi intended to analyze the current uprising and provide critical historical and political explanations to the archives. *Wujuh wa Amaken* was filmed in Turkey and aired on a small Arabic-speaking channel during Ramadan 2015. Its tone is set by dull music that is intended to create a sense of boredom. Within the miniseries, three separate stories—"Waqt Mustaqta'" (Fragmented Time), "Madinat al-Dhahab" (City of Gold), and "al-Qal'a" (Fortress)—narrate political memories of the revolution in Syria from an oppositional viewpoint. According to Haqqi, the storyline in "Waqt Mustaqta'" exemplifies how the regime sought to corrupt honest people with integrity.[39] Many critics claimed that the stories featured flimsy character development and too many direct political conversations that detracted from the narrative flow of the storyline.[40] Yet not everyone believed that this didactic miniseries had failed. Leading television editor Iyad Shihab Ahmad, who boycotted the industry for several years, agreed to edit *Wujuh wa Amaken* due to its strong political message.[41]

The past several years had witnessed heightened violence in Syria, from Asad's chemical weapons attack in the Damascus suburbs to Da'ish's augmented presence in Syria and abroad, where the group's extremist practices included public beheadings and the destruction of ancient historical sites in Syria and Iraq. In addition to criticism of stylistic issues, *Wujuh wa Amaken* met with criticism from both sides with respect to its depiction of the commencement of the uprising. Many in the opposition questioned the series' representation of the early, peaceful days of the revolution, which some saw as a frivolous gesture amid the current tragic destruction of Syrian civilization at the hands of the regime and Da'ish. Meanwhile, the Syrian regime, which deplored its oppositional stance, barred many of the miniseries' actors from leaving Syria for Turkey.[42]

Drama creators involved in the creation of *Wujuh wa Amaken* defended the miniseries. Jamal Suleiman, who played the leading role of Mazin in "Waqt Mustaqta'," contended that the miniseries gave renowned Syrian artists who had been blacklisted a chance once again in post-uprising Syrian drama.[43] This, indeed, had been Haqqi's proximate goal.[44] Khaled Khalifa, who wrote the screenplay for "al-Qal'a," contended that all three stories in the miniseries were important since they focused on the roots of the uprising and the early, peaceful days of revolt, a historical memory that the regime certainly does not want documented. At the same time, while it documents collective memory during the devastation of war, art does not have the power to solve problems caused by the cruelty of war. He stated, "On the one hand it is important to write, since most social media networks are against the revolution and the oppositional forces have little voice. I believe that it is important to shed light on the peaceful days of the revolution since these stories will help future generations

FIGURE I.1 Ali (played by Maksim Khalil) to the left and Qamar (played by Najla' Khamri) to the right in *al-Qal'a* (Fortress) in the miniseries *Wujuh wa Amaken* (Faces and Places).

Courtesy of Haitham Haqqi.

understand what has happened. Yet I acknowledge the limited power of art during revolution. Writing cannot give milk to the children and stop the bombs from falling."[45]

Haitham Haqqi argued that during that same Ramadan season most viewers preferred *Ghadan Naltaqi* (We'll Meet Tomorrow, 2015), a story of Syrian refugees in Lebanon, because of its politically neutral stance. The story centers on two brothers with opposing political creeds who are in love with the same woman, Warda. Their fighting leads to the destruction of her home, suggesting that both sides are equally to blame for the destruction of Syria.[46] *Ghadan Naltaqi* is the kind of miniseries that Khalifa classifies as "gray" (meaning without a clear position).[47] Despite positive reviews in the press,[48] many accused *Ghadan Naltaqi* of being prejudiced against the Lebanese. MTV publicly criticized LBC for broadcasting *Ghadan Naltaqi*. One scene they cite for racism showed a contentious Lebanese taxi driver beeping at another driver to speed up. When the driver responds colloquially in Syrian, the aggressive Lebanese driver exclaims, "Oh! And he's Syrian!" The Syrian driver retorts, "What do you want us to do? This is how God created us." While this portrayal of Lebanese belligerence was seen by some as racist, others argued that it accurately portrayed the way many Lebanese feel about the presence of Syrians in Lebanon. In response, screenwriter Samer Ridwan commented on his Facebook page that an official channel such as MTV should not evaluate television drama in such unprofessional terms.[49]

Furthermore, critics debated the ethics of pro-regime and/or wealthy actors in *Ghadan Naltaqi* playing impoverished refugees, who were often ridiculed.[50]

Indeed, the genre of comedy and political satire proved complex in post-uprising Syrian drama with respect to whether it was acceptable to mock suffering in this form of cultural memory construction. By 2015, the long-standing political satire *Buq'at Daw' Part Eleven* was criticized for depicting Syrians' less-than-admirable and at-times-eccentric behavior as a result of the pressures of war.[51] Rafi Wahbi argues, "You can't make comedy and make people laugh amidst the bloodshed. Making fun of the pain of real people is in my opinion not appropriate in today's context. But you have to look at individual cases." Wahbi cites the miniseries *Dhoboo al-Shanati* (Hurry Up and Pack!), written by Mamdouh Hamada and directed by Laith Hajjo, as an example of an appropriately comic miniseries. This storyline focuses on a family who discuss whether they should emigrate from Syria. After jihadists and then government soldiers occupy their home, they decide they should leave. Yet the miniseries ends with an announcement that a family of Syrians drowned as they were escaping by boat.

Despite initial concerns, according to Wahbi the miniseries has a rich history of those two towering intellectuals—Hamada and Hajjo—working as a team to engage the population in politically critical satires. Wahbi believes that Hamada and Hajjo's work stands opposed to *Buq'at Daw'*, which lost its strength after the first few seasons. According to Wahbi, *Buq'at Daw'*'s stories about jihadists simply feed into government propaganda that the regime is fighting religious fanatics and terrorists.[52] Noted screenwriter Hoozan 'Akko argues that comedies can be inappropriate since they mock the pain of real people. Indeed, he believes that creating not only comedy but any meaningful drama post-2011 is complicated, as it is difficult to gain a clear perspective or impart wisdom about the horrors now taking place. Thus he opted to write a series that is definitively not a comedy. This miniseries, called *Bint al-Shah Bandar* (Shah Bandar's Daughter), tells the story of an impossible love that takes place in Beirut in the 1800s and disregards the uprising completely. Clearly, the purpose of this series was not to construct cultural memory of current sociopolitical trauma.[53]

On the other hand, some critics and audiences have embraced comedy as a welcome diversion amid the devastation of war. The year 2015 witnessed Da'ish's decimation of Iraq's two ancient cities Nimrud and al-Hadr (March 7), destruction of the Baal Shamin temple in Palmyra (August 23), countless terrorist attacks, and the deaths of an estimated quarter million Syrians. Within hours on June 26, Da'ish conducted a series of attacks in Tunisia, France, and Kuwait, simultaneously issuing a warning that Ramadan would be a month of disaster. But on June 28 *Donia 2015*, a Golden Line production, was featured in the *Ramadan Rating* show initiating by Abu Dhabi. Episodes 18 and 19 were devoted entirely to poking fun at Da'ish. In this two-episode storyline, members of Da'ish mistakenly kidnap the housekeeper, Donia, and try to extract millions from her employees, though they are then thwarted by her escape. Screenwriter and actress

FIGURE I.2 Extremists visit the home of Fayha (played by Douba al-Dibis) and Khalil (played by Bassam Kousa) in *Dhoboo al-Shanati* (Hurry Up and Pack!).

Courtesy of Laith Hajjo.

Amal 'Arafeh elaborated on the importance of the miniseries in the collective memory of Syrians:

> In Syria there must be someone good like Donia who exists in order for the country to persist to survive. Fifteen years have passed since *Donia Part One*. I felt it was time for *Donia* to return to our collective memory. I wondered how I could resurrect this memory for Syrians and make both the *mu'arad* [opposition] and *muwali* [pro-regime] laugh. I wanted to speak about many people—people currently inside and outside of Syria. Some said, "it has been such a long time since I heard my neighbor laugh." I believe that it's easy to make people cry when you talk about the horrors people are living during the ravages of war, but it's not easy to make people laugh. I wanted to revive this memory in order to give hope for the future.

Broadcast on Abu Dhabi and Dubai, *Donia 2015* remained consistently in the top five of the rating show during that Ramadan month. It ranked second on the same day as Amal 'Arafeh's interview, while the Syrian miniseries *Chello* ranked fourth and *al-'Arrab: Nadi al-Sharq* (The Godfather: Club of the East) fifth. Some members of the press who were critical of miniseries for either adapting foreign series or focusing unrelentingly on violence and marital betrayal were especially appreciative of *Donia 2015*. They viewed the miniseries as a rarity, encouraging laughter during a time of heartbreak.[54] Shukran Murtaja, who costarred with 'Amal 'Arafeh, was proud that the miniseries brought laughter back into the Arab household.[55]

Musalsalat and the Politics of Representing Gender and Marriage: A Brief History

Currently, given the production pressures of war, debates among those involved in the industry center on their own relevance, whether storylines should escape or capture the current reality of war, in addition to considerations of memory. Yet prior to the uprising, drama creators extensively discussed the nuances of political critique. Why could some writers engage in open political discussions while others could not? These internal debates were reflected within Western academia, where vocabulary and imagery appeared that had been previously circulated among Syrians. Specifically, scholars asked why political criticism could appear in the film industry within an authoritarian state that allows no opposition in other arenas. For the most part, functionalist arguments about coercion held sway. Some scholars relied on Bakhtin's analysis of "carnival" to suggest that licensed, politically critical cultural productions incite chaos and political resistance. At the same time, many Syrians argued that the Asad regime used politically critical television productions as "safety-valves" to release frustrations. Meanwhile, scholars drew upon the theory of *tanfis*, a term used by Syrian cultural producers that means channeling frustrations into artistic forms such as television and theater to decrease the likelihood of mobilizing against the regime.[56] Indeed, prior to the 2011 uprising, the notion of *tanfis* informed most discussions of Syrian drama. However, Lisa Wedeen has argued that there was a false dichotomy between the idea of activism and *tanfis*. While she proffered the theory of *tanfis* to explain the durability of authoritarianism under Hafiz al-Asad, she maintained that artistic transgressions such as parody nourish a counterculture. Yet she also posited that these parodies allow for mutual "unbelief" in the system. In the end, this "unbelief," a state of neither faith in the system nor explicit rejection of it, encourages capitulation to Asad.[57]

In *Dissident Syria: Making Oppositional Arts Official* (2007), miriam cooke elaborated on the idea of the "pressure valve" that sustains an unjust system. She also examined the regime's Machiavellian strategy of commissioning criticism to project a democratic facade.[58] More recently, Donatella Della Ratta claimed that writers working under Bashar al-Asad no longer adhered to the politics of pretense or the "unbelief" described by Wedeen. Nor, according to Della Ratta, did they continue to struggle to retain independence or to push boundaries to keep from feeling complicit, as cooke described. Rather, as Della Ratta argued, the new generation of drama creators during the first ten years of Bashar al-Asad's rule were implicated in "the whisper strategy," a relationship based on suggestions or innuendo in which creators maintain a comfortable relationship with power by endorsing the regime's *tanwir* (enlightenment), or cultural reconstruction project. This project uses the *musalsalat* to combat corruption, gender inequality, religious extremism, and illiteracy.[59] Furthermore, Della Ratta argued that drama creators worked closely with the government on this *tanwir* project to promote personal and civic liberties with the agenda of prioritizing social over political reforms.[60]

Della Ratta's analysis posited that drama creators are no longer savvy intellectuals who engage in political critique via subterfuge; rather, they are wholly complicit with the regime. This complicity reveals a shared agenda between drama creators and the regime to resolve a perceived backwardness in Syria in their project of nation building and fails to consider how gender and marriage storylines that seemingly appear to promote social reform are, in truth, also metaphors for political reform. Ultimately, Della Ratta argued, the shared agenda of the regime and drama creators serves to reinforce the prestige and power of both parties. Unlike the intellectuals described by Wedeen, those who merely pantomimed complicity, or by cooke, those who actively camouflaged their complicity, contemporary drama creators boast of their compliance with the Asad regime.[61] Yet Della Ratta's analysis is problematic since she did not factor in voices such as Najeeb Nseir, a screenwriter who asserted that drama creators have resisted the regime steadily since the genre's inception and throughout Bashar al-Asad's rule.[62] French scholar Yves Gonzales-Quijano, too, spoke of the complicated history of drama's co-optation by the government. While his nuanced argument documented the continuation of social and political critique in these miniseries, it left undetermined whether collusion actually occurred or whether the accusations were unfounded.[63]

In any case, this academic examination of Syrian television has become largely outdated in a post-uprising context. If the regime intended to let the population engage in a "ventilation" process to prevent political upheaval, it certainly did not work. As history has shown, the Syrian uprising became the Syrian civil war. The "wall of fear" in Syria is damaged by years of open resistance, and the theory of *tanfis* no longer captures the process by which drama creators navigate censorship, intimidation, and co-optation to publish subversive work in the public eye.[64] I emphasize that these notions of *tanfis* and commissioned criticism and even the whisper strategy come from within Syrian culture themselves. When I lived in Syria from 2002 to 2008, drama creators referred to the notion of *tanfis* in response to my questions about their peers' subversive work. It appeared that this claim often stemmed from personal rivalries and the competitive nature of the industry. Drama creators are highly aware of the bitter realities that surround and inform their work. References to regime coercion and *tanfis* mechanisms occur frequently in Syrian drama, underscoring the highly self-reflexive nature of Syrian television and fact that drama creators are often their own toughest critics.

Though no longer fully applicable in the post-uprising context, these theories continue to circulate in comic form among drama creators. Hazim Suleiman's short sketch in the ninth season of *Buq'at Daw'* (2012), titled "Tanfis," is a case in point. In this sketch, Suleiman suggests that the Ba'th dictatorship is continually searching for alternative methods of *tanfis*. Nationalist (*watani*) discourse that warns that the regime is the sole protector against imperialism and foreign conspiracies serves as a form of *tanfis*, as the population swallows these narratives.[65] Nur Shishekly's "Bila Saqf" (Without a Roof) in *Buq'at Daw' Part Nine* is inspired by the real circumstances of the previous season's *Fawq al-Saqf* (Above the Ceiling) and provides a poignant example of commissioned criticism. It also illustrates the challenges writers face under dictatorship. Underscoring this ongoing circulation is my experience during the summer of 2017. In the Teh-Marbuta café in Hamra, Beirut, I mentioned the "whisper strategy" as it related to pre-uprising miniseries to several drama creators, including television editor and producer Iyad Shihab Ahmad and director Laith Hajjo. They eagerly discussed the concept among themselves. Hajjo, who had directed the first, second, and fourth seasons of *Buq'at Daw'*, described the dispensation to protest during first two seasons of the show. The "whispering" (*hamasa*), however, began during the third season. According to Iyad Shihab Ahmad, the "wall of fear" was broken once the uprising began in 2011, but much of the *tawatu'* (collusion) prior to that time was a result of legitimate fear. Those who refused to cave into the regime paid a heavy price.[66]

In *The Politics of Love: Sexuality, Gender, and Marriage in Syrian Television Drama* (2013), I polemicized about the functionalist theories of *tanfis*, commissioned criticism, and the "whisper strategy," asserting that these notions fixate on regime intent and discount the intellectuals who evaded the censors by making use of symbols and metaphors in their political critique. Along those lines, I contended that Syrian drama creators used love, gender, and marriage metaphors to engage in political critique from the 1960s onward. I argued that in the early political parodies of the 1960s through 1970s, secular in approach and entirely from a male perspective, the main concern was an embattled, subordinate masculinity within the family, which served as a microcosm of the state. Economic despair led to loss of male dignity. Furthermore, the presence of frustrated masculinity in heterosexual marital relations ruled by a wife's demands—with the recurring image of marriage as a prison—allowed commentary on economic hardship, corruption, and dictatorship. Indeed, a central anxiety was women's empowerment as a result of a suppressed masculinity, seen in marriage metaphors of the 1980s and 1990s that feature the theme of fighting domestic dictators. The 1990s also saw the development of the politics of *qabadayat* (masculine tough men) as guardians of women's sexuality.[67]

In her research on feminism and the postcolonial condition, Lila Abu-Lughod illustrated that those who seek to challenge gender roles are accused of imitating Western modernity and attacking cultural authenticity.[68] In *Screening Culture, Viewing Politics: An Ethnography of Television, Womanhood, and Nation in Postcolonial India* (1999), Purnima Mankekar examined state-run family dramas in India of the late 1980s and early 1990s. Although the dramas did not envision a radical restructuring of power relations within the family, community, or nation, women's bodies were charged as cultural identity markers and protectors of tradition.[69] Similarly, in the case of Syrian family dramas from 2000 until the 2011 uprising, women's bodies upheld and dismantled taboos. They also dichotomized Syrian women and the West by representing Syrian bodies as pure and Western bodies as impure. The construction of the *qabaday* was a central theme, too, with an evolving relationship to femininity and deep connections to political critique. The more revolutionary trends from 2000 onward, however, demonstrated that once the *qabaday* had shed the role of protector of a woman's sexuality, a truly egalitarian relationship could exist. This relationship symbolized citizens attaining their dignity and rights from an authoritarian order. Indeed, for the more revolutionary drama creators, the repressed sexuality of women was symbolic of the political oppression of an entire population. These discourses were not always chronological, and conflicting discourses and counternarratives often occurred within the same period. Despite the conflicting discourses, my argument shows that what appears on the surface to be love, marriage, and gender storylines are actually metaphors and allegories that engage in political critique.[70]

The Politics of Love examined Syrian drama in depth from the 1960s through the first two years of the uprising. While 2011 and 2012 showed increased direct political critique in certain storylines, love, marriage, and gender metaphors continued, especially in miniseries that did not address contemporary politics directly in their storylines. Avant-garde screenwriters continued to oppose the notion of the woman's body as a purity marker distinguished from the West, and this peaked in 2012 with Qoshaqji's *Urwah 'Ariya* (Naked Souls). Because *The Politics of Love* went to press during the late summer of 2013, I touched briefly in the afterword on the new challenges drama creators faced for the 2013 season, which included increased violence, the rise of Da'ish, the exodus of numerous established drama creators from Syria, and heightened production pressures.[71] In *Mediating the Uprising*, I argue that the rise of Da'ish in 2013 would usher in a defining shift in how gender and marriage were represented, which would crystalize in the 2015 season and then continue onward. Indeed, the following section examines changes in gender and marriage norms in the creation of collective memory during a time of heightened war, nostalgia for previous stability, and the rise of the destructive power of Da'ish. In the following section, I elaborate on the changed political context in which drama creators find themselves. This context includes the rise of Da'ish and religious extremism, along with evolving representations of sexuality whose counterpoint is Da'ish rather than the "corrupting" norms of the West.

The Rise of Da'ish, the Creation of Collective Memory in Wartime, and the Intersection with Gender Issues

By 2016, at least 470,000 Syrians had died as a result of the war. Ramadan 2016 was marked by continued Da'ish terrorist attacks both within and outside of Syria. The year 2017 ushered in intensified fighting, despite the declaration of a nationwide cease-fire. As fighting continued, Da'ish unleashed new waves of destruction and on January 20 destroyed part of the Roman theater in Palmyra. Airstrikes and suicide bombings continued. While Da'ish terrorized Syria and beyond, the 2017 Ramadan season began with the Kuwaiti company Zain's widely publicized television commercial asserting that the Muslim God is a God of Peace. This commercial reflects Zain's mission to teach people that Islam is a peaceful religion and that hate should be returned with forgiveness and love. Yet the act of remembering—or forgetting—in this short video clip was not without controversy. Syrian actress Yara Sabri criticized the commercial for its misuse of facts and its exoneration of the Syrian regime. Additionally, the use of a child to play the Syrian boy Omran Daqneesh ignited intense critique. Daqneesh was wounded in a regime airstrike in the Qaterji neighborhood of Aleppo; an image of him sitting vulnerable in the ambulance went viral. In the commercial, the injured boy holds up a sign stating that he responds to hate with love. Critics of the commercial reminded viewers that the Syrian regime, not Da'ish, was responsible for Daqneesh's death. While the Kuwaiti commercial was clearly not a *musalsal*, it serves as a clear example of forgetting/misremembering the state's violence. The narrative hegemony of collective memory construction is evident, in both the mechanisms of the commercial and the commercial's implication in working through traumas (or not). Here we see a hegemonic discourse occurring in which facts not just are obscured but displace responsibility from the regime to Da'ish.

Despite the criticism, certain Syrian miniseries continued to represent this violent and terrifying time as solely the responsibility of Da'ish, an elision that effectively absolved the regime for its own complicity and violence. Attacks on the Manchester arena on May 22, deadly twin bombings in Baghdad on May 30, the London Bridge attack on June 4, and the attack in Iran on June 7 corroborated Da'ish's ongoing global presence. Even prior to its release, the pan-Arab miniseries *Gharabib Sud* (Black Crows, 2017), produced by MBC 1, received media attention as it allowed viewers to enter the personal world of Da'ish in Syria and Iraq and apprehend details and anecdotes lost in the news.[72] This miniseries, which had selective English subtitles and would later be picked up by Netflix,[73] focuses on women and young children. The story reveals Da'ish's methodology: preying on people's fear to lure them to terrorism. Syrian actors were cast in leading roles, which offered complex profiles of Da'ish figures. Some individuals are cruel and corrupt, while others either have been tricked into joining or have done so out of desperation. Early on, a scene shows Da'ish members slaughtering their kidnapped victims for their organs, a practice that resulted from depleted oil revenues and the need for other sources of money. The miniseries allows us to see Da'ish techniques, including the strategic use of their followers, who are doctors, hackers, and fighters. In one storyline, a man tricks his new wife, a French woman, into traveling to the Middle East with him. She soon discovers that he is a member of Da'ish and that he is behind the terrorist attacks in London and Paris. He tells her he is Muslim and this is his fight. When she flees the Da'ish cell with a gun, black-clad women catch her and drag her, screaming, back.

As the miniseries continues, corrupt sheikhs organize a string of terrorist attacks around the world and promise the perpetrators eternal paradise. Inside the Da'ish cell, a mother realizes that the powerful emir has sexually molested her mute son. An old mufti tells his wife that she cannot leave the house. He orders a boy to watch her and make sure she works, since rest will allow sinful thoughts. The evil Khansa (played by Syrian actress Dima al-Jundi) passes a plate with a note that designates which woman receives the next martyrdom assignment. We repeatedly see Da'ish mercilessly killing doubters and preying on the most vulnerable. The miniseries also depicts how Da'ish exaggerates its reports of attacks in order to foment fear. Noticeably lacking, however, are reminders of the barbarity of the Syrian regime. The miniseries stopped at Episode 20. According to Iyad Shihab Ahmad, the already-controversial miniseries was perceived as having crossed a line when a Kuwaiti woman told the other female characters that it was an honor sleep with the *mujahidin* (Islamic guerilla fighters) and engage in *jihad al-nikah* (sexual jihad).[74]

In his article "The Arabic Fantastic and ISIS Terror: The Aesthetics of Antiterrorism and Its Limits" (2017), Jamil Khader argues that the Zain advertisement and Black Crows fail to provide a protective screen as a self-defense mechanism against the trauma and horrors of the Islamic State. Furthermore, he critiques the fact that the advertisement and miniseries present a form of moral relativism and ambiguity that ultimately humanize the terrorist. Khader proceeds to argue that framing Da'ish in the horror show genre also filled with monsters and zombies could offer a way out of this impasse. Khader also contends that current representations of Islamic terrorism fail to convey the inflammatory role that "US imperial interventionism and global war on terrorism" has had on terrorist groups. However, he fails to mention the benefit that dictatorships such as the Syrian regime reap from the focus on Islamic terror in art form.[75]

Mediating the Uprising: Narratives of Gender and Marriage in Syrian Television Drama takes an approach that is, for the most part, literary but also contains ethnographic fieldwork among drama creators. I show how post-uprising Syrian televisual culture portrays a battle against religious extremism as drama creators struggle for relevance amid wartime marketing pressures. In *Egypt as a Woman: Nationalism, Gender, and Politics* (2005), Beth Baron examined mythmaking in national narratives that identify an external enemy. In her research on women's political activism in Egypt and women's incorporation into collective memory, Baron analyzed how forgetting is central to the construction of nationalist narratives. While some memories vanish, those perceived as dividing the collective are intentionally repressed.[76]

As shown in a preceding section, numerous scholars have examined issues related to cultural and historical memory construction and the role of forgetting and memory in representations of past. According to Jeffrey C. Alexander in *Trauma: A Social Theory*, "Cultural trauma occurs when members of a collectivity feel they have been subjected to a horrendous event that leaves indelible marks upon their group consciousness, marking their memories forever and changing their future identity in fundamental and irrevocable ways."[77] In *When Memory Comes*, Saul Friedlander expanded these ideas, identifying a "working through" of the traumatic events that those traumatized individuals may attain agency.[78] In *Memory, History, Forgetting*, Paul Ricoeur traced the embroilment of memory and imagination through the Greek lineage, delineating Plato's discussion of representation of something of the past that is currently absent: "Now, to begin, do you expect someone to grant you that man's present memory of something which he has experienced in the past but is no longer experiencing is the same sort of experience that he had then? This is far from being true."[79]

During the current upheaval in Syria, some drama creators write screenplays that ignore past oppression at the hands of the regime and can be characterized as having historical amnesia. These intellectuals focus on the current troubles of war without allowing the necessary distance for "working through" the trauma. Thus the complex process of constructing cultural and historical memory is short-circuited. Furthermore, this is a way to differentiate an imagined secular vision of pre-uprising days from radical Islam as portrayed by Da'ish. At the same time, wartime marketing challenges have made drama a casualty of war, as some miniseries have capitulated to regime narratives in order to survive. Useful here is Alexander's contention that mediated mass communication, itself subject to various restrictions, allowed for some trauma metanarratives to gain hegemony over others.[80] In the case of this book, we witness how particular gender narratives attempt to gain hegemony over others. At the same time, by examining the nuances and complexities of each genre, as well as hidden gems, we may observe the survival and even flourishing of unconventional strands with the potential to cause transformation.

In *Mediating the Uprising: Narratives of Gender and Marriage in Syrian Television Drama*, which covers the commencement of the uprising but elaborates more extensively on the period from 2013 through 2018, I show that gender and marriage continue to inform drama while moving from a predominantly politically critical stance prior to the uprising to social and cultural transformation in the post-uprising period. I argue that the rise of Da'ish in 2013 marks a turning point. Indeed, dismantling sexual taboos has been less complicated, especially from 2014 onward, as many Syrian drama creators differentiate an authentic Syrian culture not from that of the West, but rather from that of extremism represented by Da'ish. This tendency crystalizes in 2015. In this context, the female body is no longer burdened by purity markers distinct from its Western counterpart. Storylines including nonheteronormative relations, previously taboo, are explored more openly and with less judgment following the uprising. In other words, drama creators find themselves in a changed political context. This new context involves the rise of Da'ish and concern about religious extremism, changed material conditions of production, and the new representations of sexuality, marriage, and gender norms in Syria. These factors are understood in relation to the conservative social norms advanced by Da'ish rather than by "the corrupting sexual license" of Western society.

Five Post-2011 Strands of Syrian Miniseries Set in Wartime Syria and Predicated on Gender and Marriage Issues

This book focuses on five post-2011 strands of Syrian miniseries, all of which reference the war and all of which ostensibly include gender and marriage issues at the heart of their storylines. These strands can be described as the following: an oppositional stance, regime propaganda, a neutral political stance, a nostalgic stance, and the "social for the sake of the social" stance. A clear-cut divide between these genres does not always exist, as some miniseries evince a mixture of these strands at various points in their storyline. While their relationships to the state, attitudes toward the past, and depictions of gender dynamics differ, each strand overwhelmingly opposes the culture of Da'ish and religious extremism. Furthermore, as we shall see, all miniseries at times fall into the trap of reproducing the regime narrative, regardless of screenwriters' intentions. This is because anti-Da'ish narratives fit easily into the regime narrative, unless those anti-Da'ish narratives also explicitly point to regime violence. It is overly simplistic, however, to place miniseries into a regime narrative because of intermittent intersections between the objects of their criticism; close analysis reveals both the screenwriters' intentions and indications of a critique of the regime.

I have computed that 211 Syrian miniseries were broadcast and produced from 2011 to 2018 (see Appendices A and B). In all, 88 percent (186 miniseries) of these miniseries were wholly Syrian, while 6 percent (13 miniseries) were Syrian-Lebanese productions and 6 percent (12 miniseries) were Syrian-dominated pan-Arab (with Syrian actors, directors, and/or writers). Since the pan-Arab miniseries included the strong participation of Syrian drama creators, I argue that they form an essential part of new trends in post-uprising Syrian drama. Of the 211 miniseries, 60 contemporary miniseries (28.5 percent) commented in some way on the current uprising and war; this figure also includes miniseries such as *al-Haibeh* (2017) and *Tango* (2018) that referred to the war only indirectly. Of this 28.5 percent that addressed the war, 29 percent (17 miniseries) had a neutral political position, 8 percent (5 miniseries) were clearly oppositional, 15 percent (9 miniseries) promoted regime propaganda, 11.5 percent (7 miniseries) were nostalgic, and 36.5 percent (22 miniseries) can be categorized as the social for the sake of social. While the nostalgic storylines did not always intend to cater to a regime narrative, they at times unintentionally reproduced aspects of the regime narrative by harkening back to a previous time period that is often perceived as stable. I placed them in their own category, though, since they intentionally often differed from that of regime propaganda miniseries.

While 28.5 percent of the miniseries touched on the war, the remaining 71.5 percent (151 miniseries) included 42 Old Damascus tales (28 percent), 13 historical and biographical storylines (8.5 percent), 34 comedies (22.5 percent), 9 escapist adaptations (6 percent), 2 police thrillers (1.5 percent), and 51 miniseries (33.5 percent) that deal with social issues without addressing the war. Several of the 51 miniseries in the non-war social strand (*al-Sarab*, 2011; *al-Ghufran*, 2011; *Urwah 'Ariya*, 2012) use marriage and gender metaphors to critique politics and society, as occurred pre-uprising; the majority are escapist and avoid politics. As we shall see in chapter 4, as the uprising continued, Old Damascus tales, in particular, captured the rhetoric of the uprising in indirect ways; however, I have not included those in the percentage of miniseries addressing the uprising. Furthermore, Old Damascus tales such as *Ayyam Shamiyyeh* (1993) have traditionally been characterized by nostalgia, a hearkening back to a perceived golden age in Syrian history before the Ba'th Party regime. This strand of nostalgia differs from the nostalgia present in narratives set in the midst of the war that choose to forget the oppression of the Ba'th Party. While I have not combined these two percentages together into one whole, the nostalgic register makes up 3 percent of the total and the Old Damascus tales make up 20 percent of the total, demonstrating the influential potential of this nostalgic feature. It is also important to clarify that all the above figures compose a rough estimate to give a general impression of the media landscape, as Syrian miniseries sometimes fall into various categories at different points in the storyline.

The overtly political miniseries addressing the war can generally be broken into two groups: those that clearly espouse a regime narrative and those that espouse an unabashedly oppositional stance. Those that espouse a clear regime narrative make up 15 percent of the miniseries that deal directly with the uprising. These miniseries, such as *al-'Inaya al-Mushaddada* (Emergency Care, 2015) and *Bila Ghamad* (Without Cover, 2016), can be used as propaganda on behalf of the regime and emphasize a stable sociopolitical environment in pre-2011 Syria.[81] While these series attempt to portray more liberal gender norms compared to the standards embraced within religious extremism, the main focus is on promoting a positive version of the political regime rather than actually changing gender norms. Many war-related miniseries serve as mouthpieces for the regime narrative, but due to production pressures, only 8 percent take an unabashed oppositional stance. Yet some screenwriters and directors choose to engage in direct political criticism rather than depend on gender and marriage metaphors, even at the risk of marking difficulties.

Those few with a clear oppositional stance have difficulty finding funding both within Syria and throughout the Arab world, namely in countries making up the GCC. An example of this pattern is Haitham Haqqi's *Wujuh wa Amaken*, which aired on a small Arabic-speaking channel during 2015. Additionally, director Haqqi had begun working on a miniseries, which would be composed of sixty episodes portraying the beginning of the revolution in Aleppo and the flight of Syrians to Turkey, with screenwriter and novelist Khaled Khalifa.[82] However, because their script told the story of Aleppo from an oppositional stance, they could not secure funding to complete the project for the 2017 drama season.[83] Khalifa and Haqqi remained notably absent from the 2018 season. Yam Mashhadi's *Qalam Humra* (2014), which was discussed earlier in this chapter and will be discussed in further detail in chapters 3 and 4, is another miniseries with a direct political stance that faced marketing issues. While *Wujuh wa Amaken* takes place before the rise of Da'ish, it examines the roots of religious extremism in Khalid Khalifa's screenplay *al-Qala'*. *Qalam Humra* shows how religious extremists took over the revolution and portrays the regime's oppressive hand.

Alongside those overtly political miniseries, 29 percent appear neutral, or "gray," as Syrians themselves refer to this phenomenon. *Ghadan Naltaqi*, which was discussed earlier in this chapter and will be discussed in further detail in chapter 5, is one of these "gray" miniseries. Another miniseries, *al-Wilada min al-Khasira*, began its first season (2011) with an extremely critical stance toward the regime, but by the second (2012) and third (2013) seasons had become more neutral in tone. To some degree, due to censorship and production pressures, it even intersected with the regime narrative at times.[84] What the above miniseries—whether pro-regime, oppositional, or neutral—have in common is that they place their storylines in the midst of war. They attempt to make gender and marriage norms more egalitarian in response to a culture of religious extremism, and they voice an increasingly critical perspective on the culture of Daʿish from 2014 onward.

The two remaining strands in miniseries taking place during the war are integral to my argument in both their nuances and their moments of intersection, though their philosophical perspectives are extremely different. These are the social for the sake of the social and the nostalgic. The social for the sake of the social strand (36.5 percent) comprises twenty-two miniseries that examine social dynamics simply as social rather than political. Some of the social for the sake of the social strands are set in the present, yet without the current political problems facing Syria; others depict imagined societies with gender and marriage norms toward which the writers aspire. More commercial pieces in this group craft stories intended purely for entertainment rather than intending to generate transformation. The nostalgic strand, on the other hand, comprises (11.5 percent) seven miniseries that lament the current bloodshed and express the explicit desire to return to a time of prewar stability. Both the social for the sake of the social and nostalgic strands of *musalsalat* focus on society and critique conservative social norms around gender and marriage. However, the former portrays prevailing social issues as deeply rooted and the present struggle to resolve those social issues as continuous with the past, while the latter glosses over past struggles and implicitly contrasts Syria's present moment with the period before the uprising, a time of freer sexual norms. Both strands, like the oppositional and neutral strands, distinguish progressive gender and marriage norms from the extremist culture of Daʿish and thus at times appear to intersect with a regime narrative. The line between the nostalgic and regime narrative strands is occasionally blurred, as regime narratives are also often characterized by nostalgia, a sentimentalizing of life before the war.

Yet the social for the sake of the social strand, which focuses on the social simply as social rather than as political allegory, does sometimes engage in subtle political critique. This critique occurs not necessarily through gender and marriage metaphors, as it has in the past, but, for example, through a passing reference to a character who was unfairly imprisoned. In this way, the social for the sake of the social strand may disassociate itself from the less critical regime narrative and nostalgic series. Indeed, I argue that positing an ongoing struggle across past and present allows the social for the sake of the social strand to take a critical stance toward the state and helps establish a collective memory of the regime's past violence, whereas the nostalgic pieces, which have become more prevalent since 2015, engage in a forgetting process that sidesteps past oppression.

Lila Abu-Lughod's formidable manuscript *Dramas of Nationhood: The Politics of Television in Egypt* centers on Egyptian melodrama of the 1990s and its quest to combat Islamic extremism and provides important analysis of the issue of nostalgia. Abu-Lughod, whose ethnographic approach to televisual culture captured the tension between Islamism and globalization in Egypt of the 1990s, demonstrated how the nostalgic register raised themes related to cultural identity and authenticity that stood in opposition to Islamic extremism. Characters in these miniseries found themselves trying to remain true to their culture despite the opposing forces of religious excess on the one hand and rootless modernity on the other. Although this media form fell under direct state control and was attacked by some as hegemonic, Abu-Lughod adeptly described the complicated negotiating process that it undertook in the 1990s. Through analysis of press reports, screenings of miniseries, and ethnographic fieldwork, she examined this televisual culture as it fought Islamic extremism to forge a national community.[85]

In post-uprising Syria, especially in 2017, the nostalgic register in television drama expresses a yearning for previous prewar days (along with an erasure of past political oppression), rather than facing the current war, religious fanaticism, or Da'ish in historical or contemporary storylines. Though this nostalgic register at times intersects with the regime narrative, it is not exactly the same as miniseries whose specific goal was to uphold the regime. The nostalgic register, which expunges references to past political oppression, may incidentally intersect with the regime narrative, but that is not its goal. Regardless of screenwriters' intentions, they may inadvertently reproduce the regime narrative because their narratives are anti-Da'ish and they do not represent regime violence. Thus the contours of the nostalgic register (as seen in *Shawq*, 2017) fit those of the regime narrative.[86] Here, rethinking marriage and gender norms is a central task. These norms aim to distinguish the current state from the time before the war, as if to say that life was freer and more inclusive before the arrival of Da'ish. Indeed, I argue that while Syrian drama had once used gender and marriage metaphors to critique the state, some miniseries now use gender and marriage metaphors to critique the culture of religious extremism and Da'ish.

Slightly different patterns emerge within the social for the sake of the social strand, which sometimes examines the current moment and sometimes imagines a future moment in which certain social problems have been addressed. Prior to 2011, Syrian screenwriters overwhelmingly sought to transform a dictatorial order to a more democratic one. Previously, gender and marriage metaphors served as political symbols, but now, some of these writers see gender and marital norms as the basis of the country's problems and choose to criticize their culture rather than political structures or leaders. These screenwriters focus on the social dislocations caused by war as well as gender and marriage norms whose conservatism appears conspicuously rigid within the desperate maneuverings of war. This focus represents a shift from pre-uprising intentions to use miniseries as a mouthpiece for critiquing and changing the political landscape. When the uprising began, some writers continued to emphasize equal gender relations to symbolize a pluralistic political order; others, who outwardly embraced the regime narrative, insisted that their emphasis was the social simply as social rather than political.[87] Other screenwriters advocate profound cultural and social transformation, in no way suggesting a return to the pre-2011 political reality, though a critique of religious extremism is ever present. Indeed, some of these writers capture the discourses of the current uprising and fixate on the refugee crisis and Daʻish rather than sociopolitical critique.

Najeeb Nseir's sketch in *Ahl al-Gharam Part Three* (People of Love, 2017), which will be described in detail in chapter 5, has been intensely criticized for exhibiting gender and marriage norms that do not exist in Syria. He states, "My critics forget that as a writer I do not always write about what I see, but rather an imagined culture that we are striving for."[88] Yet an imagined culture is not always Nseir's intention in his storylines. He is known for social realism as political allegory in both pre- and early post-uprising miniseries—*Zaman al-ʻAr* (A Time of Shame, 2009) and *al-Sarab* (Mirage, 2011), respectively. More recently, Nseir reached new heights in breaking gender and marriage taboos and criticizing hypocritical social norms in war-torn Syria in his 2018 production *Fawda* (Chaos), which takes places in the Qasaʻa neighborhood of Damascus. Here, Nseir engages in social rather than political allegory, which serves as a key example of the social for the sake of the social stance. It is this multifarious stance that I believe has the most hope of flourishing within Syrian television drama.[89] Repressed aggression, sadness, and hypocritical social stances permeate the storyline. The work is imbued with a subtle oppositional stance, as Nseir portrays the slow destruction of the human soul as a result of years of war.[90]

The different stances outlined above show that there is not just one response among drama creators. Indeed, alongside miniseries centered on war are those that feature escapist trends. These place themselves in an imaginary time and place, some being contemporary, others Old Damascus tales. Certain of these are at once escapist and indirectly capture the rhetoric of the uprising. These well-marketed escapist tales, many of which run transnationally through drama via foreign adaptations, actually make up the new trend in the Syrian drama scene in recent years and will be discussed in further detail in chapters 1 and 5. *Mediating the Uprising* underscores the understanding that drama creators are not a monolithic group but possess multifarious ways of engaging in this dramatic art form, constructing memory, and addressing trauma, with gender and marriage at the heart of their cultural and political protest. In showing this continued activism through the lens of gender and marriage, this book situates itself among other studies that have underscored the diversity of forms of protest in the Arab world.[91]

I argue that amid wartime trauma and the rise of a tragic, unprecedented refugee crisis, nostalgia, and the forgetting of past oppression at the hands of

FIGURE I.3 Fethiyyeh (played by Rasha Bilal) on the ruins of her deceased family's home in *Fawda* (Chaos).

Courtesy of Najeeb Nseir.

the regime imbued collective memory construction. Indeed, a bifurcated act of memory construction took place among post-uprising Syrian drama creators: on one hand a reimagining of a past collective memory, on the other hand an attempt to construct historical archives carried over for future generations to make sense of wartime trauma. But in the case of wartime Syria, it would be simplistic to conclude that this rise of historical amnesia in storylines is due solely to market pressures or to place these screenplays into a clear category of regime narrative. Some Syrian drama screenwriters in the nostalgic register do evince historical amnesia of past oppression at the hands of the state and choose to evoke an idealized past and present far removed from Da'ish terrorism, thus reverting to the regime narrative even when this is not an explicit intention. Indeed, for some, a return to pre-2011 days would be welcome after war.

Yet alongside recent storylines colored by historical amnesia or those that interpret current history for the future, some seek escapism while others continue along the lines of deeply rooted oppositional politics. We have also seen the potential flourishing of the social for the sake of the social strand as exemplified by Nseir's *Fawda*. At times, the regime narrative seemingly intersects with all the above stances, even those such as *Fawda* that critique society while engaging in subtle political critique. Through this argument, this book serves as a corrective to the misreading of the social for the sake of the social strand's alignment with the regime narrative. This study sheds light on the politics of remembering and forgetting in wartime Syria. In examining the collective memory construction of these *musalsalat* from 2011 through 2018, the integral role of gender and marriage storylines is evident.

This book does not conduct an in-depth analysis of *musalsalat* during Ramadan 2019, a transition year as international platforms such as Netflix sought out Syrian miniseries more than ever before and drama creators believed that many competing platforms would soon emerge.[92] During this season only two miniseries, *Tarjaman al-Ashwaq* (Interpreter of Desires) and *Musafat Aman* (Distance of Security), place their storylines directly in the uprising. While *Tarjuman al-Ashwaq* focuses on the war; *Musafat Aman* addresses the traces of the "crisis" on individual lives in Damascus as if advising viewers on the psychological process of reconstructing a society damaged by war. *Kuntak, Buq'at Daw' Part Fourteen*, and *'An al-Hawa wa-l-Jawa* (On Love and Passion) include episodes that touch on the "crisis," but other episodes do not. Still, I have included the following: a chart of 2019 series in Appendix C as well as a breakdown of the percentages of categories in Appendix D; a list of 2019 series in my filmography at the end of this book; a few examples of 2019 series in various chapters; and a brief reference to the transitions to this new season in the conclusion. This analysis further illustrates the unique characteristics of the time period of 2011 to 2018 and encourages future study.

Chapter Overview

Each chapter orients itself within a historical framework and interweaving of earlier miniseries, showing the long-standing tradition of criticism in Syrian drama. A chronology of some political and cultural events in Syria from 2011 to 2019 places each miniseries within the appropriate historical context. Chapter 1, "Mediating the Uprising," describes at further length the process by which the regime tries to control the discourse of the uprising through the media—often through gender and marriage metaphors—and the self-reflexive thought process of the drama creators themselves as they explore the state's interference on their thought processes. This first chapter examines the changed material conditions shaping *musalsalat* production and drama creators' responses to those pressures, through both their voices and self-reflexive processes in miniseries themselves that depict the regime's attempt to manipulate the discourse in the media. Furthermore, chapter 1 traces transitions and continuities in Syrian television drama from 2011 through 2018, at the same time tracing the context of pre-uprising miniseries. The chapter contains press releases, anecdotes, and interviews giving voice to drama creators as they discuss their role and that of the regime in mediating the uprising. It also places Syrian drama within larger issues of transnational Arab drama, escapism, and historical amnesia. After discussing the phenomenon of Syrian-Lebanese coproductions, pan-Arab productions, and

Lebanese solo productions to establish the more general media landscape, this chapter zooms in on the nostalgic register and the social for the sake of the social strand. Finally, the chapter ends with an examination of the self-reflexive nature in which drama creators reflect marketing and production issues in their miniseries to capture the challenges that surround their writing process.

From the next chapter onward, each chapter of *Mediating the Uprising* orients itself within a historical framework and interweaving of pre-uprising miniseries, showing the long-standing tradition of sociopolitical critique in Syrian drama. Chapter 2, "Sociopolitical Satire in the Multiyear Syrian Sketch Series *Buq'at Daw'* (Spotlight): Artistic Resistance via Gender and Marriage Metaphors, 2001–2019," addresses the roles of comedy and political satire, in particular as they relate to gender and marriage norms, in the multiyear sketch comedy *Buq'at Daw'*. This chapter appeared in an earlier, shorter version in the *Middle East Journal* (2014) and touched on the first two years of the uprising. This current chapter, which expands to the 2019 season, sheds light on transitions in the use of gender and marriage metaphors to deconstruct regime narratives due to increased bloodshed in the Syrian uprising in 2013. In illustrating these transitions, the chapter shows how some sketches on refugees and Da'ish intersected with the official regime narrative from 2014 onward, while others continued to engage in political critique of the regime. I have devoted a chapter to the multiyear sketch comedy *Buq'at Daw'* and traced the show from its inception in 2001 since I believe that it poignantly highlights transitions among drama creators with the rise of Da'ish.

Chapter 3, "The Rise and Fall of the *Qabaday* (Tough Man): (De)constructing Fatherhood as Political Protest," appeared in an earlier version capturing the first five Ramadan seasons of the uprising in the *Journal of Middle East Women's History* (2015). This current chapter begins with an exploration of drama during the 1960s and then covers the uprising through 2019. I commence by showing how, prior to the uprising, constructions of masculinity were related to an internal criticism of the state rather than being locked in conflict with issues of identity formation, cultural imperialism, and Western modernity, as in the case of constructions of femininity. Prior to the uprising, the avowed focus was on interpersonal, intimate social relationships—but gender constructions predicated the messages. Soon after the uprising, reformulations of the *qabaday* (tough man) took place against the backdrop of politics (both pro- and anti-regime), which became much more pronounced and direct in their storylines. In this chapter, I examine the fall of the *qabaday* during Ramadan 2011 with miniseries written from a reform-minded stance that reconfigure notions of the father as protector of a daughter's sexuality.

The next cluster of miniseries I examine, from 2013 and 2014, make direct references to the uprising, while fathers' impact on intimate relations is central to the discourse. Some of these miniseries depict the moment when the "wall of fear" tumbles down and citizens refuse to wait any longer. Other miniseries show how, against the background of the squashed revolutionary dreams of a secular opposition, the crisis of fatherhood is linked to an existentialist crisis of the individual. In still others, the importance of emotive fatherhood and a softer *qabaday* is the focal point. Since 2015, a time when many transitions had crystalized in Syrian drama after the rise of Da'ish, fatherhood has increasingly been used as a means of critiquing social norms rather than politics. Furthermore, from 2015 onward, during heightened trauma and war, the lens of fatherhood in the nostalgic strand of Syrian television miniseries served collective memory as a way to evoke nostalgia for life before the war. By 2018, some social for the sake of the social strands of miniseries eradicated the mythology surrounding fatherhood altogether.

Chapter 4, "The Politics of Love and Desire in Post-Uprising Syrian and Transnational Arab Television Drama," was published in a shorter version in the *Arab Studies Journal* (2016), which examined miniseries up to 2015. Through a close textual analysis of several miniseries, both prior to and since the uprising, extensive interviews, and periodicals, this current chapter, which covers the uprising through 2018, shows how at the outset of the uprising, Syrian miniseries persisted in offering coded messages of freedom and dignity when relationships were based on sexual equality. Several years into the uprising, however, the discourses became more complicated as television miniseries criticized not only the political order but also the civil war. Nostalgia and historical amnesia began to dominate thematically. This chapter also shows how post-uprising miniseries have offered varying critiques of an impotent Syria, escapist transnational Arab love stories sought by Gulf State market forces, and new narratives of resilience around assaulted women who take agency. The rhetoric of the "crisis" is captured in certain gender and marriage storylines—both contemporary and *Bi'a Shamiyyeh*—even when they seemingly ignore the uprising. At the same time, in both the nostalgic and social for the sake of the social stances, screenwriters more easily dismantle sexual taboos in miniseries of recent years as they construct a new, secular collective memory, one that stands opposed to religious extremism. This chapter shows that gender and marriage narratives within the nostalgic stance engage in a forgetting process, glossing over past oppression and recasting pre-uprising Syria as a place of freer social norms. On the other hand, the social for the sake of the social stance refuses to sentimentalize past oppression, instead viewing the struggle in gender and marriage norms as an ongoing societal battle.

Chapter 5, "The Politics of Queer Representations in Syrian Television Drama Past and Present," examines the instrumentalization of queer representations in Syrian drama from the 1960s through the uprising and ends with an exploration of recent portrayals that exhibit new advocacy directions proposed by Hanadi al-Samman; these focus on body politics.[93] I trace how in the 1960s and

1970s cross-dressing and cross-gender roles were symptomatic of the fear of impoverished masculinity. Specifically, the fear that weak masculinity would result in strong, cross-gendered women marked the miniseries of these decades. In the 1990s through 2000s, "bad mothers," absent fathers, and dictatorial fathers raised effeminate sons who were implied to be homosexual. In the 2000s, women's cross-gender roles were instrumentalized to show the harm imposed by law and culture on women, and, as Hanadi al-Samman has argued, lesbianism filled a temporary role before heterosexual relations were reinstated. Although linked with the rise of nostalgia and historical amnesia that sought differentiation from Da'ish, some politically neutral or oppositional-stance miniseries show homosexual men and women overcoming previous stereotypes and evincing new directions.

The concluding chapter, based on ethnographic fieldwork, a close viewing of miniseries, and analysis of recent media outlets and press releases, continues to give voice to Syrian drama creators by exhibiting their debates, concerns, and plans for forthcoming seasons. This chapter captures discussions and debates centered on new trends in web series initiated by *Bi-dun Qaid* that could be viewed on YouTube beginning in late 2017. These series bypassed market constraints and were able to reach wider audiences than previously permitted. While *Bi-dun Qaid* engaged in heightened sociopolitical critique and showed more graphic love scenes, the Ramadan 2018 web series *Doubt* sought to avoid all mention of current politics and instead focused on commonly portrayed topics such as betrayal, honor, and shame. The dawn of new platforms such as Netflix and the impact on Syrian television drama is also examined in this concluding chapter. At the same time, the chapter shows how drama creators continue to tackle marriage and gender metaphors in post-uprising storylines of miniseries composed of the traditional thirty episodes that catered centrally to Arab audiences.

I LIVED IN SYRIA for about a decade, conducting research on television drama. My positionality as an Iranian American woman conducting research on gender dynamics in Syria is important to state at the outset. From the commencement of my research, I have been highly sensitive to the power dynamic that exists when artistic works of protests in Syria are transported to the Western context. The majority of Syrian miniseries do not have English subtitles, which limits access by those outside the field of Arab studies or unfamiliar with Syrian colloquial. In turn, the voices of drama creators featured in these miniseries get lost in the hegemonic discourses of media outlets representing Syria. My intention in *Mediating the Uprising* is to portray drama creators struggle to claim their future as their own amid an uprising turned civil war. My last research stints in Syria were in 2010 and 2011, and since then I have spent the summers of 2014 through 2019 in Beirut observing the Ramadan drama season firsthand, interviewing drama creators, and collecting press interviews. I have also traveled to Paris extensively these past few years to interview exiled Syrian drama creators there.

I have listened to debates among Syrian drama creators in cafés, restaurants, and homes in Damascus, Beirut, and Paris and have discussed with them storylines filled with love, gender, and marriage themes. Furthermore, we have discussed production challenges, the survival of television drama during war, the trauma of war and memory construction, the ethics of representation, and the advent of experimental texts dealing with gender, marriage, and sexuality. Due to their incredible generosity and humility, I have had the chance to interview these drama creators over the span of many years. This has allowed me to see transitions in their thought process and, most importantly, to establish trust and ease of contact. All these ethnographic vignettes are included in the following pages. The diverse responses among drama creators evince the richness and complexity of this genre of art during a time of inconceivable tragedy.

The research presented in this book, which documents the survival of Syrian television drama and multifaceted aspirations for the future, serves as an essential component of heritage preservation. In recording the efforts of drama creators to create stories filled with gender and marriage metaphors to construct and preserve collective memory for later generations—some with a continual eye for political critique, others to express nostalgia for the past, others to advocate for a cultural revolution, and yet others to provide for escapism—this research serves as testament to the resilience of art and the human spirit. *Mediating the Uprising: Narratives of Gender and Marriage in Syrian Television Drama* tells the story of Syrian drama creators who aspire to relevance and for life and business to continue against a landscape of ongoing catastrophe in Syria.

1

Mediating the Uprising

Another power outage. Screenwriter 'Imad sleeps in a small room lit by candles, his laptop on the table in front of him. He awakes to the ring of his cell phone: a call from 'Adil, a Syrian producer who lives in Dubai and awaits his new musalsal. The screen shifts to focus on 'Adil. "I want you to reflect on the hard lives of four women amid these difficult conditions," orders 'Adil, surrounded by four Syrian actresses dressed in tight, provocative outfits. "You mean, they're living in our country, and you want me to show their struggles?" 'Imad asks his producer curiously. "No," 'Adil says dismissively. "They're in Dubai. But they can't go shopping in their own country. . . . Come up with a story and start scribbling." 'Adil bursts out laughing, then proceeds to say that he wants all four actresses—whom he coyly refers to as qotat faranjiyat (foreign cats)—to have equal roles and that he does not want the story to seem superficial. "I want you to say that as much shopping as they are doing here, there's nothing like shopping and partying in the discos of their own country. I want it be deep, and get it to me quickly." The next morning, to the sound of explosions, 'Imad writes about the character, Nur, waking up in Dubai and calling for the housekeeper. She drinks American coffee. When his friend calls and says the gas tank seller is in the neighborhood, 'Imad runs out to retrieve his tank. Meanwhile, the actresses in Dubai discuss how their difficulties have transformed them into poets.

After days of writing against a background of artillery, 'Imad submits his script. 'Adil complains that it is too depressing. While he wants 'Imad to reflect on these women's difficulties living in exile, he also wants him to show how these women have overcome their problems. "You can't make us cry in the first three episodes," 'Adil exclaims. Displaying his detachment from what is happening in Syria, 'Adil asks his screenwriter what is making him feel so depressed. 'Imad replies, "Ma fi shi' (it's nothing)," a phrase that implies that 'Imad, like many others in Syria, is in denial about what is happening around him.

35

On another day, the four actresses and 'Adil laugh, sing, and drink cocktails. Mean-while, 'Imad sits aboard a small truck with sheep and answers another call from 'Adil. Now the producer wants Nancy to own a Porsche and Nur to own a Range Rover. On another day, 'Imad fetches his bread and writes to the sound of exploding bombs. He notes, "Nancy is in her home, in a jakoozi, relaxed. . . ." Soon, 'Imad's house is bombed and, as smoke fills the house, he grabs his laptop. When 'Adil calls and complains about the delay, 'Imad explains that he has lost his home. He needs an advance so he can find another room to rent in which to write the last few episodes. 'Adil complains to 'Imad that his script was not fair to Nancy, who needs more scenes. 'Imad roams the smoke-filled streets, neighbors running frantically around him.

Mediating the Azmeh: Pressures of GCC Funding, the Regime's Media Drama, and Historical Amnesia

"Montij wa Katib wa Azmeh" (A Producer, Writer, and Crisis) is a short sketch written by Muhammad al-'Omri in the fifteenth episode of *Buq'at Daw' Part Ten* (Ramadan, 2014). The sketch reflects the circumstances under which Syrian screenwriters have found themselves working since the 2011 uprising due to constraints imposed by Gulf State production companies and Syrian producers who yield to their demands. Syrian drama was under direct state control when it commenced in the 1960s. From the 1990s onward, however, an increasing number of private production companies were run by rich businessmen or parliamentarians (with ties to the state) who sponsored miniseries.[1] From the 1990s through 2010, with the influx of pan-Arab satellite stations, the Gulf Cooperation Council produced and aired the majority of television shows.[2]

Prior to the uprising, Syrian drama creators complained that they were forced to change their scripts to appease Gulf State producers, who wanted more conservative storylines. In *Zaman al-'Ar* (A Time of Shame, 2009), screenwriter Najeeb Nseir sought to expose double standards that deemed a woman impure if she had sex before marriage. He consciously chose to outfit his heroine, Buthayna, with a headscarf in order to show that even a religious woman was entitled to experience premarital sexual relations. Yet his storyline caused such fury that the production company in Dubai ordered Hani al-'Ashi, the Syrian producer, to rewrite the script. Al-'Ashi subsequently told Nseir to situate Buthayna in a secret 'urfi marriage rather than an extramarital affair, a change that introduced religion to the discussion. Nseir resisted his producer initially but eventually complied. While the secret marriage was briefly mentioned, Nseir made no attempt to connect it to the larger storyline.[3]

Gulf State control of Syrian television drama, including stipulations of "no touching" and the prohibition of explicit romantic relationships, was comically portrayed in the third season of *Buq'at Daw'* (Spotlight, 2003), "al-Drama Numud-hajiyyeh" (Exemplary Drama), where events related to the couple's romance appear in the writer's head. More importantly, we see the changes he is compelled to make as he writes down their story.[4] Gulf State control is just one of the problems facing Syrian screenwriters. According to screenwriters, directors often serve as an impediment to the original storyline. Screenwriter Najeeb Nseir, for example, laments that directors (even when working with non-GCC companies) generally discount screenwriters' original text. His thirty-episode miniseries *Chello* (2015) was funded by O3 Productions (a subsidiary of MBC) and Eagle Films LLC Middle East (a studio in Dubai). Based on *Indecent Proposal* (1993), the miniseries was filled with scenes of marital passion. Yet the storyline did not develop as planned. At the Younes café in Hamra, Beirut, as the 2015 Ramadan season unfolded, Nseir said, "Once I handed in my screenplay, the director no longer communicated with me. As I view the miniseries now on television, I see that he has made many changes to my original storyline. I actually have no idea how it will end."[5] His script involved the heroine Yasmin (Nadine Nassib Njeym) sleeping with wealthy businessman Taymur (Taim Hassan) as a result of a bet. But Syrian director Samer al-Barqawi, intent on protecting his female character (and actress) from criticism, removed this crucial plot twist. Najeeb had originally wanted to include a casino scene like the one in *Indecent Proposal*, but the director refused.[6]

Nseir was dismayed that al-Barqawi and the production companies took other liberties with his script as well. 'Alia, the woman who pursues Yasmin's husband, Adam, becomes, in the miniseries, an absent mother. Her son lacks focus, wastes time with a friend who is "a bad influence," and appears to be homosexual. This depiction of family dynamics plays up the "bad mom" trope so popular in Syrian television drama and implicitly attributes the son's homosexuality to the lack of maternal guidance he has received. In this way the storyline falls into a pattern of modern Arabic literature that portrays nonconforming sexual identities as resulting from "deviant social practices"—in this case an absent mom.[7] At the end, when 'Alia resolves to focus on her son, he severs ties with his past. This entire storyline came as a surprise to Nseir.[8]

Naturally, the relationship between Syrian drama and the GCC has fluctuated. In 2005 the Syrian government was widely blamed for the assassination of Lebanese prime minister Rafiq Hariri. Gulf countries, led by Saudi Arabia and Qatar, subsequently isolated Syria. According to director Firas Dehni, the boycott of Syrian drama was a tacit movement. Still, the continued output of drama demonstrates that the GCC states never ceased to provide funding. While 2010 was hailed as a watershed year that saw the airing of thirty miniseries, some of which broke taboos related to women's rights, corruption, and Islamic extremism, a formidable challenge arrived with the Syrian uprising of 2011. At the time Saudi Arabia and Qatar spearheaded an embargo against Syria in their efforts to topple Bashar al-Asad. Dehni argues that by this time the embargo against Syrian drama was no longer disguised.[9]

At the outset many believed this embargo would lead to the end of Syrian drama. Yet while production decreased during the initial years of the uprising, Syrian drama continued, even through the advent of civil war and the rise of terrorist groups. Still, drama creators complained that they were forced to comply with GCC demands. In addition, miniseries that represented the perspective of the uprising either were not produced or were confined to smaller, less commercial channels. Director Inas Haqqi, for example, knew of one writer who was informed that MBC would fund his miniseries only if he portrayed a Saudi hero saving the Syrian revolution from the regime. She also points to *Qalam Humra* (2014), which sympathized with revolutionaries and was thus confined to the relatively unwatched channel al-Sumayriyya during Ramadan (although MBC broadcast it that fall).[10] Screenwriter Rafi Wahbi complained that Abu Dhabi heavily censored *al-'Arrab: Nadi al-Sharq*—cutting out drinking scenes, for example—during the 2015 Ramadan season.[11] Renowned Syrian screenwriter and novelist Khaled Khalifa voiced widespread concerns, stating that the uprising effectively closed the door on pro-opposition miniseries.[12] Thus the sketch "Montij wa Katib wa Azmeh" spoke to the problem of production demands with which Syrian screenwriters must contend.

"Montij wa Katib wa Azmeh" also depicted the government's effort to control discourse on the uprising. Indeed, the word "azmeh" (crisis) in the sketch's title was first propagated by the regime to deflect the legitimacy of the uprising. Indeed, "crisis" connotes jihadists and terrorists who conspire with outsiders to destabilize Syria. Furthermore, the word "crisis" simultaneously downplays the idea of revolution and, as Judith Butler has aptly argued, "manages 'the crisis.'" This is because in situations of "crisis," the population not only must tolerate social degradation and economic distress but must mute their protests. In this way the government suggests that dissent is harmful to the nation's future.[13] In *Frames of War: When Is Life Grievable?* Butler examines the visual and discursive fields belonging to the realm of war recruitment. She analyzes governmental regulation of the media and its control over the framing of events. As Butler explains, this regulation of violence is also a component of violence. Specifically, by framing the "other" in derogatory terms, the lives of those "others" are less grievable in the event that they are lost.[14]

Syrian drama creators have exposed the regime's effort to erase political injustice in comic yet moving sketches. This mediatic manipulation of war can be placed in context by looking at other war-torn societies that have similarly encouraged historical amnesia. Unlike the case of Lebanon, the Syrian civil war began as an uprising against the regime, and opposition figures still refer to its revolutionary origin. Yet the civil war in Lebanon provides an interesting point of comparison since, like Syria, it became a fertile terrain for playing out internal and external battles. Several key monographs have addressed Lebanon's erasure of memory following the war. In *War and Memory in Lebanon* (2010), Sune

Haugbolle outlines how the elite propagated amnesia, while intellectuals and artists believed that it was important to confront the pain of the war in order to move past that pain and experience cultural renewal.[15]

On the other hand, Lucia Volk's *Memorials and Martyrs in Modern Lebanon* (2010) challenges the existing literature, showing how elites built memorials for shared Christian and Muslim suffering.[16] While both of those monographs deal with postwar handling of memory, Line Khatib's *Lebanese Cinema: Imagining the Civil War and Beyond* (2008) traced cinema as one of the few arenas to confront the grotesque nature of the civil war during and after its occurrence. Khatib showed cinema both uncovering and hiding war memories, thus playing a dominant role in the writing of Lebanese history.[17] In *Mediating the Uprising*, I examine the media's quest during the current civil war in Syria to propagate historical amnesia of the ruling Ba'th Party's political oppression and downplay the fact that it was an uprising against the regime. I manifest how drama creators in Syria, as in Lebanon, work within and against these dominant, hegemonic paradigms to construct a new collective memory for future generations.

Some early post-uprising sketches in the multiyear comic series *Buq'at Daw'* (Spotlight) directly critique government paranoia as well as its manipulation of information. These sketches' direct approach swerves away from a traditional approach to critique that relies on gender, love, and marriage metaphors. In "Kull Shi' Tamam" (Everything Is Okay), for example, a Syrian news channel announces its *Mujaz al-Akhbar* (News Highlight): "The Western world is jealous of the Syrian way of life; Syrian citizens want the price of *mazotte* (cheap diesel) to increase, but the government refuses; the rise in salaries prompts citizens' concerns that the government is far too charitable to them; one thousand new homes are ready for our youth." After the highlights, "Lahza Haqiqiyyeh" (A Moment of Truth), described as a show with "credibility and transparency," commences with news broadcaster Widad holding the microphone out to an angry village. As the villager's face reddens with outrage, a voiceover says, "Our life is boring, since we have no problems. The director of our region calls us every day to see if we are okay. Our governor even leaves good night messages on our cell phone. *Kull shi' tamam.* Don't worry about us." When the voiceover ends, the villager grows visibly more irate and Widad quickly dashes off. Next, inside a factory, Widad asks a worker about his life. The worker seems agitated, frustratedly hurling his papers into the air as a calm voiceover says, "We have more than we need. We want to work more. The director refuses to have a higher salary than us, saying he is sitting and doing nothing. So, yes, *kull shi' tamam.*" Widad then speaks to a woman on the street who bangs her hand against her head in frustration as the voiceover gently says, "*kull shi' tamam.*"[18] It is important to note that while al-Manar originally broadcast this as a ten-minute sketch that clearly critiqued governmental manipulation of the media, a Lebanese station later cut it down to four minutes.[19]

Duplicitous grand narratives have been specialties of the Ba'th Party since its inception in the early 1960s. Thus it is no surprise that the regime has spun metanarratives involving terrorists and Western conspiracies in order to discredit the uprising. Using the word "azmeh" has been one method of controlling the revolutionary discourse. All who did not side with the regime were perceived as terrorists conspiring with the West. In this respect, the misogynistic miniseries *Bab al-Hara*, whose fifth season had been broadcast in 2010, was viewed by the government as having had a major influence on the uprising. Shortly after my arrival in Damascus during the second week of July 2011, drama creators planned an anti-regime protest and publicized it on Facebook. The protest was set for Friday, July 15, at the Hassan Mosque in Midan after the morning prayer. Over one hundred artists arranged to attend; however, once actors, screenwriters, and directors arrived, they texted friends not to come. The *shabbiha* (army of proxies, hated strongmen of the regime) were beating many of the participants. Police arrested writer Yam Mashhadi and the actress Mai Skaf, who later contacted the al-'Arabiya news channel and pleaded with them to publicize the injustice, hoping other nations would step in and help the Syrian people. Subsequently, the *shabbiha* harassed actor Fares al-Heloo, who would later flee to Paris, for his participation in the protest.[20]

A few days later in my hotel room as I watched the news, I saw that a Syrian Arab television channel was repeating a news ticker from actor Selim Sabry. Sabry reported that recently jailed actors had claimed upon release that the other jailed protesters they had encountered merely saw themselves as characters in *Bab al-Hara* rather than having their own political goals. The statement instilled fear in the public, as *Bab al-Hara*, imbued with nostalgia for traditions that started to fade during the French colonial mandate, is often associated with extremist trends.[21] Despite author Merwan Qawuq's intention to avoid politics and focus only on social issues in his screenplay, many argued that the show's message encouraged citizens to take up arms.[22] Some, like theatrical writer and director Talal Lababeedy, contended that it was the GCC-produced *Bi'a Shamiyyeh* miniseries, which takes place in Old Damascus during the French colonial mandate, that ignited the Syrian uprising of 2011 by encouraging civilians to arm themselves.[23] Others, such as renowned *musalsal* editor Iyad Shihab Ahmad, argued that blaming *Bi'a Shamiyyeh* was the regime's method for belittling the revolution.[24]

The regime's propaganda at the outset of the uprising, which claimed that revolutionaries were influenced by *Bab al-Hara*, was an attempt to demonize the revolutionaries and scare the local population. It hearkens back to Roland Barthes's philosophy of the death of the author, which asserts that the author's original intent in a given work is unimportant. What matters is how audience members have interpreted that work.[25] In the midst of the increasingly bloody war, and following the appearance of jihadist and al-Qaeda-linked groups (and later Da'ish), the regime downplayed the role of secular activists. Indeed, according to screenwriter Colette Bahna, the regime originally bolstered jihadist and al-Qaeda groups to reinforce their narrative of a secular state attacked by fundamentalists.[26] Emphasizing the influence of the misogynistic, religiously conservative *Bab al-Hara* on the uprising reinforced regime rhetoric that it was not a legitimate uprising but a battle between the regime and Islamic fundamentalists. It also fit with the regime's key narrative that the regime was the last bastion of secular Arab nationalism in the Arab world.

Ironically, while pro-regime sources critiqued *Bab al-Hara* for having incited the war, proponents of the uprising criticized the miniseries for presenting unsympathetic storylines and detaching itself from the protests. On May 15, 2011, al-Jazeera aired a show that accused *Bab al-Hara* actors of failing to support the uprising. The special began with footage of protests and the *Bab al-Hara* music score playing in the background. It recounted how *Bab al-Hara* ended in its fifth season, and then the real uprising picked up as if it were *Bab al-Hara*'s sixth season. Al-Jazeera then addressed the irony that certain actors, such as Mona Wassef and 'Abbas al-Nuri, had played nationalist figures in *Bab al-Hara* but stood by Asad in the uprising. In other words, al-Jazeera linked *Bab al-Hara* to the uprising but observed irony in the actors' failure to protest the regime.[27]

When *Bab al-Hara* introduced a sixth season in 2014, one article referred to the men of the show as *qabadayat min waraq* (tough men made of paper), suggesting that the miniseries had drifted away from the reality of the azmeh.[28] *Bab al-Hara* continued into its seventh season and aired on MBC and LDC in 2015. Despite the miniseries' strong viewership, the press criticized mistakes and historical inaccuracies in the screenplay.[29] Ironically, *Bab al-Hara Part Seven* and *Bab al-Hara Part Eight* (2016), which continued to heavily employ gender and marriage metaphors, had aligned itself with the regime narrative and heralded a transition in Syrian people's collective memory of the mandate period. Since, in earlier installments of the show, the French colonial presence had served as an allegory of the Ba'th Party regime, the *qabadayat* had been portrayed as fighting the colonial (regime) presence. In these seasons of *Bab al-Hara* onward, however, a concerted effort was made to differentiate the Syrian regime and the French colonial mandate.[30] Furthermore, while *Bab al-Hara* had previously been characterized by nostalgia for an imagined and unified religious community where women's bodies were markedly distinct from the predatory West, now the show disassociated itself from religion, which caused contradictions in the storyline. From 2015 onward, *Bab al-Hara* emphasized a secular and nationalist viewpoint that distinguished Syrian culture from religious fanaticism. This Old Damascus narrative echoes the contemporary narrative recited by the Ba'th Party regime that insists it is a secular regime fighting the religious fanaticism of the revolutionaries.

Despite its misogyny, the miniseries presented the neighborhood in which it was set as religiously moderate and depicted religious fanaticism in a negative light. Indeed, the miniseries redirected its focus from fighting Syrian political authority to fighting Islamic fanaticism, which stood in for Da'ish. History could, as such, be discarded in pursuit of this new goal as writers pursued the establishment of a new collective memory. In *Dramas of Nationhood: The Politics of Television in Egypt*, Lila Abu-Lughod showed how state-run miniseries in Egypt during the turbulent period of the 1990s presented storylines in opposition to Islamism. In 1993, in the service of a project to remake Egyptian cultural identity, the media were called upon to fight extremism and violent Islamic terrorists were often integrated into the plots of television shows.[31] Similarly, post-uprising television drama in Syria, in particular from 2014 onward, fixated on religious extremism and propagated the idea of an imagined secular culture under attack from Islamic extremism in the form of Da'ish.

The regime's manipulation of the media at the start of the revolution did not stop with *Bab al-Hara*. From early on, in order to portray members of the Free Syrian Army as blood-thirsty jihadists and terrorists seeking to subjugate and rape women, the regime employed a dangerous form of what Syrians have designated as "media drama." The regime forced women to testify that the revolutionaries raped them as part of this campaign to instill fear in the population. In a 2013 case, a young woman from Harasta claimed that she was raped by a jihadist, but her lie was exposed when a Syrian employee gave al-'Arabiya news channel an unedited tape of someone dictating what she was to say.[32] Similarly, the case of sixteen-year-old Rawan Qaddah enraged the population and inflamed social media. Qaddah testified on Syrian state television that her father, a member of the Free Syrian Army, had forced her to have sex with his comrades as a form of Jihad al-Nikah. Her innocent expression as she described being raped (with her mother's approval) angered the population, who believed that the Syrian regime was raping her a second time. Stories emerged that regime thugs had kidnapped and imprisoned her, and her forced testimony was the price she had to pay for her freedom.[33] The story bore witness to the Syrian regime's reliance on a gendered narrative to denounce the opposition activists in its media drama.

On July 8, 2015, as part of a regime media effort to manifest *kull shi' tamam* and distract viewers from the reality of uprising, telecasters for the show, *Ramadan Yajma'na*, interviewed Syrians about what they were watching. As it turned out, many were watching miniseries such as *Buq'at Daw' Part Eleven*, *al-'Arrab*, *Donia 2015*, *Chello*, and *Bint al-Shah Bandar*. There were no signs of war on the streets of Damascus, where citizens spoke enthusiastically about their favorite miniseries. The attempt by Syrian state television to demonstrate that all was fine in the capital was another clear case of media drama. Yet despite turbulence in the region and a string of bloody attacks by Da'ish in Tunisia, Kuwait, and Lyon, France, that Ramadan, Syrian production dominated the miniseries landscape and competed for viewership.[34] Indeed, one article decried the fact that it was virtually impossible to watch all the series airing during Ramadan.[35]

Despite the pressures of GCC funding and the regime's media drama, Syrian miniseries have thrived during the war and have engaged in innovative forms of expression.[36] In 2015, for example, Abu Dhabi initiated a *Ramadan Rating* show for the first time in drama history. Maysa' Maghribi and Wissam Braydi hosted a selection of Syrian, Lebanese, Egyptian, and Gulf writers, directors, and actors for each of the thirty days of Ramadan. Each night, the creators and actors of one particular miniseries were invited to discuss their creative process in the miniseries. Throughout the month of Ramadan the top five shows of the season were rated daily and then this new rating was publicized on the show. The top five shows usually included between three and four Syrian miniseries. These ratings were determined via cell phone submissions by audience members. Indeed, the show made heavy use of social media; guests were asked to respond to both positive and negative tweets, and the hosts frequently asked participants if they liked social media. A major issue discussed virtually every day of the show was the rise of the pan-Arab television series and the direction of Arab drama in general.[37]

As the uprising developed into civil war, lively conversations were held in the press as well as in coffeehouses regarding the role of drama during revolution (or "crisis"). Syrian dramas have varied in content, as some have propagated historical amnesia while others have set their stories during the war. The latter have experienced various levels of success or failure. Furthermore, dealing with the uprising in this art form has been difficult for even the most seasoned writers and directors. Screenwriter Fu'ad Humayra stopped writing miniseries since love stories seemed futile when his co-citizens were dying in war. Furthermore, Humayra bemoaned that no one was willing to produce a miniseries truly depicting the opposition. He attempted to produce, direct, write, and act in a new miniseries, *al-Ra'is wa-l-Nisa'* (The President and Women), on YouTube in February 2014. But the show was heavily critiqued on social media sites and proved to be a flop. The miniseries, which relied on amateur actors, portrayed the problems of a dictator and his son in relation to the various women who surround them. Humayra continued, "It cost twenty thousand dollars to produce five 10-minute episodes. I rented a large space in Jordan, but when the owner saw we are in the opposition, he kicked us out and we had to film all fifty minutes in my own apartment."[38]

Escapism in Transnational Arab Drama

While many drama creators have engaged in collective memory construction, as delineated in the introduction, others have preferred escapism from the current war. This section emphasizes the escapism that occurs in transnational Arab dramas, though they constitute just roughly 6 percent (twelve) of post-uprising miniseries. Though they form a small group, they have nevertheless prompted conversations and debates among drama creators and left an indelible impact on the media landscape. Additionally, experiments with the length of the miniseries have become increasingly popular in post-uprising Syrian miniseries, just as the experiments have similarly occurred in Turkish miniseries.[39] *Al-Ikhweh* (The Brothers, 2014) ran 116 episodes; *Alaghat Khasa* (Intimate Relations, 2015) ran 78. Each premiered prior to the Ramadan season and was filled with stories of love, betrayal, and difficult separations. While *al-Ikhweh* was based on a Chilean telenovela, *Alaghat Khasa* did not appear to be based on anything. Still, the transnational miniseries was patched together by random, and often disconnected storylines that did not always come together into a unified whole. Screenwriter Samer Ridwan contended,

> Syrian drama has declined in quality since we are creating drama in a country that is not living in a natural condition. So how can drama be natural? Art needs stability. War does not let anyone think. . . . And *al-Ikhweh* is not truly the same caliber of a typical Syrian miniseries, though it does benefit from Syrian talent. Based on Chilean telenovela *Hijos del Monte,* it was just a commercial project. *Alaghat Khasa* was also a commercial work, not necessarily because this is what the writer wished for, but because this is the kind of storyline that particular production company was soliciting.[40]

Pan-Arab adaptations based specifically on foreign films and novels once critiqued as "not resembling us" have become a fad for those hoping to escape the current reality. Yet they compose merely 3 percent (seven) of post-uprising miniseries, which is ironic given the debate and contention they have also sparked among drama creators. From *Lo'bat al-Mawt* (Game of Death, 2013—based on *Sleeping with the Enemy*) to *Law . . .* (If . . . , 2014—based on *Unfaithful*) and *Chello* in 2015 (based on *Indecent Proposal*), storylines borrow from foreign films and novels to escape politics and then adapt the details to accommodate Arab culture to please production companies. Screenwriter Reem Hanna, who has been working on adaptations since the uprising, said, "This is our only solution, since channels are asking for these kinds of escapist storylines." Hanna wrote the popular *Lo'bat al-Mawt* for the 2013 season. When asked for a story that would involve Egypt and Lebanon, Hanna decided that the storyline of *Sleeping with the Enemy* would allow travel between the two countries.[41] She referred to this new trend as "Musalsalat Zurufiyyeh. La Makan. La Zaman" (Miniseries of the Circumstances. No place. No time). Hanna went on, "One feels alienation when watching them. But at the same time, it is hard to write about something going on now, to capture the bombings and destruction of war."[42]

On another occasion, Hanna, who wrote *24 Qirat* (24 Carat) for the 2015 season, proclaimed that Syrian drama had made a huge comeback, with thirty broadcast series that year. She continued, "There has to be a kind of miniseries for everyone. Some want superficial shows; others want a deep examination of the Syrian war."[43] *24 Qirat*, directed by Laith Hajjo, recounts the story of the corrupt Yusuf, who almost drowns and is saved by Mira. Mira takes Yusuf to her house to recover. Many critiqued the storyline, saying that no Lebanese woman would bring an unknown man into her home. The miniseries was criticized too for poorly depicting memory loss. Despite the negative reception, the miniseries was often ranked among the top five on the *Ramadan Rating* show. Fans loved the beautiful clothes and shallow storyline that allowed for an escape from the devastating reality of the region.[44]

After his 2011 *al-Sarab*, screenwriter Najeeb Nseir remained absent from Syrian drama until completing the escapist tale *Chello* for Ramadan 2015. Nseir expressed how difficult it was to write about the uprising, to capture the pain of real life, and to offer insight on his viewers' daily suffering. He wondered, as well, about the wisdom of trying to do so.[45] Nseir had edited *Ma Wara' al-Wujuh* (What's Behind the Faces) for the 2014 Ramadan season, but it was not sold and therefore never aired. Nseir voiced regret that he wrote two other screenplays on the *azmeh* that were no longer in high demand. He continued, "The stations are asking for escapist adaptations and pan-Arab serials, and thus, I wrote *Chello* for this season based on *Indecent Proposal*."[46] Yet discussions in the press surrounding *Chello*, which was broadcast on Future, MBC, and Adounia, questioned the appropriateness of a plot in which a character sold his wife during the Ramadan season and asked whether this storyline accurately resembled Eastern society.[47]

The point I wish to make is that *Chello* and the discussions it raised were apolitical and did not intend to serve as cultural archives for future generations. Yet this was not true of all adaptations. In 2015, the press debated which of two different miniseries called *al-'Arrab* (The Godfather) invited more viewership.[48] The version *al-'Arrab: Nadi al-Sharq* (The Godfather: Club of the East), directed by Hatim 'Ali and written by Rafi Wahbi, was always highly ranked on the *Ramadan Rating* show. Despite Wahbi's complaints about the Abu Dhabi satellite channel, actor Jamal Suleiman acknowledged that the channel had done a great service to Syrian drama. While the hope was that a foreign film would direct public attention away from the current upheaval, many immediately associated the storyline with the Syrian regime. One press article referred to director Hatim 'Ali's *al-'Arrab: Nadi al-Sharq*, saying, "'Nadi al-Sharq': 'Dood' al-Nizam al-Suri 'Minnu w-fi'" (Nadi al-Sharq: The Smell of the Syrian Regime Is Here).[49] Screenwriter Rafi Wahbi explained the connections to the Syrian regime: "The idea of a dictatorial father crushing the will of his children is symbolic of Bashar al-Asad's rule. Also, while *al-'Arrab: Nadi al-Sharq* takes place ten years before uprising, the third part will go into the Syrian revolution." Wahbi said that his boldness in addressing politics in his screenplay arose in part from living outside of Syria while writing.[50]

By the spring of 2016, however, it was clear that director Hatim 'Ali had contracted the second season to Khaled Khalifa rather than Wahbi, with whom he

FIGURE 1.1 Bassem Yakhour (right) in *al-'Arrab (Nadi al-Sharq)* (The Godfather: Club of the East, Part One).

Courtesy of Rafi Wahbi.

was not able to reach an agreement. Khalifa acknowledged that this adaptation was not his most original work but that even adaptations provide means of indirect critique. Many characters, for example, resemble members of the regime.[51] Indeed, Khalifa was explicit with his political critique in the second season, highlighting the time period and links to the Syrian regime and referencing the regime's torture and abuse of Syrian intellectuals. The story begins when a writer named Nawras returns home after having been tortured in prison. Shortly thereafter he is arrested again for his writing. The second season also features Abu 'Aliya, whose family tortures its competitors. The season concludes with a scene in which the characters sit mesmerized in front of the television as the protests are broadcast. According to director Haitham Haqqi, Khalifa pushed the envelope further than the producer wanted, decreasing the likelihood of a third part.[52]

Many mocked this trend of foreign adaptations. On his personal Facebook page, critic 'Ammar Hamed derided Hatim 'Ali and al-Muthana Sobh's adaptation of *The Godfather*. Hamed sarcastically wrote that if the goal of adapting foreign films was to loosely fit the current context, then perhaps a good movie to consider would be *Gone with the Wind*, since it also takes place during a civil war.[53] Actress Amal 'Arafeh asserted, "The identity of Syrian drama is in danger." Pointing to the reliance on weak actresses in foreign adaptations, she said,

"Just because a girl is pretty doesn't mean she can act."[54] Zuhair Ahmad Qanoo', director of *Donia 2015*, contended on *Ramadan Rating* that the role of drama during crisis is to reveal difficulties such as water shortages, rather than to fantasize about mafia shootouts and women in glamorous dresses. He continued to say that since, unfortunately, there is no market for miniseries in Syria, drama creators submit to the demands of Gulf producers. On the same show, Wissam Braydi asked Amal 'Arafeh about her stance on joint-Arab productions. She replied, "I need to know the time and place where a story is occurring. I don't like miniseries with no place and no identity. At the minimum you can't have a Syrian mother, Egyptian father, and the child of another nationality." Her *Donia 2015* costar, actress Shukran Murtaja, added, "When someone is supposed to be poor but wears expensive outfits, this is not convincing, and people notice it and make comments. It should not be an imaginary world or you will not be able to convince viewers."

Others in the drama industry also commented on these joint-Arab productions. Actress Sulafa Me'mar stated,

> There is no doubt that the *'A'mal Mushtarakeh* [Arab joint productions also referred to as pan-Arab] have made Syrian drama lose some of its specificity that focused on the local reality of the Syrian society. . . . But on the other hand, these joint-Arab productions have had some benefits on society since at least we see a production of Arab miniseries. Even though these shared works are attractive to the viewer since they bring together different societies, I don't think they will continue for a long period of time since they represent a complicated, out of the ordinary reality.[55]

Actress Suzanne Nejm al-Din came down even harder, arguing that joint-Arab productions convey a negative view of Arab society. She questioned whether miniseries were the appropriate tool for creating Arab unity.[56] During the 2015 drama season, talk shows such as Ramadan Rating and Syria's daily drama discussion show, broadcast on the Addounia channel (led by actor Muhammad Kheir Jarrah), often asked participants what they thought of pan-Arab productions. On July 4, actress Jenny Asber, who had a role in *Alaghat Khasa*, appeared on the Addounia drama talk show to weigh in on pan-Arab productions. She indicated that a well-produced pan-Arab show would be better than a weak Syrian production. At the same time, she emphasized that any well-produced Syrian show would be better than any well-produced pan-Arab show. She also observed that pan-Arab miniseries were the current trend. Asber stated that it was good that for once they could collaborate in harmony. Asber also appeared on *Ramadan Rating*, which discussed the issue of pan-Arab miniseries throughout the month of Ramadan. On July 12, Asber pointed out that one positive element of these pan-Arab miniseries was that all the actors and actresses were stars, creating opportunities for teamwork. Additionally, she said, pan-Arab miniseries allowed Syrian actors the chance to travel and to meet new people.

The June 30 *Ramadan Rating* show featured the cast and crew of *al-ʿArrab: Nadi al-Sharq.* Actor Jamal Suleiman, who plays Abu ʿAlia (the godfather), was a leading guest. Suleiman had chosen to act in Egyptian rather than Syrian drama for four years. But during the 2015 season he acted in two Syrian productions, *Wujuh wa Amaken* and *al-ʿArrab*, the former of which was criticized for its direct political critique. Suleiman responded on June 30 that being direct can be dangerous but is sometimes necessary in art. Furthermore, he differentiated between those who watch drama solely as a form of relaxation and those who hope it will teach a lesson. When asked whether Syrian identity was lost in miniseries adopted from foreign films and novels, Suleiman said that this was not the case: "We filmed in Lebanon, but many characters resembled people I knew from Syria. When I read the screenplay I thought of several people I knew from Syria. The idea was to show the complexities in people—not just evil but also moments of good. . . . No miniseries is able to change the situation, but it is meant as stories for the people. Art is not responsible for providing a solution. That is not the duty of art. Art has to give an opportunity to understand the problem, to ask how this happened in the first place."

Suleiman was later critiqued for this stance that he expressed on the *Ramadan Rating* show, that art is not responsible for providing solutions. Yet his answer falls into the framework of collective memory, which according to scholar Ron Eyerman "specifies the temporal parameters of past and future, where we came from and where we are going, and also why we are here now."[57] In his research on slavery and the formation of African American identity, Eyerman examined theories that link collective memory to myth due to the process of mediation, negotiation, and selection of recollections. While collective memory references historical occurrences, events are often interpreted according to perspective and need. Eyerman also recounted how popular culture served as a means of transporting memories of slavery into future generations.[58] Yet not all screenwriters chose to construct collective memory, gravitating toward escapism instead. Journalist Ninar al-Khatib wrote, "It is curious that many screenwriters are adapting their storylines from foreign films earlier than the 90s and beyond. I wonder if this indicates that issues raised in an earlier time period in the West now apply to contemporary Arab society. Or simply, is it because this is just a current trend that will not continue?"[59] Screenwriter Hoozan ʿAkko argued that this particular escapism is grounded in complicated issues, underscoring the difficulty of imparting wisdom on events currently taking place. He stated, "Some miniseries that do try to place their storylines within the ʿazmeh' and provide wisdom can in the end give a wrong message. This happened with *Qalam Humra.* Many interpreted that the writer was saying we have an existential crisis because we don't have a civil society and this led to the revolution."[60]

The Phenomenon of Syrian-Lebanese Coproductions and the Rise of Lebanese Solo Productions in a Media Landscape of Pan-Arab Productions

Iyad Shihab Ahmad contended that many production companies in Lebanon stipulated that Syrian miniseries must include Lebanese actors, thereby advancing the Lebanese drama industry.[61] On June 24, 2015, *Ramadan Rating* discussed the development of the Lebanese drama industry along with joint-Arab productions since the Syrian revolution, explaining that the situations in Syria and Egypt had resulted in Lebanon's development into a veritable studio for Arab drama. The show also pointed out that among approximately seventy 2015 miniseries, only two were purely Lebanese. Tony 'Issa, a Lebanese actor, had a leading role in *Bint al-Shah Bandar*, produced in Lebanon but employing mainly Syrian actors. He argued that the role of the Lebanese is currently one of assistance since it was the presence of Syrian talent that ensured the success of the show. 'Issa also said that pan-Arab miniseries—with Syrian, Lebanese, Egyptian actors—have been good for Lebanese actors as they have benefited greatly from their Syrian mentors. Another important Lebanese actress, Warda al-Khal, contended that local Lebanese miniseries are difficult to export, which explains why the pan-Arab miniseries are doing better commercially.

On the July 1 *Ramadan Rating* show, which featured the Lebanese miniseries *Ahmad and Kristina*, screenwriter Claudia Marchalian expressed a desire for Lebanese drama to become more important in the Arab world. While joint-Arab productions were a start, she said, she hoped to promote miniseries that were purely Lebanese. Marchalian cited the Muslim-Christian love story *Ahmad and Kristina* as essential to contemporary Lebanese society. "We need to separate government from religion," she avowed and proudly identified two full Lebanese serials this year. Yet, Lebanese actor Talal al-Jordi, who had a role in *24 Qirat* that summer, contended, "At the moment, viewers enjoy Syrian-Lebanese productions, and I believe that Syrians and Lebanese help each other with drama. Because of the instability in the region, people can't concentrate and are thus, glued to the screen. However, in the future if there is peace in the region, people will not want to waste their time watching these miniseries."[62]

During Ramadan 2015, the Lebanese press ran frequent articles claiming that Lebanese-Syrian and/or pan-Arab productions presented opportunities for Lebanese drama. These Lebanese miniseries could replace dubbed Turkish serials, especially after channels in Egypt such as CBC, al-Nahar, and al-Hayat decided to drop Turkish miniseries in response to Turkey's political stance in Egypt. Lebanese drama creators hoped, clearly, that joint-Arab productions with Syrian, Lebanese, and Egyptian stars would replace the Turkish miniseries.[63] Many in Lebanon seized upon this opportunity and competition surrounding Lebanese serials increased. Marchalian's *Ahmad and Kristina* continued to draw viewers. Additionally, articles in the press carried titles such as "al-Muntij Marwan Haddad: 'Ahmad wa Kristina' Musalsal Lubnani li-l-'Adhem" (Producer Marwan Haddad States That *Ahmad wa Kristina* Was a Lebanese Miniseries to Its Very Core), stressing the fact that it was a Lebanese production.[64] Other articles included a string of Syrian miniseries in addition to *Ahmad and Kristina* and claimed they were Lebanese. For example, the article titled "al-Shashat al-Televizioniyya fi Shahr Ramadan: Tartadi Thawb al-Drama al-Lubnaniyya" (Television Channels during the Month of Ramadan Are Wearing the Clothing of Lebanese Drama) included Syrian miniseries such as *Chello*, *Bint al-Shah Bandar* (The Daughter of Shah Bandar), *24 Qirat*, *Bab al-Hara Part Seven*, *Ghadan Naltaqi*, and *al-'Arrab* as the top Lebanese productions of the year.[65] Most of these series, though written by Syrians, were produced by Lebanese companies, aired on Lebanese channels, and involved many Lebanese actors and actresses.[66] Other journalists wrote that while Lebanese drama was developing, a good screenplay was hard to find. As a result, producers were attracting viewers by borrowing texts from other films.[67]

Some journalists claimed Lebanese drama had elevated its presence in 2015 to the point where it could compete with Syrian and Egyptian drama. A few years earlier, they claimed, production companies had gathered Lebanese, Egyptian, and Syrians actors under the guidance of Syrian writers and directors and encouraged them to adapt storylines from foreign texts. This essentially stripped writers of their creative function. The screenplay *Rubi* (2012), by Marchalian, for example, was adapted from a Mexican series and starred Syrian actor Maksim Khalil and Lebanese actress Cyrine 'Abd al-Nour. *Lo'bat al-Mawt*, *Law*, *al-'Arrab*, and *Chello* were other noteworthy examples of this trend.[68] With respect to those who criticized the presence of Syrian actors in Lebanon, Sulafa Me'mar maintained that Syrians were there because of the war. Me'mar acknowledged that Lebanese actresses competed with her and that some had even asked her, "Isn't it enough that your actors are living in Lebanon?" Yet Me'mar averred that Syrians' presence in Lebanese drama had been mutually beneficial.[69]

Mufeed al-Rifa'i, the Lebanese producer of *Bint al-Shah Bandar*, admitted that people were talking about the *al-Ghazoo al-Suri* (Syrian invasion) of Lebanese drama. Indeed, many producers had been asked to exclude Syrian actors. According to al-Rifa'i, however, these demands have been ineffectual. For example, while *Bint al-Shah Bandar* is considered a Lebanese show and includes Syrian actors, *Al-'Arrab* is a Syrian show that includes Lebanese actors. Al-Rifa'i granted that Lebanese actors were learning from Syrian actors' experience, continuing on to say, "In Lebanon there is a crisis of shortage of writers and texts are stolen from foreign films and novels. There are very few Lebanese writers so they depend on Syrian writers. And with all the differences of opinion, it also comes down to what production companies are looking for."[70]

Meanwhile, violence continued to shatter Syria; by 2016 at least 470,000 Syrians had died as a result of the war. Continued internal and external Da'ish terrorist attacks marked Ramadan 2016. On June 12 a gunman first pledged allegiance to Da'ish, then killed fifty people at a gay nightclub in Orlando. On June 28 three suicide bombers with suspected links to Da'ish killed forty-one people at the Ataturk Airport in Istanbul. On July 3 Da'ish carried out suicide bombings that killed an estimated two hundred people in a heavily populated shopping district in Baghdad. Despite the reign of terror as well as the escalating refugee crisis, the press continued to discuss Syrian and Lebanese drama. Positive reviews of current storylines competed with heightened critiques of Syrian drama in the press and in coffeehouse discussions.[71] Titles of articles such as "al-Drama al-Suriyya Akalaha 'al-Ghool" (Syrian Drama Taken by a Demon) characterized that season's media attention.[72] Furthermore, production uncertainties during the 2016 season caused already-filmed Syrian miniseries such as *Ahl al-Gharam* (People of Love) *Part Three* to be delayed.[73] Despite such challenges, the Syrian drama industry offered twenty-six new miniseries. Commentary proliferated in magazines such as *Sayidaty*, *Nadine*, *Laha*, and *Hadeel*, sold at newsstands in Beirut. Many of these miniseries—whether transnational adaptations, Old Damascus tales (*Bi'a Shamiyyeh*), or contemporary stories set against the background of war—focused on heterosexual love and desire from various perspectives.

Both Syrian-Lebanese coproductions and transnational Arab miniseries faced strong criticism. Titles of articles such as "Suqut al-Drama al-Lubnaniyya al-Mushtaraka" (The Downfall of Transnational Lebanese Drama) criticized the superficial storylines of transnational Arab productions such as *Nus Yawm* (Half a Day), *Ya Reit* (I Wish), and *Jarimat al-Shaghaf* (Crime of Passion). Some critics felt that this crop of weak miniseries struggled from the outset to entice viewers.[74] In an article titled "al-Mawsam al-Suri Madrub fi 'Entizar Mu'jiza" (The Syrian Drama Season Is Beaten Up and Awaits a Miracle), critic Wissam Kan'an opined that long, boring clips had transformed famous actors such as Taim Hassan, Maksim Khalil, and Qusay Khawli into fashion models in the first three episodes of each of the season's transnational miniseries. Kan'an also argued that transnational miniseries, such as *Ya Reit*, *Jarimat al-Shaghaf*, and *Nus Yawm*, relied on advanced film techniques and beautiful scenery at the expense of the storyline. He criticized *Ya Reit* for its superficial references to the Syrian war, berated *Jarimat al-Shaghaf* for its unrealistic storyline about a Syrian escaping to Egypt (when, in reality, Egyptian doors were closed to Syrians), and chided *Nus Yawm* for showing a poor orphan girl dressed in expensive clothing.[75] Another journalist said, "*Jarimat al-Shaghaf* is not just one crime, but a television genocide."[76] Consider titles of articles such as "*Jarimat al-Shaghaf*: Nadine al-Rasi bi-Kamel Anaqatiha fi al-Habess (Nadine al-Rasi Completely Elegant while in

Prison)," which critiqued the character Jumana, shown in jail looking stylish and fully made up.[77] Journalist Rose Suleiman deplored the fact that Syrian joint-drama cooperations seemed to focus more on form and technique than on sociopolitical critique. She attributed this to marketing issues as well as the subtle embargo against Syrian miniseries. Suleiman ascribed the recent rise in escapist genres to a struggle to market miniseries dealing with the war.[78]

By 2017 an increase in confidence alongside disenchantment with Lebanese-Syrian coproductions had led many Lebanese production companies to showcase their talent independent of Syrian stars. According to Najeeb Nseir, however, these Lebanese companies broke from their Syrian mentors too soon. As a result, most of the year's solo Lebanese productions flopped.[79] Still, a June 26 episode of the Lebanese talk show *Fann al-Kheir* boasted about the large batch of Lebanese series, even as actors such as Yusuf al-Khal complained that these recent shows tended to repeat familiar themes. Many magazines also crowed about the more than nine independent Lebanese productions of the year. Although many were adapted from foreign films, this yield was still considered a landmark accomplishment. According to the Lebanese press, Lebanese miniseries were far stronger than Syrian miniseries, whose industry was on the verge of collapse. One article in *Nadine* contended that it was time the Lebanese took steps toward producing their own miniseries since Lebanese miniseries were stronger. One sign of this was that Syrians could succeed in Lebanese shows while Lebanese actors failed in Syrian productions. Author Nada 'Imad Khalil cited the Lebanese production *al-Haibeh*, which brought fame to Syrian actors like lead Taim Hassan. Khalil then mentioned two Syrian productions, *Khatun* and *Qanadil al-'Ashaq*, which, she argued, had failed despite renowned Lebanese actresses Warda al-Khal and Cyrine 'Abd al-Nour in leading roles.[80] Similarly, critic Wissam Kan'an pronounced *Qanadil al-'Ashaq* a shallow epic story that nonetheless surpassed other Syrian productions. He argued that the miniseries failed to capture audiences despite its having aired on several channels and having the benefit of Sireen's presence.[81]

These articles in the Lebanese press revealed a clear bias against Syrian miniseries and accentuated the dilemma facing Syrian television drama. While Syrians wrote and directed the summer hit *al-Haibeh*, a sensation in the press,[82] they had to depend on a Lebanese company to produce it. *Al-Haibeh*, populated with both Lebanese and Syrian actors, takes place during the uprising and tells the story of a family of arms and drug traffickers in northeast Biqa'.[83] Phrases such as "the war in Syria has changed many things (Episode Two)" testify to the ongoing reality of the war, as do references such as, in the ninth episode, brothers insisting on their preeminence as arms dealers in the face of new dealers who have established themselves during the civil war. According to Iyad Shihab Ahmad, the main character, Jabal (Syrian actor Taim Hassan), was inspired both

FIGURE 1.2 Taim Hassan (*second to left*) in *al-Haibeh Part One*.
Courtesy of Hoozan 'Akoo.

by Noah Za'tar, an antigovernment strongman in Lebanon, and also by Pablo Escobar as he is shown in *Narcos*.[84] Najeeb Nseir claimed that many viewers enjoyed this story of the weaponized hero and promised a *Part Two* in the next season. Many other screenwriters, he said, would follow suit and pick up similar storylines. Yet while Nseir argued that *al-Haibeh* should be considered Lebanese due to its Lebanese production company,[85] Reem Hanna reasoned that it should be considered a joint Syrian-Lebanese production.[86] The same dilemma related to the Lebanese production *Karamel* (inspired by the Hollywood movie *What Women Want*), written by Syrian screenwriter Mazin Taha but starring Lebanese actors.

According to Iyad Shihab Ahmad, while local channels can broadcast Lebanese miniseries starring Lebanese actors, more important channels require Syrian actors. This is due to the fact that Syrian actors are considered more experienced than their Lebanese counterparts and tend to improve the quality of the miniseries in which they appear. Nonetheless, Ahmad argued that Syrian miniseries face grave marketing and production issues. He cited *Shawq* (2017), broadcast only on OSN and a local Syrian channel, the highly anticipated *Shababik* and *Psycho*, both of which were completed but were deferred to the following season because they could not find a channel, and *Fawda*, which did not complete filming in 2017.[87]

Partially due to those marketing issues, Syrian miniseries continued to struggle for relevance. Reliance on escapist storylines and superficial depictions

of war continued, as did collaboration on pan-Arab or Syrian-Lebanese coproductions. However, during the 2018 season Syrian-Lebanese coproductions would
be reinvigorated and reach new heights of popularity with miniseries such as
Tango, al-Haibeh: al-'Awda, Julia, and *Tariq.* Alongside these trends, war plots in
some Syrian miniseries evoked nostalgia for life before the uprising and the
ensuing terrorism. The social for the sake of the social strand characterized
miniseries that both dealt with or did not deal with the war. Of the 211 total miniseries from 2011 to 2018, 73 series (34.5 percent) are in the social for the sake of
the social strand and 49 (23 percent) compose the nostalgic register (a percentage that includes Old Damascus miniseries and nostalgic series during the war),
making these the two largest strands of Syrian miniseries. Accordingly, the next
section zooms in on these strands.

Zooming in on the Two Central Strands of Miniseries: The Rise of Nostalgia and the Social for the Sake of the Social

Two central strands of miniseries, the nostalgic register and the social for the
sake of the social, place storylines in wartime Syria, though each strand also contains a substantial number of miniseries that avoid the war. The social for the
sake of the social strand comprises 36.5 percent of storylines on war, and the
nostalgic register comprises 11.5 percent of storylines on war; the social for
the sake of the social strand comprises 33.5 percent of miniseries that do not
address the war, and the nostalgic strand comprises 28 percent of miniseries
evading the war. Despite ostensible intersections, these strands represent
extremely different philosophical viewpoints. Both are social rather than political and criticize gender and marriage conventions. Yet the social for the sake of
the social strand portrays prevailing social issues as deeply rooted in history and
the present struggle to resolve those issues as continuous with the past. The nostalgic register, on the other hand, ignores past struggles; it depicts Syria's present condition as at odds with the pre-uprising period, which is romanticized as
a time of freer sexual norms. Both strands, like the oppositional and neutral
stands, distinguish progressive gender and marriage norms from the extremist
culture of Da'ish and thus, at times, similarly appear to intersect with the
regime narrative.

The trend of postwar miniseries that constructed cultural memories in the
nostalgic register, filled with historical amnesia about past oppression perpetrated by the state, culminated in the 2017 season. Yet the nostalgic register is
not new to Syrian television drama. In *A New Old Damascus: Authenticity and Distinction in Urban Syria* (2004), Christa Salamandra delineated how Ramadan
had become a season of nostalgia for Sunni Muslims. Through close viewing of
programs broadcast during Ramadan such as *Intoxication with the Past*, the folk-
lore series *Our Popular Memory*, and *Ramadan Days*, Salamandra showed how the

nostalgic register formed a key component of the regime's construction of national culture, while at the same time sowing division rather than connectedness. Her fieldwork in the 1990s centered on the reception of *Ayyam Shamiyyeh* (1993), which portrayed social life in Damascus in 1910 during the Ottoman period. This imagined age of innocence contrasted strongly with the corruption of contemporary life and provoked significant debate. While some viewers interpreted the nostalgic miniseries as a critique of the present or even a historical document of a national identity crisis, others focused on the show's inaccuracies and misinformation. *Ayyam Shamiyyeh* set a trend in Old Damascus Syrian miniseries that harkened to a simpler, more authentic past, before the contemporary identity crisis exacerbated by the French mandate and outside cultural influences.[88] Whereas pre-uprising Old Damascus tales avoided intersections with the regime narrative by using the French colonial mandate as an allegory of the Ba'th Party regime, the post-2011 nostalgic strand in contemporary series does at times intersect with the regime narrative, as it glosses over state oppression during the prewar days.

Themes of culture memory organically intersect with nostalgia, and much has been written on trauma and nostalgia in postconflict societies outside of the Syrian context. Scholars have shown that in postcolonial states transitioning to peace, the transmission of stories that ground citizens in an affirming past are often part of the reconstruction effort. Additionally, active silence about past political drama is often part of this nostalgic project. In *Ethics and Nostalgia in the Contemporary Novel* (2005), John J. Su challenges negative views of nostalgia, which he views as the central concern of the twentieth-century novel. On the other hand, Svetlana Boym in *The Future of Nostalgia* (2001) describes nostalgia as a sentiment of loss and displacement that often seeks to eradicate history and transform it into a collective or private mythology. Boym also contends that bursts of nostalgia often follow revolutions. I argue that what we see of the uprising in Syrian drama is different. Here, historical amnesia and nostalgia are part of the war media effort to discount the legitimacy of the uprising rather than being part of postwar reconstruction. This distinction points to the regime's mediative effort to manage the uprising, which is often referred to as a "crisis" rather than a revolution. Furthermore, the rise of the nostalgic register in drama, alongside the increased use of the term "crisis," is also connected to the identity politics of a secular, tolerant Syrian culture that is contrasted with the extremist culture of Da'ish.

Mudhakkirat 'Ashiqa Sabiqa (Memoirs of a Former Lover), written by Nur Shishekly and Mazin Taha, aired twenty-eight episodes approximately one month prior to the formal 2017 Ramadan season. Here, a major theme was fear: fear of bombings, fear of kidnappings, and fear of war profiteers. Intimate pleas, such as those of Hanadi to her sister Huda, evoke a deep sense of collective trauma and nostalgia for the peaceful past: "What has this happened to us? What did we do for God to punish us in this way? No one knows what got us here."[89] In *Trauma: A Social Theory*, Jeffrey C. Alexander delineates how during the cultural construction of collective trauma, the central occasion becomes not "who did this to me, but what group did this to us?" Alexander recounts how, as competing claims are made, "which narrative wins out is a matter of performative power." According to Alexander, "shared trauma depends on collective processes of cultural interpretation."[90] Eyerman expands on the mediative process that reinterprets the past and engaged in obliviousness when necessary to suit present needs.[91] The construction of collective trauma along with nostalgia toward a peaceful past surfaces on another occasion in *Mudhakkirat ʿAshiqa Sabiqa*, when Huda asserts, "For five years we have lived with fear, coldness, and humiliation. Enough."[92] Huda's statement to Hanadi situates the past as a time before suffering, which demonstrates a certain historical amnesia. This is true, also, when she says, "We used to live happily. No one was sleeping in gardens. No one went to sleep hungry. Even poor families did not put their children to sleep hungry. In five years we've grown older. Not in age, but in sadness."[93]

In a similarly nostalgic tenor, *Shawq* (broadcast on OSN in 2017) is also characterized by historical amnesia. In this storyline the days of political protest through gender metaphors are gone. Rather, the miniseries is inspired by the Hollywood production *Still Alice* (2014), which recounts the story of a dynamic Columbia University professor who is diagnosed with early-onset Alzheimer's disease. When the Syrian version commences, its thirty-two-year-old female protagonist, Shawq (meaning longing, nostalgia), is involved with Majed, who is engaged to another woman. Rather than offering a political critique, this sexual openness evokes nostalgia for Syria's simpler prewar past and distinguishes its secular culture from the religious fundamentalism of Daʿish. Even her family is nonjudgmental about her premarital relationship, as if freer sexual norms were inherent in Syrian society. This impression is also created by the fact that the storyline no longer conspicuously defines the pure female body against that of the corrupted West. Instead, the point of comparison is religious fanaticism and Daʿish. Thus, gender and sexuality predominate in the storyline to bring forth an imagined secular culture, one that forgets past oppression as it evokes nostalgia. In this way, a collective memory of a secular society arises in the gender and marriage storylines.

Shawq takes place against the backdrop of kidnappings, forced prostitution, and terrorism executed by Daʿish. In addition to highlighting the destruction Daʿish wreaks on the country, the miniseries also portrays secular war criminals profiting from the bloodshed. As Adam, the brother of the protagonist, Shawq, tells his love interest, Waʾed, "At the beginning of the 'azmeh,' my sister said that we Arabs try to eliminate oppression but end up bringing in even worse oppression in our lives."[94] Accordingly, one major storyline in *Shawq* involves Rose, the wife of Shawq's cousin, who is kidnapped and sold to Daʿish; this scenario is based on the true story of opposition activist Razan Zaitouneh, who was captured by Da'ish and disappeared. According to Iyad Shihab Ahmad, many viewers perceived this story as an example of how the regime steals even their stories.[95]

Line Khatib recounted in *Lebanese Cinema: Imagining the Civil War and Beyond* how during and after the civil war, the Lebanese developed the myth of "others on our land," which erased responsibility for the war. According to Khatib, nostalgia arose from postwar emptiness as well as longing for those simpler, romanticized days of the war.[96] In Syria, the nostalgic register acted in a similar way by imagining a rosy past that was disrupted by the interference of "others." In this way, the nostalgic register discounts the legitimacy of the uprising. In *Shawq*, nostalgia conjures prewar days when the regime was uncontested and citizens lived in an imagined peace. In both *Mudhakkirat 'Ashiqa Sabiqa* and *Shawq*, gender and marriage metaphors gloss over the oppression of the past. Through the lens of gender and sexuality, criticism is directed toward war profiteers and the devastating reality of war.

Yet it would be simplistic to say that nostalgia is the dominating theme of the gender and sexuality storylines in recent post-uprising Syrian miniseries. The social for the sake of the social, an increasingly popular genre of miniseries, presents storylines that address wartime social dynamics, especially marriage and gender, as social commentary rather than as metaphorical political critique, as occurred in pre-uprising miniseries. This genre has developed since the uprising in distinction to the politically tinged love, gender, and marriage metaphors that dominated the airwaves before the uprising. Screenwriter Reem Hanna has argued that issues of honor and shame related to a woman's body and sexuality still permeate Syrian culture; therefore, the current trend among contemporary miniseries is a prioritized cultural revolution rather than a loss of interest in politics or nostalgia for the past.[97] This point is evidenced in my analysis of *Fawda* in the introductory chapter of this book. It is true that market demands fueled the emergence of escapism in Syrian drama. Still, the production of *Fawda*, which will be examined in more detail in chapters 3 and 4, reveals that post-uprising Syrian drama continued to offer insight into the traumas of war. In producing this miniseries, drama creators explored innovative techniques and broke taboos in unprecedented ways through gender and marriage storylines.

Another pertinent example is "Imra'a k-al-Qamr" (A Woman Like the Moon), in *Ahl al-Gharam Part Three* (2017), written by Reem Hanna and directed by al-Muthana Sobh. Khawla introduces her brother, Jarir, visiting from Spain, to a young woman named Sandra. Much to Khawla's dismay, Jarir falls instead for Zaina, the young woman's divorced aunt. Despite family remonstration, Zaina and Jarir feel an instant attraction. In this storyline, sex is discussed casually, as shown when Sandra first meets Jarir and offhandedly gives him her address. Khawla and her husband are pleased, though Jarir chooses, instead, to visit Zaina, who works as a dentist in Beirut. When their families protest the marriage, Jarir proposes that they continue to live in different places and see each other during vacation. Zaina agrees. In the end, however, a jealous Sandra contacts her aunt's ex-husband, who tells Zaina that he will take their son Hani if she gets involved with another man. Jarir returns despondently to Spain.

This story treats sex as an open topic and even hints that the lovers may reconnect in the future. For now, Zaina says, her son is her priority. Since the lovers are older and independent, their union is impeded less by family disapproval than by matters of culture, law, and family logistics. Central here is the idea that though the lovers lived in the same neighborhood in Sham, they had not seen the relationship potential before them. Now, returning to each other seems impossible, which parallels the impossibility of Sham returning to an earlier state.

Hanna's exploration of more liberal sexual, marital, and gendered norms provoked criticism on social media, reflecting viewers' conservative social values. Hanna elaborated, "On social media, many wrote that I was promoting homosexuality and sex. Also, there were vociferous comments by some viewers saying that they agreed that Zaina should remain with her husband when he returned, rather than pursue her lover." Hanna added that the unhappy ending reflected her understanding that the *Ahl al-Gharam* production team preferred unhappy endings. Indeed, unhappy endings predominated in the first and second seasons of *Ahl al-Gharam*. However, she felt that the ending was open to interpretation.[98] Ultimately, the miniseries did not intend to make a political statement. Rather, it participated in a trend in which the social is shown for the sake of the social itself rather than with the submerged intention of political critique.

The Drama behind the Drama: Marketing and Production Pressures

In 2013 the phenomenon of miniseries that were produced but delayed or cancelled due to marketing and production pressures began to take root. By 2017 miniseries were frequently delayed, canceled, or shelved. Indeed, the 2017 and 2018 Ramadan season witnessed cancelations and delays of multiple Syrian miniseries due to marketing issues. Some critics and observers believed that this disruption marked the end of Syrian television drama. Najeeb Nseir and Hassan Sami Yusuf's *Fawda* was unable to complete filming in 2017 after the producer replaced director Laith Hajjo, with whom he could not reach an agreement, with Samir Husayn. *Fawda* finally appeared in 2018 and raised Syrian drama to new heights of cultural critique by fundamentally undermining traditional gender and marriage norms. Amid marketing challenges and difficulties writing and producing *Fawda*, Nseir remained committed to his writing process and went on to write other screenplays. After six months of working on a commissioned screenplay for the second season of *al-Ikhweh*, Nseir disappeared. He reappeared with a new screenplay in which he imagined postwar Syrian society. Though one production company gave itself a substantial discount on the screenplay, Nseir was still willing to write. When that agreement fell through, Nseir continued to write, though there was no production company on the horizon.[99]

Over the years, Syrian miniseries have depicted the drama behind the drama as it relates to marketing and production pressures. A particularly poignant example of this self-reflexive process is in *Buq 'at Daw'*. In the show's 2008 sketch, "Aba'd," screenwriter Adnan Zira'i illustrated the challenges continually facing directors.[100] Here, an actor approaches his director on set and asks if there is anything political, moral, social, humanistic, economic, or revolutionary in the miniseries. The director denies every count, claiming the series would never have gotten anywhere if that were the case. Then the actors and production team gather together to begin the filming process. The production team says cut, and we quickly see a small white board indicating that the miniseries the director is producing is titled *Qadayat Balad* (Problematic Issues of the Country), a title that indicates that the director is indeed predicating his story on controversial and difficult issues that he is nonetheless hoping to sneak unnoticed past censors and governmental watchdogs into a space of public consumption.

During Ramadan 2011, the first season after the uprising, *Buq'at Daw' Part Eight* addressed journalistic shortcomings in a sketch called "Ra'yak Yahemna" (Your Opinion Is Important to Us). In this sketch, screenwriter Hassan Fares is astonished to see his recent miniseries *Ayyam Majnuna* (Crazy Days) candidly discussed on television. The show's interviewer roams the streets asking people for their opinion on Fares's new work. She hands the microphone first to a butcher, who, standing on the street outside his shop, describes the miniseries like a piece of meat. She then interviews a man who rips the miniseries apart, from the terrible set decor to the poor directing. When the interview is finished and the woman leaves, he leans over to his friend and brags that he trashed the miniseries, though he had not seen a single episode. He explains that the director, who is a real snob, lives in his building, and this was his way to get back at him. Then the interviewer moves on to a tall, shy man about to get into his car, who lacks the vocabulary to describe the series and mutters the word "beautiful" over and over again as the interviewer asks him questions. After watching people judge, misrepresent, and insult his work, Fares tells his wife that he will abandon screenplay writing. He prefers to become a critic so he can evaluate others rather than let ignorant spectators belittle his work.[101]

Consider Nur Shishekly's sketch "Hayati Musalsal" (My Life Is a Miniseries), which portrays *musalsal* writers' intimacy with their audience as well as their sensitivity to socioeconomic hardships.[102] Here, Jumana is a young television screenwriter who writes for *Buq'at Daw'*. She finds herself in the tricky position of having to dodge her family and friends' pitches for sketches. Over lunch, her father-in-law advises her to write about corruption and bribery before telling her that while he will not charge for his service, he does expect that his name will appear in the credits. After the uncomfortable meal, she hurries to an appointment with the director. As she drives, discussing her ideas with the director on her cell phone, a police officer pulls her over. The officer penalizes her for talking on her cell phone while driving, not wearing her seat belt, and having expired paperwork. She begs him not to fine her and boasts that she writes for *Buq'at Daw'*. He replies angrily, "So your penalty will now even be greater! Your show has made a mockery of our occupation. It is as if you think that we are the only ones who take bribes." He proceeds to tell the story of how he moved from a small village to the city, where his monthly rent is nine thousand pounds though his monthly income is only eight thousand pounds, and how he "can't eat or drink" and "can't even think about marrying and having children." Above all, he continues, "everyone hates us and they treat us like a dog when we want to give them a ticket." Finally, it seems, Jumana has found a story, a bitter portrayal of the pressures of masculinity, worth being dramatized. She whispers, "I'm sorry. Your life truly is a miniseries."

These dramas behind the drama vary with time. Indeed, post-uprising *Buq'at Daw'* sketches often dealt with the divide between escapist narratives and those set in the midst of war. In the sketch "Pan-Arab," screenwriter Mazin Taha sharply and humorously depicts the predicament in which Syrian cultural producers find themselves as they try to determine the angle of their storyline.[103] The screenwriter Abu Dhiya' asks his producer if he liked his screenplay *al-'Aileh* (The Family), and the producer says the text needs fundamental changes. When the producer insists that he does not want a local miniseries, Abu Dhiya' asks if he prefers foreign, Turkish, or dubbed miniseries. The producer specifies that he wants the miniseries to be pan-Arab with a mix of stars from Syria, Lebanon, Egypt, and the Gulf. The screenwriter insists that this is a Syrian miniseries and thus the structure needs to be Syrian. Even when Abu Dhiya' explains that his story is about a Syrian family and so it does not make sense to include actors from Jordan, Lebanon, and Egypt, the producer still emphasizes that the show must be pan-Arab. He wants ninety episodes and stars from all over the Arab world. The producer contends that political discussion have always revolved around Arab unity, that Arab people are one, and that, thus, drama requires a unified message. The screenwriter, in turn, is shocked to hear the producer's message that he expects this miniseries to bring about Arab unity.

Then we switch to a scene when Abu Dhiya' is writing an Egyptian accent into his dialogue. He informs his wife that this represents the last time he will insist on writing a Syrian story, that the next time he will write a genuinely pan-Arab story: "A Lebanese woman married to an Egyptian man and she has a Syrian lover. Or an Egyptian woman married to a Lebanese man and she likes a Syrian." Later, the producer notifies the writer that he wants three million dollars for certain well-known stars and—alluding to the real-life popularity of Lebanese model-actress Nadine Nassib Njeym and Yusuf al-Khal—insists that he wants to hire Majed al-Nemr and Cyrine Zalam al-Layl as the stars of his show. Next, we see the director filming actors with all different accents. Even the director keeps changing his accent. We observe a Syrian mother and father with a daughter who has a Lebanese accent. A son enters and demands his coffee in Egyptian colloquial, and then a son with a Gulf accent arrives. Finally, an Iraqi lady comes in yelling in an Iraqi accent. Throughout this scene, the director speaks in an array of different accents.

Ziyad al-'Amer's "Hamlet" goes even further in recounting the mixed messages producers send screenwriters in post-uprising Syria.[104] Here, the producer tells the writer Hadi that his screenplay is good but, unfortunately, deals with the azmeh. Hadi replies that viewers have always liked Syrian miniseries for their realism, as they address the familiar. His producer responds, "You want to explain to me what reality is? I'm living it. But art is supposed to transport us from this reality." The screenwriter insists that he likes realistic texts and says, "I did try to make my text less direct and *bayna al-sutur* (between the lines)." His producer responds, "*khalina bi-l-satur* (leave us on the lines)."

When Hadi says he is not sure what to do, his producer answers that as an acclaimed writer, he should be able to figure it out. When Hadi goes home to write, he has a hard time. He tells his wife that he wants to write about the azmeh but the channels are not accepting these storylines. Hadi then discusses the possibility of writing a historical fantasy with his friend. When, later, Hadi tells his producer he is having a hard time, the producer brushes him off, insisting that if Turkish and Mexican miniseries can run a hundred episodes, he should be able to come up with thirty.

Hadi goes to the bookstore and explains his predicament to the saleswoman. He says that he needs a foreign book with a story that is far away from the azmeh. She says that there is such a book, titled *How to Get Away from al-Azmeh in Five Days*, which she has been selling to other writers like himself. Hadi later decides to write Shakespeare's *Hamlet*, since it is far removed from the azmeh. When he gives the script to the producer, he is happy. Later the miniseries is broadcast and a large audience tunes in. A man from a small grocery store asks Hadi if he chose Denmark since Syrian refugees are fleeing there. Hadi is enraged and responds that Denmark is merely where the play takes place and has nothing to do with the azmeh. At the hair salon the barber asks Hadi if Ophelia is a revolutionary or aligns with the regime. He tells Hadi not to be scared and hopes out loud that Hadi will inform him if Ophelia's father rejected Hamlet since he is a revolutionary. Hadi is upset and leaves the barber with shaving cream on face, insisting that Hamlet has nothing to do with all that. Hadi and his wife watch a talk show on which a reporter says that Hamlet reminds him of Syria: everyone conspiring against him. He also references the expression "to be or not to be," to which another man comments that *Hamlet al-Suri* (the Syrian Hamlet) will not die: "The Syrian human being has to be or not to be."

A devastated Hadi approaches the producer and apologizes, since so many viewers are connecting the plot to the azmeh, though he intended the opposite. The producer, however, does not understand Hadi's distress. He replies, "Of course it's on the 'azmeh.' This is what channels want. I want you to think of creating another show on the 'azmeh.' Everyone is talking about your show!" By now Hadi is utterly confused. This self-reflexive sketch poignantly shows the predicament in which screenwriters find themselves. It all comes down to the role of art in revolution. Though writers have a particular role in mind, they are also forced to navigate the commercial demands of production companies and hidden agendas that compete with their own vision.

2

Sociopolitical Satire in the Multiyear Syrian Sketch Series *Buq'at Daw'* (Spotlight)

Artistic Resistance via Gender and Marriage Metaphors, 2001–2019

After years of intense nationalistic "jihad" against colonialism, a preeminent government official is charged with corruption and dismissed from office. His advisor, Nader, suggests that he reenter politics via the Majils al-Sha'b *(literally "People's Chamber," meaning parliament) in order to continue his anticolonialism quest. The official shows visible disinterest in dealing with the general public, so Nader explains that giving a few hopeful speeches to local communities and posing for photographs distributing rice (creating an illusion of benevolence) would suffice to win a seat. Nader constructs his boss's new masculine image, arranging for him to deliver a speech at a funeral and hiring large muscle men with black glasses, representing* shabbiha *(Syrian regime thugs), to stand in the audience. The official's funeral speech, imbued with nationalist threats toward those who oppose stability, is tragicomically out of place, and the grievers cry and run away. As they flee, the official turns to Nader for an answer. The equally jaded Nader replies, "They're so excited to vote for you that they're racing to the polls!"*[1]

The official in the above television sketch, "Khitab Mu'athir" (A Moving Speech, 2012), appears in *Buq'at Daw'* Part Nine, and is just one representation of Bashar al-Asad as a dictator who clings stubbornly to his seat of power.[2] Hazim Suleiman, the sketch's writer, uses the disoriented (and disorienting) official to represent a dictator so caught up in defending his own position that he cannot empathize with the masses. The speech's absurdity symbolizes the dictator's inability to engage in reform that reflects the wishes of his people.[3]

Deconstructing Dominant Regime Narratives

Political stability seemed impossible when Hafiz al-Asad staged his Corrective Movement in 1970. Syria had undergone numerous coups d'état since independence in 1946. But Hafiz al-Asad managed to hold on to his power for thirty years.

Then, just as remarkably, he seamlessly transferred power to his son, Bashar.[4] An important element of the 'Alawi-dominated Ba'th regime's grip on power had been its ability to cultivate fear through storytelling. Through a grand narrative, the regime had presented itself as the last bastion of secular Arab nationalism and sole protector against imperialist threats, conspiracies, and rising Islamic fundamentalism. Accordingly, the regime downplayed defeats, suppressed counternarratives, revised reports that might undermine its leader's strength, and employed an elaborate system of rewards and punishments to ensure the loyalty of cultural producers.[5]

Syrian television drama subtly deconstructed these regime narratives and played a vital role in undermining the Asad regime while operating within the framework of government co-optation. Since the establishment of Syrian television in 1960, transgressive political, social, and economic critiques of the Ba'th socialist project and failed Arab nationalist aspirations had informed political parodies. Nihad Qal'i, already known for his work in the Syrian National Theater and referred to as the Father of Syrian Comedy, created the character Husni Burazan, while Durayd Lahham invented Ghawwar al-Tawsheh, inspired by the popular American television series *The Laurel and Hardy Show*.[6] Together, Qal'i and Lahham teamed up with actor Rafiq Sbai'i's and his character, Abu Sayyah, forming a comic trio.[7] They went on to star in Qal'i's *Maqalib Ghawwar* (Ghawwar's Schemes, 1966) and *Hammam al-Hana* (Hana Hamam, 1968), which solidified the foundation of the *musalsal* (miniseries) as its own genre.[8]

Short, satirical political sketches of *Masrah al-Shawk* (Theater of Thorns) appeared alongside these television miniseries during the 1960s. An average *Masrah al-Shawk* theater piece lasted a little over an hour and was composed of short, unrelated sketches in which actors changed roles. In the 1970s adaptations of pieces written by the late poet Muhammad al-Maghut—such as *Day'at Tishrin* (The October Village, 1974), *al-Ghurbeh* (Alienation, 1975), and *Kasak ya Watan* (Cheers to the Homeland, 1979)—brought sarcastic theater to the forefront of Syrian entertainment. These theatrical productions came to life when actors from the Omaya folk dance troupe combined song and dance with biting political critique. Hossam Tahcin Bik, who arranged songs, dances, and sketches in many of these pieces, recollects how, in light of the performances' popularity, eager fans sometimes had to wait several weeks until a ticket became available.[9] The sarcastic theater and miniseries productions of the late Nihad Qal'i in the 1960s and poet al-Maghut during the 1970s and 1980s are driven by the belittlement of ordinary men corrupted in a patronage system. Yasser al-'Azmeh's multiyear, one-man television sketch comedy *Maraya* (Mirrors) would continue Syria's tradition of sharp sociopolitical critique from the 1980s onward.

When Hafiz al-Asad died in June 2000, intellectuals felt optimistic that the young president, Bashar al-Asad, would work to reform their nation.[10] Media specialists Christa Salamandra and Marlin Dick recall that the first season of the multiyear television sketch series *Buq'at Daw'*, which openly discussed taboo topics such as state corruption, sectarianism, and villainous *mukhabarat*, reflected that hope. Dick and Salamandra document how Suriya al-Dawliyyeh (Syrian Art Production International), a television production company owned by nouveau riche Sunni businessman Muhammad Hamsho (with close ties to the regime), approached two talented young actors, Ayman Rida and Bassem Yakhour, to create a comedic political satire for the 2001 season. Rida and Yakhour chose newcomer Laith Hajjo as director, and the three of them worked together to compose this sketch-based miniseries. They planned each episode to contain three short sketches, typically written by different screenwriters. Their refreshing collaboration welcomed the participation of actors and writers. President Bashar al-Asad's 2000 inaugural address, in which he advocated tolerance of multiple opinions and a campaign against endemic corruption, inspired them to push the boundaries of censored content. Though former vice-president 'Abd al-Halim Khaddam attempted to stop the show, the president intervened on its behalf.[11] In Dick's detailed analysis of *Buq'at Daw'*'s initiation, he contends that this miniseries marks a departure from traditional *musalsalat* and introduces "revolutionary innovations in comedy form with more daring reformist content." He continues, "*Spotlight* has fused new approaches to comedy production—cinematic techniques combined with flourishes more in keeping with theater, an emphasis on collective talent over the individual, slapstick interspersed with social realism—with new, more reformist, more self-referential, more visual material."[12]

Director Haitham Haqqi argues that drama creators had been engaging in political critique for years prior to *Buq'at Daw'*. The only difference, he claims, is that while authorities previously forbade this critique, now the president actively encouraged it as part of the appearance of reform.[13] Yet Laith Hajjo, who directed the first, second, and fourth seasons, insists that the revolutionary content of the initial seasons did not result from more freedom under the regime per se. Instead, Hajjo explains, the government's promises of change inspired them, which spurred them to take risks. At the same time the censorship committee was torn between following the new president's orders and heeding the demands of the *mukhabarat*. Despite the challenges facing the creators of *Buq'at Daw'*, Hajjo contends that many of their bold sketches aired because their sociopolitical critiques were disguised to elude the censorship committee.[14]

Innovative film techniques enticed television screenwriter Colette Bahna to contribute pieces to this comedy. Although *Buq'at Daw'* was Hajjo's directorial debut, Bahna appreciated collaborating with writers to preserve the spirit of the original piece.[15] Writers barely made one hundred dollars per sketch, yet the majority noted the miniseries' immense success and agreed to contribute. Bahna argues that the spirit of cooperation that characterized the first two seasons fell victim to government-provoked personal rivalries among the creators. Afterward, she contributed only an occasional sketch and lamented the increasingly harsh stipulations censors imposed upon writers. In later seasons her sketches would appear in truncated versions, ultimately leading to her departure.[16] Bahna contends that while idea theft and the recycling of popular jokes occurred in later seasons, Hajjo employed the tools of sarcastic comedy and critiques of government corruption in *Buq'at Daw'*, which ensured its success.[17] Jihad 'Abdo, who began his acting career in 1994, was at first attracted by the show's innovative, fast-paced sketches, but fellow actors' sense of entitlement prompted him to leave after the third season. According to 'Abdo, once Hajjo left the sketch comedy went downhill because he was the only director capable of protecting creative talent and standing up to the production company.[18] Salamandra reiterated that *Buq'at Daw'* lost its initial momentum due to artistic tensions—just like the reform process it was representing.[19]

Similar government-incited rivalries plagued the artistic creators of the early burlesque, politically oriented Syrian comedies of the 1960s and 1970s. In his memoir veteran actor Sbai'i writes that once he realized the extent that Qal'i and Lahham had excluded him from their financial agreements, he refused to act in *Sahh al-Nawm* (Good Morning, 1973), even when Qal'i insisted that he join them. This marked the official end of the comic trio.[20] After Hafiz al-Asad presented Durayd Lahham with an award in 1975 for his role as Ghawwar—leaving out Qal'i, his partner and creator of the comic duo—Qal'i fell sick and ceased to participate in productions.[21] Indeed, the direct relationship between the government and the intellectuals involved in television production exemplifies the capacity of the government leaders to selectively distribute privilege. This, in turn, sows division between creators and promotes hero worship within the system.[22]

It is worth noting that despite the animosity between Lahham and Sbai'i, both maintained warm relationships with Hafiz al-Asad. In fact, Sbai'i dedicated his memoir to the late president. Both too have remained outwardly supportive of Bashar al-Asad throughout the current uprising.[23] Through this example, we see how the system's divide-and-conquer strategy interferes with creative life, encourages inequity, and ignites animosity between intellectuals who could otherwise form a unified base. The division between intellectuals and their dependence on the system's support exaggerate the veneration of government leaders, creating strong columns of support for the foundation of the political system. Jihad 'Abdo recounts how the government compelled actors to get close to the *mukhabarat*. Those who refused, like him, paid a heavy price. For seven years he landed important roles only to discover that his name had been deleted from casting lists.[24]

Following Hafiz al-Asad's death, noted actor Fares al-Heloo signed the Memorandum of the 99, calling for political reform at the start of Bashar's presidency. When Bashar clamped down on the opposition after a brief Damascus

Spring, Heloo felt the repercussions on his acting career. First, the *mukhabarat* convinced directors to offer Heloo inferior roles. When he refused those roles, the *mukhabarat* accused him of being a temperamental drunkard with whom it was impossible to work.[25] Director Samir Gharibeh describes how the government distributed privilege to certain individuals it could count on to show support even during political turmoil. According to Gharibeh, this explains why some drama creators have stood by the regime and criticized the revolutionaries during the current uprising.[26]

In my opinion, *Buq'at Daw'* follows a firmly established tradition of political satire in Syrian drama. Prior to the revolution, it proffered innovative critical sketches despite divisions in the intellectual community and attempted government co-optation. There was an element of truth in *tanfis* (airing), the government's desire to present a democratic facade, and the interest in monitoring dissent and delayed retribution. This reasoning, however, focuses on government intent and disregards the role of the artist as an opposition activist. Instead, that reasoning depicts artists as conniving with the regime. I would like to underscore the oppositional role these artists played by examining their manifold use of innuendo and word artistry to subvert regime propaganda. Many Syrian intellectuals, such as Hazim Suleiman, argue that later critiques were less fresh and surprising than their earlier counterparts and were no longer part of a larger unified project. Yet, according to Suleiman, while the project fizzled for some time, it eventually regained momentum.[27]

Furthermore, I believe these sketches must be viewed in the context of a firmly established tradition of political critique in Syrian art and culture through the lens of gender and marriage. Some fans argued that Syrian television drama—with all its stories of the *qabadayat* (tough men)—stood in stark contrast to what they saw as the current reality of cowardice and passivity in the face of political oppression. Yet actress and producer Lora Abu-As'ad argued in 2009 that the sketch comedy *Buq'at Daw'* was an example of a politically courageous show that she wished were broadcast not just during Ramadan but as a daily ritual for the population throughout the year.[28]

Several recent works have also emphasized the continuity of sociopolitical critique in post-uprising Syria. In "Prelude to an Uprising: Syrian Fictional Television and Socio-Political Critique," Christa Salamandra documented how, following antigovernment protests, observers praised a new generation of artists for finally engaging in creative dissent. Yet she countered this theory that artists had been sudden galvanized after years of torpor. Drama creators of miniseries such as *Buq'at Daw'*, she contended, had already pushed the boundaries of accepted political discourse and offered truly subversive work.[29] *Syria from Reform to Revolt, Volume 2: Culture, Society, and Religion* underscored the importance of Bashar al-Asad's initial ten years and the fact that opposition literature and culture did not suddenly appear following the revolution in 2011. Rather, it expressed continuity from Bashar al-Asad's first decade in power.[30] In her seminal chapter "Syria's Drama Outpouring: Between Complicity and Critique," Salamandra expanded on many of the activist-artists who emerged after 2011, appropriating the oppositional vocabulary of radically political drama creators.[31]

In *Dancing in Damascus: Creativity, Resilience, and the Syrian Revolution* (2017), miriam cooke powerfully delineates the story of the revolution's socially engaged artists, "artist-activists," who, through "smart-phones, pens, voices, and brushes," defended the revolution against the regime. Cooke begins her work well before the revolution and connects the dissent of the 1990s, when the "wall of fear" fell, to current revolutionary fervor among "artist-activists." She shows how the state was losing control as intellectuals critiqued its very essence. For instance, activist-intellectual Hassan 'Abbas advocated political change through culture, and novelist/screenwriter Nihad's *Silk Market* captured the regime's underground protests, thus breaking political taboos.[32] Edward Ziter's *Political Performance in Syria: From the Six-Day War to the Syrian Uprising* (2015) chronicles the adapting of theater tropes such as martyrdom by the uprising's cyber activists.[33]

In *Mediating the Uprising* I emphasize continuity in the tradition of sociopolitical critique and trace the roots of subversive drama in the 1960s during Hafez al-Asad's rule. However, a central claim in my analysis is that the rise of Da'ish in 2013 constituted a turning point. While *Buq'at Daw'* did not air in 2013, it reappeared in 2014 with sketches that harmonized with the dominant regime narrative. During the 2014 to 2016 seasons, jihadists, followers of Da'ish, and refugees were mocked. Furthermore, sociopolitical critique gave way to comic relief within the show's storylines. I have devoted a chapter to tracking *Buq'at Daw'* from its inception in 2001, well before Da'ish, to its most recent season. The show's longevity highlights transitions in gender and marriage storylines prompted by the uprising, particularly once drama creators began to strive to differentiate Syrian culture from the culture of Da'ish.

Economic Disempowerment and Suppressed Masculinity

"Al-Liss wa-l-Fannan" (The Thief and the Artist) exemplifies the distinctive satire from the first season of *Buq'at Daw'* (2001).[34] An embattled masculinity due to economic malaise and sociopolitical oppression drives this bold sketch, which fits into what Edward Ziter has identified as the trope of the "defeated performer as symbol of the silenced citizen."[35] Here, a disheveled, unemployed actor (played by Bassam Kousa) finds himself at the knifepoint of a stealthy crook (Ayman Rida) while ambling home one night. The actor laughs when the thief orders him to hand over his possessions and offers him the only belongings he has: tranquillizers and a bag of nuts.

THIEF: How are you an actor with no money? If you were truly an actor, I would have seen you on a television *musalsalat*.

ACTOR: I don't act in *musalsalat*. I work in theater, but you wouldn't recognize the kind of theatrical work that I do.

THIEF: What do I have to do if I want to go into acting?

ACTOR: Stick with your profession. To be an actor you'll have to apply to the acting institute. *If* you are accepted, you'll have to complete four years of study. *If* you are lucky enough not to get kicked out, you'll need to find a director, which requires tireless courting and schmoozing. Then you'll need to find a production company that will give you a chance. Once they accept you, you'd better oppose their competing production company. When you have achieved all those steps, the two companies will make up, and you'll be on the black list and thrown on the streets. Then you'll become a theatrical performer like me.

Here the actor insinuates that he is forced to live by his wits on the streets in order to survive. The thief then claims that art requires sacrifice, to which the actor responds, "Yes, sacrifice of your opinion and dedicating your life to paying compliments. In the end, you surrender your hands to popping pills and sacrifice your body to a heart attack." He laments that his work conditions are wretched these days: "I used to survive for the whole month by stealing from one or two individuals. Now, I work day and night and barely survive. People have no money. May God bless them, so they may bless us!" When the thief insists that he needs to swipe something of value in order to preserve the honor of his profession, the actor sarcastically mutters, "Now I understand why I'm poor. People need to preserve the honor of their profession." The allusion that he is poor due to government officials engaging in theft "to preserve the honor of their profession" recalls 'Omar Hajjo's political innuendos in *Masrah al-Shawk*.

The actor agrees to perform for the thief free of charge. They pull together a small set, the actor puts on an abysmal show, and the thief begs him to stop. Before heading off, the actor shows the thief the five hundred Syrian pounds he just swiped from his pockets. He informs the thief that he, too, needed to defend the honor of his profession. As he hands back the five hundred pounds, they laugh at their bond. In this sketch comic mishaps reside on the surface but ultimately veil deeper concerns. Beneath the messages of economic disempowerment and silenced masculinity lies a biting political commentary on a system that promotes crime to overcome economic hardship instead of fostering individual growth. The sketch blames a government that intentionally fails its citizens in order to legitimize its own position. It is not in the government's interest for citizens to effect change; rather, it supports policies that lead its citizens to scour the dirt roads for bread.

Mukhabarat and Regime Manipulation of
the Private Life of a Marriage Couple

"Quwwat al-Tawari'" (Emergency Forces) is a crafty critique of *mukhabarat* encroachment into the private life of citizens.[36] The title is a play on words referring to the repressive *qanun al-tawari'* (emergency law) established by the Ba'th regime after the 1963 military coup. We begin with two thieves, Ra'if and Hamoudi, crouching on the rooftops. They peer into a courtyard and see a man hitting his wife. They conclude that their duties as "emergency force" and "humanistic service" justify interference and descend into the courtyard. As the wife, Umm Ramzi, threatens to file a complaint against her husband, Abu Ramzi, at the Human Rights Commission, he accuses her of trying to make an international scandal of his life and continues to hit her. The thieves convince the couple to sit down, and Ra'if tells Hamoudi to bring some water. Without questioning who these men are, Abu Ramzi points the stranger toward the kitchen and asks for tea or coffee instead. The couple explains that they were fighting because Abu Ramzi accused actor Samer Qareb of wearing a wig in a theatrical production. Umm Ramzi is irate that her husband suspects all actors of wearing wigs but will never admit when an actress has undergone plastic surgery. Another fight erupts, but the husband and wife eventually compose themselves. Just as they decide to make dinner for their guests, they realize that Hamoudi and Ra'if have disappeared, along with her jewelry, their watches, and one of Abu Ramzi's socks. The story is an adroit allusion to the omnipotence of the *mukhabarat*, who take advantage of human vulnerability by stealing from the people they claim to save. Rather than being skeptical about the motives of the meddling strangers, the couple are so accustomed to the humiliations of the arbitrary emergency law that they do not ask for the men's identities.

While Bashar al-Asad's reform movement had dissolved long before the third season of *Buq'at Daw'* (2003), many sketches continued in the tradition of political critique through the lens of embattled masculinity. "Zaharat al-Intihar" (A Wave of Suicides) opens with a suicidal man named Sa'id standing on top of a building.[37] The government official (Fares al-Heloo) voices his indifference toward the report with a thick 'Alawi accent, until one of his assistants tells him that foreign news channels are filming. The official arrives on the scene and Sa'id screams that he has neither hope nor work and wishes to kill himself. The officer dismisses his next complaint about not having a home, claiming that there is plenty of housing for citizens. The officer tells Sa'id that his marital problems must have triggered his stress, to which Sa'id replies that if he had been able to marry in the first place, he would not be committing suicide.

The officer climbs to the top of the building and promises Sa'id that he will provide housing for him and his brothers, but Sa'id—whose embattled masculinity reflects the challenges of a generation of men under an oppressive regime—refuses. As a final solution, drawing on the regime's divide-and-conquer strategy, the officer finds Sa'id's two brothers, and as they ascend to the top, threatens that they will both be in trouble if they do not stop their brother. The officer leaves them alone only after he has incited tension and the three brothers begin to fight. He allows the television cameras to film the brothers hitting Sa'id. Finally, in front of the cameras the officer offers the brothers housing on behalf of the government; once they are out of the spotlight, he escorts them to jail. Fares al-Heloo recalls that the clear use of the 'Alawi accent did not offend the government. He believes that, on the contrary, officials took sadistic pleasure in watching their oppression manifest in fictitious form on screen.[38]

Attempted Religious Critique

While sociopolitical critique became the norm in *Buq'at Daw'*, even after Bashar al-Asad's failed reform movement, criticizing religious fundamentalism remained taboo. Some drama insiders, however, contend that Majed Suleiman, at the time a high officer in the *mukhabarat*, approached producer Muhammad Hamsho and director Laith Hajjo before they started preparation for the third season (2003) to suggest that rather than focusing only on government oppression, they address the "other side": religious fanaticism.[39] Thus, during the third season—which Naji To'meh directed after Hajjo quit—several sketches mocked religion. In "Teeb al-Janneh" (Heaven's Fragrance), a religious sheikh named Abu 'Abdallah (played by Fares al-Heloo) enters a jewelry shop and tells the owner (played by Jihad 'Abdo) that he wants to sell a diamond necklace. Since the now-deceased Abu Habib originally sold him the necklace, the owner tells him to contact the man's children. Abu 'Abdallah hands a ring to the owner and tells him it needs to be fitted. Clients enter as the owner begins to work on fitting the ring, but they exit as soon as they see him talking to a "ghost."

When another client picks up her jewelry, the owner asks if she sees the sheikh sitting there. She says she does not and quickly leaves. The owner faints and wakes to discover that his store has been robbed. We then cut to a scene at a night club where Abu 'Abdallah, no longer in religious garb, sits with the young men and women who helped trick the owner—a not-so-subtle accusation that thieves use the guise of religion to deceive their victims.[40] At the time, sheikhs and religious viewers actively complained about actor Fares al-Heloo.[41] This was not the only sketch in the third season that attempted to mock the religiosity of the sheikhs. Sheikh Salta, however, forbade broadcasting a different sketch that starred Ayman Rida as a sheikh who uses religion as commerce, deceiving his adherents into giving him money.[42]

Mazin Taha's "al-Anissa Shakira" (Miss Shakira) was the first sketch to poke fun at the female religious group *qubaysiyyat*, focusing on how these women infiltrate affluent society and use spirituality for personal material gain.[43] Religious adherents were infuriated by this blasphemous portrayal of the *qubaysiyyat*, arguing that while the first two seasons were exemplary in their critique of corruption, the writers' sarcasm went too far in the third season.[44] Although the Gulf States forbade the sketch, it aired on Syrian television. The late Sheikh Muhammad Sa'id Ramadan al-Buti, a Syrian *muwali* religious leader, approached Muhammad Hamsho, owner of Suriya al-Dawliyyeh, and ordered him to interdict the mocking of religious adherents.[45] Likewise, the Syrian government compelled actress Amal 'Arafeh to apologize to the infuriated public for her role in "al-Anissa Shakira." Sketches from then on avoided direct religious critiques.[46]

Actor Jihad 'Abdo, who played the part of the conned jewelry owner in "Teeb al-Janneh," interprets the government's defense of religion as an indication that it does not want to confront religious authorities. A skeptical 'Abdo argues that the Ba'th Party, which claims religious legitimacy, wishes to appear as the protector of religious sentiment.[47] Based on the regime's divide-and-conquer policy, I speculate that the regime asked the writers to address religious topics as a strategy to pit intellectuals and religious figures against each other. The regime then stepped up as the one who could solve the disagreement. Indeed, the history of the *qubaysiyyat* movement in Syria illustrates the cynical attempt of the 'Alawi regime to achieve religious legitimacy while professing to be a secular state that protects intellectuals against the rising fear of Islamification (which the government itself creates).[48] Munira al-Qubaysi founded the *qubaysiyyat* in the 1960s at the pinnacle of Islamic activism in Syria, but its activism increased when Bashar al-Asad came to power in 2000.[49] During this time, with government consent, the *qubaysiyyat* penetrated the power apparatus and *mukhabarat*. Many skeptics believe Bashar's government is on close terms with al-Qubaysi, protecting adherents while giving permission and funds to control about 40 percent of the schools in Damascus. Syrian artist 'Itab Hreib notes, "It's part of the regime's game. They claim a secular identity in order to create a modernizing image for their Western counterparts, though all the while they fuel the growth of fundamentalism and backwardness in our society. By squashing dreams, they retain control."[50]

According to renowned director Haitham Haqqi, Bashar al-Asad's support of the *qubaysiyyat* movement merely followed his father's policy of the 1980s: a concerted attempt to use the *muwali* religious groups to counter the influence of the Muslim Brotherhood, which Hafiz al-Asad crushed in the early 1980s but of which he remained wary.[51] It is noteworthy that nouveau riche influential Sunni businessman Muhammad Hamsho, producer of *Buq'at Daw'* (who is rumored to launder the funds of Maher al-Asad, Bashar's despised younger brother), is part of the state-condoned Islamic movement. Indeed, Line Khatib, who describes how Hamsho, "crony of the Asad family," won a seat in the parliament during the 2007 legislative elections, argues that the regime co-opted such nonpolitical Islamic groups in order to pit Islamic and secular groups against each other.[52]

Corruption of Government Officials, Citizen Discontent, Pressures on Masculinity

Despite the prohibition on religious satire, both indirect and symbolic political critique continues. In "Fula," a sketch from the fourth season (2004), a dancer named Fula directs a cabaret attended by leading government figures.[53] When the county expands its road, cutting into about 50 percent of her cabaret, the desperate woman seeks help from each of the government officials with whom she has had an affair, only to be rebuffed. She reminds one government official, Nazem, of how he had promised that he would help her at the snap of her finger. When he insists he must have been drunk at the time, she replies he should get drunk again and keep his promise. Her assistant then recommends she take revenge against the dishonest officials by spreading the rumor that she has contracted AIDS. The sketch ends with a scene of panic-stricken government officials in a line at the Ministry of Health, wearing dark glasses to disguise their identities.

Buq'at Daw' was delayed for a couple years due to fighting among its production team,[54] but a sixth season appeared in 2008. It did not directly address the Hariri assassination or even the 2007 presidential referendum, but several sketches were nevertheless particularly harsh in their critique of political oppression and citizen discontent through the lens of an embattled masculinity. In "Ana al-Mosta'" (The Disgruntled One), Wahid (played by Bassem Yakhour) lies in a hospital bed awaiting test results.[55] The doctor nonchalantly tells him she has both bad and good news. The bad news is that he will die in a month. When Wahid asks what the good news is, she answers, "Well, since there is nothing we can do for you, you won't have to spend all your money on medical treatments." He returns home and tells himself that, like the rest of the population, he has been forced to keep his complaints bottled up inside him for thirty years (note the reference to thirty years). He decides to express his anger, since he has nothing to lose. He begins a letter to the government, "I'm the citizen Wahid Sarkhas, and I'm hopeless." After composing the letter, an exhausted Wahid asks Abu Rami, the owner of a small shop, if he can deliver it to the post office. Abu Rami kicks Wahid out, saying he does not have the right to implicate others just because he is dying. A sickly Wahid drags himself down the street and tosses his letter in the mailbox.

When he returns, his doctor calls to tell him the hospital made a mistake; she needs to see him as soon as possible. Assuming there is a problem with his bill, he returns to the hospital. His doctor informs him that another patient died the day before, causing them to realize the test results they gave Wahid actually belonged to that patient. She explains that minor malnutrition is Wahid's only health concern. Upon hearing this, he screams, "I have to die. You have to help get me out of this predicament. I want to die." He runs to the mailbox, but just as he arrives an employee takes the letters and drives to the post office. Wahid goes to the post office, hovering over the employees, but is so frightened he cannot figure out how to recover the letter. Later, a shot of Wahid hiding under his covers is juxtaposed with one where workers sift through envelopes. In another shot, while employees continue sorting letters, Wahid climbs a high rock perched over the city. As an employee stares at the address on his letter, Wahid throws himself from the rock, and the employee mutters that whoever wrote this letter is crazy, tossing the envelope in the wastepaper basket. Wahid crashes to the ground, dead.

Subverting the Regime's Narrative of Nationalism and Terrorism Conspiracies through the Lens of Disabled Masculinity

The fourth and fifth seasons of *Buq'at Daw'* appeared on schedule, but the drama was then delayed for a couple of years due to fighting among the artists involved in its production.[56] The sixth season did not appear until 2008. In this new season, which featured several sketches that aimed to subvert the regime's narrative of nationalism and terrorism conspiracies, director Samer al-Barqawi directly addressed neither the Hariri assassination nor the 2007 presidential referendum. 'Adnan Zira'i, an influential writer from Baba 'Amru, contributed important sketches to the sixth season. His "al-Jundi al-Majhul" (The Unknown Soldier) opens with the cross-eyed Abu al-'Izz (his disability instrumentalized to evoke suppressed masculinity) and his pregnant wife, Umm al-'Izz, dancing in their home as a long line of *mukhabarat* forms outside.[57] These *mukhabarat* contend that there are terrorists in the area and they need to get to a vantage point in this couple's house to overcome them. They barge in and shoot at "terrorists" (whom we never see) from the balcony. Despite the risks, Abu al-'Izz and his wife are proud that their house is being used for nationalist purposes. Abu al-'Izz slides a tray of tea to the men, innocently exclaiming, "Who are these terrorists? Why do they want to ruin our country?"

The lights go out and their house catches on fire as the shooting continues. Umm al-'Izz goes into labor and begs her husband to take her to the hospital. He refuses, telling her they have a nationalist duty to stay home and help. As gunshots pierce the night, a baby is born into the chaos. The next day reporters arrive at the sight of their destroyed house, praising Umm al-'Izz and Abu al-'Izz for standing by the *mukhabarat* to banish the terrorists. An audibly unhappy Umm al-'Izz, holding her infant, declares that they happily sacrificed themselves for their country. Abu al-'Izz, now deaf and blind (symbolic of his further-suppressed masculinity), declares, "Allahu Akbar" (God Is Great). The sketch acts as a criticism of citizens who buy into government propaganda (which acts as a sort of *tanfis*), as well as an indictment of a Syrian government that is willing to destroy its country and citizens while professing to rid itself of "terrorists." Here, screenwriter 'Adnan Zira'i foreshadows the massive government retaliation against protestors (referred to as "terrorists) during the 2011 uprising. It is noteworthy that while the censors originally approved Zira'i's sketches, authorities arrested and imprisoned him during the spring of 2011, when they held several of his earlier sketches responsible for inciting the population. He has not been heard from since.[58]

Buq'at Daw' Post-Uprising Political Critique

Shortly after the Syrian uprising began, director 'Amer Fahd expressed optimism for *Buq'at Daw' Part Eight.* He reported that he chose from over four hundred sketches by high caliber writers such as Mazin Taha, Muhammad al-Ja'foori, and Hazim Suleiman and would begin filming on March 20, 2011.[59] "I decided to address social dramas far removed from the concerns of the people during this turbulent time," said 'Amer Fahd. "As a result, fans heavily critiqued the season, which aired in August 2011, for not portraying the country's uprising."[60]

Still I found several sketches that succeeded in subverting regime propaganda and capturing the early ambiance of the uprising. "Abu Samu'il" (The Father of Samu'il), for example, focuses on a dictator incapable of separating himself from his position of power and empathizing with ordinary co-citizens. In this sketch, the government forces Abu Samu'il into retirement after forty years of working in a position of high authority.[61] As he languishes at home, his neighbors inform him that they have appointed him president of their building's management committee. Despite his wife's protests, Abu Samu'il—who reminds us of the disoriented official in Hazim Suleiman's "Khitab Mu'athir"—yearns to take on this nationalistic responsibility for his country. He delivers a speech to his neighbors, appropriating traditional official government discourse and promoting national unity against colonialism, shame, and conspiracies. He laments that colonialism has left its traces but insists the community will beat foreign collusions. The men exchange shocked glances and begin to clap out of habit. His speech concludes, "The people choose their destiny themselves and we are against colonialism," highly reminiscent of deeply rooted official Ba'th discourse, which intensified in Bashar al-Asad's speeches after the start of the 2011 uprising. As the sketch progresses, we see how Abu Samu'il carries his dictatorial disposition into his new appointment, continually belittling his neighbors' suggestions. In another scene, he forces everyone to pick up trash and yells at them to work faster while he chats on the phone. Abu Samu'il brings militaristic order and humiliates the buildings' occupants while a neighbor, Abu Sa'id, runs to the real estate office to sell his apartment. He is disheartened to hear that prices have plummeted since everyone else wants to leave the building too.

In "Mathaf al-Shame'" (Wax Museum), a tour guide takes a group of people around a wax museum.[62] We see a statue of the last honorable employee in the country, who died of grief, hunger, and disappointment. We see, too, a statue of a *mukhabarat* officer, and the guide says that the officer viewed everyone suspiciously. His motto was, "I doubt, therefore I am." The tour guide says that these days *mukhabarat* officers pull people from their homes and make them confess to things they may or may not have done or wanted to do.

Another sketch, "Hes Watani" (Nationalist Sentiment), captures the reactions of Syrians at the beginning of the uprising, when some—subdued by government propaganda—became ultrasensitive toward any critique of Syria, claiming that it played into Western conspiracies.[63] This short sketch, which cleverly demonstrates the regime's attempt at *tanfis* and uses deceptive nationalist discourse to brainwash the masses, begins with an elderly man, Abu 'Amer (played by renowned writer and actor 'Omar Hajjo), purchasing oranges. When the merchant says the imported oranges are riper than their Syrian counterparts, Abu 'Amer grows furious and a bell rings from his head, symbolizing his sensitivity to insults to his country. Later on a service bus, a man complains about the lack of real news in their local newspapers. The man asks, "What do we care about the rise in cost of living in New Zealand? We need to know about our own country." A bell rings again, and an irate Abu 'Amer insists a conspiracy exists against nationalist newspapers. The driver, irritated by the elderly man, orders him to leave his bus.

The sketch then cuts to a scene at a restaurant where two young men complain about constant power outages. They deplore parliament's ineptitude and the government's failure to find a solution. The bell rings again and Abu 'Amer screams that the men have no right to criticize parliament, a symbol of freedom and democracy. They start fighting and the scene quickly ends. The police later arrive to arrest the elderly man at his doorstep since another young man has filed a complaint for hitting him. His wife cries, but he yells that the law in his country is fair and that there is no reason to worry. When she continues to cry, he asks her for a divorce and leaves with the police. At the police station, the young man filing the complaint explains, "All I said was that we young people can't marry since the government does not take care of us." Abu 'Amer quickly responds, "See how negatively he speaks of our country!" The irritated officer, played by Ahmad al-Ahmad, asks Abu 'Amer, "And who asked *you* to defend the government?" The officer loosens his collar and then asks, "Really, is our salary enough?" When Abu 'Amer answers in the affirmative, the irate officer kicks him out.

While the eighth season was sporadically marked by oblique references to the political turmoil, director 'Amer Fahd argued, "As we prepared for the ninth season, we had a clearer sense of how Syrian citizens interpreted the uprising, so we decided to address the situation from the perspective of the street." Though he contacted many writers, most turned him down because of the bloodshed in Syria. Hazim Suleiman accepted the offer, though, and received the privilege of writing the majority of the sketches.[64] Some fans argued that the ninth season was the strongest since the first three seasons.[65] Indeed, *Buq'at Daw'*'s coverage of the atmosphere of a nation in the midst of political upheaval contrasted with the majority of the season's miniseries, which avoided the topic.[66]

Although Suleiman was living in Dubai at the time, he kept up with his country's news as a journalist and created sketches reflecting the reality on the ground in Syria.[67] Yet Suleiman states, "The sketches don't always deal with the revolution in a direct way, but rather focus on the effects of political events on the private lives of citizens."[68] According to Suleiman, if a writer does not depict the current unrest, fans denounce him as detached, but if he addresses the politics, he is accused of engaging in *tanfis*. Suleiman believes it was still too early for drama creators to address the uprising in a neutral way, and depicting the human side of suffering is most important. At the same time, he wonders whether drama can truly depict the death and destruction currently taking place in Syria.[69]

Season Nine (2012): Marriage Norms and Daily Life in the Midst of War

The ninth season of *Buq'at Daw'* was hailed for being one of the only miniseries to address the uprising and engage in outright political criticism in 2012. Some argued that after the first three seasons, the ninth season was the strongest in direct and symbolic political critique.[70] Indeed, *Buq'at Daw'*'s coverage of the atmosphere of a nation in the midst of a major political uprising contrasted with the majority of miniseries that season, whose characters never even referred to the uprising.[71] While the eighth season was marked by sporadic indirect references to the uprising, director 'Amer Fahd explained, "As we prepared for the ninth season, we had a clearer sense of how Syrian citizens interpreted the uprising, so we decided to address the situation from the perspective of the street." Though he contacted many writers, most expressed their inability to write because of the bloodshed. As one of the few who responded that he was willing to depict the uprising, Hazim Suleiman wrote the majority of the sketches.[72]

Although Suleiman was living in Dubai at the time, as a journalist he was keeping up with news from his country to create sketches that reflected the reality on the ground in Syria.[73] Yet Suleiman states, "The sketches don't always deal with the revolution in a direct way, but rather focus on the effects of political events on the private lives of citizens."[74] Suleiman claims that if a writer does not depict the current unrest these days, he is denounced as being detached, yet if he addresses politics, he is accused of engaging in *tanfis*. In his opinion, it is still too soon to be neutral about politics and is more important to depict the human side of suffering. At the same time, he wonders whether personal drama can fully capture the death and destruction occurring in Syria.[75] Despite its audacious perspective, some critics argue that the season is less exemplary of the artistic collaboration that defined the earlier seasons. 'Amer Sheikh, for example, contends that Suleiman's hegemonic vision could have been summarized in a couple of episodes.[76]

Consider a short sketch titled "Shayef al-Bahr Shoo B'id" (See How Far the Sea Is), named for a Fairuz song.[77] A happy family wants to take a trip to the beach despite the country's turmoil. They sing and clap their hands in the car. When they take a rest stop, soldiers inform them that they have approached a military area, so they race back to their car. Later, when they stop for a bathroom break, more soldiers force them to leave. Later still, they stop to smoke a hookah and have a picnic. But then they hear shooting and once again race back to their car. The husband exclaims, "I never knew the beach was so far away." Finally, the family reaches its final destination in the corner of the mountains overlooking the city. They don't have bathing suits, and the children's feet rest in buckets. It is the nearest they will get to the beach.

"Tijarat al-Qubur" (The Tombstone Business) speaks to the issue of war profiteering.[78] In this sketch, community members become agitated over purchasing their gravestones. Abu Homam (played by Ayman Rida), the comically incoherent proprietor of a grave business, struggles to keep up with demands for spacious graves in prominent areas of the graveyard. The sketch mocks Abu Homam's disability as he stumbles over his words and ineffectively tries to convince a customer to take a grave in a remote location as bombs explode overhead. The customer cuts discussions short and drafts their contract. The sketch then jumps to a scene where two men stand in front of a fruit stand. One tells the other about new deals to purchase a gravestone in installments, and the second replies that some graveyard projects allow customers to register for large plots where entire families can be buried. The next scene cuts to Abu Homam surrounded by people holding coffins and complaining about the corpses' odor. Just as Abu Homam insists that burial sites are scarce, bombs explode and they enthusiastically agree to a mass grave for the dead.

In "al-Ghaz" (Gas), Syrians race to purchase portable gas tanks, which have become a scarce commodity. Indeed, people throw confetti in the air when gas tanks arrive in the neighborhood.[79] A father tells his daughter that a top-notch groom, Ibn Abu Yusri, Baya' al-Ghaz (the son of the gas seller), wants to marry her. He admits that several years ago, before the conflict, he made a mistake by rejecting this suitor; in today's war-ridden society, gas providers have social standing. Her mother, excited at the prospect of her daughter marrying into fortune, adds that she will ask for one hundred gas tanks as her daughter's dowry. Later, a father approaches the gas seller to say that while his son earned a degree in engineering, he would prefer to sell gas.

Gas is the subject of another sketch, "Qard Shaqsi" (A Personal Loan).[80] A husband and wife, Ragheed ('Abd al-Mon 'em al-'Amayri) and Sana' (Dima Qandalaft), wish to purchase a car in installments. Before the bank offers Ragheed a loan, the tellers ask him whether he is involved in politics and whether he smokes or drinks to test his prospects for longevity and return the bank's investment. After he passes his interview, the bank dispatches employees to question his neighbors. One neighbor insists that Ragheed is apolitical, to which the employee responds that he merely wants to know whether Ragheed pays his bills and spends reasonably. Next, the bank asks Ragheed to return to the bank in order to sign some guarantees. When Ragheed grows impatient, the employee tells him, "Don't be irritable. Don't forget that you're in a government office." Ragheed allows the men to come to his house to register his belongings as a guarantee. They take everything, from the refrigerator to the dishwasher to their son's bike. However, when the men reach for the portable blue gas tank, Ragheed rips up the papers and kicks them out.

Constructions of Masculinity as Political Critique

The ninth season of *Buq'at Daw'* explores the growing pressures of masculinity and reveals hypocritical standards of female purity. "Ma li 'Alaqa" (It's None of My Business) opens with a man, Abu Ahmad, lying next to his wife in bed one night.[81] When they hear their neighbor Bedriyyeh screaming, Abu Ahmad says, "*Ma li 'alaqa*." Another man walking through the neighborhood hears the sound and echoes, "*Ma li 'alaqa*. Maybe she saw a rat." The next evening at a café, the neighborhood men pretend they heard nothing. When one man says, "People in the neighborhood are saying Bedriyyeh was screaming last night," others feign surprise. One says, "Poor lady, living all by herself." Another exclaims, "Shame on our mustaches" (meaning shame on our masculinity). They decide to check on her, and Bedriyyeh tells them a thief stole her television and refrigerator. The men promise to help next time, yet later, when Bedriyyeh screams for help, each man says "*Ma li 'alaqa*" once more. They visit her the following day and discover that the thief stole all her furniture. In a performance of masculinity, the men vow to come to her aid next time, using the husky, drawn-out voices of *qabadayat*. As she whispers what the thief warned her he would do next time, Abu Ahmad yells out, "On my mustache, whoever touches my *sharaf* (honor) will be in trouble." They supply a whistle to blow if the thief returns. But at a restaurant the next evening, the men play cards and ignore Bedriyyeh's loud whistles.

While "Ma li 'Alaqa" highlights the hypocrisy of men who use their mustaches as a symbol of their masculinity, "Farhan" (Happy) addresses a masculinity that the dictatorial nature of marriage and family life has crushed.[82] A man says, "My name is Farhan. I have no idea why my parents named me this. I don't know what it means to be happy. I only know that I've been alive for thirty-three years, and that I expect the next ten years to be the same." Here, we have another reference to thirty years, alluding to Hafiz al-Asad's rule, with ten additional ones under Bashar. He says he wakes up early, but his wife—the dictator—does not allow him to smoke, drink coffee, or listen to Fairuz in the house. He sneaks to listen to Fairuz in a café. "If you ask me if I like my wife, I could tell you that I have asked myself that same question for the past twenty years. She does not like Fairuz, cannot have children, and does not wear tight pants. I blame my father for not letting me make this decision on my own." He recalls his oppressive father telling him that he would find an appropriate girl for him. His boss says that weak men like Farhan make reform impossible, to which he responds, "You ask why I don't defend myself. Well, it's because I can't. I no longer have a voice. I've accustomed myself to being quiet. By name, I'm Farhan. But if you ask me if I'm really Farhan, I'll tell you that I really don't know. I've been like this all my life." Ultimately, he has become so accustomed to oppression that he facilitates his own misery. Told from a male perspective, the show falls into a trope in Syrian drama that uses the metaphor of marriage as a prison to engage in political criticism.

"Ab Dimuqrati" (A Democratic Father) also alludes to the dictatorial nature of Syrian politics by depicting hypocrisy within family and gender dynamics.[83] In this sketch, Umm Nabil informs her son and daughter that their father is returning home after leaving for several years. The children soon warm up to their long-absent father. When a man calls to speak to the daughter, Roula, she is at first worried, but her father says, "Sometimes it's okay for a guy and girl to have a relationship." When Nabil wants to go out, his mother says it is too late, but the father says, "I trust him. He's young. Let him go out." In another scene, the father catches Nabil hastily hiding his cigarettes. His father immediately says, "I'm not angry. I just want you to tell me the truth. I know a lot of kids who smoke. Smoking to fit in is one thing but smoking because you want to is another thing." Later, the father allows Roula to bring her boyfriend to the house. At this, Umm Nabil kicks him out, shouting, "Go back to where you were. You only came here to cause problems." She later lets him return and viewers learn that he is not the children's real father; she discovered him in the market and asked him to act as a father figure to her children. As she apologizes for being harsh to him, he receives a phone call from his wife, who says that a neighbor greeted his daughter. He panics, exclaiming that he does not know where to hide his face from the shame. When Umm Nabil says she is surprised that he had allowed Roula speak to a man, he replies, "She isn't my child. My children aren't allowed

to stay out late. I'd never let a man speak to *my* daughter." When Umm Nabil
tells him he is crazy, he responds, "Everything is up for discussion but a man's
sharaf." Here we see a satire of the hypocrite who tries to play the part of a democratic father but in the end is caught up in notions of honor and shame that
transform him into a dictator.

Direct and Biting Political Critique in *Season Nine*

Some have commented that the courageousness of political critique in *Buq'at
Daw'* shows the indulgence of the censorship committees, which willfully coop-
erated with drama creators.[84] According to Rania Jaban, the supervisor of the
ninth season of *Buq'at Daw'*, the increasing leniency of the censorship committee allowed the 2012 Ramadan season to reach new levels of political criticism,
though the committee sought to eliminate all obvious references to terms such
as *shabbiha*. She laments, however, that marketing problems limited *Buq'at Daw'*'s
broadcast to three channels: al-Manar, al-Jadid, and al-Dunya.[85] At the same
time, renowned screenwriter Samer Fahd Ridwan argues that some journalists
apply the words "courageous" or "bold" to a miniseries to praise the censorship
committee that permitted that work rather than as a compliment to the writer,
who cleverly disguised his critique.[86]

Consider the following sketch, "Anti wa la Ahad" (You and No One Else),
written by Hazim Suleiman in 2012: A sleek, chauffeur-driven car approaches a
tall building. Jaber, a dignified, love-struck man in a gray suit, descends and
peers longingly at his office. He opens his office door and swoons, as if to a lover,
"*Sabah al-Kheir, Sabah al-Ward, Sabah al-Ful, al-Yasmin*. Oh, if only you knew how
I struggled to reach a time like this when it is just you and me." As Jaber
approaches, the camera shows that he is talking not to a lover but to his chair,
which he caresses and embraces. Breathing heavily, he proclaims, "You're my
love, dearer to me than my children, my mother, my father. You are my life. My
God, you're beautiful. I'm prepared to sell my son, wife, sister, children for you.
Allah, what fine leather. I swear nothing in this world will separate me from you.
You and no one else."[87]

As he sits in the chair, a group of department heads surrounds the secretary, carrying flowers and saying that they wish to congratulate the new director.
When the secretary approaches him for permission, he insists they remain at a
distance, since he is "sensitive." Additionally, he demands that they stand in a
straight line so no one can hide himself behind any other. He tells himself, "They
need to be aware that I'm firmly established, and that if anyone thinks about
attaining my chair, it will be the last day of his life."

Jaber's suspicions increase when the men, especially Ahmad and Besher,
enter the room. Later, a nightmare that the two men are stealing his chair shakes
him awake in the middle of the night. He calls his secretary and demands that

she proceed to the office with a file of all department heads. The next morning he transfers Ahmad from Damascus to Qamishli. Still mistrustful, he sits on his chair as his secretary and employee push him through the hallway to sign paperwork. He then desperately searches for a way to get rid of Besher. His solution for Besher's demise becomes clear when we see him visiting a room full of mourners. Two thugs (*shabbiha*) in black glasses deliver the director's chair, which he clutches during the funeral. Though Jaber has eliminated his rivals, his doubts do not fade. He dines out accompanied by his chair, shops with his wife as thugs transport his chair alongside him, and sleeps handcuffed to his chair. The sketch ends with the director surrounding the chair with piles of large brown sacks. Toting a gun, he hugs and kisses his chair, vowing, "There is no power in the world that can separate us from each other. Remember what I told you thirty years ago, 'You and no one else.'"

In this short sketch, the swooning director in love with his seat of power clearly represents Bashar al-Asad. Discussions of this sketch and others in this season of *Buq'at Daw'* reveals the split that has been accentuated among intellectuals during the uprising. Some dismiss *Buq'at Daw'*, alleging that contributors are *muwali* (supporters of the regime). This accusation is often leveled against those who criticize the regime without facing punishment. Others argue that the government is too distracted this season to pay attention and the *mu'arid* (dissident) writers will pay the price later. Yet others contend that these sketches paint a democratic facade to outside viewers.[88] Previously, such a sketch would have been held up as an example of *tanfis*. Yet if *tanfis* was intended to vent frustration to keep the population from protesting the regime, then surely it loses its meaning in today's context, when the wall of fear has been broken, and resistance has become part of daily Syrian life.

Indeed, several sketches are direct rather than metaphorical in their critique of government paranoia and its patterns of manipulating information. In the press, journalists wrote that "Syrian Arab television" saw Hazim Suleiman's strongly critical sketch "al-Ghalazeh" (Irritation) as a conspiracy and forbade it from being broadcast. Yet the government propaganda channel al-Dunya, owned by Muhammad Hamsho (director of the company that produces *Buq'at Daw'*), allowed it to be broadcast in full.[89] According to television editor Iyad Shihab Ahmad, this decision is not as startling as it appears since these issues can often be quickly addressed with a phone call and bribe between officials.[90] Hazim Suleiman himself said that these decisions are often made by one employee and can be resolved internally.[91]

In "al-Ghalazeh," Hamdi, the central character (played by Bassem Yakhour), is a simple man who has read the entirety of the new Syrian constitution promulgated by Bashar al-Asad and carries a copy with him in order to defend his rights.[92] The sketch opens with Hamdi and his friends sitting at a café. Hamdi gripes about government corruption and the necessity of having connections to accomplish anything. A man at the next table eavesdrops and tells Hamdi to calm down. Hamdi, irritated at the interference of this *mukhabarat* officer, says, "I see *you people* have changed your style. You used to wear a suit, and now you are dressed in jeans." Hamdi then takes out the new constitution and recites the article stipulating that the citizen has the right to express himself. He then turns to his friends, "So we were talking about corruption, bribes, and spies." Later, when Hamdi walks on the streets, he catches the *mukhabarat* officer following him. He pulls out his pocket constitution, holds it up, and declares, "No one is allowed to spy on another citizen unless it is a question of a nationalist emergency or crime." But on another occasion, the *mukhabarat* officer brings a colleague to help him deal with Hamdi, who is on a walk. When Hamdi holds up the constitution and says that a citizen has the right to walk where he wants, the two men arrest him on the grounds of *ghalazeh*. Here we see how even when an individual obeys written law, he or she can still be indicted through sociocultural laws.

Indeed, censorship was director 'Amer Fahd's primary concern during the ninth season of *Buq'at Daw'*. He contends that while the Reading Censorship Committee rejected some sketches, the miniseries suffered more often from being refused by the Screening Censorship Committee after sketches had already been filmed. Fahd called for more consistency between the censorship committees during its next season, since filming a sketch requires significant financial and emotional resources. Complicating his request is the fact that even when both censorship committees accept a sketch, Syrian channels such as al-Manar may reject them or cut scenes. The sketches are only occasionally shown in full on stations such as al-Dunya.[93]

Transitions: Gender and Marriage amid War, Da'ish, and a Refugee Crisis (2014–2016)

During the first few years of the uprising, writers who contributed to *Buq'at Daw'* proffered their critiques despite heavy censorship. Even after the censorship committee prohibited the use of the term *shabbiha* in the ninth season of *Buq'at Daw'*, for example, writer Hazim Suleiman portrayed a murderous *shabbhba* in "A Moving Speech." Moreover, frequent and conspicuous references to "thirty" or "forty" years reflect the regimes of Hafiz al-Asad and his son.

Although viewership decreased following the uprising, many viewers in Damascus had tuned in to *Buq'at Daw'* during Ramadan 2011 and 2012. Iyad Shihab Ahmad, who was responsible for advertising *Buq'at Daw'* during the show's initial seasons, argues that Damascus was still fairly sheltered in 2011; even in 2012, when the government placed checkpoints throughout the capital, families maintained a semblance of normalcy and gathered to watch *musalsalat* during Ramadan. While the media focused mostly on news of the uprising, it did grant some coverage to the miniseries. Yet Ahmad also points out that many Syrians in areas outside the capital no longer had television sets or even homes. Watching *musalsalat* was the last thing on their minds as they struggled to survive. As a result, according to Ahmad, the traditional idea of *tanfis* no longer applied. Watchers who had not yet joined the protests would maintain silence, meaning that they did not need an outlet to express themselves.[94] Bassem Yakhour, one of the founding actors and writers of *Buq'at Daw'*, argues that "comedy is an important weapon since it is able to simply transfer ideas and feelings to the masses. Comedy is the genre closest to the people and the safest way to reflect the reality of the situation." While he is not certain that comedy will remain popular, given the upheaval, he thinks that perhaps it will play the role of *mutanaffas* (relief) as a means of escape or as a way to breathe a little.[95]

Buq'at Daw' prepared for its tenth season during Ramadan 2013, with the production company choosing one hundred from the hundreds of sketches it received.[96] However, *Buq'at Daw'* struggled to survive the increasing bloodshed in Syria. Key actors such as the husband and wife team Amal 'Arafeh and 'Abd al-Mon'em 'Amayri fled to Dubai, and many others on all sides of the political spectrum relocated. By the spring of 2013 it was clear that the production of *Buq'at Daw'* would be delayed, since writers had not completed their sketches and the majority of the show's stars had left Syria.[97] According to Iyad Shihab Ahmad, director 'Amer Fahd hoped to film the new season in Tartus. But the production company felt this shift would be too expensive and preferred Damascus. Thus the project fell through.[98] Indeed, filming in Damascus had become challenging: cameras could not move freely among the blockades, and suicide explosions occurred throughout the city. As a result, many directors searched for more stable cities such as Tartus and Sweida in which to film during the Ramadan 2013 season, or relocated to other countries such as Jordan or, frequently, Lebanon.[99] For instance, when the Syrian Censorship Committee banned the tragicomic miniseries *Hudud Shaqiqa* (Brotherly Borders) from the 2013 Ramadan season, writer Hazim Suleiman, who had written the less-successful comedy *Abu Janti Part Two* (2012), filmed the miniseries in Lebanon.[100]

As anticipated, *Buq'at Daw'* did not air in 2013. When it reappeared in 2014, production pressures resulted in obvious changes. Many sketches now adhered overwhelmingly to the dominant regime narrative. Indeed, *Buq'at Daw' Part Ten* (2014, directed by 'Amer Fahd), *Buq'at Daw' Part Eleven* (2015, directed by Seif al-Sheikh Najeeb), and *Buq'at Daw' Part Twelve* (2016, directed by Seif al-Sheikh Najeeb) shy away from gender and marriage metaphors that engage in political critique. By 2015 *Buq'at Daw'* was criticized for unflattering representations of Syrians as they reacted to the pressures of war.[101]

A few scattered sketches during the period from 2014 to 2016, however, did employ some elements of politically motivated criticism in the spirit of previous years. In "Ehkoo" (Speak!), for example, the Editor-in-Chief orders his employees to convince others to express themselves honestly to the press. When the work-ers say that no one will talk, the Editor-in-Chief tells them that if they can't do their job, they should go home and watch Turkish *musalsalat*. But no matter how hard they push for confessions of hardship and revelations about political cor-ruption, the people remain unwilling to talk.[102]

Also appearing during these seasons were traditional societal critiques as well as unattractive portraits of Syrians at war. "Hawa Baladi" (My Country's Air) shows the hypocrisy of expatriated Syrians. In this sketch a relocated man insists he misses and adores his homeland while charging a high rent for his home in Syria. As he sells weapons, he laments that he misses Syrian air.[103] In "Ahadith 'Abira" (Passing Talk) people engage in small talk about war. A young man and woman chat on a bench about kidnappings occurring in their country; a father teaches his young son to carry a gun.[104] In "F'el-Kheir" (Acts of Kindness) every-one is scared; no one trusts each other. An elderly woman carrying heavy bags calls for assistance. When a man offers his hand, however, she rejects his help. Another man refuses a friend's financial contributions to pay back his debts. A waiter rejects the tip a customer offers at his restaurant. Another man, sus-pecting a nearby bomb, calls the police. The police ask for his address and then proceed to arrest him. As they are taking him away, a bomb goes off. He says, "That is why I called you."[105]

In previous seasons of *Buq'at Daw* and more generally within Syrian drama, marriage and gender metaphors engage in indirect political critique. During this transitional period, these metaphors comment on the current turmoil rather than more systemic political critique. The sketch "Muyul" (Inclination) depicts a young man named Hossam and a woman whom he likes. While eating at a res-taurant, he asks why, after three years together, she still wants to know his political stance; he insists that he stands with his country. Yet, his girlfriend says, "What should I tell my father when he asks? My father only knows the *muwali* and *muaradh*. Not 'I'm with the country.'" Although she begs him to change his opinion to gain her father's acceptance, he refuses.[106]

Later, when they go to a jewelry shop, the owner wants to know their posi-tion before selling the ring. Hossam refuses, insisting that he is just buying jew-elry, so the owner refuses to sell to him and kicks them out of his store. Another jeweler also kicks them out. Likewise, a man on the street will not sell flowers to them until he knows their position. Meanwhile, the woman's father won't accept Hossam because of his *muyul*. She insists that his *muyul* is different from his father's *muyul*. Her father won't accept this, though, since he believes that it is important to know a person's *muyul*. The groom also argues with his own father about wanting to marry the woman regardless of her father's *muyul*. Hossam's father retorts that he divorced his wife due to a difference in her *muyul*. Never-theless, the young couple marries without permission. This act, called "khatifa" in Syrian culture, refers to a woman being carried off by a man against her family's wishes. Now both fathers, who curse each other, throw a wedding to prevent scandal. At the wedding, everyone is angry and the father of the bride is in tears. Indeed, the crowd of guests sitting behind the bride and groom cry as if at a funeral.

The main cause of hardship in sketches about life during war was no longer a dictator and an oppressive regime but jihadist groups—namely Da'ish, which emerges as a central character during the tenth through twelfth seasons. Da'ish is also the frequent subject of jokes, often related to gender norms. This pattern of othering extremist religious elements fits in with the regime narrative and occurs in several sketches from 2014. In "Mubadara" (Initiative), Hazim Suleiman portrays extreme Islamic groups in a highly derogatory way. Two men plan to dress up as Papa Noel to distribute gifts to children in war-torn Syria because, one man tells his friends, they want to help the children forget the war. Bombs explode in the background as they talk.[107]

One of the men worries about the border guards but is eventually convinced to proceed. The two men wear bright red outfits and don long white beards. They fill bags with toys and ring a bell as they walk. Soon, however, three jihadists stop them and say they would like to take the two men to see their amir, who does not speak Arabic. The amir tells them that the red costumes will attract women and start *fitna*, as bombs continue to explode in the background. After visiting that amir, they leave with hats that are darker red, not as bright, and with blue outfits. However, they run into yet another jihadist who wants to take them to see his amir. This *Mawlana* does not speak Arabic either and hands the two men guns. In the next scene we see them walking in brown and blue outfits with vests over their outfits and sporting brown and black beards. Their holiday fun has ended, as now they resemble jihadists and are stopped at a government checkpoint. The two men explain to the border guards that they had merely wanted to be Papa Noël and distribute gifts to the children. However, the government officials do not believe them. The sketch ends with the officials insisting on taking the two men to the police station to explain themselves.

In "Tariq al-Salameh" (Road of Safety), Hazim Suleiman depicts a young couple trying to pass different borders in order to leave Syria.[108] As they escape, the sound of bombs fills the background. The couple initially dresses casually: she wears jeans and a fitted sweater, and he wears a white shirt and blazer with jeans. At the first border, they spy a group of leftists in black bonnets questioning religious people about Che Guevara. The couple quickly puts on black bonnets and red scarves and addresses the border guards as comrades. They are tested on Karl Marx, pass, and move on to the next border. At another border they see a group of jihadists referring to a prisoner as a *kafer* (sinner). The couple removes their red scarves; he dresses as a sheikh and she wears black. The jihadists say that they look good. The man, impersonating a sheikh, yells at his wife to be quiet when she asks why they are torturing the other man. But the religious man tells him that it is fine, that he does not have to get so angry. The husband retorts, "No. First she will open her mouth. Then she will start reading books, singing, and watching dubbed Turkish *musalsalat*. I need to punish her with eighty-five lashes."

When the sheikh says that is too much, the husband starts yelling at him. He says that now his problem is with the sheikh. Stunned, the jihadists let them go, and they make it to another border. The couple observes that the rebels at this border are "gray," which means that they are neither left nor right and are not even sure of their own position. In fact, the rebels have installed themselves at this particular border only because it is located near good places to eat. They agree among themselves that once they see the couple's position, they will choose the opposite. The husband and wife approach. He is dressed in white long johns and her appearance keeps changing. She removes her veil and then replaces it, unsure of what to do, indicating the pressure on a woman's body to take on symbolic value. The couple tries to confuse the border guards to keep them guessing about their political stance. The husband claims that as a citizen he is a human being, but the border guard replies that not all citizens are human beings. The border guards ask what ethnicity he is and he says, "Basmali." No one knows what that is. In the end, they succeed in confusing the border guards enough that they are able to run off. This sketch foregrounds the issue of gender and the symbolic nature of woman's body, as the removal and replacement of her veil is intended to symbolize her respective freedom and degradation.

The jihadists continue to be the subject of jokes in other sketches. When "Ila wara' Dor" (Stop, Turn, and March in Opposite Direction) commences, family members are crawling around their home, fearful of bombs.[109] Someone knocks on the door and the father, Abu Sultan, crawls to the door. He finds his neighbor, Khaldun, outside, who says that they now have new rulers from the Shishan who fought in Afghanistan. An amir (tribal chief) who has come to rule the neighborhood does not speak Arabic. His language sounds like Persian; nobody understands. In a later scene Khaldun wears a turban on his head and proclaims that women cannot go outside in public. He orders Umm Sultan back to the house. Still later, we learn that Abu Sultan was whipped for smelling different perfumes. Now women are veiled in black and Khaldun has wrapped a large scarf around his head and neck. They now call their neighborhood an 'amara (a principality or emirate). In the final scene, Khaldun resembles a cave man with long black hair. He warns that dinosaurs have invaded the neighborhood. A large dinosaur foot enters the picture, and the scene ends. Ultimately, this episode serves as a metaphor for Syria's regression since the uprising and the increasing power of jihadist groups.

The twelfth season of *Buq'at Daw'* (2016), directed by Seif al-Sheikh Najeeb, continues to mock Syrians while focusing on Da'ish and regime rhetoric. By now, the series has radically shifted from its philosophy during its initial years. The sketch "Serrahoo Bate'" (He Has an Important Secret) commences with an explosion that many think is a terrorist attack.[110] A news reporter announces this as a possibility, though not a certainty. Meanwhile, jihadists, distressed that anyone doubts that they are responsible for the terrorist attack, search for gas tanks to continue their work, declaring *Allah Akbar*. They visit the caliph, repeating both *Allah Akbar* and their intention to procure gas tanks for another attack. Though they all speak Arabic with an accent, one jihadist shoots a man who cannot speak proper Arabic. Thus, this sketch pokes fun of the jihadists, who are caricatured as obsessively reiterating *Allah Akbar* and fixating on finding gas tanks to blow themselves and others up.

"Tagheesh Iman" (Distortion of Faith) also focuses on Da'ish characters. In the background as the episode opens, large black signs state *La Alla wa Allah*, with the Mawlana sitting and reading out loud in the foreground. He proceeds to discuss the caliphate with a variety of people in the presence of Da'ish supporters, one of whom has an Iraqi accent, all the while situated in front of the black signs. Then the Mawlana mentions a new, much-requested instrument for determining whether an individual is a sinner or believer. He requests that this instrument be widely distributed. Subsequently, we see that everyone has been arrested. The Mawlana is surprised to see that his new instrument has found that all the men are *kafer* and no one is left.[111]

In another sketch titled *Buq'at Daw'* (Spotlight), a poignant parody on the sketch comedy itself, a group of actors is preparing for a chaotic *Buq'at Daw'* sketch involving Da'ish characters and heavily veiled women. *La Allah ila Allah* is written in large letters on banners throughout the location. While the filming is intended to last a few hours, morning turns into evening. Actors argue and scenes are filmed over and over again as the director criticizes them for their exaggerated acting. Finally, they go to the next scene, where the Da'ish characters continue to take the lead. The director orders the driver of an idling car to pull back from the set. Soon after an explosion occurs on the set. The actors recognize that the explosion was not part of the plan, so it appears to have been real. They all ask for God's protection as they insist they must finish the scene to complete their work for the day.[112]

Adherence to the regime narratives can be seen especially with respect to representations of Syrian refugees from 2014 to 2016. Hazim Suleiman's "al-Ustadh Najeeb" (Mr. Najeeb) describes a camp called "Hope" run by Mr. Najeeb (literally meaning pure).[113] The opening scene shows students playing near dilapidated tents, with UN cars in the background; the next scene shows Najeeb teaching children. At the sound of a supply truck, the children sprint from the classroom to the truck. Najeeb is horrified by the resulting chaos, which he views as reinforcing stereotypes about the chaotic Middle East. He declares that a photograph of the moment posted on Facebook would convey a negative image of Syrians. He encourages his students to take respectful turns, which hearkens back to orderly, structured qualities that he associates with the West. But his actions effectively "other" the Syrians he is teaching. Later, two men approach Najeeb to say they want to help distribute supplies to the camp. Najeeb refuses at first, saying that he has enough supplies and people to help. When the two men say that he can sell extra products, he makes it clear he is not in it for profit. But the men are able to convince him, since Najeeb is easily corrupted. Later, film directors ask if they can film the misery of the camp as a way to garner sympathy and attract donations, and Najeeb, now crooked, accepts. This short sketch clearly takes a pro-regime stance as it shows the chaos of the camps, including the chaotic, haphazard educational offerings. It also focuses on corruption and accuses individuals offering to support refugees of being criminal. Such representations are dangerous, making it harder for donors to trust that their money is being used for its intended purpose and diminishing the power of Syrian refugees.

Refugees are also the focus of jokes in "al-Hijra" (Emigration), by Hazim Suleiman. The sketch begins with a couple feeding their daughter, Niriman.[114] They speak in exaggerated accents and possess strange mannerisms and clothing styles. As they discuss moving to Europe, their conversation is cut short by the sound of a bomb. Niriman faints. Another couple dance in a different room, celebrating their decision to leave for Europe. The lights go out as more bombs strike. Then, the men from each sketch meet to talk about their desire to relocate to Europe. They enter a real estate office owned by Abu Rabi' and declare their desire to go to a democratic country where they have freedom. When Abu Rabi' says that he just works in real estate, Abu Shawkat convinces Abu Rabi' to play along so they can make money. Since neither of the customers is wealthy, the two crooks tell them to gather more people—whoever has a car or home to sell. We then see a large group of Syrians gathered in front of a bus for Belgium, France, and Germany, and they are all driven away. The men who stole their money are unconcerned about where the bus is going, but it is clear that they are in danger. As the sketch ends, bombs explode in the background.

"Al-Hijra ila al-Watan" (Immigration to the Country) continues the theme of refugees.[115] A young man, Bassam, complains to a friend about the difficulty of life in Syria. He claims that going to "red hell" would be better than their situation in Syria and that he should live somewhere with governing law—like France, Austria, or Germany. After he travels to Germany, however, Bassam wonders about his assumptions about the existence of law there, given the degree of corruption he finds. The sketch intends to show that the Syrian refugees have managed to corrupt even the Germans. Bassam asks, "Are you sure we are in Germany or are we really in Sweda?" He notices that everything is paid with bribes and in the end wishes to return to Syria, where at least he is familiar with the corrupt system that surrounds him.

A sketch titled "al-Hijra ila al-Watan" occurred again the following season. In this storyline people stand in line in Germany, claiming to be Syrian.[116]

A corrupt German officer, Franz, who was also present in the eleventh season's "al-Hijra ila al-Watan," tries to distinguish Syrians from non-Syrians, realizing that many individuals are claiming to be Syrian in order to receive refugee status. The officer asks the refugees why they are in Germany now. One man says he has come since Germans are generous; one Chinese woman rocks back and forth and answers incoherently. While he accepts individuals who are clearly not Syrian, the officer immediately says that one young man in dark sunglasses and a black blazer is a liar, troublemaker, and imposter. The final examination line is filled with a similar assortment of individuals—among them, a man in a white turban as well as the same Chinese woman from before—claiming to be Syrian. The officer's assistant, 'Abdu, asks them final questions to prove they are Syrian. The last question is, "What could one buy in Syria for one thousand pounds before the 'azmeh?'" The young man with dark sunglasses starts crying, remembering all that he had bought before the war, and everyone else is startled and unable to answer. It appears, in the end, that the young man who has been refused is the only genuine Syrian.

Buq'at Daw' 2017: Gender, Marriage, and Escape from the "Crisis"

Buq'at Daw' Part Thirteen (2017), directed by Fadi Saleem, was produced the last year of the official contract with the production company.[117] This year's sketches departed from past years' by incorporating some sketches that mocked the current turmoil and others that ignored the current reality altogether. Critic Wissam Kan'an deplored the absence of a narrative thread through the majority of sketches, which appeared to have lost the spirit of sociopolitical critique that made *Buq'at Daw'* famous.[118] My own viewing found scattered sketches that continued to present love, gender, and marriage metaphors, some of which ignored the current war, while others engaged in indirect political criticism. I also located several sketches that engaged in subtle political critique of both the United States and Syria without relying on marriage metaphors.

I commence with several of the sketches that include love and marriage storylines that ignore the uprising altogether. In "Jiran al-Ridha" (Neighbors of Delight), one young man tells another that his neighbor has complained that he cleans his clothes on the balcony.[119] That same young man accuses a female neighbor of playing her television too loudly. Annoyed at each other's complaints, they fight. She pours water on him as he walks up the stairs with his groceries and refers to him as "Judy" to indicate that he is not a "true man." Her reactions to him reveal her perception of normative masculinity and her prejudice and hostility to other versions of masculinity as represented by this man. Nevertheless, in the final scene we see that the man and woman have resolved their issues, and they talk about how much they love each other.

In "Zawjat al-Strategiyyeh" (Wife of Strategy) a mother advises her daughter, Su'ad, to nag her husband all the time when she wants something.[120] It seems he has secretly taken another wife; Su'ad assures her mother that she will make him pay. But much to her mother's dismay, when Su'ad's husband arrives, she is nice to him, cutting up apples and bananas for him while he sits in front of the television. Later the husband dies, and Su'ad's brother-in-law informs her that her husband had another wife. She says she knew but pretended she did not. This way, her husband always felt guilty and wanted to make things up to her. Indeed, because his second marriage was hidden, he did not divide his belongings between the two wives. Likewise, when her brother-in-law says that he wanted to bury half his money with him, Su'ad responds that she already buried a check for half his money with him. The mother is surprised at her daughter's intelligence and survival skills.

In "Wajba Khafifa" (A Light Meal) a mother is upset that her daughter has married a poor man named Sobhi.[121] When Sobhi's mother-in-law asks him when he will find work, he responds, "Inshallah, in the next two days," a Syrian expression that means "perhaps never." Sobhi then takes his wife to a restaurant; she is veiled and Sobhi is wearing outdated clothes, so everyone questions what they are doing there. His wife wonders if he borrowed the money for dinner, and he retorts that she should stop nagging like her mother and enjoy the evening. Everyone stares as they order many dishes. One couple says that perhaps they are the type of people who hide their wealth. Sobhi burps after dinner, orders desert, and whistles for doggy bags. When the bill comes, Sobhi asks what a bill is and then complains that it is too expensive. He asks what happens if someone does not have money to pay. We quickly move to the next shot, which shows police escorting Sobhi out of the restaurant as he tells his wife not to worry, that he will be in prison for only a few days and then will return home. Meanwhile, an engaged waiter and waitress feel inspired by Sobhi and begin to plan their honeymoon, regardless of their financial constraints.

"Al-Rajul al-Mithali" (An Exemplary Man) reminds us of the hypocritical father we saw in "Ab Dimuqrati" in the ninth season of *Buq'at Daw'*. As the sketch begins, Abu Fathi tells his friend Qaysar that he imprisoned his daughter in the home after he heard that she was in love with a young engineer from a good family.[122] Qaysar expresses shock, proclaiming that love is beautiful and wondering why, when love is celebrated everywhere else, it is not allowed in Arab culture. Qaysar tells Abu Fathi that imprisoning his daughter is wrong and that he should meet the young man. On another occasion, Qaysar is playing cards with his friends when one of them admits he hit his son for smoking. Qaysar claims that his friend should have talked to his son instead of hitting him.

Then we turn to a scene in Qaysar's home. As Qaysar comes home, his wife and daughter are scared; his son gets rid of his cigarette by throwing it off the balcony. Qaysar is furious since his wife has not cooked anything. When she tells him she has gotten a job, he says she cannot work, since she can barely manage the house. Then his daughter approaches to tell him that a young man wants to ask for her hand in marriage. Qaysar is angry because his daughter already knows the young man, and he assumes she has been sneaking around behind his back. Then he belts his son, who is still out on the balcony. When a neighbor stops in to inquire about the commotion, Qaysar says that he was helping his kids resolve a problem with PlayStation. The neighbor leaves, commenting that Qaysar is an example for all. Here, Qaysar's hypocrisy is evident; indeed, hypocrisy is a recurring theme in the 2017 Syrian miniseries.

Some of the marriage metaphors of the season also engage in indirect political critique. In "Da'it wa Laqaynaha" (Lost and Found), a man looks forward to his wedding night, exclaiming that he has waited forty years for this night.[123] As he enters the room, viewers hear the sound of a horse neighing. But the man is not able to perform, and it appears that he is impotent. His wife assures him that he is not the only man to experience performance anxiety on his wedding night, but he orders her to bring him *zanjeel* and honey. When that does not work, the frustrated man demands cinnamon, then caviar. After repeated, unsuccessful attempts, the couple moves to the living room to talk. The man declares that he has yearned to be with a woman for forty years and regrets that he is unable to perform, then questions why he has accomplished close to nothing in all those years. In order to calm his anxiety, his wife helps him calculate that he has not lost time but has worked, taken public transportation, and tended to government bureaucracy as well as numerous other responsibilities. Once he realizes that he has indeed worked hard during the past forty years, he feels less anxiety and is ready to try again. Once more, horses neigh in the background as he sets out for the bedroom. This episode describes the pressures that affect masculinity and sexuality, while the time span of forty years designates the period of the Asad rule. The sketch is a poignant example of political critique that remains alive in Syrian drama, even in *Buq'at Daw'*, which lost much of its critical edge in recent years.

In "Bi-l-Geenat" (In the Genes), As'ad grows annoyed with his wife Laila's constant singing.[124] Even their daughter, Fairuz, always sings. When As'ad criticizes Fairuz, she insists that her singing is not in her hands—for nine months when her mother was pregnant, her parents were always singing. As'ad, however, is frustrated. Having been fired from his job, he cannot find work to support his family. Laila's father advises her not to bother her husband. She then asks her father how he is doing. He laments that he is alone, feels sick, and has many expenses. He gives her a list of his complaints, but then they begin to dance together. Later, when their neighbor, Umm Tariq, dies, As'ad begs Laila not to sing at the funeral gathering. When, despite his request, she begins to sing, he makes her leave. At home, he tapes her mouth shut. Subsequently, a scene shows Fairuz singing as Laila starts to dance.

The taped mouth is a recurring trope in Syrian culture and symbolizes the burden of freedom on citizens accustomed to dictatorship. In *Dissident Syria: Making Oppositional Arts Official*, miriam cooke analyzes Muhammad al-Maghut's *I Shall Betray My Homeland*, in which al-Maghut laments that freedom, so difficult to grasp, can be negotiated only with mouths taped shut. Cooke continues on to describe the image of mouth taping found in Hassan 'Abbas and Ahmad Maala's *Citizen Guide*.[125] In "Bi-l-Geenat," just as Laila joins her daughter in dancing, a devastated As'ad starts to clap and throws himself from the window. The newspaper report of his death announces that a man threw himself out of a window for unknown reasons, like many other men in that neighborhood. In this way the sketch provides a subtle reference to the pressures that unemployment and a dearth of opportunity exert on masculinity. Yet the critique is camouflaged by the episode's focus on Laila's singing, which is responsible for the couple's marital problems.

In "Na'am—La" (Yes, No), a husband says "la" (no) to everything, even when he means "yes." He even says "no" when asked if he loves his wife and children. His family, wanting to cure him, asks if he loves the government. He responds, "nnnnnnnnnnn," and then says "yes" and is seemingly cured. He repeats, "My name is Salim. I love the government. I love my wife. I love my mother-in-law." Now he says "yes" to everything. His wife questions what he would say if asked if he would divorce his wife. He says "yes," he would divorce her. His wife grows upset and threatens to leave him.[126]

In addition to sketches featuring escapist marriage metaphors and sketches that engaged in indirect, subtle political critique, there were also sketches in the thirteenth season that referred to the current war. In "Titanic 2," Mo'taz has a long-distance conversation with Rose, a woman with whom he was involved six years ago, before she left Syria for London.[127] He tells her in broken English, "No food. I'm hungry, no electricity." His friend hits a pan to make the sound of a bomb as Mo'taz tells Rose how scared he is. He then texts Rose a picture his friend takes of him with fire in the background. He tells her that he regrets that he did not leave with her six years ago, imploring her for help: "No water. No heat. No electricity, no gas, I miss you." When she asks him to marry her, he agrees to meet her in Beirut. The friend makes the sound of another bomb as Mo'taz repeats over and over again how much he loves her.

When Mo'taz tells his family that his beautiful Rose is coming to Sham (Damascus) and that he will marry her, his father throws fruits and vegetables on him. His sister asks him if she is beautiful like the Western women on television, but his mother says, "She's a foreigner. Why not marry a girl of Sham, a girl from your own neighborhood?" Despite the exorbitant cost, Mo'taz's sister convinces her furious mother to accept this marriage. Mo'taz cries and promises his family as well as neighbors that Rose will help them all leave Syria. The whole family travels to Beirut for the wedding day. They clap for Mo'taz until he takes off his new bride's veil so he can introduce her to his family and friends. At the sight of this elderly Western woman, both his parents faint. His mother lies on her bed, lamenting that "I would have preferred being bombed to living here in humiliation without any electricity . . . with bombs on top of my head."

After the wedding night, Rose asks for Nescafé and he feeds her bread with yogurt in bed. He asks her about traveling, and she answers with her mouth full. His mother and father continually ask him when they will leave, but Mo'taz tells his parents that they all need to be patient, and they throw tomatoes on him in frustration. Later, on the rooftop overlooking Sham, like the scene in the movie *Titanic* and with the *Titanic* music score in the background, Mo'taz and Rose wave in the wind. He asks her when they will leave for London, but she does not answer. Two months pass. Every time he mentions traveling, she changes subject. By this time the entire neighborhood is counting on Mo'taz and Rose to help them relocate. Meanwhile, as the family sits at the table and eats, Rose exclaims that she would like to eat kibbeh every day, and she also wants to smoke a hookah. Her wig falls off and Mo'taz's parents are dismayed. Rose continues to eat as they start to take food off the table.

One evening he suggests that they talk about their plans to travel, and she replies that she prefers to remain in Sham. She says that it is beautiful in Sham and the food is delicious. When he reminds her of the war, she insists that one day the war will end. He says that there is no electricity, but she retorts that they have each other in the darkness. He asks her about her money, and she responds that she gave all her money to charity. Then she says that she feels nauseous and may be pregnant. Upset, he goes outside and calls for security officers, saying he found a foreigner eating trash, brought her into his home, found incriminating equipment, and now realizes that she is a spy. He then gives the police his address so that they will come for Rose.

The three-part sketch "T . . . Rambo," written by Diana Fares and directed by Saloom Haddad, ridicules the artificial masculinity of Donald Trump and critiques his disrespectful behavior toward women.[128] According to Iyad Shihab Ahmad, the writer and director dedicated several sketches to mocking Trump as a way to please Bashar al-Asad, especially after Trump expressed harsh words for Asad.[129] The first sketch begins with people in the streets carrying American flags and pictures of Trump and cheering for "T . . . Rambo." Trump (played by Saloom Haddad) emerges from his car surrounded by women and tailed silently by Melania, to whom Trump is routinely disrespectful. In a later scene, enthusiastic crowds also applaud Hillary Clinton (played by Wafa' Moussalli) as she steps from a car wearing a bright red pantsuit. In the second sketch, Trump appears buffoonish onstage amid projected images of him bullfighting, his red matador's cape assuming the shape of a penis (symbolizing his false manliness) as the audience chants for T . . . Rambo. This second sketch focuses on Trump's disdain for women, shown through his bullying of Hillary during their debate.

Yet Hillary is not depicted in complimentary ways either. She appears hypocritical and evasive as she avoids answering debate questions, and Trump's accusation that she created Da'ish seems to reflect the perspective of the screenwriter.
In the third and final installment, Trump's disrespect toward women is high-
lighted through his behavior toward Melania. In a live interview he speaks for
her even when she is asked direct questions and focuses his attention on her
body and sexuality rather than her intelligence. At the end of this third and final
sketch, we see Barack Obama and Trump walking on a red carpet and entering
a limousine, along with former president George W. Bush and his first lady Bar-
bara. Next there are images of the Washington Mall with American flags wav-
ing in the air, as Trump is sworn in. The scene shifts quickly to Trump in a
swimming pool dressed in a bathing suit and sporting a red tie. He drinks
cocktails and laughs with the women who surround him. Then cannons shoot
into the air and bombs fall in Syria. Trump continues to laugh in the swimming
pool. Smokes and bombs continue to shower Syria, which is shown going up in
flames. And then the words: "The end." This three-part story propagates the idea
that America is responsible for instability and danger in the world. In the eyes
of the Syrians, it does not matter if the president is Trump or Clinton. This
criticism of the United States, rather than the Syrian president, is telling, as it
points to the new direction taken by *Buq'at Daw'*.

The thirteenth season contains direct criticism of the Syrian regime in addition to neutral marriage metaphors and criticism of U.S. politics. In "Umm
Mas'ud al-Ruzz" Part Two, a corrupt officer is hard on people. He then imagines
a graveyard where he lies dead. Umm Mas'ud (also played by Ayman Reda for
comic relief) scolds him and forces him to admit that he has hurt others. For
example, he has cheated people of *mazzote*. In the end, it turns out that this
sequence was a nightmare. Yet when he wakes up, he hears Umm Mas'ud's voice
telling him that if he makes mistakes, she will be watching and will punish him.
She then tells all the oppressed people to sleep well since she promises to watch
over them.[130]

In "al-Khat Ahmar" (Red Lines) by Diana Fares, employees at a meeting ask
the director about the "khat ahmar" (red lines) that they must avoid.[131] The director says that "khat ahmar" is like a jinn: it appears and disappears when you
least expect it. In another meeting a young woman asks another director what
is considered "khat ahmar," and he says it is something that is not uttered or
written. When she requests medicine, she learns that this is also considered a
"khat ahmar." A different director says everything is "khat ahmar" and that this
definition comes as an "order from above." When an employee expresses the
group's desire to identify the needs of the people, the director says this, too, is
"khat ahmar." Yet another director tells a group that all is "khat ahmar." Each
director ultimately gives nonsensical explanations for "khat ahmar." Then we
enter a private home and see a couple fighting. The wife says that she wants to

take the children out, but her husband says that this is "khat ahmar." She wants to visit her sister, but he says that this is also "khat ahmar." Another girl works on her laptop, and her brother says this is "khat ahmar." She says she is talking to her friends and they are "khat ahmar." Then a young man goes jogging and a large red line appears before him. Thus, this sketch attests to the difficulty Syrians have freely expressing themselves in a society where everything is "khat ahmar." Diana Fares's previous Trump sketches had served to distract the government from this kind of potentially dangerous criticism.

THE MULTIYEAR SYRIAN SKETCH SERIES *Buq'at Daw* commenced in 2001 as a sociopolitical satire that took gender and marriage metaphors to new heights of political critique. Indeed, even the direct political critique was so astute that many academic debates on *tanfis* centered on this particular sketch series. Through the years gender and marriage metaphors focused on suppressed masculinity as a result of political oppression, and this chapter has shown *Buq'at Daw'* engaging in political critique of issues related to masculinity from 2001 through its subsequent seasons. There were notable transitions during the uprising. While the 2011 season, for the most part, avoided any mention of the uprising and of contemporary politics, the 2012 season introduced incisive sociopolitical critique within the context of the uprising. This chapter has also manifested that the ninth season (2012), filled with oppositional sketches, included storylines such as "Ab Dimuqrati" and "Farhan" to indirectly critique dictatorship and its negative effects on men. Indeed, several sketches in 2012 critiqued government paranoia and manipulation of information directly rather than relying on traditional gender, love, and marriage metaphors.

While the sketch comedy came to a halt in 2013, it resumed during the 2014 season. From this time onward, gender and marriage metaphors continued amid themes that centered on war, Da'ish, and the refugee crisis rather than political critique. This period also witnessed a slow transition in critiques of masculinity. This chapter has also shown examples of the social for the sake of the social strand as well as the nostalgic strand, which grew stronger during this transition period. Despite the frequency of these less-political strands, the 2017 season also contains marriage metaphors and gender metaphors that engaged in indirect political critique, as well as several sketches that took on politics directly.

All of this attests to the fact that political criticism is still very much present in Syria's cultural spirit, despite the heavy hand of censorship. *Buq'at Daw'*, whose self-reflexive nature has been noted, consistently serves as the foremost example of the connection of Syrian drama to events on the streets. It also uniquely demonstrates the debates and ideas circulating among drama creators carefully marking transition periods. Indeed, while *Buq'at Daw'* did not appear during the 2018 season, its fourteenth season, directed by Seif al-Sheikh Najeeb, appeared with new innovations in 2019. Rather than referring to the uprising directly, the season highlights insecurities and troubles that accompany moments of "crisis." Take, for example, the sketch "Mudira al-Sa'da" (Director of Happiness) by Mazin Taha, in which a committee discusses what it needs to do in order to make people happy; when one member of the committee advises the committee chair to raise salaries, he retorts, "Money does not bring happiness." One young man arrives smiling and announces that the more unhappy he is the greater his smile, while another man enters the scene with a forced smile that turns to intense crying.[132]

Or consider the sketch "al-Jumhur" (The Masses) by Adham Marshad, which foregrounds gender issues, namely masculinity, by depicting two 40-year-old men lamenting that they will never marry since they will never have the economic means. At one point the men stand in front of a restaurant and watch others consume sumptuous meals as they describe what they would love to eat.[133] Another sketch, "Khali Shawarab 'Ala Janab" (Let's Put Mustaches Aside), written by a screenwriting workshop, also focuses on masculinity. The sketch portrays three men with oversized mustaches and deep, masculine voices who are trying to flee Syria and are concerned about leaving with dignity. When a stereotypically feminine man with a soft voice hands out fake passports to the three men, who have shaved their mustaches, the men display depression and internal conflicts involving new, mustache-less identities. Clearly, these men view mustaches as symbols of masculinity and dignity.[134] And so these sketches, ranging from ten to twenty minutes rather than the typical forty minutes, reveal war-torn Syria at a moment of deep economic crisis; some refer directly to the war, while others exhibit war's effects on individuals. Additionally, an innovation this season involves the introduction of certain sketches written by a workshop of unnamed authors, attesting to the cooperative nature of the sketch comedy.

3

The Rise and Fall of the *Qabaday* (Tough Man)

(De)constructing Fatherhood as Political Protest

Samia, a university professor, implores her son Rashad to stay away from Hisham, an opposition activist. Soon after, Rashad slams Hisham's door on her when she insists that a movement that disrespects women and is stained with blood will never bring about freedom. At home later that day, Samia blames her husband, Safwan, for his disengagement from family life, saying, "You were always chasing after money, cars, and business deals. You neglected your relationship with your son, and that's why he's now involved with Hisham. You can't convince him to come home since you don't have a normal father-son relationship with him." When Safwan claims that he just wanted to give his family a respectable life, Samira retorts that his drinking escapades and love affairs brought dishonor to the family.

Broadcast in Ramadan 2013, Hala Diab's "al-Samt" (Silence), a three-episode story in the miniseries *Taht Sama' al-Watan* (Under the Nation's Sky), directed by Najdat Anzour, concentrates on the father figure's absence, which Diab holds responsible for the disintegration of families during the uprising. Diab's story aligns with Nancy Chodorow's theory that the sexual division of labor in child rearing—with women solely in charge of maternal care—encourages men toward hypermasculinity.[1] Not only does Safwan's paternal disengagement trigger aggression in his son, but one daughter, Ruba, starved for paternal affection, enters an 'Urfi marriage with a wealthy man in Dubai, and another daughter, Razan, pursues a classmate in order to obtain a Canadian visa. Diab attempts to find neutral ground by blaming both sides of the uprising, and "al-Samt" portrays those like Samia who choose silence.

Cultural producers have accused Anzour of propagating a pro-regime narrative. Thus it is not surprising that "al-Samt" blames ordinary citizens and flawed social foundations rather than the oppressive political structure for the current Syrian tragedy. In addition to depicting the opposition as thirsty for revenge, aggressive toward Christians, and disrespectful of women, it blames a distant paternal figure for the damaged interpersonal relations that weaken society from the ground up. Even the presence of a strong mother figure in the family cannot compensate for the absence of the emotionally connected father. Scholars have shown that one cannot take for granted that the patriarchal nature of the discourse on new fatherhood has changed gender roles when a new father image is presented. Indeed, some privilege an analysis of fatherhood from a feminist perspective over one that assumes the positive impact of increased paternal involvement. Furthermore, they say, when analyzing paternal participation, one must consider whether male domination continues in the work place as well as in the home.[2]

Yet there is evidence in "al-Samt"—including Samia's strong presence in the home and workplace and her intellectual vigor—that Diab's image of fatherhood is not predicated on the image of the domineering man in the home and workplace. Instead, she deconstructs the figure of the *qabaday* and shows that an affective father—responsible for more than just finances—inspires love relations, thereby creating a stable foundation for both family and society. While before the uprising gender and marriage metaphors were a way to critique dictatorship, some post-uprising miniseries in line with the regime narrative, such as "al-Samt," now focus on societal ills to evade politics and place responsibility for hardship on the people rather than the Ba'th Party regime.

Theoretical Foundations of Masculinity and Fatherhood

The term *qabaday* is believed to originate from the Arabic verb "to grasp or hold" (*qabada*); the same term is found in Turkish (*kabadayi*), meaning "bully, tough."[3] According to avant-garde screenwriter Najeeb Nseir, who now lives in Beirut, there used to be a Robin Hood or knightly element to the *qabaday* representations in Syrian culture. The element of aggression, however, dominates in Syrian miniseries, and the term has also been used to designate criminals and troublemakers.[4] Renowned Syrian director and producer Haitham Haqqi—who currently resides in Paris and writes articles on behalf of the uprising—echoes that the word *qabaday* originally had dichotomous meanings suggesting either the honorable or violent man but that the aggressive denotation won out.[5] 'Alawi Screenwriter Fu'ad Humayra, whom the regime incarcerated during the summer of 2013 and has lived between Syria, Jordan, Lebanon, and Paris since the uprising, laments this consolidation of meaning, which he associates with the rule of Bashar al-Asad since 2000.[6] Noted actor Fares al-Heloo—who escaped to Paris after participating in the anti-regime protests staged by intellectuals on July 15, 2011, at the Hassan Mosque in Midan—contends that the fantasy of *qabadayat* fighting colonial powers in the Old Damascus tales reached an all-time high in popularity during Bashar al-Asad's presidency. According to al-Heloo, Ba'th Party politics during Bashar al-Asad's rule encouraged images of glorious men fighting

French colonialism as a tactic to divert attention from their oppression at the hands of the regime.[7]

The importance of *qabadayat*, or masculine tough guys, in Syrian television drama cannot be overstated. On September 19, 2009, actress Lora Abu-As'ad appeared on *al-Jazeera Mubashar* to answer questions about Syrian drama. One man expressed disappointment that Syrian drama is nothing but the story of *qabadayat*, which, he believed, is a far cry from the current reality, where Syrian men cower in the face of injustice. Art, he stated, is supposed to reflect reality and provide solutions to the troubles of the time. In response, Abu-As'ad cited various miniseries that did expose societal problems and offer solutions. I argue further that those stories, which depicted vainglory *qabaday* fighting colonial powers, were in fact not devoid of a political message. The strength of the *qabadayat* was intended to contrast with the current reality of an impoverished, politically oppressed manhood.

The *qabadayat* in Syria have counterparts with varying cultural meanings in other national contexts. Luigi Achilli's study of the performance of Palestinian manhood in al-Wihdat camp in Jordan demonstrates how the term *dawawin* designates a thug in the negative sense but also connotes more positive, nationalist attributes of a man who evinces anger toward the state. While prior to the 1970s the *dawawin* was the ideal form of resistance masculinity, it later signified dangerous, immoral men, and the pious *shuyukh* took over as a positive form of resistant masculinity. Similar to the *qabadayat*, who in the Syrian context of *Bi'a Shamiyyeh* tales valiantly fought off the French powers yet remained committed to providing for their families, the Palestinian refugees Achilli described in recent years have navigated between the hegemonic masculine ideal of resistance nationalism and the docile, patient pattern of behavior—traditionally attributed to the feminine realm—that allows support for families and integration into Jordanian society. I argue, however, that these are not unrelated realms, since the position of male financial provider and protector of woman (and their bodies) enhances patriarchy and fits neatly with the strong *qabadayat* role in the Syrian context.[8]

In her works on Egyptian film, Viola Shafik poignantly describes how the term *futuwwa* connoted chivalrous qualities before going on to designate "thug, bully, or racketeer" in colloquial Egyptian. According to Shafik, the term *futuwwa* later gained the positive, high moral standing associated with *ibn al-balad* (often defined as "authentic Egyptian"). This was useful since it suited the low budget of Egyptian film in contrast to the thug genre in Western traditions. Thus unlike Syrian *qabadayat*, which had a wholly political connotation of men with muscles and drawn-out voices fighting the oppressive state, the *futuwwa* character, with high moral standing rather than strong bodily confidence, allowed renegotiation of masculinity according to the technological capacities of Egyptian film.[9]

Walter Armbrust, however, addresses the issue of the tough guy in his research on Egyptian actor Farid Shauqi from a slightly different vantage point.

Armbrust shows how Shauqi's media image of a hardy masculinity closely cor-
responded with the stereotypical Middle Eastern honor-shame complex that
underscored the man's sexual protectiveness of his womenfolk. At the same
time, the egalitarian nature of his marriage to Hoda Sultan allowed the media
to portray the opposite of the tough guy image. Thus, he could present himself
as a tough guy as well as an egalitarian husband, negotiating these terms in both
his personal and professional life.[10] Constructions of masculinity—the rise and
fall of the *qabaday*—in Syrian televisual culture also stand in contrast to Wilson
Chacko Jacob's monumental *Working Out Egypt* (2011), a study of "effendi masculinity" during the interwar years of the early twentieth century. Jacob's book demonstrates the effendi's determination to eschew colonial depictions of the East
as passive and feminine as opposed to the virile and energetic West, spurring
discourse on Egyptian manhood characterized by physical strength.[11] I show how
constructions of masculinity in televisual Syrian culture prior to the uprising
as well as during its first two years, in contrast to "effendi masculinity" dynamics,
which were concerned with Western imperialism and articulating an Egyptian
modernity, were related to an internal critique of the state. (De)constructions
of fatherhood in both pre- and early-uprising Syrian drama, which were directly
related to the rise and fall of the *qabaday*, allowed political critiques to cross over
red lines and question the very foundation of regime legitimacy.

Exploring (de)constructions of the *qabaday* and fatherhood as a subtle
method of engaging in political critique or, more recently, to advocate for the
social for the sake of the social, this chapter situates itself within a growing field
of masculinity studies. R. W. Connell's groundbreaking work speaks of "marginalized masculinities" to delineate how men in weak positions negotiate their
place in hierarchies of class, gender, and race. According to Connell, the patriarchal position is alluring to men since it is through these power dynamics that
men achieve hegemonic masculinity over women. Central, too, in Connell's
analysis are the relationships of dominance and subordination between different
groups of men.[12] Salwa Ismael examines the interactions between young Egyptian men and the government in her ethnographic work on gender and the state
in Cairo. She argues that on top of their daily confrontations with the state, the
disruption of their masculine identity hinges on the changing position of women
in the household and public sphere. A major issue she finds in these masculine
constructions is that marginalized men assert their own hegemonic masculinity
by seeking to protect women from immorality. Thus, as the state humiliates
them, men seek to reinstate their power in the family structure, specifically over
female sexuality.[13] In a different vein, Marcia Inhorn argues in *The New Arab Man:
Emergent Masculinities, Technologies, and Islam in the Middle East* (2012) that Connell's theory of hegemonic masculinity fails to take into account the shift in
men's perspectives on masculinity due, for instance, to novel health technologies
introduced to the region. Through the lens of men's quest for fatherhood, her

research, even as it essentializes masculinity, renders men's lives more visible and shows how some men debunk traditional notions of patriarchy.[14]

In *The Politics of Love* I delineated how political parodies of the 1960s through 1980s focused on embattled, subordinate masculinity within the family, where loss of land and economic malaise led to the loss of dignity among *qabadayat*. When a man showed his dominance over or was violent toward a woman, that behavior was depicted as part of a vicious cycle of state violence affecting vulnerable men. Indeed, the act of hegemonic masculinity was meant to show man's political vulnerability. By 2000 the term described one who fights the occupier, guards female sexuality, and protects one's family honor. Soon after, certain writers began to define the *qabaday* as one who does not repress female desire. The more avant-garde elements of Syrian drama prior to the uprising depicted the *qabaday* as attaining true manhood only after he allows for a woman's sexual freedom.[15]

It is noteworthy that through the years both male and female screenwriters in Syria have worked to debunk the notion of the *qabaday* as tough man and instead depict a more gentle masculinity in their storylines. Within this broader trend of the *qabaday*'s rise and fall, and in the context of disguised political protest, the propagation of emotive fatherhood has been integral. Central to my argument is the notion that constructions of the *qabadayat*, along with all love, gender, and marriage metaphors, were inherently linked to political protest prior to the uprising. Since the uprising, however, screenwriters have been much more vocal about their political positions and have not always couched their ideas in metaphors. Especially from 2014 onward, drama creators whose work embraced the regime narrative, as well as those with a nostalgic viewpoint, eschewed politics in their gender constructions and instead focused on societal reform. These miniseries differentiated "secular" Syrian culture from religious extremism as represented by Da'ish. Yet the storylines that aligned with the regime narrative should not be confused with storylines that consciously explored the social for the sake of the social. The latter category, while expressing sympathy for the uprising, sought apolitically to distance itself from religious extremism. This distancing appears on the surface to intersect with the regime narrative. At the same time, other writers with an outwardly oppositional stance continued to use (de)constructions of the *qabadayat* through the lens of fatherhood as a means of advocating a more pluralistic political order.

Paternal Paradigms of the 1960s and 1970s:
The Rise of the *Qabaday*

In the first Syrian dramas of the 1960s and 1970s, cultural constructions of the responsible father as provider abounded. This figure translated into a marginalized man who lacked financial capability and could not meet his societal responsibility. It followed that the subservient father figure commented on man's insubordination by the state. These miniseries do not address the psychology of the children but focus on the man's role as a "deadbeat" father, his economic marginalization and emasculation within his family. As I have argued above, Jacob's *Working Out Egypt* demonstrates that the West portrayed the East as a feminized and sensualized body, which prompted the emasculation of men. "Effendi masculinity" arose from fear of the masculinization of women. On the other hand, in the anti-feminist current of Syrian television drama of the 1960s through 1970s, the power-wielding wife dominates the silenced father, and fear of emasculated women abounds as men are subdued by the state. Thus, concern over "othering" by the West takes a backseat to the notion that the emasculation of men results from subordination by the political order, and thus construction of the *qabaday* is linked to internal political protest in Syria. In *Milh wa Sukr* (Salt and Sugar, 1973), a miniseries that takes place three years after Hafiz al-Asad's Corrective Movement, the father figure is rendered so unimportant that the browbeaten Yassin—who lives in fear of his powerful wife Fatoon—admits that his father was infertile, and so his mother married someone else in order to conceive him. In this nonsensical family narrative, the father figure is portrayed as impotent as well as invisible.

Another crucial component of this period is that as men are subordinated by the state, they lash out with hegemonic masculinity as part of the vicious cycle of violence. In the *Wayn al-Ghalat?* (Where's the Mistake?, 1979) episode "Azmet al-Sakn" (The Housing Crisis), the police catch Ghawwar and his wife on the roof eating nuts while the famished children have nothing to eat but cement. Ghawwar explains that when their "bag of cement finally arrived, the thieves stole the cement and left us with the kids." Meanwhile, Ghawwar yells at his wife to raise his children properly. The episode suggests that the housing crisis has resulted in the emasculation of a generation of Syrian men and that the political system sustains the cycle of aggression toward the wife and children, as we saw in the previous chapter. The father figure of lost dignity culminates in the theatrical production *Kasak ya Watan*. Here, Ghawwar's daughter Amal (hope) dies due to government corruption. Officials blame colonialism and the loss of Palestine for Amal's tragic death. Yet their nonsensical explanations serve to subvert the regime's nationalistic and pro-Palestinian credentials. Utterly impoverished, Ghawwar proceeds to sell his sons. In the end, when his martyred father calls him from heaven, Ghawwar lies to him about his well-being. But when his father asks if he is missing anything, Ghawwar replies, "We're not missing anything but a little dignity." The father then realizes that his son deceived him. He had died for his son's generation, yet his son has not recovered his dignity despite his father's sacrifice. His fatherhood is thus rendered void.

Patriarchal Dictatorship's Mark on Children and
Their Love Relations in Contemporary Tales

Zuhair Boraq and Riyad Na'san Agha's *al-Tabibeh* (The Doctor, 1988), directed by Muhammad Ferdos Atassi, focuses on the effects of patriarchal dictatorship on children and their intimate relations. In *al-Tabibeh*, Dr. Medhat is the dictatorial father figure who stifles the dreams of his daughter, Sawsan, who wants to join the theater and marry the man she loves. Ultimately, it is the sudden softening of the dictatorial father, not Sawsan's own power, that grants her the freedom to determine the course of her life. Her initial submission—her willingness to study medicine and reject the man she loves—is symbolic of the discontent voiced by a generation of Syrians who did not act upon their words. The miniseries not only shows the power of the dictator to grant dignity and freedom to its citizens but serves as a blueprint for a society that can engage in discourse and find common ground. *Al-Tabibeh* shows the viewer that to create a democratic society, resistance and determination to maintain autonomy must meet a dictator's will. The story's elaborate metaphor lays bare the perils of patriarchy from the government to the home.[16]

It is not only the dictatorial father figure who negatively impacts his children. In *Laysa Saraban* (It's Not a Mirage, 2008), Jalal is a liberal screenwriter who fights fanaticism and laments the failure of others to engage in dialogue. Yet as a father, he rejects that same dialogue. Having sent his son 'Amer to obtain a university degree in an unnamed country of the West, he refuses to support 'Amer's choice to return to Syria. To no avail, during one of his visits 'Amer begs his father to allow him to remain at home. While he cites the philosophy in his father's novels that allows for freedom of choice, Jalal exclaims that "literature is one thing, and life another."[17] In the end, 'Amer returns as a close-minded sheikh in response to the disruption of social norms he experienced in "the West." Jalal, whose son now perceives him as an infidel, laments to his wife Hanan that a wall stands between him and his son. His friend Michel tells him, "We're also wrong. When he refused to return to 'the West,' we forced him. In truth, we weren't that democratic with him." Michel's wife, Sama, states, "We're democratic from the outside, but we need to be democratic from the inside."[18]

Ashwak Na'imeh (Soft Thorns, 2005) presents the recurring trope of the oppressive father who monitors his daughter's sexuality. When a schoolteacher, Hanan, catches her neighbor beating up his daughter, Marah, she tells him, "We're in the twenty-first century—you can't imprison girls anymore."[19] But the father ignores Hanan, punishing Marah for merely opening the window for fresh air. As a result, Marah rebels. Her grades slip as she flirts with Shadi, who insists that she come to his place. Despite her rebellion, she immediately reverts to traditions, telling Shadi that if he loved her, he would ask for her hand from her parents. Even so, when she returns home late, her father hits her again. When the story ends, Marah has gone mad and is peering out the window, lipstick smeared on her lips. In this story a different kind of father, a liberal-minded television scriptwriter, counterbalances the dictatorial father figure. The scriptwriter's wife has passed away, so he steps into the maternal role for his two daughters. At the beginning of the story, he cooks and cleans, but in the end, he tells his children he can no longer act like a woman and wishes to get married. Thus his maternal fatherhood—and the new father figure that the show offers—is not intended to subvert gender roles.

Qulub Saghireh (Small Hearts, 2006), written by Reema Fleihan, a Druze from Sweda, also underscores the effects of paternal dictatorship on family dynamics. When the story opens Salam has returned home late and Karim, who must adjust his teaching responsibilities to accommodate his wife's position as a social worker, is cooking in the kitchen. The adjustment of Karim's paternal role arises not from commitment to gender equality but due to Salam's longer hours at work. Thus, Karim fits into Oystein Holter's "new circumstance" model of fatherhood, in which change occurs due to the family's evolving situation.[20] Their relationship is strained when Salam becomes embroiled in a case of orphanage corruption, child rape, and abduction. Karim, disgruntled by the hours he spends monitoring the children, insists that raising good children should constitute each parent's primary contribution to society.

Adding to the discontent is Farid, Karim's colleague who insists that "real men" should control the household. When Farid's wife tells him that her son is coming home late, he orders her to stop nagging and let their son be a man. Influenced by Farid, Karim in turn refuses to help around the house. We see role models reinforcing gender constructions when their son Oussama tells his sister, "I'm a man. A man doesn't work in the house." When his sister responds that their father helps, Oussama tells her that their father no longer participates in household chores.[21] Disquiet mounts as Karim becomes more dictatorial and their parents separate. During this time Karim realizes that he is no less a man when he assists with the children and he mends his relationship with his wife. Karim and Salam's happy ending is juxtaposed with the abusive marriage of his colleague Farid, who represses his wife. While Salam and Karim have healthy, satisfied children, Farid's drug-abusing eldest son is incarcerated. Thus, *Qulub Saghireh* deconstructs traditional conceptions of the *qabaday* and promotes a new model of nondictatorial fatherhood. According to Yara Sabri (who played Salam), "In our society the preponderant idea is that the father guarantees the financial well-being of his family, while the good mother remains at home. Most believe that even when the mother works it should not be allowed to negatively impact family life. In miniseries such as *Qulub Saghireh* we seek to present new models." Indeed, dramas of pre- and post-uprising shed light on multifaceted discourses of fatherhood. According to Sabri, in our consumerist society where all have television in their homes and are tuning into miniseries, dramas should be simple and easy to understand and continue to have a huge influence on hearts and minds.[22]

Quyud al-Ruh (Bonds of the Soul, 2010) focuses on the vicious cycle of familial dictatorship. Written by Reema Fleihan and Yara Sabri, *Quyud al-Ruh* commences in 1983 with three women having babies as their husbands linger in the corridors. Fittingly, paternal politics and their impact on children is one of the central themes of the miniseries. According to Sabri, while in *Qulub Saghireh* the open-minded father is negatively affected by his colleague, in *Quyud al-Ruh* the dictatorial father, Abu Rami, fails to provide for his household from the outset. His stay-at-home wife, Umm Rami, focuses on their two sons and daughter.[23] When he and Umm Rami divorce, their son, Rami, vows to his mother that in the future he will not make his wife and children suffer as his father has. Yet as time passes, Rami's severity with his wife, Roula, and his son, Mahmud, reveals the vicious cycle of paternal dictatorship.

Due to lingering cultural acceptance of the powerful *qabaday*, the issue of patriarchal dictatorship is not without nuance in Syrian drama. In *Abna' wa Ummahat* (Sons and Mothers, 1993), the absence of the strong father figure in the life of Iyad (later called Victor by his French mother) serves to emasculate the young man. His character follows a common trope in Syrian televisual culture, in which a man is so oppressed by the system that he has lost what are considered his "masculine" qualities and becomes "soft." In this miniseries, the absence of the strong father figure's guidance effectively robs his son of traditional masculinity. This miniseries contrasts Syria's femininity to its Western counterpart—and focuses on the importance of culture and remaining true to the nation. Indeed, throughout the miniseries, love for the homeland is viewed as an essential aspect of masculinity. Thus, Victor's "softer" masculinity, which results from his upbringing by a Western woman, is portrayed in an entirely negative sense.[24]

The Fall of the *Qabaday*: Ramifications of Engaged Fatherhood on Men's Interpersonal Relationships

Alongside traditional notions of masculinity, gentler images of manhood emerge from miniseries that deconstruct the *qabaday*. Some of these miniseries show how emotive paternal involvement contributes to the father's emotional well-being and increases his capacity to love. The equilibrium of the paternal figure is seen as essential to cultivating a stable society, which, during this time, was a coded strategy for liberal screenwriters to advocate conditions that would end dictatorship. Fatherhood is one of the central themes in Yam Mashhadi's *Takht Sharqi* (Eastern Bed, 2010). As the storyline commences, Sa'ad is on the verge of a divorce from his volatile wife, Lina. When he informs his father that Lina always leaves the baby with her mother, Abu Sa'ad says, "And how about you? Time passes and never comes back. Don't think the baby can't feel. The baby can feel from early on."[25] Abu Sa'ad warns him that if he continues this way, Lana will never forgive him. Furthermore, denied paternal care, his daughter will not experience normal emotions in her relationships. Heedless of the consequences, a fed-up Sa'ad divorces Lina. According to Iyad Shihab Ahmad, who edited this miniseries, "Mashhadi's intention was to show the impact of societal norms on women. Lina's illogical behavior is not a judgment of her, but rather an indictment of society that turns her into an imbalanced individual."[26]

The turning point comes when, to pressure Sa'ad, Lina drops the sick baby off for him to watch. Sa'ad confides to his friend Y'arib that he must be the worst father in the world since he feels no love for his daughter. Fatherhood, he admits, is not a central aspect of his identity. Yet as Mashhadi sensitively portrays, Sa'ad gradually grows attached to his daughter. Studies such as Palkovitz and Palm's "Transitions within Fathering" underscore the way in which Sa'ad's harmony with his young child in turn gives him new organizational skills and psychological balance in his personal life and legal profession. He gains the ability to shift from parental to professional mode and evinces more self-control than ever before.[27] Not surprisingly, Mashhadi emphasizes her desire to resist stereotypes of the nurturing mother and disciplinarian father in *Takht-e Sharqi*, as well as to show changing roles in response to changing circumstances.[28]

The love story of a young Syrian medical student, Tariq, and Greta, who is half German and half Syrian, explores a father's duty to choose the right kind of mother. Tariq confides in Y'arib that since Greta (also a medical student) will be the mother of his children, he is uncomfortable with the fact that she had sexual relationships before him. Y'arib answers, "At least you know. She doesn't claim to be a virgin while secretly she had twenty previous relationships."[29] Greta's father possesses similar cultural hang-ups. When he returns to Syria, he reminds Greta that if a man is serious about a girl in Syria, he and his family will ask for her hand. When she reminds her father that he lived with her mother before marriage, he retorts that they lived in Germany. Later, when her father spies her departure from Tariq's apartment, he accuses her of abusing his trust. According to Iyad Shihab Ahmad, who edited the miniseries, Greta's father represents the Syrian man who is still influenced by his roots even when he has traveled to faraway countries such as Germany, suggesting that the transformation of social mores will take generations.[30] Yet actor Fares al-Heloo, who played the role of Greta's father, contends that his character's thinking had progressed over time, even though he still viewed his daughter as his possession, a reflection of his honor.[31]

Khaled Khalifa's *Zaman al-Khawf* (A Time of Fear) centers on the difficulty of fatherhood against a backdrop of political turmoil in the country and region. Khalifa maintains that the leading father in this miniseries, Abu Sobhi, defies stereotypical depictions of both liberal and stern fathers. Instead, he appears to be in the midst of an existential crisis, the cause of which is the dictatorship and its effects, including regional defeats, which broke the spirit of generations.[32] The story commences in 1982 when a paranoid regime that has just put down the Muslim Brotherhood in Hama imprisons suspects, including secular liberals, who express opposition. Abu Sobhi has taken a second wife, Bedriyyeh, and no longer lives with his wife and children. In the first episode, Zekiyyeh (Zeezee) bursts in on her father and demands that he return home. Abu Sobhi protests, "She came to remind me of my paternal duties and to treat me like a deadbeat father!" Meanwhile, his home is in a state of chaos. When Zeezee returns home late one evening, her mother declares, "This is what happens to a girl when there's no father to raise her."[33] In a telling scene, Zeezee tells her father that an absent father is a dead father.

ABU SOBHI: Maybe you have a father who isn't strong. I made mistakes. But I provided.

ZEEZEE: We don't want money from you. We want to see you in the morning and hear you say "good morning." I want to return home from college and tell you what happened that day.

ABU SOBHI: Your mother knew my dreams, but she put an end to them. My dream was to become a painter. After I graduated from law school I got engaged. She asked me why I wanted to paint, since that wouldn't give us bread. She insisted that I become an employee. When I was an employee she said the children needed more money than I was making. She assured me that I should not look at bribes as bribes, but rather as gifts. After all that, I have the right to live my life and accomplish my dreams.[34]

As the story progresses into 1984, Abu Sobhi's existentialist crisis intensifies as he informs his son that he has decided to follow his desire to be an artist. Time passes. Abu Sobhi succeeds as an artist and relinquishes his role as provider. Even as his desire for his wife increases, his children's lives slide into disarray.

Despite his failure to provide traditional paternal authority, Abu Sobhi becomes the father Zeezee had always wanted. When Zeezee decides to pursue her doctorate in France, she asks her father, who understands her and to whom she feels close, for a plane ticket and promises that she will work and pay for her studies. Her mother, on the other hand, is unsupportive. When Zeezee refuses her brother Hussain's corrupt money, Abu Sobhi admits that Zeezee gives him hope because she wants to succeed on her own. He asks why Hussain has become involved with the mafia and wonders about the deterioration of his progressive values. Hussain responds that when Israel invaded Beirut, their time had ended, and now that Saddam Hussein has invaded an Arab country, their moment in history was really over. He continued, "I envy Zeezee. I want her to fail. If she succeeds it means we were wrong."[35] Subsequently, Hussain runs into Zeezee in

Paris and promises her a house on the Champs-Élysées. She refuses, saying that he was her first hope and first disillusionment.

The story concludes when Bedriyyeh, Abu Sobhi's former wife, stabs her tyrannical husband and is placed in prison for five years. Abu Sobhi tells his wife to decide what to do with Bedriyyeh's young son from a previous marriage. With all their children out of the house, raising Bedriyyeh's son gives them a chance to fill the emptiness. Umm Sobhi cries as she confronts the state of her own children: Zahra, having been embroiled with the *qubaysiyyat*, married a man in Saudi Arabia who does not allow her leave the house, and is pregnant; Sobhi has left the mafia and escaped to the mosque; and Hussain is a leading mafia figure. Only Zeezee, who has just obtained her doctorate, has succeeded. She rejected patriarchal dictatorship as well as religion and money. As pointed out by Iyad Shihab Ahmad, Zahra and Sobhi's subjugation to religion along with Hussain's subjugation to money reflect a dictatorial society in which individuals feel secure only when enslaved.[36] In Paris, Zeezee meets up with her cousin Jalal, who escaped Syria after calling for the Syrian army to leave Lebanon. Both Zeezee and Jalal escaped patriarchy; Zeezee's father had become her friend and she had insisted on her freedom. Likewise, while Jalal's father maintained his role at home, Jalal had repudiated patriarchal dictatorship. At the commencement of the miniseries, neither father could communicate effectively with his children. Both children rejected their father's role as mere financial provider.

According to Haitham Haqqi, who produced this miniseries, the strength of *Zaman al-Khawf* is its ability to peel back layers of deceit to reveal the inner soul of the Syrian family. Haqqi details government protests against the miniseries' references to the uprising of the Muslim brotherhood and imprisonment of liberal intellectuals, as well as its critiques of Syria's refusal to withdraw from Lebanon and of the *qubaysiyyat*, which, Haqqi argues, was buttressed by the regime.[37] So controversial was the miniseries that when it first aired, ten minutes of each episode were randomly cut to remove references to Hussein's imprisonment as well as scenes involving the *qubaysiyyat*. The cuts resulted in heavy criticism of Inas Haqqi's directorial debut.[38]

Ironically, Khalifa's earlier miniseries *Sirat al-Jalali* (A Portrait of the Jalali Family, 2000) met with positive responses from the government as well as general public.[39] In this miniseries, too, marriage, gender, and love revolve around fatherhood and serve as metaphors for societal malaise. One character, a well-known playwright named Wahid, experiences an existential conflict when he finishes writing his play, *Ahl al-Hubb* (People of Love), but can't produce it in Syria for political reasons. Unlike Abu Sobhi, Wahid has always insisted on making his living solely from his theatrical productions, which means that his wife, Lobna, has to borrow money from her family to pay for their son's operation when he falls ill. Their marriage unravels and Lobna leaves him. A solution is found when he leaves for the Gulf to make money and she promises to wait for him. In

FIGURE 3.1 Roula (played by Karis Bashar) (*left*) and Bashar (played by Wa'el
Ramadan) (*right*) in *Sirat al-Jalali* (A Portrait of the Jalali Family).

Courtesy of Haitham Haqqi.

Sirat al-Jalali, then, Khalifa portrays a father who did follow his dreams, only is
forced to put them his dreams on hold to provide for his family—a subtle critique of a political order that crushes dreams and expectations.

Constructions of Fatherhood on Post-Uprising Drama

The fall of the *qabaday* culminates in Ramadan 2011 with two reform-minded
miniseries, Najeeb Nseir's *al-Sarab* (A Mirage) and Fadi Qoshaqji's *Ta'b al-Mishwar*
(Exhaustion of the Journey), that focus on the father as protector of a daughter's
sexuality. While these transitional miniseries do not refer directly to the uprising, they posit that a more liberal approach to fatherhood, one that does not
focus on guarding a woman's sexual purity, underlies a more democratic political
order.[40] During the first two years of the uprising, these metaphors about fatherhood poignantly debunked the whole system of dictatorship. Radical storylines
in which fathers shed the role of protector of female sexuality continued to
employ sexual metaphors as political critique, even when the uprising was not
mentioned.

In *al-Sarab*, Wahbi is a liberal man who offers his children a good deal of
freedom. He even embraces the idea that his children have the right to engage

in sexual relationships prior to marriage. Yet when Wahbi discovers that his daughter, Rana, is not a virgin on her wedding night, he strikes her. This reaction was the result of Najeeb Nseir's compromise with Hassan Sami Yusuf, his co-screenwriter, who believed such a liberal reaction to be unfathomable. This artistic compromise produced contradictions in the text, and Nseir lamented that, in any case, the miniseries had little impact during Ramadan 2011. Because it was broadcast on Syrian television, and because many newscasts interrupted the miniseries due to increasingly bloody protests, many viewers did not see it in whole and very few commented.[41]

Screenwriter Fadi Qoshaqji's *Ta'b al-Mishwar* was one of the first completed miniseries scheduled to be broadcast during Ramadan 2011.[42] With the uprising and subsequent marketing complications, however, Bana Production Company pulled it just hours before the start of the season. Then, despite the fact that many in the industry feared that the Gulf States were leading an embargo against Syrian television miniseries, Abu Dhabi, a leading Gulf State producer of Syrian television miniseries, broadcast it immediately after Ramadan, September 2011.[43] Here, father figures illustrate the hypocrisy of a generation of men. Maysa's father offers her freedom and assures her that he will accept any man she chooses. Yet when he spies her leaving an older man's apartment, it proves too much for him. Later, his son, Kifah, falls in love with Suheir, a divorced woman with a son, and he refuses to accept the match. Suheir, too, faces resistance from her liberal-minded father, Zafer, after she is caught alone in the office with Kifah before her divorce is finalized. He soon comes around, though, and in one of the final scenes, Zafer is interviewed on television about personal status laws. The other interviewee accuses Zafer of imitating the West; Zafer answers that every human has the right to freedom and that men and women should always be judged equally. Zafer posits that an egalitarian approach to romantic relationships sets a standard for a healthy society. Indeed, the repression of female sexuality is portrayed as a mechanism of dictatorship. While previous miniseries showed a version of fatherhood in which men repress female sexuality, here we see a novel approach, in which fatherhood functions to break down dichotomies.

Khaled Khalifa's *al-Miftah* (The Key, 2012) also contained no direct links to the uprising, but there are indirect references to political corruption through the lens of fatherhood. The story revolves around Laila and Mas'ud. As Mas'ud struggles in his life, Laila pressures him to make more money. At the same time, she is not maternal toward her son, and although she does not return sexual favors, she is receptive to receiving gifts from men other than her husband. As the story begins, a friend informs Mas'ud that she saw Laila out at a restaurant with a businessman. When he confronts Laila, she insists that she loves him and only goes out with other men for material pleasures. Mas'ud consequently divorces her, claiming to feel less of a man for being cheated on publicly, then quits his job and becomes corrupt in his effort to make a better living. Abu Zuhair, whom Mas'ud sees as a father figure, serves as the conscience in this story. Abu Zuhair asks Mas'ud why he has suddenly become hostile, and Mas'ud responds that it is better to be mean than "dumb as a donkey." Mas'ud insists, "You're either a *qatel* or *maqtul*" (a killer or killed). But Abu Zuhair says this is not true: "This kind of talk is wrong. You can be *sharif* (honorable), live *sharif*, and die *sharif*. Why had you placed all these conditions? Do you have proof of Laila's infidelity? A crime needs proof. In your eyes no one has dignity. So now you are *wahesh*."[44]

Abu Zuhair also observes that men want to be forgiven for their mistakes but do not grant the same compassion to women. Here, we see the main father figure connect corruption with hypocritical social norms. On the other hand, as with Lina in *Takht al-Sharqi*, the mother figure, Laila, is depicted as unmaternal. Indeed, her own mother was unmaternal and oppressed her father, who preferred to live in a garage than with his wife who was cruel to him. Parenting, then, is not inherent to man or woman, and both have a responsibility to the family. Because of its intense critique of corruption, *al-Miftah* was cut from Addounia and Syrian Arab Television channel before the completion of the show.[45] Yet Sharbatji insists that the role of art is not to teach a lesson or hold others to account. Rather, the true role of art is to transform "poison into a cure." He differentiates the story's critique of corruption from those miniseries that engage in impolite tirades under the banner of freedom of opinion.[46]

The next cluster of miniseries I examine from Ramadan 2013 and 2014 refer directly to the uprising and discuss the impact of fatherhood on intimate relations. These storylines explore existential issues about relationships rather than the political metaphors of a father's waning role as protector of female sexuality. Some of these miniseries depict the moment when the "wall of fear" tumbles down and citizens refuse to wait any longer. On April 20, 2013, renowned director Muhammad Ferdos Atassi began filming the first scenes of *Watan Haff* (Bare Homeland), written by Kamil Nasrawi, in Damascus. Atassi had not directed for several years, but now codirected with Muhannad Qateesh. Each director took on fifteen episodes.[47] The first episode of *Watan Haff*, titled "'Ala al-Hiyad" (Neutral), was directed by Atassi and employs themes related to fatherhood as the backdrop for political critique. In this tragicomic episode, which refers to current bloodshed in Syria as "al-azmeh," a young man, Sroor, yearns to marry Heniyyeh, whom he has courted for six years. But Abu Heniyyeh does not want his only daughter to marry a man who makes a modest living selling *za'tar* and cheese *feta'er*. Knowing that his daughter is not the studious type, his condition for accepting Sroor's marriage proposition is that Heniyyeh pass her baccalaureate. What Abu Heniyyeh does not foresee is that the eager young man,

FIGURE 3.2 Mas'ud (played by Bassem Yakhour) (*left*) and Laila (played by Amal 'Arafeh) (*right*) in *al-Miftah* (The Key).

Courtesy of Khaled Khalifa.

exasperated with waiting, hires tutors for her. After six years of struggling, she finally passes.

When Heniyyeh and Sroor announce her success, Abu Heniyyeh declares that they now have to wait for the azmeh to end before marrying. The furious groom threatens to wait no longer. Heniyyeh runs after Sroor as her mother glares at Abu Heniyyeh. Sroor's humiliating wait for Abu Heniyyeh's approval mirrors the use of waiting as a critique of the lack of opportunity in the Ba'th regime, a trope poignantly analyzed in Christa Salamandra's research on *al-Intizar* (Waiting). Here, characters wait in a debilitating limbo for better prospects that will never come.[48] Sroor's refusal to wait any longer and Heniyyeh's assertive disobedience of her father offers a new fatherhood paradigm in which the father's final word no longer counts. Whereas the trope of waiting was previously used to symbolize exasperation with a political order that ignored its citizens' needs, in this story, we see individuals rebelling again it.

Yet the harsh realities of an uprising, police arrest, and government's crushing of the revolt compels the characters to continue to wait. It is Friday, a day of mass protests, and Sroor and Heniyyeh search for a sheikh to write their marriage contract. Dressed in wedding attire, they stroll past a protest, hoping to grab two witnesses. As protestors yell, "*Wahed, Wahed, Huriyyeh*" (We are one,

FIGURE 3.3 Heniyyeh (played by Lina Diab) and Sroor (played by Muhammad Hidaqi) in prison on the day they hoped to get married, *Watan Haff* (Bare Homeland).

Courtesy of Muhammad Ferdos Atassi.

one, freedom), the bride and the groom join them in chanting. When the police incarcerate them, Heniyyeh assures her fiancé, "Don't worry, they'll see that we weren't demanding our rights and then they'll let us out." One week later, the police release them after they sign a contract promising never to protest again. Mishaps continue to prevent the couple from consummating their marriage. In these early days of the uprising, traditional notions of a father who regulates his daughter's intimate relations no longer apply. Although Abu Heniyyeh serves a traditional paternal role, he no longer control who his daughter loves. Yet the bitter realities of an oppressive regime that crushes the uprising compel the couple to continue to wait. This stasis directly parallels the aborted revolution, its citizens awaiting a modicum of justice.

Yam Mashhadi's bold oppositional miniseries, *Qalam Humra* (Lipstick, 2014), shuffles back and forth in time between the main storyline (which commences in 2010) and prison scenes in 2013—and also takes on the theme of refusing to wait. Against the background of the squashed revolutionary dreams of a secular opposition, the crisis of fatherhood and motherhood is linked to an existentialist crisis of the individual. As the story begins, the central character, Ward, critiques the individual's refusal to make change due to his or her paralysis by fear: "Fear. Fear controls you. Someone else can make you feel fear. You're scared to age; scared of death; and scared of what comes after death. You're a lump of fear."[49] Jeffrey Alexander examines the impact lay trauma theory has had on Latin American scholars whose studies focus on trauma incurred by recent dictatorships. Alexander points to the increasing body of literature that examines the trauma that has resulted from the repression of difficult events.[50] Similarly, in a strain of Syrian television drama prior to and following the uprising, fear emerges as a central form of trauma inflicted by the Ba'th Party regime on its population. Following the uprising, we see a concerted effort on the part of screenwriters not only to describe that fear but to overcome it.

In *Qalam Humra*, Ward is unhappily married to Ghassan, a dedicated father who reminds her that they need to work things out lest their son, Bahar, pay a price for their divorce. Syrian miniseries often focus on the importance of family and reconciliation.[51] In this story, however, though Ghassan is a gentle husband and good father, Ward asks for a divorce, since she is no longer sexually attracted to him. She falls in love with Taim, who, at first, refuses her advances because he is trying to reconcile with his estranged teenage daughter, Luna. Taim fears paternal responsibility, and his relationship with Luna is fraught with tension. Luna plays loud music to block his attempts to converse and threatens to leave once she is eighteen. Another fatherhood storyline runs parallel to that of Ward's husband, Ghassan, and love interest, Taim. Ward's colleague, Hazim, yearns to leave his wife, Bassima, but hopes that she will take the initiative. When Bassima announces that she is pregnant with another baby, a miserable Hazim remains in his marriage. In this storyline, too, the responsibilities of fatherhood entail a loss of individual fulfillment and imprisonment in a dead marriage. Despite Mashhadi's boldness as an oppositionist screenwriter, many critics in the drama industry saw her depiction of the religious extremism that followed the uprising as a compromise the screenwriter, who still lives in Syria, was forced to make.[52]

Both *Watan Haff* and *Qalam Humra* depict fatherhood in the context of characters who attempt to overcome fear by refusing to wait any longer. Both end with aborted efforts to change, paralleling a revolution that was aborted due to political oppression. These miniseries tellingly portrays the futility of protest in a repressive political order. The state's capacity to create a "politics of pretense" in which citizens act "as if" they believe, in order to enforce obedience and prevent rebellion in the first place, has been powerfully depicted by Lisa Wedeen in *Ambiguities of Domination: Politics, Rhetoric, and Symbols in Contemporary Syria* (1999) and miriam cooke in *Dissident Syria: Making Oppositional Arts Official*. This, too, is the central theme in *Sa-Na'ud Ba'da Qalil*, which was produced by Clacket and would be broadcast on MBC during Ramadan 2013. Written by actor-writer Rafi Wahbi and directed by Laith Hajjo, the events shifted between Syria and Lebanon, yet the majority of the miniseries was filmed in Lebanon.[53]

With the participation of Syrian actors such as Basel Khayat, Qusay Khawli, 'Abed Fahd, Sulafa Me'mar, and Kinda 'Aloosh, the miniseries, which for the most part evinces neutrality with respect to politics, tells the story of a middle-class Syrian family that immigrates to Lebanon because of increasing bloodshed, thinking they will be gone for a few days, then months, then years.

FIGURE 3.4 Ward (Sulafa Me'mar) (*right*) and Sebah (Reem 'Ali) (*left*) in prison scene, *Qalam Humra* (Lipstick).

Courtesy of Yam Mashhadi.

They leave behind the widowed father, Najeeb, played by Durayd Lahham, who joins them later because of illness. Wahbi was inspired by the Italian film *Everything Is Fine*, where a father voyages to see his children, hoping to discover whether they had accomplished their dreams. Having first written the adaptation as a series of five episode stories several years earlier, Wahbi had originally imagined the family would travel within Syria. Ultimately, because of political circumstances, they traveled much further.[54]

The story commences with the widowed Najeeb, who lives in the Old City of Damascus and denies the political upheaval in Syria, although bomb sounds reverberate in the background. As Najeeb describes the "perfect" lives of his children, who live in Lebanon, their problems unfold before us. One third of the show passes, and Najeeb prepares to surprise each child in Beirut. First, he visits Dima, whose husband has discovered her affair. Najeeb feels the tension in their home but does not acknowledge it. Next, he visits Sami, whose wife has asked for a divorce. Najeeb senses that something is off and tries to help by telling his Lebanese daughter-in-law that her strength will keep her home intact. His son, Karim, whose wife is visiting her family in Beirut, spends the evening with his lover and returns home late. Najeeb does not allow him to explain. Then Najeeb visits Fu'ad, who is being visited by the mafia. Fu'ad tells Najeeb that the men surrounding him are his employees, and Najeeb chooses to trust him. When he visits Raji, his ex-fiancée Nura is there and Najeeb wants to believe that she and Raji are back together. Najeeb's denial about the country, which runs parallel to his denial in his fatherhood role, can be seen in the following conversation:

NURA: Are you with all the killing?

NAJEEB: The regime is fighting to defend the country from terrorists.

NURA: They're revolutionaries.

NAJEEB: Don't you see them on the news admitting their crimes?

NURA: Are you for killing?

NAJEEB: Should you ask that question? Was I ever for violence?[55]

Najeeb's discussions with his children represent the many viewpoints of Syrians and in this way fall into the neutral strand of post-uprising miniseries. Actress Sulafa Me'mar explains, "We will get all perspectives, pro-regime, against regime, and those who are neutral and why they are neutral."[56] In each child's house, the ailing father finds a problem he tries to solve. Despite his efforts, however, the problems grow worse, and he questions whether he was a good father. When he tries to address his children's financial problems by selling his house in Damascus, he becomes nostalgic, revealing how personal issues become entwined in national issues. Wahbi elaborates, "We are dealing with the 'azmeh,' attempting to remain neutral. While the current crisis is filled with stories that will give us drama for the next ten years, the events are still in process, and it is hard to treat them only from one perspective. Instead, we decided to treat them from a human standpoint." Wahbi, who also plays the artist-son, claims they hoped to avoid categorizing certain persons as good or evil. Because of Durayd Lahham's presence, Wahbi says that there are some elements of comedy here and there.[57]

The miniseries ends with Najeeb lying alone in the hospital. Bombs drop near Najeeb's shop in Old Damascus and a radio announces that Israeli has bombed a research center and that the regime will never accept the enemy, Israel, in the region. The ending powerfully illustrates the regime's desire to keep its population in denial by feeding it propaganda about its nationalist credentials. The father figure Najeeb—whose denial about the live of his children runs parallels to his denial about the political upheaval in his country—represents the Syrian who has lived in the "city of fear" all his life. Indeed, he represents a generation of Syrians who knew the government was lying but acted as if they believed in order to survive. It is not that Najeeb is ignorant and does not see, but that fear traumatizes him. According to Iyad Shihab Ahmad, this form of thinking still influences Syrians, and to this day, when they watch the uprising on television, many say, "*Ma fi Shi*' (It's Nothing)."[58]

Najdat Anzour's miniseries *Taht Sama' al-Watan* (2013) is composed of three-episode stories that deal directly with the azmeh in Syria from the perspective of the regime, for the most part, and focus on various symbolic meanings of

FIGURE 3.5 Raji (played by Rafi Wahbi) (*left*) and Mariam (played by Dana Mardini) (*right*), *Sa-Na'ud Ba'da Qalil* (We'll Return Soon).

Courtesy of Rafi Wahbi.

fatherhood. In the first story, "al-Hamidiyyeh," written by Fadi Qoshaqji, the father, Abu William, is a loyal nationalist figure determined to remain in war-torn Homs despite the bombings and power outages. His daughter, Violet, following his lead, does not wish to leave, though she is engaged to Somar, a young man who lives in Damascus. Anzour portrays tensions within previously-caring relationships with remarkable poignancy. When a neighbor, Ilyas, is kidnapped, Violet's brother, William, refuses moral support, since he accuses Ilyas of being a *shabbiha*. On another occasion, William tells Ilyas's sister, Roula, that they were slaves for forty years to a government that would not allow people to open their mouths and that the government's brutal suppression of the uprisings compelled the rebels to resort to arms. Roula responds that the people "need to be crushed. They're backward and know nothing of freedom." When William retorts that his father, too, always refused to acknowledge the corruption of the state, Abu William says that he is only concerned about Syria's well-being. He then turns to Roula, objecting to her claim that her fellow citizens should be crushed. As he insists that both sides of the conflict are terrible, Anzour's camera zooms in on images of ruins. When Abu William finally agrees to leave Homs, the family moves to Geramana; the story ends with Abu William in the hospital waiting for an operation. After he tells Violet that he is not scared of death but wants to die in Homs, we see a picture of his house in Homs, destroyed.

While in "al-Hamidiyyeh" the central father figure represents the nationalist Syrian who yearns for peace, in "Nazuh" the father figures manifest the differing political opinions in Syria both within and across generations. In this story, Jumana, a screenwriter, has a supportive marriage with Hisham, an artist. Jumana is hired to complete a miniseries in three months. Just as she hopes to start, they hear that Hisham's parents' neighborhood was bombed. Jumana fetches them and listens to Hisham's father, Abu Hisham, blame America for the turmoil, citing a conspiracy against Syria with the goal of getting a hold of Syria's oil. Soon after, Jumana's parents also flee their neighborhood and Hisham picks them up. Not too long after, Hisham's sister Maysa's building is decimated. His sister, her husband, Jamil, and their two children join them. Abu Hisham, who believes the government's side of the story, counsels his son-in-law:

ABU HISHAM: You can get fifty thousand liras compensation from the government.

JAMIL: I lost my house built on ten years of effort and you want me to accept fifty thousand as compensation?

ABU HISHAM: So is this the freedom you want?

JAMIL: I just want to live in peace. Now I'm a refugee.

ABU HISHAM: Look at the army protecting you. What else do you want? Look at all the kidnapping, bombing. Do you like what happened in Iraq? This was the most secure country in the world. We could go out at night and be safe. This is the freedom you want?

Jamil's young son laments to his father, "My friends have died. My school is gone. Before I was best in school, we were all living happily. Why do these people want to ruin our country? What did we do to them?" Finally, Jamil, ashamed to live with his in-laws, leaves to find a job to give his wife and children a better life. "Nuzuh" ends after only two episodes, leading some to think censors had cut it. Screenwriter Nur Shishekly, however, insists that she planned the story to have two episodes.[59] Shishekly claims that the popularity of this two-episode story, which was based on personal experience, is due to the fact that every Syrian family has been touched by this refugee crisis. So many Syrians have fled their homes or have family members who have fled that the story touched connected with a large percentage of the population.[60]

"'Aziza min Baba 'Amru ('Aziza from Baba 'Amru) by Hala Diab describes how religious figures exploit the vulnerability of the impoverished in the Za'tari Refugee Camp. The storyline, which falls into the strand of miniseries that from 2013 sought to differentiate Syrian culture from Da'ish and religious extremism, also underscores fathers' key role in selling daughters. The lascivious sheikhs claim they should marry the girls to protect them, even informing the jihadists that marrying raped girls is an act of jihad. In this tale, fathers, with the cooperation of mothers, sell their daughters to religious fanatics. When gossip circulates that a man raped Hanan, a fifteen-year-old girl from Homs, Hanan insists that this is not true. Her father, fearful that she will cause a scandal, sells her to Yusuf to marry, even though she yearns to continue her studies. Yusuf then rapes her on their wedding night. Also in the camp, 'Aziza's fourteen-year-old daughter Zeina is unable to go to the bathroom due to trauma she underwent in Baba 'Amru. The sheikh tells 'Aziza she should marry off Zahra; after all, 'Aisheh married at the age of nine. But when he tells 'Aziza that he is willing to marry Zahra to help out their family, a furious 'Aziza tells him he should be ashamed to think like that at his age. The sheikh responds, "This is the only solution. I want to give you money. I'm doing what is *halal*. I want to help. I've given you lots of food. I won't be able to continue doing this." 'Aziza's husband says they need to accept Zahra's marriage since they need the money to cure Zeina. Yet the miniseries ends with their son Ali barging in on the wedding ceremony with a gun to prevent his father from selling his daughter to this hypocritical sheikh.

Some screenwriters who are not associated with the regime, but who nevertheless do not wish to associate with the opposition, focus on aspects of law and culture responsible for the azmeh. Mazin Taha's *Sukar Wasat* (A Medium Quantity of Sugar, 2013) portrays injustice as the basis of the azmeh. While the storylines of *Watan Haff*, *Sa-Na'ud Ba'da Qalil*, and *Taht Sama' al-Watan* occur during the uprising, *Sukar Wasat* commences in central Damascus in the year 2010 with Nabil and Jumana, an unhappy couple with a son. The story critiques social and political oppression through the lens of problematic paternity rights. While Nabil, an engaged father, refuses to compromise his honesty at work, Jumana, who takes bribes, insists, "This is the system. If you resist corruption, you won't be able to live a decent life."[61] When Nabil finds out that Jumana aborted their baby, he divorces her. In revenge, she denies his paternity rights. Nabil's predicament in *Sukar Wasat* discloses how unfair laws allow women to deny men the right to fatherhood. Jumana's behavior is calculated to manipulate, control, and seek revenge on Nabil, an honest man who strives to resist corruption. When Nabil goes to his son's school, he learns that Jumana has forbidden this contact, and the school threatens to call the police. Nabil asks, "What kind of law is this? A man just wants to see his son. No law can keep me from seeing my son."[62]

Furthermore, when Nabil's father is swindled and loses his property, they are forced to move to a haphazard zoning area where Jumana does not allow him to take his son. Nabil relies on the court to grant him visitations with his son once a week. As Nabil and Jumana argue at the court, Taim wanders through the streets and is hit by a car. The story ends with Nabil and his girlfriend wheeling his handicapped son as a tearful Jumana laments her behavior. *Sukar Wasat* belongs to a trend of miniseries that begin their storylines prior to the uprising; it then attempts to make sense of the crisis without referring directly to politics. Taha, who based the miniseries on his experience of being denied paternity rights, said that the story touched many others with similar experiences. He elaborated, "For years I had to wait hours in front of the home of my child's mother, and was barred from seeing him at school lest they call the police. In this miniseries, I hoped to show that while custody should go to the mother, there are circumstances when the law unnecessarily abuses fathers."[63]

Like *Sukar Wasat*, *al-Qurban* (Sacrifice, 2014), written by Rami Kousa and directed by 'Ala al-Din Kawkash, commences in Damascus in 2010. While *Sukar Wasat* avoids direct commentary on politics, *al-Qurban* refers to the politics of the secular opposition in the year prior to the uprising. Here we have the figure of Salem Bik, a wealthy businessman involved in the illegal trade of ancient national treasures and also the father of a handicapped son, Ward. As Salem Bik stomps on the secular opposition, his son yearns for his attention. Ward tells his father, "You have property, but I'm not property. Try to find time for everything."[64] Salem Bik promises he will try to become a better father, but Ward tells him not to promise: "You see the world like a chess game. You see everything as black and white. Everyone has a role and a place with you except me."[65] Ward is devastated when he realizes how many lives his father has damaged.

The miniseries ends with Salem Bik, who has escaped Syria and broken with the regime, saying on television: "This is a failed regime; a regime that just kills. The Syrian people are great. This is a revolution of people searching for dignity. This regime should step down."[66] In *al-Qurban*, the father figure of Salim Bik represents hypocritical members of the regime who benefit from opposition politics abroad, although they once actively crushed the secular opposition. While the miniseries begins critically, the ending focuses on the corrupt members of the uprising, which appears to be a compromise with the regime narrative.

In *al-Wilada min al-Khasira: Menbar al-Mawta Part Three* (Born from the Loins: Platform of Death, 2013), filmed in Beirut although the events actually took place in Syria, the *mukhabarat* allows the evil security officer, Ra'oof, out of prison to serve as an agent of chaos at the onset of the uprising. After this decision, the decent security officer, Fayez, leaves the *mukhabarat*, declaring that Ra'oof is like a cancer that will spread and destroy their country. During previous seasons of *al-Wilada min al-Khasira* (2011 and 2012), which began with an oppositional political perspective but eventually took a more neutral stance, Ra'oof dreamed of having a son and treated his daughter, Hanin, disrespectfully. In the third season, Ra'oof's dream becomes a reality when Suzanne marries Ra'oof at gunpoint and births their son, Munir, shortly thereafter. Meanwhile, Ra'oof humiliates countless people. Though he is unkind to Hanin, she loves him and adores her baby brother. When the civil war erupts, Hanin participates in demonstrations despite her father's anger; he beats her when she insists on participating. Yet in the midst of the larger story of Syria being devoured by civil war, Ra'oof reveals a different side to his character by nurturing his son.

When Hanin can no longer tolerate her father, she decides to leave with Munir. Shortly after she leaves, a man who was tortured by and seeks revenge on Ra'oof kidnaps them. Ra'oof loses control when he learns that his son is kidnapped, but he does not care what happens to Hanin. In the end, the men kill Munir, knowing that his death will destroy Ra'oof. They throw Hanin a bag with the murdered baby boy inside, which Hanin carries home, then confronts her father: "You killed everyone—you killed all of us—cry—all the black in your heart—that feeling of all the people you killed. All the sons you killed."[67] Ra'oof later goes on a shooting spree. In this miniseries, then, paternity represents overarching themes of reconciliation and revenge and reveals the vicious cycle of violence that occurs when revenge becomes a dominating principle.

The filming of the third season of this politically critical miniseries was not without controversy. During the filming process, the screenwriter, Samer Fahd Ridwan, was arrested as he returned from Beirut to Damascus, accused of failing to seek permission from the censorship committee to produce his miniseries. Shortly after, director Rasha Sharbatji stepped down and Seif al-Din Sba'i assumed the directorial mantle. This replacement resulted in the toning down of the show's political criticism; storylines tended to be more neutral and at times even intersected with the regime narrative. Ultimately, the plot portrayed oppressed citizens as thirsty for revenge and perpetuating violence that could be avoided through reconciliation.[68] Screenwriter Fu'ad Humayra was arrested shortly after he posted this statement in defense of his colleague Ridwan on his Facebook page: "The regime views writer Samer Ridwan as a terrorist. But all he has done is protest the killing, destruction, spying, corruption, deception, hypocrisy of the regime, all of which make him a terrorist in the eyes of the regime. For them, his words are more dangerous than *al-Jabhat al-Nusra*."[69] In my view, Rafi Wahbi's *Halawat al-Ruh* (2014), a story of an estranged Syrian family uprooted by war, serves as a stunning example of the transformational power of art. Constructions of fatherhood in this series accentuate political protests, which Wahbi claims is possible in his script because he lived in Lebanon, far away from Syrian censors.[70] Nevertheless, Wahbi elaborates on the difficulties of production amid war:

> Due to financial troubles and production mishaps, we were still filming *Halawat al-Ruh* until two days before Ramadan ended. We completed filming the last episode just forty-eight hours before Ramadan was over. I was still writing through Ramadan and it was quite an adventure to produce my miniseries. I had hoped that we would complete the filming before the start of Ramadan, but due to budget constraints we had fallen behind. Some actors had to leave and this negatively impacted episodes twenty-nine and thirty. Neither of these final episodes appeared as I had originally written them. Although it aired on Abu Dhabi, like *Sa-Na'ud Ba'da Qalil*, it was not that successful in the commercial sense.[71]

This miniseries, which tried to objectively show all sides of the conflict, also incorporates the topic of waiting and was arguably the most popular of the 2014 season. In this storyline, Sara's Syrian mother, Ruba, has divorced her Egyptian husband, Jamal. During the uprising, Ruba travels to Egypt, and Sara joins Jamal, a media star, in Dubai, hoping he can help establish her career as a journalist. Jamal, however, is so engrossed in his own work that he ignores his daughter. She, in turn, refuses to wait for his attention. She leaves Dubai for Beirut without even informing him, and tells her mother: "I wanted him to hold me, to help me accomplish my dreams. I wanted the scent of a father to surround me. But I didn't even see him."[72] Ruba scolds Jamal, who does not even realize his daughter had gone: "You were never a father to her, or a husband to me. Please just try to be human. Is it that hard to be a human being?"[73]

In Beirut, Sara meets Isma'il, an opposition activist, who asks her to travel with him to Homs to film a group of men who have broken off from both the official Syrian army and the free Syrian army. Rather than fight, they have dedicated their lives to protecting ancient national treasures. Sara calls her parents to ask their advice about the trip. Ruba, who is absorbed in news of the regime's chemical onslaught and a possible U.S. strike, does not answer the phone call. Neither does Jamal, who is occupied with news reporting. Sara decides not to wait for their approval but travel to Homs, where she and Isma'il begin filming. Soon after, jihadists kill the majority of their companions. Isma'il escapes and Sara is held for ransom. When Jamal is sent an internet clip showing that Sara has been kidnapped, Ruba tells him that this is his chance to finally be a father. Jamal communicates with the leading jihadist Sheikh Abu Rabi' and agrees to comes to Syria to film a live interview with him in exchange for Sara's freedom. In a touching scene, Jamal finds Sara in the room in which she has been confined. She touches Jamal's face, grasping for the father she never had.

The importance of emotive fatherhood and a softer *qabaday* is central to this story. Years earlier, Jamal had left his lover, Sara, to fend for herself during a story on the Sabra and Shatilla massacre. Although he became a media star, the residual guilt destroyed his personal life and he was never able to love again. His subsequent marriage to Ruba ended in divorce and his relationship with his daughter lacked meaningful connection. When jihadists kidnap Sara, though, Jamal is given another chance to be a good father. The story's thread about Jamal and his girlfriend Sara parallels the thread about his daughter, Sarah and Isma'il. Unlike Jamal, who behaves in his own self-interest, Isma'il dies for the sake of bringing Sara back safely to Beirut.[74] The story ends with Sara sitting by the waterfront with Ruba, acknowledging that if there were more people like Isma'il, who sacrifice to keep their promises, then Syria would survive the crisis. Here, the dominating principle is reconciliation rather than revenge. Again, fatherhood is an instrument of this point.

FIGURE 3.6 Isma'il (played by Maksim Khalil) (*left*) and Sara (played by Dana Mardini) (*right*) in *Halawat al-Ruh* (Beauty of the Soul).

Courtesy of Rafi Wahbi.

The Ramadan seasons of 2015, 2016, and 2017 saw a contradictory dramatic culture, one that oscillated between escapism and realism. Fatherhood emerged as a dominant theme that evoked nostalgia for prewar life. Whereas in pre-uprising days, fatherhood served as a central means to critique the Ba'th Party regime, now, later seasons witnessed a sense of yearning for life before war. In this construction of collective memory, some writers forgot the regime's history of oppression and focus instead on the tragedy and terrorism unleashed by Da'ish. Others writers acknowledged past oppression but wondered if the uprising was worth the death and destruction it has caused. Still others blamed the corruption of petty employees and businessman, rather than the oppressive political apparatus, for having caused the "crisis."

Let me first begin with miniseries that confronted the war to some degree. Laith Hajjo's *al-Nadam* (Regret, 2016), written by Hassan Sami Yusuf and produced by SAMA, was broadcast on al-Jadid and was based on his novel *'Atabat al-Alam*. The first episode begins with the statement, "I may be wrong, but that does not mean that you are right." The miniseries, written in a nostalgic register, moves back and forth in time. The present is black and white; the past is colorful. The scene opens in 2016 in black and white. The narrator of the miniseries, 'Orwa, a screenwriter, asks how Syrians reached a point of disaster where terrified people run haphazardly in the streets and heavy smoke permeates the air. The narrator queries, "How do we avoid this nightmare? Damascus is the oldest city in the world. We are the oldest and we still sing of Yassamin. Three million Damascus inhabitants now live in other places."

The story centers on Abu 'Abdu, his wife, and children. Abu 'Abdu hails from an impoverished family. When he helps slaughter an animal as a young boy, he acquires a reputation for fearlessness and efficiency. He becomes the most famous butcher in the country and founds his own factory. Now as a father, he behaves like a dictator and crushes his own children. When Nada's fiancé, Hisham, is arrested and tortured, Umm 'Abdu dies and Abu 'Abdu becomes sick. Nada waits for her fiancé but then marries. Once she is married, her fiancé reappears. In another thread, 'Orwa, a novelist and screenwriter, marries a young woman, who later becomes sick. His brother 'Abdu marries a young woman whom he oppresses, while stealing his father's fortune for himself. 'Abdu then becomes a corrupt minister, establishing a shady link to the regime. However, even as the miniseries emphasizes the theme of political injustice, it also emphasizes the theme of regret. The color scheme underscores this dichotomy and suggests that despite oppression and dictatorial authority, life used to be colorful. Regret points to the existence of tragedy: wounded before, the country has been ripped apart by war. At the same time, the word 'regret' might be an innocuous term that would be likely to clear the censors.

Screenwriter Najeeb Nseir asserts that the father figure is inspired by King Lear and so is not entirely original. Likewise, Nseir points out, critiques of corruption are not new to Syrian drama but had been happening for years in prewar storylines. As an added critique, Nseir compares *al-Nadam* to *Bab al-Hara*, both filled with prayer and religious symbolism.[75] Iyad Shihab Ahmad argues that the miniseries' emphasis on regret suggests that, life was better before the war erupted. Thus, in his opinion, this storyline falls into the regime narrative.[76] Haitham Haqqi criticizes the miniseries' explicitly symbolic coloring. Yet, he concedes that perhaps this was a strategy to get past the censors. Haqqi notes that depictions of people fleeing the city during the bombing scenes signal that the government is responsible for the bombs. Thus the writer is indirectly critiquing the government-instigated war. In this way, *al-Nadam* was the most critical miniseries of the season.[77] It was also well received by the press, reviewed as humanistic and complex, involving direct political discussion between the opposition and pro-regime individuals, imprisoned individuals, and the *mukhabarat*. It was also informative, depicting even the security apparatus of the oppression in detail. According to one journalist, "It opened up Syrian wounds—presented the war as a mirror, and allowed us to see layer over layer of wounds.[78] While many of the other miniseries were criticized for lack of depth, *al-Nadam* was seen as a highlight.[79]

On the other hand, *Bila Ghamad* (2016), situated during the uprising, offers a direct governmental perspective, not even attempting neutrality. Here, the father figure, Sheikh Sa'id, ignores his wife and young daughter, who is dying of

FIGURE 3.7 'Orwa (played by Muhammad Nasr) in *al-Nadam* (Regret).
Courtesy of Laith Hajjo.

leukemia. As his friend warns him that his fanaticism will hurt the country, he preaches that the country is abandoning Islam and advocates for a Syrian Islamic state. At the same time as he is neglecting his daughter, he secretly marries another young woman, strikes and then secludes her. A hateful character who rallies people into extremism, his behavior contrasts with that of Majed, who works for the government, serves in the military, and risks his life to protect the citizens. Majed even disguises himself in order to gain entrance into a jihadi cell. Though the character of Sheikh Tawfiq represents moderate Islam, we also see the roots of religious fanaticism, which is a central theme in this season.

Ayyam la Tunsa (2016) begins in 1990 and continues through the uprising. While focusing on individual dictators in the family, the series also explores religious fanaticism and the rise of Da'ish. Its storyline is based largely on Khaled Hosseini's *A Thousand Splendid Suns* (2007), which takes place in Afghanistan during the rise of the Taliban. *Ayyam la Tunsa* occurs in Syria during the bloody war and rise of Da'ish, and features a father figure, Jalal, who is weak and vulnerable. His affair with the servant, Nur, results in her pregnancy. In response, his wife, Malak, the dictator of the family, forces Jalal to divorce Nur and banish her to a secluded place. As the story progresses, the oppressed becomes the oppressor. Because Jalal oppressed Nur, she is subsequently oppressive with her daughter, Mariam, whom she forbids to leave the house or talk to people on her own. Angered by her mother, Mariam runs away to her father, but her illusion that he will provide a more supportive environment for her fades quickly. Under pressure from Malak, he refuses to take her in. When she returns home, she discovers that her mother has drowned herself. Later, Jalal takes Mariam to his home, but is cowardly because of Malak and marries her off to a corrupt religious man. In the meantime, terrorism surrounds them. When Mariam and Laila try to escape the husband, Da'ish members catch them and send them back, even when they insist that they will be beaten up. This miniseries underscores the destruction of the human soul, as victims become victimizers, individuals can't survive outside prison walls, and religious fanaticism accelerates in the midst of the Syria war. The weak father figure cannot combat the oppression in his marriage or the forces of religious tradition and fanaticism around him.

In *Mudhakirat 'Ashiqa Sabiqa* (2017), the idea of paternity is again used to evoke nostalgia. Here 'Abed is not present for his wife, Diala, or his daughter, Talia. Indeed, neither parent is present for Talia. 'Abed defends himself, asserting that he must follow "the laws of war." 'Abed explains to his wife that in war, one is either "the killer or the killed, oppressor or the oppressed."[80] When Diala recovers from a near-fatal shooting due to 'Abed's war trade, she asks for a divorce. 'Abed responds, "I never wanted the war to beat me, and maybe that is what made me lose you and my daughter. I'll do exactly what you are asking for, not because I'm weak."[81] Indeed, 'Abed's inability to be a good father parallels Diala's own inability to be maternal and nurturing. As Diala engages in an affair with Bassel, he too becomes disconnected from his wife and infant son, calling his own paternity into question. Whereas paternity or lack of paternity in pre-uprising miniseries assumed political meaning, from 2015 onward, in miniseries like *Mudhakirat 'Ashiqa Sabiqa*, paternity-related themes are used to evoke nostalgia.

Some dramatic storylines are unrelated to war in Syria except that their storylines engage in an indirect critique of the current bloodshed. In *Lestoo Jariya* (2017), which does not refer to the uprising, a dictatorial father creates a vicious cycle of dictatorship. Ghaleb and his sister grew up with an oppressive father. Ghaleb now oppresses his wife. His sister Muna, a female version of Ghaleb, tyrannizes the men with whom she forms relationships. In one scene, when a man says he loves her, she stops the car and forces him out. In another scene, she stomps on the flowers of young cousins who are staying with her mother. Mona later apologizes to the man she loves, justifying her behavior by explaining that she had herself been oppressed. By the end of the story, Mona has overcome this psychology of oppression. As we will see in the following chapter, this miniseries was viewed in the press as an indirect critique of Da'ish.

Also discussed in the next chapter are Old Damascus tales that relay indirect messages about the current political situation. Hoozan 'Akko's *Bint al-Shah Bandar* (The Daughter of Shah Bandar, 2015), however, gained publicity due to the fact that it was set in Beirut in the 1800s and because it did not have a message related to the current uprising in Syria. Though the majority of the main actors, the director, and the writer were Syrian, it was considered a Lebanese production.[82] ʿAkko wrote the screenplay in 2011 after completing his screenplay *Asʿad al-Waraq*, but no one wanted to sponsor it at the time. Later, when he settled in Lebanon, he rewrote it, focusing on Syrian-Lebanese relations in the late Ottoman period. A Palestinian producer who owns a company in Lebanon bought the miniseries. Though the miniseries was technically a Lebanese production, ʿAkko acknowledges that many in the industry considered it Syrian.[83]

At the beginning of the story, Abu Raghad is the imposing father who stands at odds with his eldest son, Raghad, who has arrogantly cursed the Sultan. The quiet younger son, Zain becomes the chosen one for *zaʿim* in his father's eyes. Though Zain is in love with a young neighborhood woman, his father forces him to marry one of Shah Bandar's daughters. The eldest daughter, Niriman, chooses to be his bride. Devastated, Zain disappears after the marriage, and everyone believes he has died. Raghad then becomes *zaʿim*. Eventually, Raghad finds Zain, who has changed his name to Yusuf and wants distance from his family. Zain/Yusuf insists that his family killed him when they forced him to marry against his will.

During my fieldwork, when I asked ʿAkko if this dictatorial father was a metaphor for a political dictator, he made it clear that he intended no such message and had chosen a story that had nothing to do with the uprising. E. Ann Kaplan, in *Trauma Culture: The Politics of Terror and Loss in Media and Literature* (2005), delineates the importance of nuanced positioning with respect to trauma. The extreme positions of trauma are occupied by those who have lived through the traumatic event and those involved impersonally from afar. In between these poles are various positionalities, including those of people who know trauma victims or absorb aspects of trauma through stories or accounts they have heard.[84] ʿAkko believed that his positionality, far removed from the horrors of war in Syria, delegitimized any attempt at interpretation. "After all," he said, "I sit in the Expresso café in Beirut, writing and living comfortably. What right do I have to impart wisdom on the uprising?"[85]

While all the male characters refer to each other as *qabadayat* in *Bint al-Shah Bandar*, it is not the typical "tough man" miniseries. Indeed, it warns women to refrain from quick judgment. While Niriman judged Raghad as an aggressive *qabaday* who gazed unembarrassedly at her standing in her window, Zaid (who was on his way to visit another young woman) ignored her. Niriman interpreted this behavior to mean that Zaid was respectful, while Raghad had no shame. In the end, she realizes that she misjudged both brothers. Actress Sulafa Meʿmar contends that though *Bint al-Shah Bandar* takes place in 1800, it departs from traditional Old Damascus tales. Specifically, it depicts the relationship between money and power in Beirut when it was separated from the governance of Sham. The producer, Mufeed al-Rifaʿi, contends that it was the best production of the year in terms of the storyline, actors, and production value, that he focused on

FIGURE 3.8 Niriman (played by Sulafa Meʿmar) (*left*) and Shalabiyyeh (played by Dima al-Jundi) (*right*) in *Bint al-Shah Bandar* (The Daughter of Shah Bandar).

Courtesy of Hoozan ʿAkko.

the beauty of the filming, and that its importance arises from the fact that it does not engage the Syrian azmeh. Accordingly, the miniseries was produced without delay by a Gulf State company.[86]

Whether or not storylines were set in the midst of the uprising, some miniseries of the 2018 Ramadan season attempted more radical breaks with the mythology of paternity, as a new collective memory was constructed. While Daʿish is not mentioned and the "crisis" is referred to only subtly, the storyline clearly attempts to establish a secular, liberated culture as opposed to one immersed in religious extremism. This emphasis emerges clearly in the role of fatherhood. ʿAbd al-Majid Haider's *al-Gharib* (The Stranger, 2018), based loosely on Alexandre Dumas's *Comte de Monte Cristo* and inspired by Victor Hugo's *Les Misérables*, never mentions the war, though there are indirect references to the azmeh. Broadcast in January in advance of the season and again during Ramadan on the al-Jadid channel, this storyline presents Kamal Mussalam as an honest government employee with a wife and baby girl. Kamal repudiates any corrupt behavior, but early in the story, is framed by his corrupt brother-in-law, Raʾoof, and found guilty of drug trafficking. After twenty years in prison, he learns that his mother died and his ex-wife has married Raʾoof. As he embarks on a journey to prove his innocence, he discovers not only Raʾoof's current money laundering practices but also the fact that it was Raʾoof who framed him years ago. At the heart of the story are two paradigms for paternal figures: one a liberating mechanism in children's lives (Kamal) and one a form of dictatorship that crushes children's wills (Ra'oof). The storyline features a secular, more liberal culture, where women are not judged and children are encouraged to make their own decisions and accept responsibility for their choices.

Kamal's relationship with his daughter, Yara, fits the affective paternal role. Once reunited, their closeness is exemplary, and they confide in each other as friends. Kamal has no difficulty seeing Yara on campus with her boyfriend, Tareq, and he supports her decision to follow her passion for theater instead of studying medicine, as recommended by her mother. He assures her that he trusts that she will make the right choices and take responsibility for her decisions in her relationship with Tareq. Yara is strong; she encourages her half-sister, Rihan, to remain committed to the man she loves despite family objections. She tells her sister, "When you know you're right, then you won't allow others to raise their voice and force you to do things differently."[87] Kamal, who realizes that he is dying from a sickness he contracted in prison, tells his daughter that he wants her to be strong when he is gone. While Kamal is honest and allows Yara her freedom, Ra'oof is restrictive. He judges her for having a boyfriend and deplores the fact that Kamal is accepting. He calls Yara *feltaneh* to denounce what he sees as "loose" behavior. At the same time, Ra'oof crushes the love interests of his own children, even causing the death of the young woman his son loves.

The stories related to paternity in *al-Gharib* occur within the larger context of a drive for more relaxed social norms. This is evident in Kamal's love story with his ex-wife, Nidal. Years earlier, he divorced her when she doubted his innocence. Then, when she found herself on the streets as a divorced woman, she accepted Ra'oof's marriage proposal. While Kamal's family cuts her off due to her behavior, Kamal understands her desperation and refuses to judge her. Even so, screenwriters 'Abd al-Majid Haider and 'Ala' 'Assaf reveal and criticize a brief moment of hypocrisy when Kamal expresses to his friend that he is hurt that Nidal married another man. His friend responds, "You're always ready to place your mistakes on the shoulder of others rather than take responsibility."[88]

While Da'ish is not referred to directly, the story involves an avowedly secular culture. Likewise, while the uprising is not directly named, scattered references to the azmeh evince a nostalgia for the security of previous times. For instance, Kamal unveils Ra'oof's money laundering business, which he blames as the cause of the azmeh. Sahar, Tareq's older sister, tells Kamal, "I wish there were more people like you, who think of others first. If that were the case, we would not be where we are now."[89] Kamal repeatedly expresses his desire to protect the country. Yet, at the same time, the story sends mixed messages. Despite the push for more liberal social norms, the idea of "ghalta" (a mistake, referring to sexual relations outside the framework of marriage) still predominates. The storyline continually emphasized that a "ghalta" should be avoided as when, at one point, Sahar tells Kamal that she had made a mistake, "ghalta," with Ra'oof, when she had found herself responsible for raising her brother and sisters and had searched for a means of survival. She continually beseeches Kamal to forgive her, but he expresses his bafflement. He wonders why he needs to forgive her, since he is not her father or brother. Still, while Kamal is baffled, he never states clearly that there is no reason to judge her.

Mixed messages regarding women's sexual conduct are present in other narrative threads throughout miniseries. Tareq blames Sahar when their younger sister disappears, revealing his obsession with honor and shame. At the same time, we see Tareq's hypocrisy: he slept with a former girlfriend one night while in a relationship with Yara, yet his younger sister's innocence is of such vital importance that when Ra'oof dishonors her, Tareq kills him in a fit of rage. Kamal takes responsibility for the crime, sending Tareq away and allowing himself to be imprisoned again. When Tareq admits the truth to Yara, though, she tells him to turn himself in and prove her father's innocence. Later, Tareq turns himself in to the police, admitting that he committed an honor crime. Thus, while the issue of honor and shame occurs in this storyline, it falls within the context of a new, secular culture, one imbued with nostalgia for the past.

The emphasis on the independence of the individual and freedom from paternal dictatorship is manifested in the story of Mustafa, Ra'oof's illegitimate son. When Ra'oof discovers his son, he offers to support him financially and give him his name. Mustafa rebuffs his corrupt father, protesting angrily, "I don't need anything from you. I don't need anyone to acknowledge me."[90] In the past, oppressive paternity symbolized regime dictatorship, and a more liberal paternal model served as a metaphor for a democratic political order. However, in *al-Gharib* this is not the case. The shift uproots the myth of fatherhood as it follows the trend toward the construction of a secular collective memory. There are no references to the current war, only the occasional mention of an azmeh. Additionally, corruption and dishonesty are at fault for the azmeh, rather than the Ba'th Party regime.

Other recent miniseries ignore the azmeh, uprising, and rise of Da'ish altogether as they attempt to reconfigure paternity according to a new, secular collective identity. Iyad Abu Shammat's *Tango* (2018) is loosely based on a seventy-episode miniseries from Argentina, and avoids the mixed messages of *al-Gharib*. In this miniseries, which falls into the social for the sake of the social strand, the war in Syria is evident only by a few references, such as when a friend brings 'Amer sweets from Syria or when 'Amer tells his wife that they need to work hard now that they are living in Lebanon. The connection between masculinity and fatherhood is evident in the storyline of police detective, Jad, who faces a marital crisis with his wife, Samar, who is not interested in giving him the baby he so desires. His crisis of masculinity becomes so acute that at one point he suspects she is having an affair, barges into the apartment, and strikes her.

Indeed, new configurations of paternity are the heart of *Tango*'s storyline. Sami's realization that his deceased wife, Farah, had an affair during his marriage injures his masculinity to the degree that he questions the legitimacy of his infant son, Shadi. He angrily refuses to raise another man's son and requests a DNA test. Yet he soon abandons his pride and continues to devote himself to being Shadi's father. He even refuses to get a DNA test when the child's relatives demand it. During this new cultural configuration, the fact that Sami's wife had sex with another man, as well as the fact that he may be raising another man's child, no longer bruises his masculinity. Indeed, we soon learn that he knew all along that Shadi was not his son. To avoid losing Shadi, he runs off with him, tearfully confiding to his friend Lina, "But I was the first to hold, bath, dress, and feed him. I stayed up late with him when he was sick. I was the first who dreamed of his future and I hoped to give him a life better than what I had lived."[91] Sami later emerges from his hideout and hands Shadi over to police custody for the DNA test. As viewers, we experience his bond with his son, even though there is no biological connection. The story's message is that Sami is Shadi's father even though he has no literal paternity.

An essential component of the storyline is that while Sami is depicted as an exemplary father, women in the miniseries—such as Lina and Farah—are not portrayed as exceptional mothers. Lina often leaves her son unaccompanied at home, and Farah often leaves her son with Sami so that she can spend time with her lover. However, these portrayals of women are not intended as critique. Rather, the nuances and complexities of women shown in the motherhood role resist essentialized notions of motherhood and fatherhood and thus open the potential for new configurations of gender and marriage norms.

In *Fawda* (2018) Najeeb Nseir challenges traditional notions of paternity and masculinity in various storylines set in the midst of the chaos of war and serves as one of the most innovative, avant-garde miniseries in the social for the sake of the social strand. This latest setting contradicts his previous stance of avoiding the current upheaval in his screenplays. He asserts, "As a screenwriter if I'm going to film my miniseries in Syria today, it isn't possible to ignore the war. Miniseries that place their storylines in current day Syria and disregard our current reality, alienate the viewer and fail to impart a message."[92] In this storyline, Zeidan is so in love with Fethiyyeh that he has no problem raising her child (who he thinks is his missing brother's child) as his own. Initially, his sense of masculinity is insulted when Fethiyyeh describes the passion she and Fares, his brother, felt for each other. Yet he quickly comes to terms with the situation, rips up her marriage contract with Fares, and marries her. Here, Nseir deconstructs the importance of biological fatherhood, erasing its inherent link to masculinity. This storyline also deconstructs the towering myth of marital law, which is reduced to a piece of paper that can be ripped apart and thrown away.

In another storyline in *Fawda*, a young woman, Dana, dreams of finding her father, who divorced her mother and disappeared from their lives when she was just eleven years old. She tells her ailing mother, "My life is ruined without him. I want my dad to protect me. I want someone who'll be responsible for me."[93] Her mother laughs sarcastically at her daughter's false expectations of her absent father. In this way, too, Nseir deconstructs the myth of fatherhood. On another occasion, Dana lashes out at her mother, who has fallen in love with another man. Her mother breaks into tears, "For the first time I feel I'm a woman. Your father left. I hope you find him. Go and see for yourself who he is and how oppressed I was with him."[94] Here, the absent father figure, mythologized in Dana's eyes, symbolizes an oppressive force that stifles her mother's newfound chance to love. At the same time, his absence allows for Dana's independence, self-confidence, and freedom of movement.

DRAMAS OF THE PRE- AND POST-UPRISING engaged in multifaceted discourses of fatherhood. These discourses are inherently linked with the rise and fall of the *qabaday* and fervently portray its impact on love relations. Prior to the uprising, while the avowed focus was on interpersonal, intimate relationships in society—specifically, constructions of gender and metaphors about marriage and love—in truth, politics lay at the heart of the messages.[95] Soon after the uprising, reformulations of the *qabaday* took place against the backdrop of politics (both pro- and anti-regime), which became much more pronounced and direct in the storylines. In this chapter I argued that, in actuality, the rise and fall of the *qabaday* took place twice prior to the uprising. First, this occurred when the *qabaday*'s aggressive nature won out over the more generous, noble aspect of masculinity; the second occurrence was when writers reconstructed a gentle, emotive masculinity that replaced aggressiveness. After the 2011 uprising, according to Haitham Haqqi, those displaying combative, aggressive behavior were no longer referred to as *qabadayat* but rather as *shabbih*.[96]

Post-uprising transitional miniseries in 2011 and 2012, such as *al-Sarab* and *Mishwar al-Tariq*, which made no reference to the uprising, showed that fatherhood that is not concerned with protecting a woman's sexuality is the foundation of a democratic political order.[97] These fatherhood metaphors continued in a long line of sexual metaphors used as political critique and movingly functioned to undermine dictatorship during the first two years of the uprising. Some miniseries during the 2013 and 2014 Ramadan season portrayed fatherhood's impact on intimate relations within the context of the uprising. These storylines prioritized individual experiences rather than the dynamics between a less patriarchal father who no longer regulated his daughter's sexual identity. The eradication of the "wall of fear" as well as the refusal to wait any longer were recurring themes in some of these storylines.

The rise of jihadist influences and Da'ish in 2013 changed storylines, as many screenwriters increasingly worked to portray a culture distinct from a culture of religious extremism. These shifts often played into the regime narrative, as seen in Anzour's three-episode story "'Aziza min Baba 'Amru." By 2015, the violent presence of Da'ish crystalized into a strong sense of nostalgia for a prewar past, and fatherhood was often instrumentalized to evoke this nostalgia. As war and destruction intensified in Syria from 2015 onward, storylines continued to be marked by the deletion of past oppression and the perception of Da'ish and conservative social norms as the new enemy. Indeed, some storylines in the 2018 season no longer called out the dictator as paternal figure but deconstructed the myth of paternity altogether as part of the process of constructing a new, secular collective identity. Yet the regime narratives and nostalgic register, as well as neutral strands, must be distinguished from the social for the sake of the social strand, which had no political agenda. In a case like *Fawda*, we can sense that the screenwriter feels empathy for the uprising. However, the central focus in *Fawda* is the liberation of the female body in a war-torn society with problematic social norms. Whereas in previous miniseries such as pre-uprising *Zaman al-'Ar* and *al-Sarab* Nseir used sexuality to show that freer sexual norms symbolized a free, democratic political order, *Fawda* can be categorized as social for the sake of the social, documenting the need for a cultural revolution to reform society itself.

Certainly, fatherhood continues to serve a key role in Syrian drama. This is true specifically in the 2019 miniseries *Turjuman al-Ashwaq*, originally slated to appear in 2018 and delayed because political opposition expressed in the text forced drama creators to make changes before the 2019 season.[98] Here, Najeeb, having left Syria years earlier due to his oppositional politics, returns to Damascus during the uprising when his daughter, Anna, is kidnapped. This absent father's search to discover his daughter symbolizes his search to reunite with Syria. Though she is killed by Da'ish, she appears to Najeeb in a hallucination, telling him, "Don't leave Damascus. I'm like Damascus. Don't leave me."[99] Or consider *Musafat Aman*, the story of Sarab, whose husband, Jalal, immigrates to Germany and lives with another woman. He returns to Damascus only when his daughter, Rawan (who left her mother's house in anger), contacts him to say that his absence has destroyed her mother and made her completely unapproachable. When Jalal returns unexpectedly and inquires about Rawan, Sarab retorts, "All these years you have been gone and now you want to play the part of an exemplary father?"[100] In both series, the absent father figure returns to Damascus in search of his daughter, who, to a certain extent, represents Damascus; thus the father figure is positioned as protector of Damascus.

4

The Politics of Love and Desire in Post-Uprising Syrian and Transnational Arab Television Drama

Sham refuses to follow her mother's traditionally gendered advice: withhold sex before marriage to increase a man's desire. Her mother warns that she risks being discarded by the man if she gives in to his longing. "Are we at war?" the baffled young woman asks.[1] As their love develops, Mansour struggles to accept that he and Sham have the right to experience premarital sex. In the end, his conservative mind-set wins. He dumps Sham, with whom he had shared harmonious love and seduction rituals, to marry Dima, who chose not to have sex before marriage. Yet their union is sexually incompatible, and he cannot consummate the marriage on their wedding night. The story ends with a frustrated Mansour running through the streets in the direction of a brokenhearted Sham while his confused and pregnant wife looks on in confusion.

The failure of the central love story in the Syrian television series *Nisa' min Hadha al-Zaman* (Women of the Time) traces a lover's emotional struggle in a country being destroyed from within and from outside. The series, produced by the Syrian company Qabnad, aired in spring 2014 on MBC 1 in advance of the Ramadan season. Filmed in Damascus, the thirty-three-episode miniseries grapples with many controversial Syrian familial issues. The show's writer, Buthaina 'Awad, and director, Ahmad Ibrahim Ahmad, address taboo topics such as premarital sex, masturbation, menstruation, and the imported hymen wrap women use to fake virginity on the wedding night. Prior to the 2011 uprising and the "fallen wall of fear," several miniseries tackled heterosexual love and seduction. *Nisa' min Hadha al-Zaman*, however, was more radical in exploring a man's layered internal struggle with traditional social values and critiquing male sexual privilege. It also allowed viewers to observe intimate moments between lovers.

The miniseries takes place in Syria three years into an uprising that has tipped over into civil war and portrays relationships as private, gendered battles for power between men and women. While some of the stories seem exaggerated, the strongest moment is located within Sham and Mansour's intimate love story. His shifting philosophical positions along with close-ups of both Mansour's sinister and tender facial expressions and shots of him holding Sham reveal his inner struggle, since he loves Sham and yet is obsessed with her sexual past. As her lover acts hesitant and judgmental, Sham steadfastly refuses to allow either social norms or her mother's bitter past to guide her actions. Her ultimate self-destruction is a testament to the dangers of falling in love. It also bears witness to the centrality of the body in social critique. This emphasis on the body contrasts with the use of gender and marriage metaphors for political critique that characterized pre- and early-uprising miniseries.

In her seminal book *Sexuality and War: Literary Masks of the Middle East*, Evelyne Accad perceived issues related to sexuality at the heart of problems in the Middle East and called for a revolution that sought a fundamental change in traditional relations of male supremacy in sexual and familial relations. Through analysis of Lebanese literature during the civil war, she argued that both male and female novelists linked sexuality and war. Both men and women connected sexuality and women's oppression, yet while women searched for alternatives, male writers adhered to historically accepted models.[2] In *The Politics of Love*, I argued that, blossoming amid persistent authoritarianism, pre-uprising *musalsalat* written by both men and women served as an invaluable artistic venue through which political and social opposition reveals the deceit of official Syrian regime narratives. Some screenwriters showed that it is only when the *qabaday* sheds himself of the role as protector of a woman's sexuality that a free Syria could emerge.[3]

Narratives were destined to change when, on March 6, 2011, twelve schoolchildren were arrested and tortured for writing graffiti demanding the downfall of Bashar al-Asad's regime. Their treatment incited a national uprising. Transitional miniseries of 2011 and 2012, many of which were written and filmed before the regime's brutal response to the uprising, continued to use gender metaphors as political critique without referring to the current violence on the ground. As shown in chapter 3, the critique of the *qabaday*, who repressed women's sexual desire, persisted as an indirect critique of dictatorship in Syria prior to the uprising and during the first two years.

Led by Abu Bakr al-Baghdad, Da'ish (ISIS) was formed in 2013 out of al-Qaeda in Iraq and soon went on to capture large swaths of territory in eastern Syria. A terrorist organization specializing in guerilla warfare, it flaunted public beheadings, rape, and barbaric gender laws. In 2014 the uprising became a civil war. Concurrently, a transition occurred in Syrian drama with the advent of pan-Arab, escapist genres such as *al-Ikhweh*. Although very little flesh is shown on screen due to conservative Gulf State production stipulations, sex is no longer taboo, since the use of sex helps screenwriters disassociate themselves from religious extremism. Alongside those escapist narratives are stories like *Nisa' min Hadha al-Zaman* that are set against the background of war and radically dismantle traditional gender norms without using these storylines as metaphors of political critique. Though this is not true of pre-uprising drama, post-uprising dramas that outwardly embraced the regime narrative, as well as those that may also have sympathized with the uprising, increasingly focused on social norms rather than political critique in relation to love and sexuality in their storylines.

By 2015, as Da'ish's terrorism and religious extremism became more predominant in Syria's civil war, another transition occurred in Syrian television drama. In two miniseries during this time, female bodies symbolizing the nation are conspicuously unburdened of the need for male protection. These miniseries, *Ghadan Naltaqi* (We'll Meet Tomorrow) and *Bi-Intizar al-Yasmin* (Waiting for Jasmin), depict sex workers or rape victims as simultaneously pure despite the violence of their treatment and ultimately as representative of an assaulted Syria. These miniseries show rape from the outside, meaning the symbolic rape of Syria by outside powers, as well as rape from within, meaning the literal rape of women by internal war profiteers. These narratives, which present an implicit or explicit pro-regime stance, seek to differentiate a progressive Syria from its radical Islamic other.

Through a close textual analysis of several miniseries prior to the uprising as well as a close reading of a full range of post-2011 miniseries, interviews, and periodicals, this chapter shows that at the outset of the uprising, Syrian miniseries offered coded messages about the correlation between freedom, dignity, and relationships based on sexual equality. Several years into the uprising, however, the discourses became more complicated as television miniseries critiqued not only the political order but also the bloody civil war. Nostalgia left its mark too, as sexuality reflected critiques of an impotent Syria, escapist love stories, and narratives of resilience around assaulted women. This chapter shows how post-uprising television miniseries overcame stagnant models of national honor and provided multifaceted spaces for recreating social ties. While prior to the uprising these gender, sexuality, and marriage metaphors served as methods of engaging in political critique, increasingly in the uprising turned civil war, the social for the sake of the social and nostalgic strands predominated alongside miniseries that catered to an unabashed regime narrative.

The Rise and Fall of the *Qabadat* as Protector of Female Sexuality

As shown in chapter 3, at the advent of Syrian drama in the mid-1960s politically engaged writers such as Nihad Qal'i and Muhammad al-Maghut focused on territorial loss and economic discontent as the main causes of man's lost honor. Throughout the 1960s and 1970s, "weak masculinity" symbolized man's oppression at the hands of the regime. The depiction of a male character such as Ghawwar al-Tawsheh dominating a woman symbolized a vicious cycle of state violence that caused vulnerable men to lash out with violence. At the same time, screenwriters did not fixate on women's sexual transgressions as sources of family dishonor. As the Ba'th Party became further entrenched and men were increasingly politically marginalized, though, Syrian drama increasingly portrayed male aggression toward women who deviate from social norms.[4] This continually changing issue should not be conflated with the stagnant perception of the Middle Eastern honor-shame complex that has been so popular among Orientalists seeking to denigrate and "other" the Muslim world.[5] Through the years, screenwriters' depiction of the *qabaday* as simultaneously less and less able to provide for his family and assert power over his womenfolk worked as a critique of authority outside the family. From 2000 onward the increasing emphasis on the *qabaday*'s role of protecting a woman's sexuality and repressing her desire has symbolized the vicious cycle of state violence toward its citizens.[6] In the 2010 miniseries *Abu Janti*, the central character, Abu Janti, is a content albeit poor man who drives someone else's taxi for a living. His optimism wanes as his misfortunes multiply. As he loses power outside the home, he seeks hegemonic masculinity over his sister, 'Awaf. Consequently, when he hears her on the phone with her love interest, he calls her a "slut" (*feltaneh*) and belts her.[7]

Representations of masculinity in Syrian drama from the 1960s onward primarily spoke to state and regime legitimacy rather than cultural authenticity. At the same time, anxiety over Western cultural imperialism and its role in Syrian identity formation is central to postcolonial discourses.[8] Coinciding with Bashar al-Asad's ostensible reforms, Syrian family dramas from 2000 onward pushed further in social and political critique. Women during this time were sites for both upholding and dismantling taboos as well as constructing Arab women's identity in contrast to an immoral and predatory West. As was the case with secular progressives in Egypt, many screenwriters argued for a moral modernity that distinguished itself from the West by rejecting what was perceived as the sexual immorality and individualism of the Western paradigm.[9] The yet more revolutionary trends of Syrian *musalsalat* seek to overcome this East-West dichotomy. These miniseries demonstrate that the *qabaday*'s disavowal of his role as sexual repressor is necessary for gender egalitarianism, which resonates with citizens attaining their dignity from an authoritarian order. Indeed, for these contemporary drama creators, the sexual repression of women symbolizes the political oppression of an entire population.[10]

In Syrian drama prior to 2011, writers such as Najeeb Nseir, Yam Mashhadi, and Muhammad al-'Oss often portrayed seduction rituals as rooted in unequal power struggles. A woman sharing her body with a lover outside marriage risks the end of a relationship and even death. Miniseries such as *Sirat al-Hubb* (A Portrait of Love, 2008), *Zaman al-'Ar* (A Time of Shame, 2009), *Qa' al-Madina* (Lower Parts of the City, 2009), and *Taht al-Medas* (Trampled Upon, 2009) tackled the issue of honor crimes. In *Taht al-Medas*, 'Afaf's fiancé forces her to have sex with him. After he dies, she runs away so that her premarital sex will not be uncovered. When her brother finds her in hiding, he kills her. According to screenwriter Merwan Qawuq, known for his conservatism, this miniseries revealed the dangerous temptations of long engagements.[11]

Alongside this traditional notion of masculinity, other miniseries deconstructed the *qabaday*. As a softer male figure emerged as a metaphor for a more pluralistic political order, some screenwriters examined women's rights to equally access love and sex. Khalifa's *Zaman al-Khawf* explores the breaking of taboos, discussed in the context of paternity in the preceding chapter. Zeezee, for example, broke from patriarchy when she had a highly visible love affair with an older professor and refused to hide the affair from her family. Her affair, as well as her refusal to listen to her parents, was depicted as natural. Hazar is widowed when her poet husband Najeeb dies. Najeeb's best friend, George, tells Hazar that she has been a symbol to him. She responds that she does not want to be a symbol; she is a woman with human feelings.[12] Many years later she has a love affair with Jalal, who is much younger. They travel to Beirut together but she refuses to accompany him to Paris, instead returning to Damascus. Later, she has a love affair with George, which breaks another taboo. At the end of miniseries, Saddam has invaded Kuwait. Many characters experience existentialist crises due to the fact that one Arab country has occupied another Arab country.

In *Zaman al-Khawf*, sexual freedom is associated with the unseating of dictatorship. Zahra, on the other hand, becomes controlled by *qubaysiyyat* religious groups and thinks that her body's physical needs are sinful. In an important scene, Zeezee is hosting a graduation party and Zahra refuses to join the fun. Instead, she dances erotically in front of a mirror, getting lost in the music she hears and touching herself. Then she cries, overwhelmed with guilt.[13] In the next scene Zahra is back in her women's prayer group. One young woman says she had a friend who "gave everything to her neighbor." He then left her to be with another woman and now her friend is no longer a "girl" (meaning virgin). Another man has asked for her friend's hand in marriage, but she is not sure what to tell her family. She fears that they may slaughter her. At the same time, she does not want to marry under false pretenses and burn in the fires of hell.[14] Thus, for Khaled Khalifa sexual freedom means political freedom and escape from bondage; he focuses on the psychology of those who choose bondage.

In chapter 1 I showed how in *Zaman al-'Ar* (2009) screenwriter Najeeb Nseir foregrounds political corruption, as opposed to a woman's sexuality, as a source of shame. While he originally wrote that the veiled Buthaina had an extramarital with her neighbor Jamil, his Syrian producer, under pressure from their GCC counterpart, compelled him to revise the plot so that the sexual relationship occurred within a legitimate but secret marriage.[15] This pressure reveals discomfort with the legitimacy of a woman's sexual desire outside the framework of marriage. Yam Mashhadi's *Takht Sharqi* (2010) also explores unequal sexual standards in Syria through the recurring trope of the half-foreign woman. Adding a Western component to the Syrian woman's identity allows screenwriters to overcome negative judgments toward "sexually liberated" Western women and also to question this clash of cultures.[16] In this miniseries, Mashhadi examines the way sexual taboos indelibly shape relationships between men and women. For example, Greta, born of a German mother and Syrian father, is honest in her relationship with Tareq. She recounts previous lovers, laughs wildly, and makes a conscious choice to sleep with him. In turn, he falls prey to social norms, disrespects her, and doubts her suitability to mother his children.

Director Rasha Sharbatji portrays the sexual nature of the relationship between the two characters in scenes in which the pair appear under wrinkled silk covers, haphazardly pulling on their clothes on when her father comes home early. Actress Sulafa Me'mar contends that her character, Greta, expresses her feelings honestly and is not afraid of social taboos. While some fans criticized their premarital sex, Me'mar insists that drama must be explicit, since sex is an important part of intimate relationships.[17] Nevertheless, Tareq's need to possess Greta and his chronic jealousy nearly destroys his lover. After he discovers that she has not thrown away a box of mementos from past lovers, she cries out, "You made me what you wanted. You transformed me into girl who lies in order to hide things; a girl imprisoned in her home so her jealous lover won't get upset. You turned me into a lonely girl who can't choose."[18] In this final fight, he says he never trusted her. She retorts that he isn't able to trust himself. When he insists that he was trying to turn her into "a respectable woman in this country," she slaps him and he walks away. By exposing the double standards regarding a woman's sexuality, Mashhadi calls for a softer *qabaday*.

The 2011 season began on July 31 in the midst of an extraordinary turnout of protesters, which the regime brutally repressed. Several of this season's miniseries, written before the uprising, painted portraits of love and seduction from various standpoints, poignantly illustrating how it is simpler to explore masculinity, even different layers of masculinity, than to represent contradictory ideas about femininity, given that women are both the object of desire and expected to uphold unrealistic standards of purity. One miniseries, *al-Ghufran* (Pardon), broadcast on a Dubai satellite channel, offers an alternative and more egalitarian understanding of financial responsibility.[19] In this storyline 'Azza decides to marry Anjam even though he does not have the means to be the sole breadwinner of the household. In order to alleviate the financial burden and demonstrate her commitment, 'Azza gives up her *muqaddam* and *mu'akhar*.[20] Yet Anjam reads these choices as indicating that there is something wrong with 'Azza. *Al-Ghufran* affectingly shows that just became a man is able to shed his financial responsibilities and is given the opportunity to have a more nurturing, emotive role does not mean that he will stop acting as protector of a woman's sexuality. Indeed, when 'Azza embarks on an extramarital relationship that is alluded to, but not shown, on-screen, Anjam is unable to forgive her, even when she repents. The writer, too, does not pardon her. She covers herself with a veil, enters a loveless union, and pleads for God's forgiveness.

Another miniseries, al-Sarab, explores secrecy in intimate relationships through the lens of a woman who is half foreign. Al-Sarab's writers, Najeeb Nseir and Hassan Sami Yusuf, present the varied consequences of speaking openly about past sexual encounters. Rana, who is half Russian and half Syrian, tells Hossam, "The Arab woman isn't supposed to have feelings. When she does, she is vilified. What—only men have hormones? Here I am, just me, in front of you. Do you want me to be Arab or Russian?"[21] Hossam's true stance emerges when he discovers Rana is not a virgin on their wedding night. She explains that she could have undergone an operation to repair her hymen, but refused to base their marriage on a lie. Despite her instance that she made this "mistake" (ghalta) when she was a teenager long before they met, Hossam is unable to accept that he is not the first man in her life. Hossam's friend Fares critiques him, "The problem isn't with Rana, it's with you. You want to be a qabaday. We—Arabs— deep inside are against love (al-hubb). But love isn't a crime."[22] Fares later says, "Look at us Arabs. If we go to Europe, we can marry a woman who has had five relationships before. But if we take an Arab girl, she needs to be pure."[23] Hossam and Rana separate, but the ending leaves room for reconciliation. The story aligns with Nseir's philosophy that men and women face the same standards when it comes to premarital sex.[24]

Other miniseries from the 2011 season, which also do not refer to the uprising, offer an ever-more critical position on sex and social taboos in Syria. Fadi Qoshaqji's Ta'b al-Mishwar challenges the notion that female sexuality serves as the marker separating East from West. In this miniseries, when Homam declares his love for Ghorub, she immediately tells him about her previous sexual relationships. He contends that it is fine that she has experienced sexual intimacy since he considers her a foreigner (she has lived abroad in the United States for twelve years). She retorts that she is a Syrian woman. Throughout the story, Homam struggles with Ghorub's previous sexual experiences. Despite the criticisms of neighbors, Homam visits Ghorub's apartment often, but there are no sex scenes between them. The only intimacy is conversation. Ghorub's sexual activity in previous relationships does not extend into her relationship with Homan.

The 2012 drama season began with the bombing by the Free Syrian Army of the National Security Building in which three of Asad's inner circle were killed. This marked the start of the war between the Free Syrian Army and government forces in Aleppo. With the death toll rising daily, the Ramadan season that took place from mid-July to mid-August was considered one of the bloodiest months of the uprising to date. Laith Hajjo directed Urwah 'Ariya (2012), which was produced by Syriana and Clacket and does not refer directly to the uprising. In deconstructing traditional female gender roles and exposing the hypocrisy of the *qabaday*'s norms regarding honor and shame, screenwriter Fadi Qoshaqji challenges the Syrian dictatorial order. Rather than directly addressing the upheaval, Qoshaqji offers a trenchant critique of the injustice of love and marriage in Syria. This sidelong critique of political injustice echoes those of the avant-garde pre-uprising miniseries.[25] In *Urwah ʿAriya* Ruba has had several extramarital affairs before she meets Salah. Though he is merely her friend, Salah struggles to accept Ruba's past infidelity, since it indicates that she is impure. Ruba herself refers to her "dirty past" (*al-madi al-wasaq*). Eventually, Salah forgives her. Soon, Ruba openly expresses her love (*hubb*) and desire (*ʿishq*) for Salah, and gradually begins to believe she deserves love despite her past "mistakes." However, her past escapades are depicted within the storyline as a *ghalta* she made within an abusive marriage.

In the current storyline, though Ruba and Salah are shown holding each other and sleeping in the same bed, they do not have sex. The idea is that she has repented. Their story contrasts with the story of Anjam and Nadia, Ruba's only friend who does not judge her. The first sex scene between Anjam and Nadia occurs after a tearful Anjam expresses his despair over his fruitless search for his biological father. Nadia holds Anjam and the scene ends. In the next scene we see Anjam in the living room, his shirt unbuttoned. She exits the bedroom and looks at him with concern, afraid that he may now break up with her. He reassures her that their intimacy has made them one and that he will not judge her. Though the sexual act takes place behind the scenes, the couple discuss sex openly, a shift from typical storylines. Ultimately, though, Anjam arbitrates morality, making the decision for both of them that their relationship is acceptable.

Though they do not allude directly to the uprising, the above miniseries communicate messages about the dignity and freedom that result from relationships based on sexual equality. Specifically, the *qabaday* attains true manhood only after he allows for a woman's sexual independence. However, with the exception of the relationship between Nadia and Anjam in *Urwah ʿAriya*, none of these miniseries explored a current, openly sexual premarital relationship. Instead, they question a woman's past "mistakes" or, as in the case of ʿAzza, an indiscretion arising from a marital crisis. The main point of *al-Sarab, Taʿab al-Mishwar*, and *Urwah ʿAriya* is that women's extramarital sexual behavior should be forgiven in the same way men's "mistakes" are forgiven so they can move on with their lives. On the other hand, *al-Ghufran* takes a more condemnatory position on woman's sexual choices, since ʿAzza serves penance for her mistake. Although these screenwriters appear to pose premarital sexual relations as potentially equitable, the female body is nevertheless a dangerous site of seduction. The control of sexuality through the tool of forgiveness or penance ultimately positions women as subjects of male authority.

Ramadan 2014: New Directions

In her edited collection on trauma, Cathy Caruth contends that trauma "does not simply serve as record of the past but precisely registers the force of an experience that is not yet fully owned."[26] According to Caruth, traumatic recollection does not constitute simple memory. Indeed, it is characterized by its inability to access the past. She goes on to argue that "the transformation of trauma into narrative memory that allows the story to be verbalized and communicated, to be integrated into one's own, and others' knowledge of the past, may lose both the precision and the force that characterizes traumatic recall."[27] Caruth maintains that the unattainability of a story does not indicate the negation of a "transmissible truth."[28] Some critics have adamantly dismissed Caruth's insistence on the "unrepresentability" of trauma. For instance, while E. Ann Kaplan argues for a nuanced understanding of the phenomena of dissociation and generational transmission of drama, she believes that representations of trauma can at times allow for a "working through," a shared understanding that can be invaluable in the healing process.[29]

Rafi Wahbi's *Helawat al-Ruh*, deemed the most popular miniseries of the 2014 Ramadan season, evokes love as a central theme and shows the invaluable nature of this "working through" process described by Caruth. The story takes place amid bloodshed. Dramatic scenes bear close resemblance to daily scenes of war on news channels. Yet love blossoms between journalist and documentary filmmaker Sara and Isma'il, a young man in the opposition who convinces her to travel with him to Homs to film a group of men protecting ancient Syrian treasures. He promises to bring her back safely to Beirut and she agrees. When jihadists kidnap Sara and hold her for ransom, it is Isma'il's love for her that leads to her safety, as he willingly gives up his life for her. In the last episode, Sara tells her mother that if there were more people like Isma'il who remain committed to their promises, Syria would be able to overcome its current tragedy. In a June 2014 interview in Beirut, Rafi Wahbi said,

> In my own miniseries, I am also trying to call upon love, to inspire the individual to return to their core emotions. In my storylines, love is not just love, but a nationalistic project. Since I am based in Beirut, my stories are also able to bypass the Syrian censors, and thus, I am able to be honest and direct in my sociopolitical critique. . . . I believe that we screenwriters cannot ignore the death and destruction that is happening in Syria, and we have to talk about it since it has affected us all. As I said before, Syrian drama has been distinguished for talking about the details of daily life. You can't write a miniseries and pretend that there is no bloodshed, war, and injustice ravaging Syria now. And so, I create a love story, such as *Halawat al-Ruh* and connect it to what is happening now in Syria.

In this section, I focus on two Ramadan 2014 miniseries, set in Damascus and Dubai, whose stories explore the politics of love, seduction, and marriage, in one case through representation of war and the other through complete escapism. *Nisa' min Hadha al-Zaman*, which began this chapter, takes place against the ravaging background of war and reveals faulty love and seduction rituals (*al-mujtama'*). Thus, "society is sick" (*al-mujtama' maridh*) and unable to cure itself. This illness has led to the current azmeh—a term that cultural producers use to depict the current political upheaval in Syria. In contrast to previous miniseries, the love relations at the heart of this miniseries are metaphors for broader turmoil, rather than being critiques of the Ba'th regime. 'Awad and Ahmad perceive any solution that will end the destruction as necessarily emerging from a reform of social norms within Syria. The cultural producers writing and directing the show, all of whom were residing in Syria at the time, blame social norms rather than the dictatorship of Bashar al-Asad for the current "crisis."

The second miniseries, *al-Ikhweh*, takes place in a transnational space, Abu Dhabi, and thereby distances itself from Syrian national culture and events. Escapist in philosophy, the story makes no reference to the uprising. Adapted liberally from a Chilean telenovela, *Hijos del Monte* (2008–2009), the miniseries consists of 116 episodes filled with love, betrayal, and sex. Its codirectors, Seif al-Din Sbai'i and Seif al-Sheikh Najeeb, hoped the show would break the Turkish telenovela's hold on the market. In this telenovela, influenced by new market constraints on Syrian drama producers, sex is no longer taboo and seduction is no longer dangerous, though it is, ironically, less revealing than Syrian series of the time. The miniseries generated a buzz, and numerous articles featured interviews with the actors from *al-Ikhweh*.[30]

Nisa' min Hadha al-Zaman: The Dangers of Love and Reform from Within

Screenwriter Buthaina 'Awad, who is also a journalist based in Syria, praised *Nisa' min Hadha al-Zaman*'s director, Ahmad Ibrahim Ahmad, who worked closely with 'Awad during the writing process.[31] Ahmad, who made a splash in 2010 with *L a'nat al-Tin* (Curse of the Clay), did not know 'Awad prior to her debut script. He stated, "She first gave me one hundred pages, and I liked the story. She kept writing and sending me another hundred pages. I told her what needed development and we discussed themes. I consider myself an artistic supervisor and always work closely with writers on their scripts." According to Ahmad, despite the azmeh, life continues: "True art requires a concentration that is impossible to achieve now. Yet, despite the tough conditions of filming, drama continues to thrive and people are still watching. Our audience always craves something new, and our viewers felt the miniseries was new in that it dealt with personal issues such as a woman's menstruation cycle or China-manufactured virginal membranes, which were not spoken of in Syrian drama before."[32]

Nisa' min Hadha al-Zaman adopts the form of a nontraditional visual novel in which several stories coalesce.[33] The story begins by zooming in on a television screen depicting war in Damascus. Gunshots fill the air, and men, women, and children flee dilapidated buildings. Amid the uprising, power outages, and bombings, the story focuses on the lives of the three central female characters, Sham, Layal, and Dima. The next scene opens in court. Layal's husband, who came from Europe to marry a "pure" Syrian woman, divorced her when he realized she was not a virgin on her wedding night. At court, Layal's lawyer, her friend Dima, asks why she did not use a manufactured hymen to fake her virginity. At the same time, Dima reminds Layal that they live in an Eastern society and should follow its norms, saying, "Look at me, I'm twenty-nine years old and no man has touched me." Layal angrily responds, "Go ahead and live with your Turkish telenovelas and your dreams." Meanwhile, their friend Sham, a psychologist, tells her mother, Farida, that her clinic is filled with patients experiencing the war trauma. Farida, an emotionally scarred woman who directs a feminist charitable organization, insists that most of Sham's patients must be women, since "men can make even the best of women go crazy."[34] According to 'Awad, "To assert her presence, Farida is an example of a woman who believes that it is in imitating "masculine" behavior that she can attain her freedom. Although she directs a foundation for women's rights, she stomps on the vulnerable women working for her."[35]

As the story continues, it follows Layal, Dima, and Sham. Layal, who has no supportive family to rely on (her father breaks down from the stress of war), begins an affair with an elderly man who gives her the furnished apartment, clothes, and jewelry of which she always dreamed. Dima dreams of Turkish telenovela heroes. She often runs her hands down a poster of Turkish heartthrob Muhannad in her bedroom, whispering that they will be together again, a subtle and rare reference to masturbation. From the beginning of the miniseries, Sham is the most balanced female character. She refuses to let her lover, Mansour, transform her into an injured "Farida." Despite Farida's warnings that a woman should not "give everything" to the man, because then he will move on, Sham willingly "gives" herself to Mansour. Their love scenes are among the most intimate shown in Syrian drama. We see Sham in her negligee beside Mansour, drinking whisky before and after sex. Candles light the apartment as he leads her into the bedroom, and they hold an explicit conversation in which she takes agency, telling him she desires him. Nevertheless, their relationship unravels.

Intertwined amid stories of these friends are stories of other suffering women who sometimes profit from the inequalities of love relations. Suzie is the mentally ill daughter of corrupt Abu Mayar, whom the government supports. She spends her time getting one cosmetic surgery after another. Her brother asks her the point, since she can't maintain a relationship for more than a week; instead, she spends her time physically and emotionally abusing her housekeepers. 'Aisha is a veiled woman activist whose father was a political prisoner. She is in love with Suzie's brother, Mayar, a Facebook activist resisting the government narrative that the opposition is composed of terrorists. While he professes a secular worldview, he is in love with 'Aisha, who belongs to the more liberal forces of the Islamic groups. In the end, she betrays him, though we never learn the details. Mayar decries Syrian society on his Facebook page, "Separation of religion from God, separation of politics from morality; separation of the killer from the issue he is fighting for," and is later arrested.[36] Director Ahmad describes the heavy criticism he faced from individuals who were insulted that 'Aisha, a veiled woman, engaged in a sexual relationship. Certain scenes, in which they closed the door of a room they were in together, or when he was drinking whiskey, her veil removed, and his shirt unbuttoned, made clear to viewers that they had had sex. "Many were outraged by this," Ahmad said, "but this exists in our society. Veiled women also have premarital sex."[37]

Shaqaf is a calculating novelist who denounces the hypocritical insistence that a woman remain a virgin before marriage. Yet while she speaks out against society's disrespect toward women, she stands by the novelist Sami, who writes about the liberation of women while physically and emotionally abusing his wife, Faten. According to Ahmad, the story aims to show the hypocrisy of the Arab intellectual who compromises his fundamental values in his quest to reach his goals.[38]

The scene at court when Faten demands a divorce is of fundamental importance since sex is explicitly discussed. Faten tells the judges that her husband treats her like a housekeeper, does not respect her, and cheats on her, but they respond that this is not grounds for divorce. However, when she accuses him of not fulfilling his duty as a husband (the duty of having sex), the judges express shock. Sami promises to remedy the situation. In a scene shortly thereafter, Sami plays with Faten's hair, caresses her, and then leads her to the bedroom. In another scene, as he is writing in the living room, she expresses desire. He puts down his work and leads her to the bedroom, saying he doesn't want to be accused of "falling short of fulfilling his duties again."[39] While we never actually see them in bed, the intimate conversation between them suggests that they have had sex. But Sami becomes destructive again, and the closest Faten gets to intimacy is to walk into the bathroom as he is masturbating.[40]

There are no children at the outset of this miniseries, underscoring the impotence of love relationships. Initially, we see Laila's frantic drive to have a child with her abusive husband, Wa'el. Multiple hospital consultations and several rounds of in vitro fertilization fail. A friend advises Laila that the issue is Wa'el's sperm and they concoct a plan to trick him into thinking he is donating his sperm. We never learn the details, but it is clear that they have used another man's sperm. Subsequently, her son is born. In one of the final scenes, Wa'el over-hears that the child is not his son and beats his wife and son up. We first hear Laila and the baby's screams, then blood splatters across the windows. Wa'el kills the one baby born in the story.[41]

Yet, the solution is reform of Syrian society not escape to the West. After Sham and Mansour break up, she marries a Syrian doctor who resides in the United States, saying she tested love in Syria and failed. A few months later, she returns to Syria, utterly destroyed, to learn that her mother has died of cancer. Symbolically, her destructive experience abroad shows that Syrians must reform social norms from within rather than trusting foreign interference. Through the lens of love, the miniseries demonstrates Syria's post-uprising impotence and its mistrust of foreign intervention, a recurring trope in Syrian television drama. Ahmad comments that, "Societal drama deals with the impact of the crisis on the life of the Syrian citizen, without political commentary. The text had a cour-age that we did not see before in Syrian drama." He continued, "Syrian society must change its traditions and way of thinking."[42] According to Ahmad, people now have the false idea that cultural producers outside Syria oppose the regime and those inside Syria support the regime (*muwali li-l-nizam*). This is not true. At the same time, art should not be direct in its political statements."[43]

'Awad commented that she received many critical emails and Facebook mes-sages from both inside and outside Syria. In response to some who protested that the miniseries does not represent *their* society, 'Awad underscores that she depicts female conditions that afflict certain women in Syria, but not all women. "The story," according to 'Awad, "is about how women deal with their problems and sometimes even bring problems upon themselves."[44] In this way, *Nisa' min Hadha al-Zaman* employs faulty love dynamics as metaphors for malaise, which, in turn, leads to societal unraveling. As a result, it is social relations rather than the government that have precipitated Syria's problems. Many have applauded *Nisa' min Hadha al-Zaman* for its bold stance on social issues during the upris-ing, including television editor Iyad Shihab Ahmad, who praised the miniseries for taking risks, breaking taboos, and exploring what many Syrians consider to be shameful (*'aib*) stories of open love relations, desire, and betrayal.[45]

Al-Ikhweh: Escapism via a Latin American–Adapted Miniseries

In April 2014, *al-Ikhweh* began airing on Abu Dhabi in advance of the formal Ramadan season. With noted stars from Syria and the Syrian diaspora, as well as from Egypt, Lebanon, and the Gulf, this telenovela sparked conversation, inter-est, and criticism. Taim Hassan, who stars as Nur, said in an interview in *Nadine* that while some people pejoratively describe *al-Ikhweh* as engaging in "*takhrib al-aqul wa-l-qayyam*" (ruining of minds and values), he does not agree, saying,

"This is not the time for a show of pure entertainment value, and this kind of show is better than those dealing directly with current bloodshed and destruction in Syria."[46] Yet some articles in the press critiqued this trend toward long, superficial, Western-style telenovelas.[47] Others criticized these telenovelas as promoting unrealistic stories of love and betrayal. As this type of telenovela was inspired by a Chilean telenovela, critics claimed the show did not represent the Arab world.[48] Despite the criticism, it was the most talked about telenovela throughout Beirut in June 2014, as everyone prepared for the Ramadan season to start. Its popularity reflects more generally the popularity of shows that serve as a visual opportunity for viewers to escape the conflict plaguing their day-to-day lives. Fashion and entertainment Magazines such as *al-Manara*, *Nadine*, *Kul al-Usra*, *Alwan*, and *al-Jaras* filled magazine and newspaper kiosks in Beirut offering interviews with individual actors involved in this Syrian experiment in the long transnational telenovela.

Despite its success in the media, many in the Syrian drama industry are quick to critique this new development in Syrian drama. Screenwriter Inas Haqqi has been producing short YouTube documentaries called *Under 35* on the opposition movement since the uprising. She contends, "*Al-Ikhweh* does not intend to take any sides in the Syrian uprising. It denies any connection to Syrian society and one feels alienation and exile when watching it." According to Haqqi, this genre of telenovela is in demand now since many producers prefer not to deal with the uprising. She continued, "Syrian drama was known for its political messages, so this new trend of escapism (*tahrib min al-waqi'*) is lamentable for the industry."[49] Director Ahmad Ibrahim Ahmad argued that *al-Ikhweh* is mere imitation. He went on to say, "Syrian miniseries are important because they are relatable, and have a sociopolitical message. But there is a political goal of this new wave, enticing the masses to escape their current reality and just become numb."[50] Screenwriter and novelist Khaled Khalifa has claimed that since the uprising, Gulf channels will not air pro-opposition miniseries.[51] Najeeb Nseir predicted for years that Turkish telenovelas would both influence and take over Syrian miniseries, since the masses wanted to watch open sexual relationships, drinking, and casual party scenes. He also notes that it is hard to write about people's pain during the revolution: "What kind of wisdom can I impart when we are dealing with the daily tragedies of the population?[52]

Al-Ikhweh opens with the wedding celebration of Nur and Maria. Mira, her mother Faten, and their lawyer Asil barge in and derail the wedding with a video of Nur's late father, Farid Nuh, telling his sons that Mira is their sister. As Nur and his four brothers were adopted and Mira is his one biological child, Farid leaves Mira 50 percent of his company as well as his private property. He urges his sons to welcome Mira into the family. Complications arise when Mira and Nur fall in love and Mira tries to break up his relationship with Maria. When Nur falls for Mira, Maria discovers that she is pregnant. Her parents display a completely novel reaction in a Syrian drama to a child conceived out of wedlock. Her mother is excited because now Nur has to marry Maria, while her father is only mildly disgruntled about the effect her pregnancy will have on his reputation. In this way, the theme of having children out of wedlock is important in that it means love and premarital sexual relations do not pose any danger to the female body. When Karam learns that his son, Zain, is the biological son of 'Amir, with whom his wife has had a lengthy affair, he forgives her. His acceptance of Zain as his own son contrasts with Wa'el's reaction in *Nisa' min Hadha al-Zaman*, which is to kill Layla's son when he realizes he is not his biological child.

In this imaginary country, characters throw around English words and expressions and play American music. Their way of life, including their clothing, is far removed from contemporary Syrian reality. With the exception of a single, albeit significant, expression, there is no reference to the uprising. After the shock Mira's sudden introduction to their family, the brothers agree that they need to be united in order to defeat Mira and her mother. The expression used to convey the importance of their family unity is *id wahdeh* (one hand).[53] Syrian rebels use the expression to proclaim a unified front needed to defeat the government, while the government employs it in order to galvanize the support of the nation in fending off foreign interference.

While themes involving sex and sexual affairs pervade the miniseries, not much sex is actually shown. Hanni and Massa's honeymoon scenes are artificial and clunky. Scenes of Massa in her wedding gown are generic and detached. Later, Fadi's sexual encounter with his new love interest, Selma, occurs off screen. This approach reveals the stipulations placed on the Gulf State production company in comparison to a miniseries produced in Syria such as *Nisa' min Hadha al-Zaman*. Furthermore, words like *qabaday* are tossed about frequently, and much of the sex occurs within a more acceptable Eastern framework than the original Latin American telenovela.[54]

Nseir reiterates that *al-Ikhweh* is a Latin American miniseries but that it is inspired by conservative elements of Arab culture. After Sara's affair with 'Amir is revealed, Massa's father refers to a traditional honor crime when he tells Sara that her father would have killed her if he were alive. Faten marries Riyad secretly, establishing their sexual relationship within the framework of a secret Islamic marriage. Nseir also points to Maria and Nur's divorce and the issue of her *muqaddam* and *mu'akhar*.[55] Other Syrian cultural producers have identified loopholes in the text. Screenwriter Inas Haqqi argued that because Syrian writers wished to avoid including the homosexual relationships present in the original miniseries, they relied on repetitive and clichéd romantic storylines. She also indicated there is no adoption in Islam, yet a solution to this contradiction was not offered in the text.[56] The disconnect with Arab culture is felt throughout the storyline, and when Mira tells Nur the truth, that she is not the daughter of Farid Nuh, the shocked man yells sarcastically, "Are we in a Mexican or Indian film?"[57]

Drama creators are mixed about the kind of affect they believe *al-Ikhweh* will have on the industry. Even after the telenovela ended, Facebook pages featured critical commentary about betrayal stories during Ramadan along with dismay that Syria was unrecognizable. Screenwriter Iman Sa'id observes a striking disconnect between the realities of ordinary men and women within the Arab world and the stories of betrayal and babies out of wedlock in *al-Ikhweh*. Despite this shortcoming, she says, many people in Lebanon and Abu Dhabi avidly watch *al-Ikhweh*. She finds the popularity of the show particularly troubling, especially because other Syrian directors and writers may mimic its content.[58] According to Inas Haqqi, the main culprit in the destruction of Syrian television drama is Bashar al-Asad's regime, which maintains a tight grip over Syrian Television. As a result, directors and screenwriters depend on the Gulf Cooperation Council for airtime. Haqqi points out that the Gulf does not accept miniseries that treat the revolution from a civil society perspective, and they have their own production conditions.[59]

Transnational experiments—whether lengthy telenovelas such as *al-Ikhweh* or thirty-episode miniseries—are filled with sex and betrayal. Yet, ironically, some are conservative in outlook due to GCC producers' stipulations on drama creators.[60] Consider *Law . . . (If . . .* 2014), a thirty-episode miniseries adapted from the Hollywood movie *Unfaithful* that represents the escapist trend so popular among producers today. Starring Lebanese stars Yusuf al-Khal and Nadine Nassib Njeym the adaptation reveals discomfort with a woman's sexuality outside marriage. In *Law . . .* , the husband, Qais, is detached from his family, which causes his wife, Laila, to be lonely. This loneliness leads to an affair with another man. In the American version, the husband, Edward, is depicted as engrossed in his work yet still devoted to his family and wife, Connie. And though Connie's affair was due to suburban boredom, Edward eventually forgives her. On the other hand, in the Syrian version, not only does Qais not forgive Laila, but Laila does not forgive herself. Her regret leads to cancer. While she wastes away, Qais refuses to lift the burden of her all-consuming guilt.

The bored, bourgeois housewife in a loveless marriage who has a passionate affair with a younger man, goes mad, and then dies, is a familiar type that has appeared in world literature for generations. Consider, for example, Gustave Flaubert's *Madame Bovary* and Leo Tolstoy's *Anna Karenina*. The former commits suicide by swallowing arsenic, and the latter throws herself onto train tracks. While the women in these novels revolt against their conditions by committing suicide, in *Law . . .* Laila is punished by her regret that turns to cancer.

Screenwriter Najeeb Nseir's thirty-episode *Chello* (based on *Indecent Proposal*) was broadcast on Future, MBC, and Adounia and is another pan-Arab production with Syrian, Lebanese, and Egyptian characters. Here, Yasmin and Adam are music students who are very much in love and marry despite her

FIGURE 4.1 Nadine Nassib Njeym (*left*) and Yusuf al-Khal (*right*) in *Chello*.
Courtesy of Najeeb Nseir.

mother's protests. While initial scenes portray their passion for each other, they wait until they are married in Episode 2 to have sex, both in bed and in the car. In debt and needing money after their theater space burns down, Yasmin and Adam encounter the wealthy Taymour Bik, who sees Yasmin and makes a bet that money is more important than love. He says he would pay one million dollars to spend one night with her. At first Yasmin and Adam refuse, but then Yasmin convinces Adam to play a trick on Taymour, and she promises she will not let him touch "a hair on her head." Though we do not see what actually transpires, Yasmin reassures Adam that nothing happened. Adam, however, is consumed by jealousy. When Yasmin finds out she is pregnant, he wants her to do a DNA test. They fight, Adam leaves the house, and Yasmin miscarries the baby. He spends the night with 'Alia, who is in love with him, and we assume they sleep together. Afterward, Yasmin and Adam separate, and Yasmin begins to see Taymour. She had sold the antique cello given to them by their mentor when she was poor and now Taymour wants to buy it for her. But Adam is the one who ends up buying the cello, and when Taymour sees the love for Adam in Yasmin's eyes, he lets her go, saying that she will never look at him in the same way.

The story ends with Adam and Yasmin standing together. And then the story flashes back to the scene of that mysterious night. Yasmin slept on the couch and Adam resisted 'Alia. Neither had betrayed the other, as shame kept them both in check. In his miniseries, Najeeb hoped to expose the double standards between men and women. However, though he succeeded in showing more explicit sex scenes than in previous miniseries, his philosophical intentions were hampered. Specifically, the fact that nothing of a sexual nature occurred outside the couple's marriage represents a compromise in that the story was acceptable to the Eastern audience.[61] Heated discussions circulated in the press about this story. Many critics questioned whether the topic of selling a wife was appropriate for the Ramadan season. While some maintained that the events and characterizations clashed with the reality of Eastern society, others insisted the drama was more accurate.[62] My point, however, is to show that transnational drama often involves stories of love and sex; however, due to GCC constraints, writers are often forced to make compromises.

These GCC productions stand in contrast to Syrian miniseries such as director Najdat Anzour's *Imra'a min Ramad* (Women of Ashes, 2015). Produced by Syriana under the supervision of Diana Jabbour, *Imra'a min Ramad* was a classic regime narrative during a moment, five years into an uprising turned civil war, when quite a few miniseries were released. In this storyline, Jihad suffers from mental illness after the death of her son, Yusuf, in an explosion. She runs a sewing factory with brutal authoritarianism, crushing everyone she encounters. When she sees a woman taking care of her orphaned nephew, also named Yusuf, Jihad insists on adopting the boy and does everything in her power to force his family into agreement. A turning point occurs at the hospital when Jihad meets Qamran, a kind security officer, and they fall in love. Qamran sees that Jihad is ill and is patient with her. When Jihad is with Qamran we see her softer side, the side she revealed before her son was killed.

Increasingly, Syrian production companies have become more lenient in their depictions of sex as they propagate an outward regime narrative and attempt to construct a secular cultural memory. This strategy effectively "others" the more religious elements in society. This is particularly true in a miniseries like *Imra'a min Ramad* that is filled with images of army men fighting jihadists and terrorists. Furthermore, because the Syrian producer was not limited by a GCC production company, he portrayed the premarital sex scenes between Jihad and Qamran without restraint or judgment. The miniseries showed bedroom scenes as well as intimate scenes in the kitchen, when a bare-chested Qamran kisses and holds Jihad. Whereas, previously, these scenes were used metaphorically to critique the political order, they now uphold the existing political order. It is noteworthy that the miniseries refers to the uprising not as the "azmeh" (crisis) but the "ahdath" (the events), a term also used to describe the regime's razing of Hama in 1982.

Nationalist leaders are now depicted as decent as opposed to being war profiteers. When the army fights jihadists, the jihadists are clearly foreigners on Syrian soil. Other storylines also portray religious extremism in a negative light. Nisrin and Yamen love each other, but since they are from different Islamic sects, her brother refuses to acknowledge their love. The lovers lament their country's current obsession with sectarian differences. In time, they marry. Later, Abu Yamen tells his infant son that Syria belongs to him, and he hopes that he and his friends will cherish their country. In the end, victory belongs to Syria's security officers. Qamran succeeds in finding Jihad's son, who was kidnapped by a childless couple. Jihad has healed and the ending is hopeful. This storyline clearly rehearses the regime narrative, lacking even a gesture toward objectivity. And though it shows people's brutality during war, the drama places blame for the current turmoil on human nature rather than the government.

Women's Body as Raped Nation and the Presentations of a Gentler Manhood

The equating of a nation and *its* honor with a woman's body and *her* honor has deep historical roots in Syria and beyond. In *Sexuality and War: Literary Masks of the Middle East* (1990), Evelyne Accad showed contrasting representations of a wounded Beirut during Lebanon's civil war. While male author Elias Khoury depicted Beirut as a whore in *al-Jabal al-Saghir*, female author Etel Adnan portrayed the city as a girl raped by countless men in *Sitt Marie-Rose*. According to Accad, while Khoury's account condemns the woman as a sinner, Adnan's commiserates with the woman as a victim of male violence.[63] In *Colonial Citizens: Republican Rights, Paternal Privilege, and Gender in French Syria and Lebanon* (2000), Elizabeth Thompson poignantly depicted how rebel propaganda linked men's honor and the nation's women during the armed resistance against French colonial rule from 1920 to 1926. This nationalist propaganda encouraged men to protect their women from rape, revealing deep-rooted gender anxieties and contributing to the notion that Syria was a nation of men.[64] In her seminal study *Egypt as a Woman: Nationalism, Gender, and Politics* (2005), Beth Baron showed that rape committed in Egypt by foreigners was perceived as having besmirched the honor of men. This perception paralleled the concept that the violated nation itself required male protection.[65]

In this section I contend that in two miniseries during the 2015 season, a shift occurred in terms of how "pure" women's bodies symbolized the nation. As Syria plunged into further destruction, a temporary suspension of "honor" codes occurred in 2015 in the depiction of a pure woman's body as symbol of the nation. Here, instead, we have a raped or prostituted woman symbolizing a nation under assault. Rather than representing these women as disgraced, these miniseries feature gentler and less judgmental masculine figures. These men view women as pure and noble. In the context of a nation under assault, this depiction, itself, marks a temporary suspension of norms of acceptable female sexuality. There are some nuances in these portrayals. Yet for the most part men continue to act as arbiters of a woman's purity. Furthermore, labeling women more liberally as "pure" serves a purpose, allowing storytellers to contrast their secular collective values with those of the "othered" Islamist and/or terrorist groups such as Da'ish. This process of constructing a collective memory entails selectively forgetting the Ba'th regime's history of bolstering Islamic groups such as the *qubaysiyyat* as well as perpetuating the myth of a secular regime fighting the Muslim Brotherhood.

Ghadan Naltaqi, perhaps the most popular miniseries of the season, is a musical, visual miniseries that breaks new ground in film technique. Written by Iyad Abu Shammat and directed by Rami Hanna, it was produced by Clacket and broadcast on LDC and Abu Dhabi.[66] While accused of being anti-Lebanese and making fun of Syrian refugees, it was nevertheless in the top five of the Ramadan Rating show every day. Some criticized the miniseries' lighting for being too dark, but Reem Hanna contends that the director dimmed the lighting on purpose.[67] Through its stills and close-ups, the miniseries creates haunting scenes in which refugees wait in a run-down apartment complex in Beirut, some falling prey to Da'ish while yearning to leave Lebanon for a new life in Europe. *Ghadan Naltaqi* adopts an arguably neutral stance toward the conflict, as love intersects with politics. The main storyline follows two brothers, Mahmud (in the opposition) and Jabir (pro-regime), as well as a woman named Warda, who is loved by Jabir but loves Mahmud.[68] Mahmud tells Warda that they have lost the country but that freedom, justice, and the homeland are worth fighting for. She responds, "Love is the one thing that we can willingly die for."[69] Yet fear surrounds Warda at all times; her door has a triple lock that she fastens when she enters her room.

One evening Warda is on the verge of intimacy with Mahmud in her room. Shocked that she is still a virgin at age thirty-six, he refuses to have sex with her. In Arabic, the expression indicating "you're still a girl" is understood as "you're still a virgin." In a play on words, Mazin, a refugee boy, appears from his hiding place under the bed and asks Warda, "Why doesn't Mahmud like girls? He was making fun of you since you're a girl."[70] Later, to deter Jabir's advances, Warda lies and tells Jabir that she had sex with Mahmud, arousing his jealousy. Such an announcement of premarital sexual activity is atypical in Syrian drama. In this anomalous moment, Warda asserts agency without fearing male judgment.

Politics and love continue to intersect in the storyline as Jaber accuses Mahmud of being a thief and opposition activist. As they fight, Jaber yells, "You've ruined the country. Look what you've done to us. Now because of you, our country is with Da'ish." Mahmud retorts, "But they aren't us. We didn't create them. The regime created them to say, look they are better." Jaber responds, "Then it is not a regime, it's a super regime!"[71] Tension rises until, one day, the two brothers fight violently in Warda's apartment. In the end, as a result of their fighting, her house burns down. This fight and its consequences symbolize the way in which both sides are equally responsible for burning Syria. According to Haitham

Haqqi, this scene dramatically symbolizes the politically neutral stance of the miniseries, which blames both sides for having caused the war that has ripped the country apart.[72]

During the fire, neighbors call the police and the three characters are escorted to a police station, where Warda is forced to submit to a virginity test. In a dark room, a doctor removes his gloves as Warda cries in the corner. Warda is declared a virgin. Jabir is relieved, but the issue is of no significance to Warda. Soon after, Mahmud is diagnosed with liver failure. Since no one else can help him, Warda desperately tries to pay for his weekly medical treatment. Distraught, she walks the streets at night, followed by a car that asks her price. With tears in her eyes, she names the amount she needs for Mahmud's care. Though we do not see them having sex, Warda walks home crying. The next morning, however, she has forgotten her sorrow as she focuses on taking Mahmud to the hospital for his treatment. In this miniseries, Warda's prostitution represents love and commitment, and her body symbolizes an innocent Syria that has been raped and exploited by all sides. It was her desperation that led to prostitution, yet Warda also exercises agency, having made her own decision to raise money for Mahmud's care by using her body. Furthermore, her matter-of-fact approach to extramarital sex with a stranger deromanticizes the female body and its traditional associations with purity.

Drama creators such as Hoozan 'Akko believed the miniseries to be in poor taste, since it mocked the pain of ordinary refugees.[73] Indeed, the construction of a new, secular collective memory disassociates itself from Islam, often in ways that attempt to be comical. In early scenes, Warda attracts the attention of Mahmud by, as her friend Khulud teaches her, allowing her headscarf to fall and reveal her hair when she speaks to him. Scenes show Warda adjusting her headscarf in front of the mirror. Indeed, the scene in which she pulls her veil down as she talks to Mahmud by the door is comical. At the same time, though, she independently decides when and where to wear the veil. The same can be said of other characters and storylines. Umm 'Abdu yearns for a divorce, threatening to burn herself if her husband does not concede. When he finally grants her a divorce, financial constraints require them to live in the same room together. Amusingly, every time Abu 'Abdu enters the room, she screams that he is not permitted to see her and dons her headscarf. This scene pokes fun at the religiosity of the refugee community, while at the same time exhibiting a woman's agency. Abu 'Abdu has pronounced the triple divorce formula, and now his wife can use this as an excuse to cover herself in his presence and avoid dealing with him.

Simultaneously, clear identity politics surface as the show builds an identity that resists religious extremism. When Abu 'Abdu's son Jamal is caught looking at women, his father punishes him by shaving his head. As seen in other miniseries such as *al-Wilada min al-Khasira*, the ritual of head shaving, or "drawing a map on the head," is a traditional punishment in the Syrian military and symbolizes the individual's vulnerability in the face of power.[74] In another scene, when the boys play ball outside their run down building, Abu 'Abdu deflates the ball, pronouncing it an instrument of the "Satanic West." Ultimately, Jamal becomes an extremist, tries to kill his sister's husband, and joins Da'ish. When Abu 'Abdu tries to find his son, he is captured by Da'ish and beheaded live on television. This trajectory of extremism acts as an "othering" mechanism for identifying an extremist religious culture. Nevertheless, the miniseries also includes subtle critiques of the regime. Creators lament Abu Dhabi's choice to cut out important political scenes, such as when Mazin talks to Khulud about Jaysh al-Hurr (FSA).[75]

Bi-Intizar al-Yasmin, written by Oussama Kawkash and directed by Samir Husayn, takes place five years into the war and can be categorized within the nostalgic register. This miniseries underscores the plight of internally displaced Syrian populations who have lost their homes to shelling, live in public gardens, and are victimized by war criminals. These people contrast with wealthy people living in safer, upper-class areas and experiencing a completely different reality that involves dancing and partying. Party scenes portray young people drinking and disrespecting their parents. Hiba complains that her mother has a "phobia to the azmeh" and will not let her leave the house. She yells at her mother, then spends the night elsewhere. Hiba's friend lives with a man with whom Hiba falls in love. At the same time, Abu Salim, his wife, and their two daughters live in the garden. Lamar finds shelter in the garden with her small son and daughter since her husband went out for bread and never returned. Umm 'Aziz catches on fire after Abu Shawk (literally father of thorns), a war profiteer and criminal, harasses her.

The screenwriter's critique focuses on Da'ish, religious fanaticism, and war profiteers rather than regime oppression. Throughout the story, flashes of news programs reveal that terrorists are destroying Syria. Lamar experiences a flashback in which she waits in her apartment with her husband while people with black flags fire shots in her neighborhood. Abu Shawk tricks Lamar into trusting him to find her husband but kidnaps her daughter, Nur, instead. Though not shown, it seems he rapes her and intends to sell her body parts. When Lamar tries to save Nur, Abu Shawk and another man rape her, connoting the rape of the nation. Rida, a drinker who lives in the garden, rescues them and brings them home to his family. In her examination of the revolution of 1919 in Egypt, Beth Baron had shown how the rape of Egyptian women by the enemy became a collective dishonor and national disgrace. Many women refused to testify against the British in order to prevent shame from falling upon their families. Baron delineated how village rapes subsequently become an integral part of collective memory.[76] In contrast, in *Bi-Intizar al-Yasmin*, Lamar does not bring shame upon her community. As she seeks to overcome her trauma, she is reintegrated into society. *Bi-Intizar al-Yasmin* serves as a telling example of the nostalgic register, which, in glossing over past and present oppression, intersects with the regime narrative.

Still, Lamar is further traumatized when she watches a YouTube clip of Da'ish beheading her husband. With time, though, Lamar heals. Rida takes her to her destroyed home in Homs and tells Lamar that the human has become like a rock.[77] Lamar eventually falls in love with Rida, and thus resilience produces a new chance at love. Lamar's purity remains untarnished by her rape; likewise, Rida's masculinity remains intact, despite his failure to protect her. The first episode had employed a phrase, *al-Hubb wa-l-Harb ma Yejtame'u* (love and war may not meet), that is undercut by the reality that love saves Rida. Falling in love with Lamar and her children has given him a reason to live. Clearly, the traditional impediments of honor and shame have not prevented Rida from loving Lamar, despite her having been raped. In one of the final scenes, Rida plays in the snow with Lamar's children and she looks on smiling. They both agree that they must not let the cold enter our hearts. Lamar says, "Sham looks like a bride," and Rida, referring to Lamar, responds, "The most beautiful bride."[78]

New Trends: Gender, Marriage, and Sexuality in Contemporary Tales

While *Ghadan Naltaqi* and *Bi-Intizar al-Yasmin* are set in the middle of war, other miniseries—especially those involving transnational experiences—focus on gender and marriage storylines and mention the war in passing. While not all of these miniseries retain elaborate goals of social transformation, many can be categorized as social for the sake of the social because of their complete disassociation from a political agenda. Lebanese screenwriter Claudia Marchalian's sixty-episode *Samra* (2016), directed by Rasha Sharbatji, was broadcast prior to the Ramadan season.[79] Produced by Sabba Media and composed of Egyptian, Syrian, and Lebanese actors, this miniseries on nomadic people falls into the category of *'Amal Mushtaraka*. While edited and directed by Syrians, it was considered a Lebanese production with a pan-Arab cast.[80] The storyline begins with a group of doctors who are en route to provide medical assistance to Syrian refugees and stop by a camp of nomadic people. The Egyptian doctor, Tamer, and a nomadic woman, Samra, fall in love. Another doctor's friend's brother is kidnapped, ends up with jihadists, and is slowly brainwashed. Many fans perceived this miniseries as a superficial examination of Syria through the doomed love story of Tamer and Samra, who, in the end, is killed by her cousin to expunge the shame she brought to her family by marrying the Egyptian doctor. Even as fans expressed sadness over the honor crime in the storyline, actress Nadine Nassib Njeym (who played Samra) was attacked on social media for saying that while her daughter must remain pure, her son is permitted to have premarital sex. Many were

outraged that while drama strives to support equality by exposing double standards related to female sexuality, this well-known actress would reveal her
real-life hypocrisy.[81]

Claudia Marchalian's *Ya Reit* (2016), which takes place in Lebanon, was also
critiqued for its superficial portrayal of the uprising. Famous Syrian actors Maxim
Khalil and Qais al-Sheikh Najeeb and Lebanese actress Maggy bou Ghossen star
in this pan-Arab miniseries that the press extensively discussed.[82] The storyline
centers on Iyad, who lives in London with his daughter and girlfriend Jenna, and
Iyad's estranged family, who has been displaced by the war and now resides in
flimsy, handmade houses in Lebanon at the border with Syria. Iyad and Jenna
return to Beirut so he can visit his dying mother. Soon after their arrival, Iyad
has an affair with Tina, who is in a relationship with Jenna's brother. Despite
the affront to her dignity, when Jenna realizes Iyad is having an affair, she fights
to win him back. While Syrian drama both prior to and following the uprising
often possessed a "politics of dignity,"[83] dignity is not linked to politics in the
storyline of *Ya Reit*, which can be seen as a light social piece. Indeed, the miniseries was critiqued for its superficial treatment of the Syrian civil war. Throughout the miniseries, only short-lived and undeveloped storylines relate to Syria.
For example, Yezen tells his brother, Rami, that no country wants Syrians; thus,
he wants to escape via a boat in the sea. Even though this risky act might be
considered suicidal, it would be preferable to living in exile.

Jarimat al-Shaghaf (2016), written by Nur Shishekly and directed by Waleed
Naseef, is a pan-Arab miniseries starring Egyptian, Lebanese, and Syrian actors
that takes place against the backdrop of recent Syrian history. While the treatment of the war is superficial, the rhetoric of war is often captured indirectly in
dialogue. In *Trauma Culture: The Politics of Terror and Loss in Media and Literature*,
E. Ann Kaplan examines how cinema can be unconsciously complicit with hegemonic political forces. As institutional forces "manage" the "crisis," cinema
can allow the "forgetting" of collective traumas.[84] In this respect, storylines
such as *Jarimat al-Shaghaf* capture regime rhetoric that effectively delegitimizes
the uprising. While the miniseries does not explicitly address the uprising,
it alludes to it through the subtle mocking of popular revolutionary terms
and expressions.

The central storyline of *Jarimat al-Shaghaf* is as follows: 'Ows, a lady's man,
is having an affair with a woman on the second floor of an apartment building.
When the woman's husband walks in, 'Ows jumps from the second floor balcony
onto the first floor balcony. At the very same moment, another man enters the
home of his wife Jumana, a woman on the first floor. Both Jumana and her husband momentarily see 'Orwa before he jumps from the balcony onto the ground,
and then we hear a gunshot.[85] 'Ows thinks that his lover upstairs has been killed
by her husband, but in reality the man on the first floor has committed suicide.
Jumana is accused of killing her husband and imprisoned until proven innocent.

Meanwhile, 'Ows escapes to Egypt and becomes an actor, as his mother and sister, Haifa, search for him. 'Ows is tormented by the belief that he is responsible for his lover's death. Meanwhile, his wife, Rania, is devastated that he has abandoned her. Jumana, when freed, seeks both dignity and revenge.

"Dignity" has been a key term in Syrian protest drama since the political parodies of the 1960s and has been a central demand of the resistance movement since 2011. In writing about Egypt, Diane Singerman argues that dignity is necessarily a gendered concept, a demand that "the state must respect the integrity, safety and autonomy of the body."[86] Prior to and through the early years of the uprising, screenwriters criticized a regime that continually violated its citizens' dignity. Likewise, the notion of dignity predicated storylines about gender and marriage.[87] Yet, at the height of the violence and destruction of Da'ish, when the establishment of a secular collective memory is imperative, the search for dignity now appears in a negative light in some storylines. In *Jarimat al-Shaghaf*, statements from the current uprising that are mirrored in the storyline now assume a belittling quality. For example, when Rania leaves her in-laws, Haifa tells her mother, "Rania has left to search for her dignity."[88] In another scene that recalls the language of revolutionaries, Rania tells 'Ows, "I have lost everything in my life. I have nothing more to lose. Come back and divorce me. I thought you were a man."[89] Yet, while Rania speaks of dignity, her behavior as she chases 'Ows shows no awareness of the true nature of dignity.

Jumana's story, which also captures the vocabulary of the uprising, revolves around her search for dignity, which prevents her from getting revenge. Upon her release from jail, Jumana seeks to punish 'Ows for ruining her life. This drive leads her to self-destruct. Set on revenge, she says, "I didn't start this war, but I'll lose it."[90] In another instance before leaving for Egypt, Jumana tells her friend, Haifa, "I have lost everything and have nothing else to lose. My whole life I was afraid. But that is true no longer."[91] In yet another scene, Haifa asks her mother what happened to justice. Her mother says, "Truth always knows justice," and Haifa responds, "Justice? Then what do you call what has happened to us?"[92]

The miniseries avoids any direct comment on the uprising yet employs the vocabulary circulating during the uprising about the philosophy of love, forgiveness, and revenge. The story in which victim becomes aggressor and is consumed by the need for vengeance captures the critiques lobbed against the protesters by regime apologists. This is poignantly depicted in the story of Jumana, who uses her oppression to justify becoming, herself, an oppressor. In this context, the issue of dignity cannot be used in the service of political critique.[93]

While the transnational miniseries above dealt superficially with the uprising, others operated wholly in the *ma fi shi'* (it's nothing) mode. *Nus Yawm*, written by Samir al-Salka and starring the popular Lebanese duo Nadine Nassib Njeym and Taim Hassan, is one such example. The miniseries, which made no reference to the uprising, was discussed regularly in the Arabic press that summer.[94] Based on *Original Sin*, starring Angelina Jolie and Antonio Banderas, this adaptation was broadcast on DRAMA, MDC, and al-Jadid. When the storyline commences, Njeym's character Maysa' is a woman who survives as a thief and con artist. Many criticized the cruelty of Njeym's role, for which she eventually apologized.[95] By the end, perhaps due to this criticism, director Samer al-Barqawi repositioned her as both oppressed and oppressor. However, in my opinion the storyline is not convincing, since the character harms her lover, Mayar, to the extent that it is difficult to imagine that Mayar could still love Maysa' or that she truly loves him. In the U.S. version, the leading female character steals everything from her lover; in the adaptation, she repents. However, the producers defended their choices as more acceptable to an Eastern audience. According to Taim Hassan, these adaptations work in the new context only if they convince viewers of the authenticity of the story, so changes had to be made to the story. Despite its faulty storyline, the miniseries was known for its suspense and drew large audiences.

Transnational miniseries are varied. Some, such as *Ya Reit* and *Jarimat al-Shaghaf*, superficially capture the rhetoric of the uprising, while others, such as *Nus Yawm*, ignore the war altogether. Contemporary Syrian miniseries similarly offer a broad range of escapist tales, superficial treatments of war, and storylines caught in the webs of a war-torn society. Qoshaqji's contemporary tale, *Nabtadi Mnein al-Hikayeh?* (2016, Where Do We Begin the Story?), is another example of a storyline that has been critiqued for its surface treatment of the war. It tells the story of Layal and Bashir, who broke up after a decadelong but unmarried romance. When the story begins in 2015, Bashir and Layal have just reunited after a year and a half separation. The story repeatedly rewinds to Damascus in 2000, when Bashir met Layal for the first time. Layal admits that she just separated from a man with whom she was intimate. Bashir, who defends premarital sex, often allowing his son private time with his girlfriend, struggles with Layal's past, telling his friend that she is like *al-watan* (the homeland) and it is hard for him to imagine her with someone else. Here, Screenwriter Fadi Qoshaqji advocates for civil marriage as he exposes both the faulty logic of connecting a woman's "pure" body with the nation and the problematic tendency to link a woman's sexuality to larger social issues.

On June 18, social media debated whether or not the miniseries promoted premarital sex. Bashir's choice to enable his son's intimacy with his girlfriend was the subject of much critique. One man wrote on Qoshaqji's Facebook page that this miniseries did not accurately portray the Arab world. Qoshaqji defended himself, saying that the miniseries was not all about sex. Najeeb Nseir, a leading Syrian screenwriters who exposes hypocrisy toward premarital sex, offered a different critique related to the miniseries' portrayal of sexual relations, contending that all storylines that normalize premarital sex must provide context for the characters to be believable. He maintained this miniseries should have offered more background to help the audience understand the reasoning behind the characters' liberal attitudes. He also identified casting issues, since Layan and Bashir lack chemistry.[96]

Furthermore, drama creators such as Reem Hanna critiqued the *ma fi shi'* mentality of the miniseries: "When you see the streets of Damascus you're not reminded of any war. It's only in discussions when they talk of the war, and fear of getting hurt or kidnapped, that we are reminded that this storyline is taking place against the background of war."[97] Haitham Haqqi critiqued the miniseries too, objecting to a cab scene in 2015 in which a character complains about the sound of bombs despite the fact that the audience hears no bombs.[98] Indeed, the miniseries represents Damascus as beautiful and peaceful.

Some surface political conversations about the unrest occur toward the end of the miniseries. In a scene set in 2011, characters watch the television news as the country is torn apart. Bashir's friend critiques the opposition for not verbally negotiating a solution. Layal watches the shootings on television and cries, telling Bashir that she feels cold. On their honeymoon, Bashir and Layal say that *Inshallah*, the country will become as it was before. But Layal adds, "not exactly like before." Bashir says his headaches begin in 2011 with the story of the "crazy war," with "the *azmeh*, *thawra*, whatever you want to call it."[99] He could not stand seeing his country ripped apart, he says. In this way the writer connects Bashir's headache and illness to the azmeh, blaming opposition activists rather than progovernment forces.

In *Nabtadi Mnein al-Hikayeh?*, a storyline within the nostalgic register that denied the Syrian regime's oppressive past, the theme of premarital sex was no longer taboo. Another miniseries, *Ahl al-Gharam*, which was delayed the previous year, returned for its third season during Ramadan 2017. While premarital sex and seduction are not taboo here, either, storylines are more nuanced rather than simply falling in the nostalgic register within a regime narrative. Produced by Sama Art International and O3 Productions, *Ahl al-Gharam* aired only on LDC and was not well marketed; it did not appear on Syrian channels.[100] The two seasons prior to the uprising focused on conventions and traditions obstructing true love. For the most part these stories end unhappily, with some lesson to be learned. The third season continues along those lines but introduces the element of war as an impediment to love. *Ahl al-Gharam Part Three* is made up of five-episode stories by different writers and directors, featuring actors with differing political stances. The stories evince varying degrees of neutrality with respect to the current upheaval as well as varying degrees of nostalgia for the past. Writers and directors involved in this miniseries had mixed reviews of the experience. Najeeb Nseir lamented that there storylines did not cooperate and conflicts arose among the directors.[101] Despite the tensions, my close viewing of each storyline shows that the screenwriters and directors overwhelmingly rebuffed the idea that a woman's purity distinguishes her as non-Western. Instead, they present a new, nonextreme, secular culture that impacts sexuality, marriage, and gender. While some of these storylines engage in political critique and others are neutral, there are also those in the social for the sake of the social strand that do not engage in political critique. Thus, the miniseries represented several of the divergent directions of post-uprising miniseries, even as they uniformly distinguished a secular Syrian culture from the culture of religious extremism as represented by Da'ish.

In *al-Hubb al-Mustahil*, written by al-Muthana Sobh and directed by Hatim 'Ali, the main love story involves Dr. Rafiq Selim (played by Jamal Suleiman) and Sama (played by Kinda 'Aloosh). When Rafiq, a dedicated Syrian bachelor and surgeon, sees Sama's exhibition, he is immediately enamored. Rafiq generally tries to block out the news, believing that what is happening will happen no matter what. The politics in this storyline seem fairly neutral. Sama works with Syrian refugees and is fully attuned to the devastation surrounding her, revealing to Rafiq that she is numb after the past five years of trauma. Rafiq, on the other hand, does not become emotional about the bloodshed.

As Sama and Rafiq's friendship deepens, he expresses his love for her, but she holds back. Finally, she confesses that she has the same cancer that killed her father and sister and does not want to get romantically involved. Rafiq insists that her avoidance of pain will strengthen the cancer. Rafiq is not concerned about Sama's previous relationship and never asks if it was intimate. This nonchalance attests to the continued campaign by post-uprising screenwriters to impose more balanced norms regarding gender and sexuality. Eventually, Sama surrenders to love and she and Rafiq get engaged. She decides to go to Sham to close her art workshop and gather some belongings. Rafiq later receives a call informing him that Sama was killed when a bomb fell on her house. He confides to his friend Randa that it is ironic that she died only once she had overcome her fear of cancer. Thus, the storyline conveys the impossibility of love when it accompanies war. While the war is not ignored, it is also not referred to as a "crisis," and as Rafiq watches explosions on the news, it is not clear if Da'ish or the government is responsible for the bomb that strikes Sama's house in Damascus. Indeed, the possibility of the government's involvement is fundamental to the storyline.

The third five-episode story, "Ba'dak Habibi" (You're Still My Loved One), written by Najeeb Nseir and directed by al-Muthana Sobh, continues the story of the young Christian and Muslim couple, Mirna and Fadi, from "Ya Mariam Ya Bekr" (Oh, Virgin Mary) in *Ahl al-Gharam Part One*, who could not marry because of religion. Nseir intended to tell the same story twenty years later, only with a female Muslim and male Christian whose parents opposed the union. At the same time, Nseir wanted to portray the couple's different options and circumstances.[102]

In the storyline that takes place twenty years later, Mirna is a widowed woman with two sons. Her son Qaysar knows she loved someone before his father and jealously monitors her. She tells him, "Your generation should be different. But you're still thinking of honor and shame. What about your studies and culture? What will you do if you meet a woman who had lovers before?"[103] Her other son, Fadi, tells his brother that she is free to live her own life. He has no issue with his mother having loved someone before or even presently.

Mirna tells her friend that she often thinks of Fadi. In the past when she had problems with her husband, she wondered if her marriage with Fadi would have been stronger. As a mother, she continually tells her sons that times have changed. She does not realize that her son Fadi is in love with Mira, a surgical dentist. Mira just so happens to be the daughter of Fadi, her former lover. When the story commences, Mira and the younger Fadi are in love, yet they worry about their families' reactions. When Mira's family suspects she is in a relationship, they ask her maternal uncle to survey her. Ironically, while he is married, he is having an affair. When Mira sees that her parents allow her sister, Maysoun, to marry an American Christian, she assumes they will accept Fadi. Fadi takes Mira to meet his mother, who leaves the table when she realizes that Mira is her old lover Fadi's daughter. While she eventually accepts their relationship, Mira's family remains adamantly opposed.

Mira later tells Fadi that marriage is not important, reminding Fadi that his mother is still in love with the man she was forbidden to marry. The fact that she married another man did not eradicate her original love. When Mira's hypocritical maternal uncle informs her that she is their ʿard and sharaf (honor and shame), Mira replies that no law or contract will stop them from loving each other. Mira tells her father that she loves Fadi. He assures her that it is her right to love, but when the relationship becomes more serious her family and community also have a right to decide. In the end, Fadi visits Mirna and tells her to keep her son away from his daughter. Meanwhile, Fadi and Mira can be seen on the street, showing their affection for each other. Thus, in this miniseries love is shown as more important than marriage. In this case the couple decides that they will not marry and have children. Instead, they will love each other outside the formal marriage relationship.[104] Critics claimed that Nseir represented an unrealistic culture of premarital dating and sexuality, one that does not exist in Syria. However, he decried the way his story was directed, claiming that intimate details that support Mirna and Fadi's love story were erased. For example, in the beginning, when Mira's father Fadi (played by Bassam Kousa) is driving in a car and hears music they listened to together in the 1980s, Nseir intended to show that Fadi was reminded of his former love. He gets out of the car and looks around as if searching for her. To Nseir's dismay, the director used the standard miniseries theme music of Syrian musician Taher Mumalli. Thus, when Fadi gets out of the car and looks around, the scene appears out of place.[105]

Matar Aylul (April Rain) was written by Iyad Abu Shammat and directed by Hatim ʿAli. When the story starts, Sami, who reviews foreign films on a radio talk show, is engaged to Mona, a jealous young woman. The sound of bombs is often heard throughout this storyline. According to director Laith Hajjo, since the screenwriter, Hatem 'Ali, is in the opposition, he did not want Taher Mamilli (generally believed to be aligned with the regime) to do the music score. Instead, he chose random Western music. Furthermore, since he does not live in Syria, he thinks there are bombings every moment. The result is Western music juxtaposed with the sound of bombings to portray a continual semblance of war.[106]

The storyline commences when Sami's ambitious ex-girlfriend, Matar, returns from London and visits him. Matar had left a few years earlier to pursue her career. Now, she explains that she had to go, try, and fail in London in order to realize what she had left behind. Matar then amends her observation, saying that, in truth, she does not think that she failed, since her experience has helped her realize what she wants. She tells Sami that she tried to love someone else who was not a nice person. Sami discloses he was admitted to the hospital because of her, and she apologizes for the pain she caused him. He acknowledges that he still loves her but that he has another woman in his life. The sound of bombs fills the air as they speak.

Later, when Sami discovers that his current girlfriend, Mona, records their conversations in his apartment, he breaks up with her and reunites with Matar. Scenes show them dancing in his house to the continual sounds of bombs and Western music, both American and French. Sami tells Matar he still loves her. While pre-uprising miniseries asserted they were not promoting either Western individualism or liberal sexual standards, these concerns no longer dominate during this time period in which Syrian culture revealed its secular rather than religious values. An indecisive Sami marries Mona and then quickly divorces her. He and Matar reunite. When Mona claims she is dying, Sami returns to her again until he realizes Mona's deception, at which point he tries to mend his relationship with Matar. She initially refuses him, leaving for Dubai but returning the next day. Their mutual friend, Jalal, says that they need to be together: Sami marries and divorces in a day and Matar travels and returns in a day. Matar and Sami ultimately decide to leave Syria and travel to Dubai together. In the end, this story is about second chances and forgiveness. Director Laith Hajjo noted the positive ending as a response to complaints about the negative endings of *Ahl al-Gharam* in previous seasons.[107]

On the other hand, *Shukran 'ala Nisan*, written by Iyad Abu Shammat and inspired by the American romantic drama *The Vow*, does not mention the uprising.[108] In the American version, Paige and her husband are happily married. After a car accident, she recovers but has amnesia and no longer remembers her husband. She pines for a former lover with whom she had broken up years earlier. In the Syrian version, Nada walks in on her husband, Riyad, cheating on her. Distraught, she drives off and gets into an accident. As a result, she develops amnesia. When she feels repelled by her husband, no one will help her. Her father, who wants her to stay married rather than coming home a divorced woman, refuses to tell her that she asked for a lawyer just before her accident. Gradually, Nada remembers and then locates her former boyfriend, Farid. She learns that on the night they had planned to escape together, she had cold feet. Farid says that his life stopped at the moment Nada married another man. In the meantime, Nada finds more and more proof that Riyad had been cheating on her. She stops worrying about what her family thinks and hurries to the place she and Farid planned to meet years earlier. Their current reunion offers them the happy ending that would not have been possible in her youth. Director Laith Hajjo said that after fans complained about unhappy endings in the first and second seasons, they made some of the storylines more hopeful.[109]

Lestoo Jariya (I'm Not a Slave Girl), written by Fathallah 'Umr and directed by Naji Tom'eh, is an unrealistic contemporary miniseries that, unlike the majority of stories in *Ahl al-Gharam*, emphasizes a man's extreme fixation with a woman's sexuality rather than the current uprising. While Da'ish is not mentioned by name, both the husband's exaggerated virginity fetish and his conviction that he owns his wife are constant reminders of that culture. One newspaper article about the show is even titled "Fath Allah 'Omar '*Lestoo Jariya*' Aw al-'Aish ma' Da'ish" (Fath Allah's 'Omar "I'm Not a Slave Girl" or Life with Da'ish).[110] In this storyline, Mayce and Ghaleb are in love and get married. On their wedding night, Ghaleb is devastated to discover that she is not a virgin. She then remembers a story she had blocked out since childhood about a family friend who raped her. Ghaleb, who does not believe her innocence, strikes and curses her. Mayce fears that if Ghaleb sends her back, her family will slaughter her; they make a deal that she can remain with him as his slave woman.

Ghaleb solicits advice from a sheikh, who tells him not to mistreat Mayce. While the sheikh believes Mayce's story, Ghaleb tries to force confessions from her. He hits her, calls her a liar, and informs her that he will marry her friend Nahed, a veiled woman who looks honorable. He tells Mayce, "I'm going to marry Nahed. I love that she puts her eyes down when I speak to her. I feel like a man when I'm in the presence of a woman like this. She's shy. I feel I'm the first and last man in her life."[111] Nahed refuses him, but Ghaleb lies and tells Mayce that she agreed to marry him. She faints and the doctor discovers that she is pregnant. When Ghaleb complains to his mother about Mayce, she says, "You're an oppressor, the son of your father."[112]

He reunites with Mayce, promising that he will try to overcome his jealousy. But he continues to doubt her innocence, insisting that she had lovers in addition to her rapist. He admits to the doctor that he fears he will become impotent from his doubts. Ghaleb then tells Mayce that he will allow her to leave the house and see her family but contends that she does not have the right to protest his relationships with other women. He telephones Safa', a woman who went to college with Mayce and who is depicted as a stereotypically "loose woman." At first, she hangs up on him, but later, she agrees to meet him. They flirt and he advances her money to work with him. Still, after all that he has done to her, Mayce loves Ghaleb. She assures her sister that Ghaleb behaves this way because he loves her. Throughout the miniseries, Ghaleb is portrayed in a negative light and Mayce is shown as overly submissive. It appears that, in an attempt to reconfigure gender norms, the screenwriter is critiquing Ghaleb's insecurity and Mayce's submissiveness. Yet the depiction of Safa' as a "promiscuous woman" reinforces stereotypical gender images; likewise, the depiction of veiled Nahed reinforces stereotypical images of devout woman.

Ghaleb continues to waver about Mayce, and he flaunts his affair with Safa'. Mayce finally breaks down and tells Ghaleb that she is carrying his baby girl. Upset, he fears his daughter will turn out like Mayce. When his mother begs him to be nice to Mayce or divorce her, Ghaleb has a moment of kindness. As soon as Mayce confides to her former professor that Ghaleb has become kind, though, he again becomes moody. He begins a relationship with Qamar, whom he marries. As his new wife milks him for money, Mayce has a baby girl. Her former professor advises Mayce to ask for a divorce, but she insists that she has surrendered to her fate. Meanwhile, Qamar treats Ghaleb poorly. When he begs for love, she tells him to have some dignity. The sheikh tells Ghaleb that he will continue to love this abusive woman as punishment for how he has treated his wife. When Mayce's baby girl is diagnosed with terminal leukemia, Ghaleb does not care, even when she dies.

Later Ghaleb, destroyed by Qamar, seeks to win Mayce back. By now, though, he has irreparably broken their relationship. She leaves, with music emphasizing her confidence. She has patiently forgiven him in the past but is moving on, understanding that divorce is the best solution. Though the ending is open, it hints that she will find love with her former professor, who has become her friend and confidant. In this storyline, love, gender, and marriage are used to differentiate Syrian culture from the extremism of Da'ish. While some pre-uprising miniseries upheld the sanctity of marriage and pushed for communal over individual values,[113] individualism, personal liberty, and divorce are now encouraged in this storyline.

While *Lestoo Jariya* does not refer directly to the uprising, *Shawq*, written by Hazim Suleiman and directed by Rasha Sharbatji, is set several years into the uprising turned war. During Ramadan 2017, *Shawq* was the miniseries that dealt most directly with dignity. The central character, *Shawq*, lost her parents when a bomb hit their home and now lives with her brother, Adam. Despite her circumstances, she refuses to accept anyone's pity. When Majed tells Shawq that they can no longer continue their affair since he will marry his fiancée in the coming week, she is startled when he expects a more emotional reaction. Accordingly, Shawq cuts off all contact with him to protect her pride.

Premarital sex is depicted without judgment in this storyline. At the beginning, we see Majed visiting Shawq for intimate moments, though the scenes are not sensationalized. When they break up due to Majed's upcoming marriage, Shawq expresses no regret that they have slept together, as she has known from the beginning that their relationship would end. When Majed tells Wa'el about their breakup, Wa'el does not express concern about honor or shame. Rather, he is angry with Majed for hurting Shawq. When he tells Shawq that he knows, Shawq says she does not regret it. She insists that it was not Majed's fault, since he was honest with her from beginning. Wa'el is surprised at her decision, but still mentions nothing about honor or shame. It is clear, too, that Majed and his fiancée, Nada, had slept together and Nada's mother wants her to marry for the prestige. When the relationship ends, though, neither family expresses concern connected to honor or shame.

Majed approaches Shawq's cousin Wa'el, with whom she is close, and says he is not sure why Shawq has not responded to his messages. Wa'el explains that Shawq wants to protect her pride. When Shawq realizes that she is increasingly forgetful, she sees a doctor, who asks if she has recently experienced trauma. Tears fall as she remembers the death of her parents. Shawq is diagnosed with early-onset Alzheimer's but hides it from her relatives. Still, they eventually find out. Majed too learns that she is ill and tells her he wants to be there for her, but she says that she does not need him to play the role of the hero. Majed realizes he needs to stand by Shawq and breaks up with his fiancée, Nada. Nada continues to fight for Majed, and her mother laments that she has no dignity left. Overall, through its focus on Shawq's plight, the story falls into the category of miniseries that uses dignity to evoke nostalgia. Shawq symbolizes Syria; her sudden and tragic demise symbolizes the unexpected destruction of Syria, a country that Amin Hamada writes, "had been previously filled with love, security, and happiness."[114] This nostalgic story intersects with a regime narrative since Syria was, in truth, far from glorious before the uprising. Like regime narratives, *Shawq* employs historical amnesia as it evokes regret at the upheaval of war and nostalgia for former times.

In his seminal research, Eyerman explores how the past is often reshaped and re-presented to fit generational or individual needs, especially in cases where there is a political motive. He continues his study by offering various perspectives on collective memory, such as Barry Schwartz's contention that "given the constraints of a recorded history, the past cannot be literally constructed; it can only be selectively exploited." Eyerman then expands on theories that associate collective memory and myth due to the negotiation and selection process.[115] Raz Yosef, in his examination of the politics of loss and trauma in contemporary Israeli cinema, cites E. Ann Kaplan's contention that "forgetting" is not always innocent and analyzes society's decisions to not talk about an event or talk about it in a way that dismisses past traumas, engaging in collective "amnesia."[116]

This nostalgia and historical amnesia further crystalizes as the story concludes. Shawq's brother Adam loves Wa'ed, a young girl who is forced into prostitution with a corrupt man named Jamal. She tries to break away from that life, but Jamal will not allow her. Wa'ed tells Adam that she is dirty and begs him to stay away from her, but he continues to love her. At one point when she is missing (kidnapped by Da'ish) Adam yearns for her. When his cousin Sulaf says she has heard scandals related to Wa'ed, he tells her not to judge. Thus, Wa'ed illustrates the suspension of rules governing honor and shame. Beyond that, the situation points to a culture of sexual liberty that arouses historical nostalgia, glosses over past oppression, and assumes the evolution of freer sexual norms. In the final episode, a written narration says that after Wa'ed was freed, she and Adam marry and travel to Germany. The written-out afterword at the end of the miniseries states that there could be no definite ending to this story taking place during continued war. We learn a few facts in this afterword: having refused to leave Sham, Shawq names her daughter after the city. Shawq dies in the middle of 2016. After her death, Majed leaves for Beirut with his daughter Sham. This last fact suggests that the city Sham continues to live but in exile.

Screenwriters' commitment to overcoming hypocritical social norms that no longer resonate during wartime peaked during the 2018 Ramadan season. Iyad Abu Shammat's *Tango*, perhaps the most popular miniseries of the season, refrains from demonizing 'Amer and Farah, who embark on a secret extramarital love affair. Rather, the screenwriter sympathetically accentuates the coldness of 'Amer's wife Lina and her disinterest in having sex with him. Yet throughout the season, social media rehashed and dissected the theme of marital betrayal in *Tango*. In a televised interview, Daniella Rahmeh (who played Farah) was asked if she had difficulty playing an unfaithful woman and if she worried that fans would hate her. When Rahmeh responded that she empathized with her character, the interviewer expressed concern because she appeared to be defending infidelity.[117] In an interview the following day, Bassem Moghniyyeh, who played Farah's husband, was asked the same question. He expressed his fundamental opposition to adultery.[118] Yet even as the theme of marital betrayal aroused controversy, *Tango* remained one of the most popular miniseries of the season, due to its suspense, plot development, convincing examples of Syrian-Lebanese cooperation, examination of oppression and injustice, critique of hypocritical social norms, and high artistic value.

The increasingly open engagement in societal critique and issues related to female sexuality can be seen in *Shababik*, which was produced in 2017 but broadcast in 2018. The miniseries consists of thirty separate episodes featuring two central characters always named Imad and Rahaf. In "al-Lahaf" (The Blanket), written by Bassam al-Salka, Imad and Rahaf are a poor, unhappily married couple struggling to survive. Imad, who is dissatisfied, lacks stable employment, while Rahaf, who is upright and honest, gives private tutoring lessons. One afternoon as she returns home, a cab driver kidnaps her. She asks for him to buy her food and gives him her clothes in order to gain his trust. When he leaves in search of food, she manages to escape with a blanket wrapped around her.

When she returns home late at night and explains what happened, Imad is suspicious and claims that the situation is shameful to him. He will not let her go to the police to report the incident for fear that it will cause a scandal. Frustrated with his refusal to help her, she hysterically tears apart the blanket she is wearing. They are both astonished when countless loose bills emerge. While Rahaf wants to take the money to the police, Imad, now calm, reassures her that he no longer doubts her honor. He says that she can choose to hand over the money to the police or she can give their son a better life. As with each independent episode of the miniseries, the ending is left open so the viewer can decide the outcome. Due to Rahaf's integrity, the viewer imagines that she will take the money to the police; perhaps she will even leave Imad, who doubted her when she needed his trust.

This post-uprising episode critiqued traditionally masculine notions of honor along with suspicion toward the female body and may be more thoroughly understood by comparing it to the story upon which it was based. In 2008 an episode titled "al-Lahaf," written by Rania Bitar and Nur Shishekly and directed by Zuhair Ahmad Qanoo', was featured in the miniseries *Wajh al-'Adala* (Face of Justice). This earlier version begins with Ruwayda leaving a boutique with bags of expensive clothing. A flashback then shows Ruwayda, newly married to Riyad. They are in love but poor. One evening when they take a cab home, the driver hits Riyad and takes off with Ruwayda. When Riyad wakes up, fearful of scandal, he refuses to call the police. Ruwayda manages to escape with a sheet around her and returns home. The neighbors call the police, but Ruwayda and Riyad refuse to cooperate. Riyad is upset and does not believe that Ruwayda did not let the kidnapper touch her. When the cab driver arrives in her apartment and hurts Riyad, Ruwayda shoots at him. Riyad is taken to the hospital and she is escorted to the police station. Yet Ruwayda has a smile on her face, as she has discovered the money hidden in the blankets. In this version, the ending is clear: Ruwayda and Riyad become rich. Riyad's suspicion is not problematized, since in this storyline money solves the issues of honor and shame. Contrastingly, the 2018 version conspicuously showcases the problems of honor and shame and refuses to reduce these problems to matters of class. The open ending in the new version compels viewers to confront hypocritical standards of female sexuality and unfair judgments of raped women, as it also examines Rahaf's integrity.

In *Fawda*, which is, in my opinion, the strongest miniseries in the social for the sake of the social strand of the 2018 season, Najeeb Nseir continues to critique troubling notions of honor and shame as well as the institution of marriage. Selwa, who is divorced, falls in love with Rateb. Her son, Seif, is outraged. When he becomes aggressive and orders her to be "honorable," she calls him the "son of Da'ish," then continues that he can kill her if he would like, but that his obsession with defending his honor is nonsensical given that a bomb could fall on their heads at any moment.[119] Rateb, a lawyer, forges a marriage contract for Selwa to show her son when he harasses her. After a prolonged conflict with her son, Selwa moves in with Rateb and behaves as if they were a married couple; their personalities change quickly once constrained by marriage dynamics. Rateb curses the day he forged the contract for the institution of marriage that he despises. Their love story ends in divorce.

In another storyline, Dana's ailing mother, Wissal, and Abu Kheil are shown in bed together. In the next scene, Abu Kheil tells Wissal he wishes to marry her as soon as possible to avoid judgment. But Wissal asserts that she does not care about what people think and that marriage is unnecessary.[120] Though Najeeb Nseir expressed disappointment that the director omitted certain character details in this story, he was pleased that the bedroom scene between Wissal and Abu Kheil was preserved. "We are in the midst of war, death, and suffering; there is no place for obsessions with issues of honor and shame."[121] A later scene, which I argue is one of the most explicit in Syrian drama in terms of expressing sexual desire, shows Wissal and Abu Kheil washing dishes together, hands touching and bodies rubbing against each other.[122]

Critiques of double standards toward the woman's body are present to an unprecedented degree in *Fawda*. When Fethiyyeh announces her secret marriage and pregnancy to Zeidan, he assumed the baby belongs to his brother, Fares, who has gone missing. In the eleventh episode, Fares, who had been arrested for his Facebook posts and is finally set free, returns home to find his wife pregnant and married to his older brother. He is utterly confused when everyone assumes the baby is his. He later approaches Fethiyyeh and asks who the father of her baby is, since they never consummated their marriage. Fethiyyeh cries, confessing that she has no idea; there were four men who gang-raped her. Fares is upset, but not because Fethiyyeh has been hurt. Instead, his rage springs from the fact that her body was shared with other men. She pleads with him in her own defense. Angered, he storms out. From that point onward, he leaves his "dishonored" formerly beloved for his brother. Shortly afterward, he pronounces the three-time divorce formula to Fethiyyeh in front of Zeidan and two witnesses so that their marriage is officially dissolved.

Nseir poignantly addresses Fares's condemnation of Fethiyyeh as well as a society that irrationally blames women for violence perpetrated against them. When Zeidan disappears (drafted into the army reserves), Fares refuses to help Fethiyyeh, who is alone, cold, and hungry in her room. He refers to her unborn child as "a disaster," and contends that she is cheating on Zeidan by not telling him the truth about the rape. Yet Fethiyyeh fears Zeidan will "slaughter" her if he learns the truth.[123] Despite his threats, Fares ends up supporting Fethiyyeh's lie to avoid scandal and protect her from Zeidan's wrath. As seen earlier, in the nostalgic *Bi-Intizar al-Yasmin*, a raped woman symbolized a violated Syria, engendering both compassion and forgiveness. In this storyline, however, Nseir captures the judgmental cruelty directed toward raped women as well as the impossible standards expected for a woman's body.[124] *Fawda* elevated the social for the sake of the social miniseries to greater acclaim. It also established new potential avenues to explore in upcoming seasons.

Honor and Shame: Old Damascus Tales, War, and Historical Revision

Old Damascus tales were traditionally filled with images of French colonial presence and featured themes involving gender and marriage norms. Prior to the uprising, these tales served as metaphors and allegories that allowed for an indirect critique of the Ba'th Party regime.[125] In recent years critiques of both religious fanaticism and outdated requirements for female purity have increased in frequency. *Bi'a Shamiyyeh* tales often revise collective memory by rewriting traditional notions of honor and shame, though at times contradictions arise. Furthermore, in recent years these tales have transformed the collective memory of this time period and used them to take on contemporary issues, causing all sorts of historical revision. As seen earlier, indirect use of the terminology of the current uprising along with indirect references to Da'ish has occurred in some post-uprising contemporary tales. Similarly, popular *Bi'a Shamiyyeh* miniseries, which have had multiyear installments, such as *Tawq al-Banat*, *Khatun*, and *Bab al-Hara*, contain marriage and gender metaphors with contemporary implications.

While the first season of *Tawq al-Banat* (The Necklace of Girls, 2014) focused on the role of women in the resistance against the French, the second season, which centered on black magic, was less female-centric and lacked the charisma of the first season. Both seasons showed woman as active outside the household, but they did not reconfigure norms relating to honor and shame. By 2016, the storyline diminished women's activity outside the home and reaffirmed honor and shame values. In this third season, Salhiyyeh's husband accuses her of being "impure" on her wedding night. Her father, Abu Talib, is prepared to kill her until several midwives declare that she is *Tahera* (pure). The show declines to critique this custom. The fourth season of *Tawq al-Banat* (2017) commences with the kidnapping of Abu Talib by war profiteers and rabble-rousers, which obliquely reminds us of Syria's current turmoil. When he escapes his kidnappers, he and his wife try to persuade a reluctant Salhiyyeh to get married. Umm Talib and her daughters even consult a sheikha for guidance in influencing Salhiyyeh. Soon, Abu Talib realizes that the evil Na'amat was behind his kidnapping and also behind the killing of his young son. Mariam, Mal-al Sham, and their mother try to convince Abu Talib to take a second wife so that he can have another son who carries his name. The sheikh confirms for Abu Talib that his conditions qualify him for a second wife: his first wife is no longer of child-bearing age to grant him a son. The miniseries' attempt to be progressive, communicating that a man should take a second wife only under certain conditions, was undermined by its basic premise, which advocates for polygamy.[126] Evident in the fourth season of this miniseries is the battle of cultures of which screenwriter Reem Hanna spoke.[127] Although the open ending concludes with a farewell until the fifth season, it became clear at the start of Ramadan 2018 that there would be no fifth season at the time.

While *Tawq al-Banat* couches a woman's honor in her "pure" body, other Old Damascus tales reconfigure the issues of honor and shame. Among Old Damascus tales, *Khatun* was one of the most popular, thanks to its strong female lead.[128] In *Khatun Part One* (2016), the French colonel of Lebanese origin, Karim, seduces the leading character, Khatun, after a horse hit her and he saw her without a veil. Though Karim is already married, but wants to marry Khatun as well, since she is the daughter of the powerful *za'im* (local leader) and proximity to her will allow him to spy on her neighborhood. With the help of a nurse, he repeatedly visits Khatun's room at the hospital. When people in the neighborhood spread rumors about how Karim saw Khatun without her veil, the situation becomes a scandal. The scandal is amplified when Khatun's sister-in-law Na'mat spreads the news that Karim is seeking Khatun's hand in marriage though she is already engaged to her cousin, Fahd. Na'mat encourages Khatun to flee on her wedding night, lest her new husband discovers the love between Karim and Khatun. When Khatun flees, her father Za'im Abu al-'Izz and brothers are humiliated and respond that "the scandal can only be cleansed with blood."[129] Her fiancé Fahd, his mother Umm Fahd, and other angry relatives are upset that Fahd's dignity was damaged and want Khatun to be killed. Al-Zaiba, a nationalist hero who fights the French, does all he can to prove Khatun's innocence. Later, when she is married and pregnant, he ensures that an honor crime is not committed against her.

While the *za'im* does not want his innocent child to be killed, Khatun's brother Ayub is determined to kill her. Here, even while others strive to uphold the practice of an honor crime, the father figure assumes a new leniency when he learns that his daughter is pregnant. Still, Abu Fahd telling the *za'im* that he may remain *za'im* only if he repairs the damage his daughter has caused. The first season ends after Fahd and Ayub find Khatun, and Ayub points a gun at her head. In *Khatun Part Two* (2017), al-Zaiba kills Fahd and then prevents Ayub from killing Khatun. When the *za'im* goes to see Khatun, he first he points gun at her head while she hugs his legs and cries. She assures him that she did not commit a sin but tells her father he can kill her. She takes the gun and points it at herself. However, he refuses to kill her, saying that he regrets only that she ran off without his counsel.

Since Abu al-'Izz had refused to kill Khatun, he loses his position. Khatun's brother 'Izz al-Din refuses to see his sister, since she is the reason her father lost his position. But he will not hurt her, since she is of his blood. Meanwhile, as the men fight to replace Abu al-'Izz and become *za'im*, al-Zaiba fights a nationalist struggle against the French. The women express a desire to fight alongside the men. When the neighborhood, Harat al-Amara, is surrounded, Khatun comes up with an idea to make poisoned food that the soldiers will eat. The drugged soldiers are no longer alert, and the plan is to transfer food to the neighborhood. The food is distributed, and al-Zaiba proudly tells Abu al-'Izz that the plan was Khatun's idea. When her older brother, Forough, under the influence of his wife Na'mat, tries to kill her, the other men hold him back and the women declare, "So you're trying to make yourself out to be a man?"[130] While the story attempts to overcome traditional understandings of honor and shame, these notions are nevertheless ingrained in the community. Umm Fahd has made a scandal of Abu Fahd's alleged relationship with Samiha, and Abu al-'Izz says that the honor of people should not be taken lightly.

The issue of reconstructing family honor occurs throughout the miniseries. Khatun becomes a nationalist hero against the French, and Abu al-'Izz forgives her for marrying Karim. He tells her that even if whole world is against him, he is with her. He says, "You lifted my head and made me proud. Don't cry—be illuminated like Sham."[131] He dies shortly after. Despite reform-minded instances related to honor and shame, the miniseries contains contradictions. Na'mat unleashes evil on the neighborhood, causing one of her sisters-in-law to miscarry. She is also responsible for the kidnapping of Khatun's newborn son. Still, when her evil is discovered, her parents stand by her. Na'mat's father regrets that the neighborhood was harsh with Abu al-'Izz when he refused to discipline Khatun after her honor was questioned. As his own daughter now faces severe rebuke, he now realizes how hard it is for a father to punish his own child.

Yet the parallel between Khatun, who married a man she loved, and Na'mat, who unleashed evil in the neighborhood, reveals that issues related to honor and shame have the same significance as much greater crimes. Also, when the French want to kill Khatun because she is responsible for the deaths of many French soldiers, al-Zaiba charges the neighborhood with protecting her since she is their *'ard* and *sharaf*, terms that reinforce traditional notions of honor and shame. Furthermore, when the French are about to hang Khatun (before al-Zaiba saves her), she announces in front of the whole neighborhood, "Please forgive me. I didn't obey my father or follow our customs and traditions. Lift your head, oh, brothers and sister. I'm not sad to die. I died for Sham. The pure land of Sham."[132] While *Khatun* ended by announcing a third season, director Tamer Ishaq made it clear that this announcement was not accurate. He said that the first and second seasons were filmed together, providing integrity to the storyline, and he did not wish to now introduce an unintegrated third season.[133]

In the second season of *Khatun*, as with the first, the wartime atmosphere is felt indirectly. For example, Harat al-Amara is surrounded and food supplies are blocked off until al-Zaiba agrees to surrender. While Abu Fahd wants to give up so that the neighborhood does not die of hunger, Abu al-'Izz insists that it is better to die of hunger than to eat food gotten through humiliation.[134] This sentiment echoes the value placed on dignity throughout the uprising. On another occasion, the evil Na'mat says that some play revolutionaries while most go hungry. This statement recalls animosity directed toward revolutionaries in Syria.[135]

Bab al-Hara Part Eight (2016) continues to construct a new history, focusing on societal advancement.[136] As shown in chapter 1, new seasons of *Bab al-Hara* manifest disjunctions from previous seasons. Although the miniseries remained popular among the general public, it was criticized in the press and called a "disaster in drama."[137] Gender and marriage themes in this season establish a progressive culture that resists religious fanaticism. Julie, a Syrian lawyer, arrives in the neighborhood to offer Syrian women an avenue to divorce. The show roots this effort in the *Sharia*, which is tradition in Syria rather than France. At the same time, the storyline critiques several conservative traditions and social norms. Sim'u is depicted as an impotent religious fanatic who cheats his neighbors. When he beats his wife, Delal, her family supports her decision to divorce him. The evil Sheikh Fekri, who conspires with the French, says that Umm Bedri should consummate her marriage with another man before returning to her husband, since her husband pronounced the divorce formula three times. Abu 'Isam agrees to marry Umm Bedri. In the end, however, the good Sheikh 'Alim realizes that since Abu Bedri does not even remember pronouncing divorce, the formula is void.

Bab al-Hara Part Eight also addresses issues of honor and empathizes with women. 'Aisha flees into al-Nems's home since her brother Laban, against her will, has written her a marriage contract to a criminal. Al-Nems does all he can to protect her and they fall in love. Later, 'Aisha works in the home of a wealthy family, and Abu 'Isam accompanies al-Nems, who would like to ask for her hand in marriage from her brother Laban. While 'Aisha insists that her brother will never forgive her, Abu 'Isam helps them reconcile. However, on the wedding night, Laban kills her. Abu Zafer then wants Abu 'Isam to step down from being *za'im* since he did not know how to protect 'Aisha. Here, an honor crime triggers political turmoil in the neighborhood. This takes place against the background of new gender norms in the neighborhood with the dramatic aim of disassociating Abu 'Isam's ideology from religious fanaticism. When Delal participates in women's marches and is seen unveiled in the neighborhood and in the newspaper, Abu 'Isam defends her and even encourages her education. He also helps her divorce Sim'u, who is impotent. The story occurs in the context of battles against the French, so that a clear distinction remains between the Syrian regime and the French. Even when women, including the lawyer Julie, her friend

Khaldiyyeh, and Abu 'Isam's daughters, Delal and Sharifa, protest the Syrian government, it is clear that the French are shooting at them. The storyline does not intend the French to stand in allegorically for the current Ba'th Party regime as occurred in prewar seasons of *Bab al-Hara*.

The press extended their criticism of *Bab al-Hara Part Nine* (2017) to historical inaccuracies, faulty storylines, and contradictions within characters who carried over from previous seasons.[138] As in *Khatun* and *Tawq al-Banat*, there are moments in *Bab al-Hara* that reveal the present. In earlier seasons, during fighting scenes against the French, the battleground always seemed far away from the neighborhood. Now, however, the gunshots sound as if they are next door, a striking similarity to scenes in miniseries set in current war-torn Syria. Furthermore, in *Bab al-Hara*, like in *Khatun* and *Tawq al-Banat*, the competition to become *za'im* is central to the neighborhood, even as the men fight the French. As shown in the previous season, *Bab al-Hara Part Nine* is being read as an allegory of the current bloodshed in Syria. Thus, the storyline explains the roots of Da'ish from a faulty historical perspective. According to Iyad Shihab Ahmad, for example, *Bab al-Hara* used to be an allegory for fighting the Ba'th Party regime through the lens of the French mandate powers. Now, the focus is on fighting the French colonial presence and outside interference in general (not as an allegory of Syrian government). The main point, now, is the fight against outside conspiracies and religious fanaticism rather than political oppression.[139]

In *Bab al-Hara Part Nine*, women's protests amid new configurations of honor and shame remain a central theme. Storylines in this season focus less on women's bodies, in an attempt to make Abu 'Isam and other men in the neighborhood appear more open minded and to disassociate them from religious extremists. Accordingly, women's concerns are defended in an unprecedented way. For example, when Sara thinks her husband will take another wife, he assures her that he will not. When Booran's husband takes a second wife, Abu 'Isam is critical of his behavior. Yet these characters demonstrate contradictory instances of extremism. For example, Delal's participation in the women's manifestations in the previous season had led to her photograph in a newspaper. Now in the ninth season, at the barber shop when 'Isam is cutting Zafer's hair, he finds a picture of Delal in the newspaper in Zafar's pocket. 'Isam begins to scream about his honor, and he and Zafar fight.[140] Many neighborhood men surround them, and Abu 'Isam joins, spitting on Zafer, and contending that this matter involves honor and blood. When Abu Zafer sees Abu 'Isam, he expresses contrition, acknowledging that there have been problems between them in the past, but that honor is not a game. He says he will do exactly as Abu 'Isam asks. He kisses Abu 'Isam's head and is forgiven. Abu Zafer's wife claims that everything is Delal's fault, since she was in the manifestations in the first place, but Abu Zafer takes responsibility. While there are such moments that reveal a less reactionary stance toward women's equality, contradictions continue to abound.

When a young woman staying with Umm Hatim's family looks out the window at her cousin, Umm Hatim is furious. She tells the young woman that she cannot look out the window anymore, since if people see her figure by the window, they might assume one of her daughters is looking at a man and spread rumors.

The public assumed that there would be a *Bab al-Hara Part Ten* the following year, and rumors abounded about actors returning and others leaving the show. Rumors spread that Mu'taz would take a second wife when Sarah was proved barren, and that 'Isam would marry a fourth woman, the lawyer Judy. Yet on the eve of the new season, the channel on which the miniseries would be broadcast remained a mystery. Once the new season started, it became clear that *Bab al-Hara* would not run this season due to disputes between the director and producer as well as criticism of the miniseries, which was now deemed a failure despite its popularity. At the same time, actors gave interviews promising a tenth as well as eleventh and twelve season.[141] Indeed, a tenth season appeared in 2019 with an entirely new cast of characters and, though the miniseries was an Old Damascus tale, directly used the terminology and themes of the current uprising. For example, French warplanes (similar to modern airplanes) descend upon neighborhoods full of internal refugees seeking shelter.

SINCE ITS ADVENT IN THE MID-1960S, drama has sought to transform social norms by focusing on intimate relations. During the 1960s and 1970s writers addressed man's oppression at the hands of the regime. Territorial loss and economic difficulties were the main sources of the *qabaday*'s lost honor rather than the sexual transgressions of their female relations. Over the years, as the *qabaday* became less able to provide for his family, he became more fixated on guarding and repressing the sexuality and desire of his female relations. While representations of masculinity in Syrian drama addressed regime legitimacy, representations of women were embroiled in issues of cultural authenticity. In the years prior to the uprising, some contemporary Syrian drama screenwriters portrayed the sexual repression of women as symbolic of the political oppression of the entire people. In some avant-garde storylines, the *qabaday* initially declined when he gave up his role as protector of a woman's body. During the initial years of the uprising, several transitional miniseries continued to present coded messages of equality, dignity, and freedom where the *qabaday* did not repress the sexual desire of his female relations. At this time, Syrian television writers of various political perspectives dealt more than ever with formerly taboo topics of love, sexuality, and betrayal, in order to impart some modicum of wisdom to the work of understanding the growing bloodshed in Syria's war. In these miniseries, however, the central focus was on forgiving a woman for her past "mistakes." The female body still appeared as a dangerous site of seduction.

With the increased bloodshed of an uprising turned civil war and the brutal violence of Da'ish, drama screenwriters persisted in creating a plethora of love and marriage metaphors to navigate a changing market and devastated nation. The ongoing presence of pan-Arab escapist dramas marked a transition in 2014. While the theme of premarital sex and seduction was no longer taboo, little sex and seduction took place on screen. Some Syrian-produced miniseries, such as *Nisa' min Hadha al-Zaman*, which set their storylines against the background of war, had as their avowed intention the reexamination of issues related to sexuality. But by blaming women for their actions and positioning women as subjects of male authority and judgment, they fell short of reconfiguring gender norms. During this time, screenwriters focused on Syria's impotence, a phallocentric concept that ultimately served to reify woman as objects. Although they ultimately fell into the trap of presenting women as a symbol of the nation, they attempted to evince the importance of social reform from within while underscoring a secular collective identity in contradistinction to Islamist militants.

By 2015, as the nation sought to survive amid further assault, Da'ish became a central theme in Syrian drama. Here we witness a temporary suspension of honor codes and an attempt to present new narratives of resilience around noble and exemplary women who have been sexually assaulted. Yet this temporary suspension of gender norms does not entail sexual equality. While Warda in *Ghadan Naltaqi* establishes her own patterns of sexual behavior without fearing a male response, Lamar in *Bi-Intizar al-Yasmin* is a beneficiary of a temporary moment of crisis and war. She symbolizes a victimized Syria who is forgiven. Indeed, even Warda takes on the symbolism of Syria, a Syria destroyed from within and without, and thus no longer subject to former standards of judgment. This attempt to reconfigure gender to promote a "secular" identity as opposed to religious extremism still revealed a tendency to cling to stale models of national honor.

During the 2017 Ramadan season, in their gender constructions, miniseries such as *Mudhakkarat 'Ashiqa Sabiqa* and *Shawq*, which also place their storylines in the heart of the azmeh, evoke nostalgia for previous times and evince a collective amnesia to past political oppression. These two miniseries served as poignant examples of how the nostalgic register could intersect with the regime narrative, even unwittingly. During that same season, *Ahl al-Gharam Part Three*, with a series of different writers and directors, offered storylines with various degrees of nostalgia, political neutrality, and oppositionist stances. It also supplied social for the sake of the social storylines. All episodes worked to differentiate a secular collective memory from one steeped in religious extremism.

In 2018, *Tango* and *Fawda* went even further in critiquing notions of honor and shame for the purpose of reforming cultural norms and constructing a new, secular collective memory. Both fell within in the social for the sake of the social strand, though *Tango* touched very indirectly on the uprising, while *Fawda* was set in the Syrian uprising turned civil war. As both these miniseries aspire to overcome hypocritical social standards, there is no intention to evoke nostalgia for former times. While *Tango* avoids political critique altogether, *Fawda* subtly evinces its oppositional stance through the social critique at the heart of its storyline—specifically, Fare's unjust imprisonment, Zeidan's sudden drafting into army reserves, and the chaos of a neighborhood that is flooded by internally displaced Syrians. As opposed to the nostalgic register, which may unconsciously fall into the regime narrative as it reveals historical amnesia, the social for the sake of the social strand, *Fawda* in particular, sets itself apart through the cultural reconfiguration of societal norms.

Indeed, in the 2019 season, while only six miniseries touched on the war, the majority with a neutral political stance, one—*Musafat Aman*—took the social for the sake of the social strand to new heights. *Musafat Aman* promotes fair and equitable social norms and a softer masculine figure. This can be seen in the figure of Yusuf who helps Nur, who was pregnant but aborted her baby out of desperation when her lover left. At the hospital Yusuf covers for her, revealing his unjudgmental personality; later they become engaged. At the same time, we have the storyline of Sarab, whose husband has been in Germany for over two years, and who embarks on an affair with her friend Nihad's husband. When Nihad finds out about the affair, she refuses to forgive her husband, despite his attempts to win her over again. Eventually, he packs his suitcase to leave. At the door, Nihad announces that she will ask him a question; if he can answer it, she will forgive him and they can start over. Her question is, "If I had been the one who had the affair, would you have been able to show me forgiveness, the same forgiveness you now ask of me?"[142] Her husband looks at her blankly, unable to answer, and then leaves. His action demonstrates the double standards of a man who wants forgiveness for his extramarital affair yet can't consider the possibility of forgiving his wife for the same grievance. The series speaks to ongoing concern about hypocritical standards that require change to make Syrian society more just. Furthermore, as we will see in the next chapter, several post-uprising storylines involving nonheteronormative relations, previously taboo, would be explored more openly, with less judgment and for the purpose of societal critique.

5

The Politics of Queer Representations in Syrian Television Drama Past and Present

Buq'at Daw' *did not appear during the 2018 season but reappeared with sharp sarcasm in 2019 as writers analyzed their war-torn society. In a sketch titled "al-Mas'ul Namudhaji" (An Exemplary Authority Figure) in Episode 1 of* Buq'at Daw' *Part Fourteen (2019), written by Muwaffaq al-Mas'ud, a Japanese transgender woman, Sakura, has introduced a robot, Yong, who will serve as an exemplary authority figure, rejecting bribes and conducting honest work. Sakura has designed Yong to look Syrian yet think like the Japanese. Sakura herself is dressed in a silk blue gown with a traditional brown rectangular hat (both items traditional Japanese garb), with a yellow shirt and makeup slathered on her face. Even though her language and gestures are incomprehensible as she mimics Japanese, the Syrian assistant understands and translates for her. As the assistant introduces Yong, the director of the office refers to Sakura as "he" despite the assistant's insistence on the pronoun "she."*

While the transgender aspect of the storyline provides a troubling comic relief, the focus of the sketch is the robot, Yong, who serves as a model official, refusing to allow any kind of unethical or indecent office behavior even as employees are arrested for dishonesty. When Yong sees a young man on the street corner complaining about his personal difficulties along with the trash littering the streets and the high price of potatoes, Yong says the situation is a shame and promises to help. Later, when Yong calls out on the director for using the office phone for personal use, the director has Yong arrested by three men in suits who tie him up and then electrocute him, saying they brought him to Syria to help the country, not to destroy it. At the end of the sketch, an electrocuted Yong is returned to Sakura, who holds her hands in prayer and then escorts him out. Sakura's transgender identity, intended as a secondary plot line and as comic relief, reveals that despite certain attempts to deal respectfully with matters of sexuality, which we will examine in this chapter, queer spaces are often used for humor of a derogatory nature, even in the most recent Syrian Ramadan season.

Historical and Theoretical Frameworks for Queer Studies

Middle East queer studies, as poignantly argued by Hanadi al-Samman and Tarek El-Ariss, often operates within a binary model in which the East is viewed as pre-modern and bound by tradition and the West is viewed as modern. Through their examination of literature and culture, al-Samman and El-Ariss propose an engagement with the intricate sites of meanings that move beyond viewing queer identities in the Middle East through an imperialist and colonialist gaze.[1] In "Out of the Closet: Representations of Homosexuals and Lesbians in Modern Arabic Literature," al-Samman illustrates how modern representations of male homosexuality in the Arab world are instrumentalized to show the Arab male's loss of manhood and disempowerment by the state. On the other hand, female homosexuality is firmly situated in a heterocentric discourse that allows for lesbianism to exist as a transient condition to heteronormativity. Al-Samman emphasizes how this contrasts with medieval traditions that allowed mutations in representations of same-sex "definitions and practices."[2]

In *Crossing Borders: Love between Women in Medieval French and Arabic Literatures*, Sahar Amer explores the formative role that Arabic eroticism had in influencing alternative sexualities in Old French literary texts, sexualities that otherwise would have remained ignored. Her study shows that while same-sex sexual practices were considered taboo in the medieval West, this was not the case in the medieval Middle East. Amer's study reveals the debt that the Old French tradition owes to the Arabic literary homoerotic tradition. She also shows that, since it was seen as emerging from the East, lesbianism was believed to be a menace in the European Middle Ages.[3]

Joseph Massad argues that Edward Said could easily have added "sexual deviant" to his long list of Orientalist tropes due to Western perceptions of sexual depravity in the East. In his monumental *Desiring Arabs* (2007), Massad shows that the Orientalist fantasy once viewed the Arab world as degenerate due to its homoeroticism, licentious sex, and its fluid gender spaces. Yet with the colonial gaze, the West turned that framework around and instead judged the Arab world as backward and oppressive of the rights of homosexuals. Massad also expands on how some Arab writers since the middle of the nineteenth century would adopt Orientalist judgments about a degenerate Arab Islamic civilization and would imitate the colonial gaze in their portrayals of queer subjectivities.[4] Furthermore, Khalid Hadeed argues that due to homosexuality's menace to accepted constructions of masculinity, its depiction in modern Arabic literature is one of political and social emasculation, as well as corruption.[5]

In this chapter I critique the instrumentalization of queer representations in Syrian drama from the 1960s through the uprising. I trace how in the 1960s and 1970s, cross-dressing and cross-gender roles were symptoms of the fear of impoverished masculinity. Likewise, fear of strong cross-gendered women

emerged. In the 1990s through 2000, "bad mothers," absent fathers, and dictatorial fathers raised effeminate sons who were, it was implied, homosexual. In
the 2000s, women's cross-gender roles showed the dangerous role of law and culture on women, and lesbianism or transgender served a temporary function
before the reinstatement of heterosexual relations, as al-Samman has argued.
While many post-uprising miniseries continue to propagate previous discourses, a few noninstrumentalized roles show homosexual men and women
overcoming previous stereotypes and possibly evidence a new direction. These
recent portrayals exhibit new forms of advocacy, as proposed by al-Samman; they
focus on body politics rather than gender politics.[6] I argue that these recent
renderings are efforts by screenwriters to construct a collective memory with
different characteristics and values than those of religious extremists and Da'ish.

Male and Female Gender-Crossing Roles, Cross-Dressing, and "Women" with Mustaches in the Early Subversive Drama of the 1960s and 1970s

Television in Syria laid its foundation amid a tense political atmosphere, shortly
before the unraveling of the United Arab Republic. From this rocky foundation
sprouted a culture of political parodies and social commentary concerning the
lives of Syrian citizens.[7] As shown in chapter 3, the early Syrian political parodies of the 1960s through 1970s were secular in approach and represented a
male perspective. The main concern of these parodies was an embattled, subordinate masculinity within the family, which served as a microcosm of the state.
Loss of land and economic malaise led to loss of dignity among men who from
time to time are referred to as qabadayat. The presence of frustrated masculinity
in marital relations governed by a wife's demands—with the recurring image of
marriage as a prison—commented on economic hardship, corruption, and
dictatorship. Women's empowerment as a result of suppressed masculinity
emerged as a fear during this time, as men's pride indeed suffered due to territorial loss and economic discontent. This loss of pride was not, however, because
of the sexual transgressions of the women in men's families. When a man showed
his dominance over a woman or was violent toward her, it was depicted as part
of a vicious cycle of state violence causing vulnerable men to be violent rather
than as an example of powerful hegemonic masculinity. Indeed, the act of hegemonic masculinity was meant to show man's political vulnerability.[8]

  In this context male gender-crossing roles were directly linked to concerns
about impoverished masculinity, while female gender-crossing behavior reflected
a fear of female empowerment. Images of men wearing wigs and cross-dressing
while women became bullies recurred in the early political parodies of Ghawwar Tawsheh and Husni Bik. During the early 1960s Lahham, Qal'i, and Sbai'i
acted in a series of fifteen disconnected television episodes in a studio in Beirut.

These episodes were written by Qal'i, directed by Naqoola abu Samah, and produced by al-Sharikat al-Televizion Lubnan wa-l-Mashriq.[9] *Maktab Mu'amalat Zawjiyya* focuses on Husni Bik's attempt to oversee Ghawwar's engagement. When Ghawwar and Husni Bik enter the prospective fiancée's home, her unnamed father remains silent while the aggressive mother, Su'ad, makes impossible demands. Their son, Ahmad, who is stereotypically effeminate, has a stutter and behaves passively—a result, the show implies, of his upbringing by a dominating mother. Ahmad's homosexuality, however, is not addressed directly. This trope of the effeminate young man abounds in Syrian television drama and points to the negative consequences of political oppression. As Khalid Hadeed argues, due to homosexuality's threat to dominant constructions of masculinity, its portrayal in modern Arabic literature also portrays political and social emasculation as well as corruption.[10] Similarly, Hanadi al-Samman argues that modern Arabic literature engages in a form of constructivism that suggests that homosexuality is the result of the political and economic oppression of Arab manhood.[11]

The fear of role reversal is the subject of Episode 10, "Safaqa Rahiba" (A Good Deal), which addresses marriage issues and gender subversion. The episode opens with Husni toiling in the kitchen as his children's noise fills the house. The eldest son, Ghawwar, tells his father, "It's your fault. You're weak and afraid of your wife. You're doing all the work while Mother visits friends." Ghawwar convinces his father to divorce his wife. Together, they break into the safe of Amin Bik (who happens to be in his office with his lover, Selma) to finance the divorce. Just as Amin calls the police, Amin's suspicious wife, Soo, enters the office. Moments later, Ghawwar, dressed as an elderly lady with a headscarf covering part of his face (and mustache), comes out the office and presents "herself" as Husni's mother, who is in the process of marrying her son to Selma. Ghawwar exclaims, "Someone who cheats with money is better than someone who steals the honor of people by messing with their women." "She" inches closer to Soo and attempts to kiss her on the cheek, causing Amin Bik much discomfort. This Bakhtinesque carnival, in which men disguise themselves as women and engage in a gender-bending masquerade, appears throughout these disconnected episodes.

Originally produced in Beirut and then broadcast by Syrian Arab Television, *Maqalib Ghawwar* (1966) portrayed embattled masculinity with a subtle focus on political critique. That same year, the second Ba'th coup established Salah Jadid as president and Hafiz al-Asad as defense minister. Due to the *idafa* construction of Arabic, *Maqalib Ghawwar* translates into either "Ghawwar's Tricks" or "The Tricking of Ghawwar." Both titles explain the loosely jointed miniseries, which follows an exchange of pranks between Ghawwar, Husni Bik, and Abu Sayyah and shows Ghawwar constantly attempting to replace Husni Bik as performer in Abu Sayyah's café, often consigning both Abu Sayyah and Husni Bik to an asylum. Men touch their mustaches repeatedly in the midst of carnivalesque gender masquerade as a tribute to male honor. Additionally, *Maghalab Ghawwar* explores the concept of female purity. The female body is not so much an identity marker but an indicator of and reaction to male subservience. Ghawwar arouses Abu 'Antar's suspicions that Husni is having an affair with his daughter Fasiha, and to wash away the shame, a frightened Husni agrees to marry her. Husni reluctantly agrees to all conditions, and Fasiha (a male actor playing a woman) appears before him. When he sees his unattractive wife, Husni refuses to proceed with the marriage, and Abu 'Antar beats him up. On another occasion, Ghawwar disguises himself as a female passenger in Husni's cab and gets out close to Husni's house. As he makes Husni wait in the cab, Ghawwar informs Husni's wife that "she" is now married to Husni. Consequently, Husni's wife leaves him. At the end of the episode Husni finds Ghawwar's sandals in his car, revealing Ghawwar's tricks.

Abu Sayyah and Husni Bik later team up to bring down Ghawwar, who has effectively ruined their lives. Husni grudgingly shaves off his mustache (or manhood) and disguises himself as Fatema to convince Ghawwar to fall in love with "her." Ghawwar immediately senses something familiar about Fatema. He tells Fatema that he wishes to marry her. Abu Sayyah convinces him to give his half of the café as Fatema's dowry. On their wedding night, Ghawwar is shocked by what he sees behind the scenes and checks into an asylum. Unbeknownst to the remorseful Husni Bik and Abu Sayyah, Ghawwar realizes that his bride was Husni Bik and has a trick up his sleeve. Ghawwar threatens to kill himself unless he sees his beloved again, so Husni dresses up as Fatema again to visit. Then Ghawwar exposes Husni as a man dressed in woman's clothing and accuses him of being "the crazy one." The doctors put Husni back in the mental hospital and discharge Ghawwar.

The theme of men cross-dressing as women occurs in the context of marriage as a prison governed by a dictatorial woman in *Milh wa Sukar* (1973), a three-episode miniseries that takes place three years after Asad's Corrective Movement. The symbolic prison of marriage is illustrated by the way Fatoon torments her passive husband, Yassin, who at one point hides under his bed to escape her wrath. Meanwhile in the concrete jail, Ghawwar and his inmates put on a performance for Mother's Day in which, despite his protests, Ghawwar is required to veil himself as a woman. Still, he insists on keeping his tarbush and mustache, which lends a carnivalesque quality to the show.

When Qal'i ceased to write theatrical productions in the mid-1970s, Lahham benefited from the creative genius of Muhammad al-Maghut, a Syrian poet born in the city of Salamiyyeh. *Wayn al-Ghalat?*, written by al-Maghut and Lahham, addresses corruption, the housing crisis, and the unimportance of an academic degree. Composed of independent episodes, this miniseries was based on sketches for *Masrah al-Shawk*, written by actor 'Omar Hajjo.[12] In *Wayn al-Ghalat?*, al-Maghut offers an stronger antigovernment critique than in previous miniseries. In the episode "al-Bahth 'an al-Wazifa" (Searching for Employment), the men's central fear is role reversal and emasculation. In one scene, Abu 'Antar and Ghawwar, dressed in women's clothing, cook with stolen items, impersonating housewives. Using stereotypically feminine gestures, they complain that they have no idea how to cook and clean and blame their families for not teaching them to manage a household. They add stolen potatoes and pictures of tomatoes to the soup, which contains no meat, since meat is expensive. The scene symbolizes job scarcity, ineptitude, and oppressed masculinity.

Kasak ya Watan was one of the most politically critical productions of the era. The play aired on television and was referred to as a *musalsal*. In it, Bakhtin's carnivalesque vision, subversions, multiplicity of styles, and conflicting points of view resonate strongly.[13] Lahham plays Ghawwar, the impoverished son of a martyr whose infant daughter, Amal, dies due to the neglect of officials. The show unveils the hollow rhetoric by which the regime claims to be the loyal protector of Arab nationalism as we see sacrifices made by unsung heroes. The storyline also critiques the regime's scapegoating of colonialism, imperialism, and Israeli occupation rather than addressing its own failed policies. The political critique is introduced and then later interrupted at various times by a chorus. Bakhtin's border transgressions and eradication of conventional rules through both festivity and anger set the tone for the subversion of the regime narrative.

Sabah al-Jeza'iri, wearing a tie and dress suit, introduces actors who also appear in the chorus. Hossam Tahcin Bik emerges wearing a long yellow wig and mustache, making stereotypically feminine gestures. Al-Jeza'iri announces that when he had tried to become a television broadcaster, problems with his identity cards meant he was sent over to the chorus as a sentimental female singer. "She" walks toward the stage with effeminate gestures. The chorus is filled with characters wearing pots on their heads. Other carnivalesque features interrupt the acts when they become politically charged. At one point early on, Ghawwar tells his unborn daughter Ahlam that her grandfather was a martyr and that men went to war as if going to a wedding, an acknowledgment of the unsung heroes sent to die for the regime.

A chorus interrupts. A short unrelated skit features an Egyptian woman, Fadhihha, who insists that her friend 'Atiyyeh is not a man but a woman. 'Atiyyeh (Hossam Tahcin Bik), wearing a mustache, pink headband, purple sleeveless shirt, green pants, and silver purse, performs a cross-dresser busy putting on makeup. When al-Jeza'iri refers to her as "anissa" (miss) "she" demands to be called "madam" in the same way "her" father preferred to be called "madam." The scene ends by returning to Ghawwar, who is waiting for an ambulance to take his wife to deliver their babies. The ambulance is late, and a midwife (a man clad in a black veil and overcoat) delivers three boys and baby girl Ahlam. At another point, the chorus appears in a hospital scene. Hossam Tahcin Bik takes on the role of an official representing the doctor, who blames imperialism and colonialism for the death of Ghawwar's daughter. When Ghawwar asks the official if he really believes that colonialism killed his daughter, we are interrupted once again by the disconcerting chorus.

In this way, the chorus distracts from intense political discourse. Cross-dressing and gender subversion also disorient the viewers in order to communicate more radical views, the aim less to show the fluidity of genders than for carnival effect.[14] Indeed, cross-dressing, which eradicates "socially imposed sex roles," plays a strong part in Bakhtin's carnival and allows for social and political inversion. Yet we see that this cross-dressing propagates misogyny. Indeed, cross-dressing men evoke laughter as they subvert the regime narrative but do not ultimately suggest the fluidity of gender roles. The focus remains on men's fear of female power, a power that evolves from "weak" masculinity.[15] As Judith Butler argues, "This failure to approximate the norm, however, is not the same as the subversion of the norm. There is no promise that subversion will follow from the reiteration of constitutive norms; there is no guarantee that exposing the naturalized status of heterosexuality will lead to its subversion. Heterosexuality can augment its hegemony *through* its denaturalization, as when we see denaturalizing parodies, which idealize heterosexual norms *without* calling them into question."[16]

"Bad Mothers," Passive Fathers, and Effeminized Sons

From the 1990s onward the miniseries demonstrates heightened sensitivity to women's concerns. Yet traditional paradigms of masculinity continue to dominate, along with illustrations of "bad mother" and "absent father" figures. The tendency to blame the "bad mother" has bridged contexts and historical periods. In "The Making of Bad Palestinian Mothers during the Second Intifada," Adania Shibli astutely examines how the media cast Palestinian women as bad mothers for allowing their children to die at the hands of the Israeli military during the Second Intifada.[17] With respect to fatherhood in Syria, my research has shown a gradual construction of a softer *qabaday* in contemporary tales from 2000 on. Screenwriters have shifted their focus from fathers as protectors and financial providers to more emotionally connected fathers or entirely absent father figures. The new masculine ideal became, I argue, an affective father who inspires his children's relationships and offers a stable social foundation. The absence of this ideal is shown as having serious consequences on manhood.[18]

Khalid Hadeed has argued that representations of homosexuality in modern Arabic literature have sought to contain its menace through what he coins as "epistemic closure," which aligns male homosexuality with passivity and femininity with inferiority to a sexually dominant masculinity. He locates this essentialist paradigm of closure in Sa'd Allah Wannus's *Tuqus al-Isharat wa-l-Tahawwulat* and in 'Ala' al-Aswani's *'Imarat Ya'qubyan*. These two miniseries demonstrate gender anxieties caused by the heightened presence of homosexuality as they narrate developmental deviance.[19] In the same way, *'Abna wa Ummahat* and *Rasa'il al-Hubb wa-l-Harb* (Letters of Love and War, 2007) show homosexuality resulting from the "epistemic closure" of the recurring trope of bad mothers and absent or domineering fathers.

In *'Abna wa Ummahat*, Abu Iyad is married to Marseille, a French woman who lives in France with their son Iyad, whom she calls Victor. Marseille is shown as a selfish and absent mother—a symbol of corruption, immorality, and the individualism often associated with Westernization. Abu Iyad laments to his daughter that before he married a foreign woman, people warned him that the child would not belong to him. She is now pregnant with a new baby, and when Abu Iyad travels to France for the delivery, the viewers meet Victor, who is quiet and effeminate. Victor reinforces the message about his mother, whose selfish Western individualism results in denying her son the guidance of his father. As with the character of Ahmad in *Safaqa Rahiba*, the stereotypically effeminate man recurs in Syrian televisual culture, a sign of such extreme oppression by the system that the man loses his masculine qualities. In *Abna' wa Ummahat*, writer Jamal Baghdadi goes further by blaming the strong Western mother for emasculating her son.

In Reem Hanna's *Rasa'il al-Hubb wa-l-Harb*, Nassin is forced to marry the strongman lieutenant colonel Nazem against the backdrop of Syria's interference in the civil war in Lebanon. After the Israeli invasion in 1982, Nazem leaves with the Syrian army to fight in the civil war in Lebanon. In a deconstruction of traditional gender roles, Nassin starts a sewing business to support her young son and daughter. Though Nazem physically and mentally abused Nissan, she remains loyal to him when he is taken as a political prisoner and becomes a national hero. At the same time, she has nightmares that he is angry with her for leaving the house, and she begs him to understand that she needs to support her children. According to editor Iyad Shihab Ahmad, Hanna intended to criticize Syrian interference in Lebanon. However, the *mukhabarat* instructed director Bassel al-Khatib to revise Hanna's original screenplay to show Nazem as a war hero adored by his wife at the end of the story.[20]

On the other hand, Hanna argues that Nassin's surprising adulation of Nazem reflects her intention to show an individual's simultaneous love and fear of the oppressive patriarch (representing the dictator). In this scenario, an individual who is unaccustomed to freedom unconsciously reaches for shackles.[21] The authoritarian father figure of Nazem, who later becomes an absent father figure, also impacts the adopted son, Rouhi. Rouhi recalls a childhood without a father figure and surrounded by women who stepped in as a mother figure. Due to cultural taboos, Hanna could not make Rouhi openly homosexual, but the text hints that homosexuality is a consequence of growing up without a present father figure.[22] Nevertheless, the son and daughter come into their own and flourish outside traditional gender roles only after the dictatorial father has disappeared. Rouhi is drawn toward design and fashion, and Zana pursues higher education.

While "weak, effeminate" masculinity resulting from "bad mothers" and "absent fathers" is the dominant trope in the majority of pre-uprising miniseries, *Abna' al-Rashid: al-Amin wa-l-Ma'mun* stands out as an innovative miniseries that explores the homosexuality of Harun al-Rashid's son Muhammad al-Amin, who became the sixth 'Abbasid Caliph after the death of his father. Rather than suggesting that strong mothers and absent fathers cause homosexuality, the miniseries tells the story of a strong mother who tries to suppress her son's nonheteronormative sexuality because of her political ambitions. In portraying the life al-Amin, known for his attraction to eunuchs, the miniseries *Abna' al-Rashid: al-Amin wa-l-Ma'mun* added a nonheteronormative storyline to the long-standing tradition of engaging in political critique through the lens of love.[23]

The Politics of Cross-Gendered Women, Transgender Men, and Lesbians

The male perspective of the early political parodies of the 1960s through 1970s would come full circle with *Ahlam Abu al-Hana* (Abu al-Hana's Dreams, 1996), a miniseries starring Durayd Lahham that consists of a concatenation of short episodes centered around the main character, Abu al-Hana, who is married to Khayroo. In "Ham al-Khanum" (A Woman's Concerns), writers communicate the struggle of gender subversion by underscoring male nightmares of female empowerment. The episode starts with Khayroo asserting a new independence by refusing to cook and do household chores. As she spends her days reading and educating herself, Abu al-Hana finds himself in the kitchen cutting vegetables, hanging clothes, and washing floors. More and more women follow Khayroo's example while neighborhood men engage in household chores. In another scene, Khayroo tells Abu al-Hana that some women have accomplished major things and she, too, wants to participate in elections. She also wishes for equality between men and women. Abu al-Hana tears up the papers she has given him and tells her that these ideas upset men.

The episode ends with Khayroo emerging from her room in a pants suit and bearing a strong resemblance to a man. She says she intends to undergo a sex-change operation to become a man and that she would like for her husband to become a woman. Though depicted comically, her proposal mirrors male nightmares that women's empowerment will result in their economic and political downfall. The episode is reminiscent of Lahham and Qal'i's early comedies, which emphasize the connection between female emancipation and male oppression. Significantly, when women in this miniseries cross-dress or assume stereotypically masculine behaviors, they trigger men's fear of emasculation rather than deconstructing gender norms to benefit all parties. However, in the next two miniseries we will study, gender-crossing women are instrumentalized to critique the legal and social oppression of women in the family and community. Gradually, a feminist perspective absent in the early political parodies of the 1960s and 1970s begins to assert itself.

Ayyam Shamiyyeh's 1993 story of the "mustache guarantee" that led to the loss of masculinity and then reinstatement served as an example of constructions of masculinity in Syrian television drama of the 1990s.[24] Khayri al-Dhahabi's *Hasiba* (2006) serves as a leading example of the social construction of femininity. When the miniseries commences, cross-gendered Hasiba has tied her hair in a turban and is wearing a ragged pair of pants and shirt, toting a gun alongside the men. After French forces terminate the rule of King Faisal in Syria, Syrians revolt against the colonial mandate. Alongside her father and other men, Hasiba participates in the Great Syrian Revolt of 1925 against the French in the Jabal-Druze mountainous region. At this time, she is not fully cross-gendered. Rather, she exhibits an intermediate gender with attributes of both male and female. Hasiba and the men are stationed in the mountains, where the French shoot at them. Meanwhile, in the cities, men say that the *qabadayat* are protecting them. The French examine a picture of the most dangerous revolutionaries: Sayyah and Hasiba (who they think is a man). Yet Hasiba's romantic interest in a man who fights alongside her underscores the distinction between gender ambiguity and sexual orientation, since her cross-gendered presentation does not indicate her sexual attraction to women. When the revolt ends, Sayyah and Hasiba knock on the door of their relative, Haj Hamdani. As Sayyah touts his efforts to defeat the French, Hasiba waits alone.

Hasiba becomes a more traditional woman when Haj Hamdani wants to marry her and his sister, Khaldiyyeh, advises her to remove her male attire. When Khaldiyyeh asks Hasiba how she lived in the mountains with all those men, Hasiba laughs, "Men? In the mountains they weren't men. They were my friends and brothers. We were all similar. French bullets made us the same."[25] Gradually, though, we see her domestication. She becomes pregnant and refuses to return the arms to her father when he wants to fight in Palestine. The story of Hasiba becoming more traditionally feminine is contextualized within other stories of women who are debilitated by masculine traditions as they try to find space for themselves. Hasiba's sister-in-law kills herself, her daughter goes mad, and Hasiba herself commits suicide at the end. This consciousness of the overpowering nature of traditional masculinity provides a subversive counternarrative throughout the miniseries.

As shown in stories examined earlier, cross-gender self-identification, gender-crossing roles, and male-presenting female characters with a gender ambiguity distinct from their sexual orientation were used to critique women's oppression. Another miniseries, *Ashwak Na'imeh* (2005), contained a feminist perspective that sought to elevate women's status but did not advocate sexual freedom. This limitation manifested in continual references to Eastern morality in opposition to the perceived looseness of the West. In one scene the school principal, Hanan, tells her students, "You have to make sure that love doesn't lead you down the wrong path. Don't let a *ghalta* today influence your future. We Easterners have an ideal of love. We live among our family, neighbors, and relatives. Let's think of love in term of everyone we love."[26] Likewise, a father tells his daughter, "Our religion and culture does not allow us to go out half naked. The problem is that we're trying to imitate the West. We shouldn't imitate their bad qualities. We reject their culture."[27]

When the story begins, Nidal (a typically male name meaning struggle), who is a male-presenting female high school student, has just attacked a classmate who was mocking her masculine behavior. Nidal is called into the office of the principal, Hanan, and expelled for one week. At home Nidal watches television in sweats, dances, whistles, and is treated as if she were family son. Nidal's freedom contrasts with the condition of her classmate, Mara, who opens the window for fresh air before her father angrily closes it. Mara's father hits his daughters even after Hanan emphasizes that fathers cannot strike their daughters in the twenty-first century.

Nidal's identification as male, we learn, was imposed on her during her childhood. When Nidal's mother was pregnant, her father had so yearned for a son that when his child was born female he refused to look at her for three months. After that her parents decided to dress and raise her as if she were a boy. When she got older she liked the freedom this "game" affords her compared to her older sister Nada's treatment. After Nidal returns to school post-suspension, her teacher tells her parents that her behavior is not "normal." Nidal's father becomes defensive, however, and informs the teacher that she has the right to deal with only Nidal's studies, not her personal life.

When a television program on transsexuality and sex reassignment surgery is broadcast, Nidal watches with avid interest, then informs her parents that she desires a sex change. The storyline subsequently explores being transgender rather than cross-dressing. While her father agrees that she can have a sex change, her mother does not. Nidal asks her mother why she does not want a boy, and her mother says she wants only what was given to her by God. However, her father responds that he and Nidal will go and see a doctor who conducts sex reassignment surgery. The doctor says they have been doing that in extreme cases in Syria for years but will not do the sex reassignment surgery for Nidal.

He tells Nidal's father that, instead, she needs a psychologist to convince her that she is a girl. When they leave, the doctor says to himself that, in truth, the father needs a psychologist. The second and third doctors also refuse, insisting this surgery is only for individuals with a "real problem." Nidal and her father decide to find a doctor in another country. Nada regrets that her younger sister, Nidal, wants to become a man, but Nidal responds, "You don't want me to become a man since you're scared of having a brother who'll tell you what to do." Nada responds, "Is that how you see a man? Just giving those orders. A man also has problems. His life's also complicated."[28]

When Nidal, dressed in a cap and sweats, visits the principal, Hanan, she tells her that 99 percent of girls are "stupid" and she intends to undergo an operation to become a man. Nidal laments that girls dream only of getting married. Hanan later calls a doctor and explains that Nidal's "problem" is not a surplus of masculine hormones. Rather, gender is a social issue for her. She would like to become a man because she perceives that men are powerful while women are weak. Law and tradition are the impetus behind her desire to change. To help Nidal accept her femininity, Hanan uses reverse psychology. She tells the other schoolgirls to treat Nidal as if she were a boy. At first, Nidal is thrilled. But she gradually starts to feel left out. When her classmates crack jokes, they ask her to leave so that she can feel what it is like to be a man.

Nidal's perception of herself changes at the moment of her sexual awakening. At a fabric shop, a young man, Adnan, flirts with Nidal. Subsequent scenes show her peering at herself in the mirror and letting her hair down, then gradually putting it back in a ponytail. In sweats and a cap with her hair tied back, she returns to the same shop and flirts with the young man, who gives her flowers. As the story develops, it is evident that her strong masculine drive does not mean that she will be sexually drawn to women. Nidal continues thinking about the young man and asks her mother what it feels like to be in love. At the shop on another occasion, he calls her "anissa" (young girl) and another woman asks with surprise, "What? She's a girl?" As Nidal begins to identify as a woman, she reads about important woman. She tells her sister that even women have the ability to accomplish important feats.[29] Nidal's fantasies continue; she imagines herself in a wedding dress and calls Adnan's name as she sleeps.

When Nidal tells Hanan that she needs her help to become "a girl," Hanan reminds her that she claimed all girls were silly and weak. Nidal expresses her anxiety about her father's reaction, but Hanan assures her that if he sees that she is happy, he will accept this change.[30] Nidal enters the shop wearing makeup and giggles when Adnan looks at her, removing her cap. Later scenes show Nidal embracing a feminine identity. She wears tight shirts and makeup and lets her hair down to her shoulders. When her father sees her putting on lipstick, he asks why she has changed. She answers, "I'm comfortable like this. I want to be a girl just as God created me. I played the role of a boy but it tired me and I can't anymore."[31] At first her father does not talk to her anymore, but Nidal tells him that these days a daughter is just like a son. She reminds him that she is studious and has dreams for her future just like a son. He then comes around and says that when he sees Nidal and Nada he feels he owns the whole world.[32]

Nidal's story advocates not for sexual freedom but for respect and equality. When Nidal believes that all girls must fit the mold of wife and mother, she prefers the role of son. When she falls in love, though, she embraces her femininity. Ultimately, the miniseries operates within an Eastern framework and does not address the issue of sexual liberation, a distinction between Syrian culture and the West. This storyline that explores transgender identity uses woman's bodies to mark differing versions and perceptions of cultural identity and authenticity. The two-episode story "Sabi aw Bint," written by screenwriters Yezen Atassi and Lobna Haddad, opens with a crisis of femininity. In the opening scene we see a traditional construction of femininity, as Lulu washes the dishes in her clean and pristine kitchen. When she leaves for work, a biker catcalls her and another driver yells that she is driving like a woman. Once she reaches the office, she learns that although she has worked for seven years without taking a vacation, her boss gave one of her less-deserving male colleagues a coveted position. Her boss tells her that in the future she will marry, take maternity leave, and have other responsibilities. Lula is devastated men determine her destiny. When Lula complains to her fiancé, 'Abed, he not only agrees that maternal duties will one day consume her time but also recommends she wear makeup and let down her hair as other women do. Furious, Lulu rises, bumps into the waiter, and faints. The next scene shows Lulu waking up in a hospital with her best friend Judy and her fiancé. Then she steps into the bathroom and screams. The doctor comes and tells her that he has discovered a mass between her legs and she must choose whether to continue as a woman or become a man. Despite 'Abed's protests, she says she has to think about what is best for her as an individual.

The doctor tells her that currently both sexes are present, but that after the operation, only one will remain. If she decides to become man, she will have to have hormone treatment. And if she decides to continue as a woman, they will remove the male organ. She asks about "muyul" (sexual attraction), and the doctor replies that attraction will depend on her gender choice, thus reinforcing a heteronormative binary that discounts same-sex desires and practices. If she remains a woman, she will be attracted to men; if she becomes a man, she will be attracted to women. Lulu inquires whether she will be able to have sex and produce children, and the doctor assures her that this will be possible even if she becomes a man, as her body takes on more masculine features: lower voice, facial hair, broader shoulder, larger shoe size, shrunken breasts. He tells her that she will need psychological help to adapt to her new body. Evident here is Judith Butler's statement, "The heterosexual logic that requires that identification and desire are mutually exclusive is one of the most reductive of heterosexism's psychological instruments: if one identifies as a given gender, one must desire a different gender."[33] Thus, in the storyline there is no room for nonheteronorma-tive gender/sex identification. The idea of her continuing with her previous fiancé is not even a consideration in the storyline if she decides to become a man.

Lulu reflects on the problems women face in her country. For example, if a man rapes a woman, he is given the chance to ask to marry the woman her raped in court. If she accepts, he is judged innocent. Another example is that a woman cannot pass citizenship to her children and a husband can prevent his wife from leaving the country. Lulu tells her best friend Judy, "A girl has a hard time in this society. She can't live as she wishes. Everyone is ready to pounce on her for mak-ing one mistake." But Judy reminds her that a man has responsibilities toward his relatives and community and also faces difficulties. She continues, "Even we liberated women expect a lot of men. We take no responsibility for household expenses." Judy acknowledges that they live in a "masculine society" and laws and rules benefit men. Yet, she says, men's laws have positive and negative reper-cussions for both sexes. Still, Lulu sees a sex change as a golden opportunity to eliminate the hardship she faces as a woman. She exclaims, "I'll be the best man in the world, because I'll understand what a woman loves, what she hates. Lucky be the woman who marries me." Lulu then tells her distressed fiancé that she has decided to become a man.

In a subsequent dream sequence that features an operation and hormone therapy, Lulu is transformed to Lu'ay, a "real man." Whereas the miniseries started with Lulu washing dishes in an immaculately clean home, Lu'ay now smokes a cigarette in a messy home with clothes scattered everywhere. He tells Judy that he saves so much time by not applying makeup or getting manicures, and he wishes he had been born a man. Judy complains about her fiancé, and Lu'ay comforts her. In the evenings he frequents cafés and flirts with women, gets drunk and sleeps around. Soon, Lu'ay asks Judy to marry him. Shortly after their marriage, Lu'ay begins to feel affronted if any other man looks at Judy. He gets in fight and covers Judy with a shawl, accusing her of wearing revealing cloths. He continues to go out drinking and embarks on an affair with his sec-retary. Eventually Judy leaves him, addressing not Lu'ay but Lulu, her friend: "You [use of female gender] once said that if you become a man, you would be exem-plary. Now look around you. Dishes piled in the sink; mustiness, the smell of smoke, aggression, and jealousy. You're doing everything you accused men of doing and worse."[34]

The dream sequence abruptly ends. We return to Lulu, a woman, sitting at a table, furious with her fiancé. 'Abed calms her down and apologizes, saying that he merely asked her to take care of herself. Startled by the glimpse of her life as a man, Lulu lets her hair down and embraces her femininity. Though the West is not referred to explicitly, a clear anti-Western subtext runs through the two-episode story. While screenwriters Yezen Atassi and Lobna Haddad challenge traditional gender roles by reconstructing masculinity and femininity, their deconstruction rejects Western individuality in order to reinforce Eastern notions of community and family.[35]

While the miniseries appeared to be avant-garde, in fact it carried a conservative message, one that championed rather than destabilizing heteronormativity and refused to challenge binary sexuality. All the images of Lulu/ Lu'ay—whether washing dishes as a female or surrounded by a mess as a male— rely on traditional, stereotypical constructions of gender until, in the end, she lets down her hair and becomes a traditional woman. Furthermore, the dream sequence requires her to gain a penis to enter the male domain. She can pursue her dreams only so long as they do not interfere with the traditional Eastern framework. Adding to the traditional trappings is the fact that heteronormative sexuality was never in question in the show. If Lulu had decided to become a man, "he" would have been attracted to women. Remaining a woman, she maintained an attraction to men and revealed her desire for children. Thus, the transgender storyline was instrumentalized as a way to show how Eastern culture must avoid the individualism of the West rather than challenging identity categories or questioning the heterosexualization of the social bond. As stated by Judith Butler, "Gender norms operate by requiring the embodiment of certain ideals of femininity and masculinity, ones which are almost always related to the idealization of the heterosexual bond."[36]

Though the storyline about alternative sexuality was destabilizing, in the end, heteronormativity won. Yet I identify one nonheteronormative triumph in this storyline. This relates to Judy, who often addressed Lu'ay in the female gender, both before and after they married. When she breaks up with Lu'ay, she emphasizes that she is talking to "her" (use of female gender) not as Lu'ay but as her friend Lulu. This dynamic does indeed destabilize the practice of heteronormativity and disrupt social norms. Judy can be seen as transgressing the boundaries of normatively gendered relationships, though the story ends with a confirmation of heteronormativity.

The miniseries *Ahl al-Gharam* was aired in two installments in the 2007 and 2008 Ramadan seasons and was composed of a series of independent episodes addressing love. Most episodes concluded that traditional customs and rituals lead to the demise of relationships. In the second season story "'Alemooni" by 'Ahad Fakhoori, Iman and her family return from Saudi Arabia to a small village in Syria where their relatives live. Iman has three sisters, and her parents had always wished for a son. Upon their arrival, the cousins dance and gossip as Iman self-consciously watches the young women. The director leads us to believe that Iman is of an ambiguous gender. She dresses in pants, wears no makeup, and is not typically feminine. She prefers the company of books to people. At eighteen, she has not yet experienced her menstruation cycle. Her mother asks Fariha to try to teach Iman femininity, and Fariha uses this as an excuse to see her boyfriend. While serving as Fariha's alibi, Iman meets Fu'ad, who had been infatuated with Fariha but quickly falls for Iman. When Iman returns home, she plucks her eyebrows to appear more attractive to Fu'ad.

The scene of Iman plucking her eyebrows provides material for a queer reading of the interpersonal dynamics. When Fariha sees Iman struggling, she instructs her to lay her head on her legs so she can help pluck her eyebrows. We see a moment of discomfort as Iman settles her head on Fariha's bare legs, the background music contributing to the sexual tension. Fariha asks why Iman is closing her eyes, and Iman shouts in pain as if to distract or disorient to viewer. At the same time, this scene clearly points to gender fluidity, as Iman displays both manly and womanly inclinations. In addition, the moment of sexual tension suggests that Iman is attracted to women. The next scene, however, places the viewer back within a heteronormative storyline. Iman wears a tighter, more feminine sweater and skirt when she goes out with Fariha to see Fu'ad. Here the social construction of gender, as well as fluidity, is evident.

The next day Fu'ad tells Iman he had dreamed of her, and they make plans to marry. Iman insists that she wants to finish high school since she must be educated to raise good kids. Fu'ad accepts her conditions. However, Iman returns home to a distressed household; Fariha was caught when she left to meet her lover. Both Iman's aunt and mother exclaim that having a daughter is a curse. Fariha's punishment is extended to Iman, who can no longer meet Fu'ad. Confined to her room, Iman reads, much to the dismay of her mother, who believes that girls use education as an excuse to engage in "loose behavior." To the mother, Iman's interest in continuing her education is gender-discordant. Iman asks her mother if she can leave and uses the opportunity to see Fu'ad. However, she returns home with intense stomach pain. After the doctor examines Iman, the mother praises the doctor, who has discovered that Iman displays a male physiology and may, accordingly, undergo sex reassignment surgery. Her parents avidly support this move. Iman does not have a say in the decision-making process, as doctors diagnose her and suggest that she will need psychological counseling to align her body with her self-perceptions after sex reassignment surgery. A queer reading of this outcome suggests that despite the presence of male hormones, Iman, now "Ayman," might retain his attraction to men. This explains the doctors' emphasis on the fact that "he" would need a psychologist to align "himself" to "his" new gender. We are reminded again of Judith Butler's point about the arbitrary rules that predicate heterosexism and that require each given gender to desire a gender other than the one an individual inhabits.[37]

In the following scene, Ayman appears as a man for the first time as he is shaving. His mother and father express gratitude for a surgical intervention that finally gave them a son. In the case of Lulu, the presence of both male and female organs allowed her to choose between genders. In this storyline, the masculine organ is dominant and Iman does not have a choice. The family decides not to return to Saudi Arabia but to live in a Syrian neighborhood where no one knows them. Meanwhile, Fu'ad is devastated that Iman has disappeared. When he asks Fariha where Iman is, she responds that Iman does not exist. The cousins are upset too, since Ayman knows everything about them and they fear his reaction.

The show never reveals Ayman's feelings toward his new gender, just as it reveals nothing of Iman and her feelings. Perhaps this omission symbolizes confusion about her sexuality. The first indication we have that Ayman may long for Fu'ad is when he tells his father that he misses the neighborhood. However, his father says a man should not miss anything. At the park, Ayman sees Fu'ad sitting alone on the bench. He wants to talk to him but refrains. When he senses Fu'ad's discomfort at being surveyed, he walks away and the story ends.

Ahl al-Gharam Part One and *Part Two* sought to expose the incompatibility of love stories and societal norms. Correspondingly, the episodes typically concluded with failed relationships. The episode "'Alemooni" tells the story of parents who yearned for a son and were thrilled at any chance to have one. Complicating an understanding further is the possibility of reading scenes through a queer lens. Iman's embarrassment at laying her head on Fariha's lap cannot be taken for granted. The thwarted love between Iman and impoverished Fu'ad shifts into questions about whether Ayman's newfound freedom as a male will allow him to approach Fu'ad, tell him who he is, and embark upon a secret love affair. Though Iman's doctors recommended that she see a psychologist to reprogram her mind to match her physiology, the question remains, will Ayman reset or cede to his desires for Fu'ad? Though Fu'ad still desires Iman, could he love Ayman? Cultural norms and homophobia might prevent requital, but Ayman's continued love for Fu'ad suggests a queer storyline of male-male love.

A queer reading could also perceive of a Laila and Majnun storyline, with Fu'ad as the love-struck Qais, who goes mad pining over his lost love. This transforms the Laila-Majnun story into an impossible male-male love story, an unsuspected space for expressing alternative attachments. As Judith Butler has argued, "The practice by which gendering occurs, the embodying of norms, is a compulsory practice, a forcible production, but not for that reason fully determining. To the extent that gender is an assignment, it is an assignment which is never quite carried out according to expectation, whose addressee never quite inhabits the idea s/he is compelled to approximate."[38]

Thus far, transgender and cross-gender storylines were instrumentalized to relate to law and women's political rights rather than sexual liberation. Neither was lesbianism explored other than to be represented as reprehensible. Indeed, there is much silence surrounding the taboo subject of women-women sexuality in Islamic societies.[39] Hanadi al-Samman has argued that passing references to lesbian relations are only "a prelude to, or a temporary replacement of, normative heterosexuality."[40] A case of lesbianism in a pre-uprising drama was *Ma*

Malakat Aymanukum (Those Whom Your Right Hand Possesses, 2010), by director Najdat Anzour, which presented an Islamic feminist perspective and critique of conservative religious trends. The script denounces the religious extremism of the female *qubaysiyat* and terrorist groups. In one scene, a sheikha from the *qubaysiyat* named Anissa Haja holds religious sessions in her home. The script suggests that she is attracted to female students in her prayer group and emotionally manipulates them. One flashback shows a girl in the prayer group crying as she remembers Anissa Haja looking lovingly at her, asking if she wants to marry, then telling her to come close and intimately resting her hand on her head. Returning to the present time, the girl's tears indicate her guilt at having engaged in illicit sex.[41]

Anissa Haja's insecurity about her sexuality and morality makes her harshly critical of her students to the degree that she becomes a hated figure in the miniseries. Furthermore, Anissa Haja and the terrorist Tawfiq are on close terms, working together to repress young women. The pairing of the lesbian and the terrorist, the two most hated characters in the miniseries, along with the correlation between lesbianism and religious hypocrisy point to the taboo nature of lesbianism in Syrian culture.

In his study of 'Ala' al-Aswani's *Yacoubian Building*, Michael Allan argues that joining "along parallel tracks," Hatim Rashid, an openly gay newspaper editor, and Taha al-Shazli, a poor man who is a terrorist, breaks the divide between the gay-friendly First World and socially conservative Third World. According to Allan, bringing the liberated homosexual and repressed religious fanatic together along a common storyline (both characters, who have engaged in sodomy, are murdered) breaks down the binaries implicit in homonationalism.[42] I argue, however, that this is not a liberation of the binaries since negative judgment is implicit in the link between homosexuality and terrorism. While the binary is indeed broken, the result is not positive. In the case of *Ma Malakat Aymanukum*, Tawfiq is a religious fanatic and terrorist linked to Anissa Haja, a religious fanatic and closet lesbian. The effect is to dehumanize both the Muslim and the lesbian, coloring her as a charlatan religious fanatic who tortures the young women in her prayer group.

Post-Uprising Queer Storylines

Post-uprising discussions with drama creators address nonheteronormative relations more openly than before. In an interview on Syrian drama in 2016, Reem Hanna had told me that the miniseries *Nazik Khanum*, which she was in the process of writing, would have an openly gay male character.[43] Najeeb Nseir discussed with me how in post-uprising Damascus there were now openly gay spaces such as those found in Beirut.[44] I argue that the fact that screenwriters are exchanging views more easily on formerly taboo topics such as homosexuality intersects with the construction of a new secular collective identity that stands in contrast to religious fanaticism as represented by Da'ish.

This is not to say that all post-uprising miniseries will overcome stereotypes and the much-critiqued "epistemic closure" discussed by El-Ariss and al-Samman. In the miniseries *Gharabib Sud*, jihadists rape young boys, once again linking homosexuality with rapists.[45] Several sketches in *Buq'at Daw' Part Thirteen* continue to propagate stereotypes. In "Mashakil Teqaniyya," a gay man who works on a drama set has stereotypical gay mannerisms and cross-dresses with a yellow wig. He is dishonest and causes problems to disrupt rehearsals so he can travel with his boyfriend, Johnny.[46] "T . . . Rambo" portrays Donald Trump and Hillary Clinton in the midst of a preelection debate. Clinton is depicted as corrupt, though she conspicuously advocates for homosexual (*muthilin*) rights.[47] In "Umm Sa'id al-Ruzz," Ayman Rida appears once again dressed as a woman for comic effect, as if to demonstrate the absurdity of a man consciously choosing to inhabit a female body.[48]

Another case in point: the portrayal of the stereotypically effeminate homosexual man who pulls up in front of Abu Kheil's shop in search of drugs in Episode 9 of *Fawda*. Nseir had originally imagined a spoiled teenager with enough money to buy hashish to distribute among his friends. However, the director, Samir Husayn, transformed the character into a gay young man searching for hashish who emerges seemingly without context.[49] His flirtation with Abu Kheil (who sells hashish) and his subsequent and humiliating ejection from Abu Kheil's shop in the ninth episode play upon prevailing stereotypes. When he reappears in the twenty-third episode, pulling up his car in search of Abu Kheil, Dana and Fares mock his appearance. Fares conjectures that he is high on hashish. In this way, the prejudicial colonial gaze, which once perceived the East as morally depraved, again links depravity, drug abuse, and homosexuality. This is especially ironic given the West's current perceptions of the East as being repressive. Mazin Taha's Syrian-Lebanese comic production *Julia* (2018) tells the story of an actress who inhabits each of her roles and thus forgets her real identity. When she plays the role of an *Imra'a Mustarajila* (A Manly Woman), she becomes an aggressive, slovenly, and oppressive male-presenting female named Juliano, who mimics the stereotypical gestures of hypermasculinity.

As seen in the examples above, many of the problematic frameworks and stereotypes from pre-uprising miniseries abound. I do not argue that a clear shift in narrative occurs with respect to portrayals of queer spaces. However, *Sa-Na'ud Ba'da Qalil* (neutral) and *Qalam Humra* (opposition stance) stand out as isolated post-uprising storylines that include nuanced depictions of nonheteronormative spaces and desires. Both miniseries intricately weave a queer storyline into the miniseries as a whole. As al-Samman has delineated, few works of modern

Arabic literature render queer characters sympathetically, focusing on human emotions and biological difference rather than gender constructions.[50] Both these post-uprising miniseries fall into that rare category. While there is some instrumentalization for a political message, both portrayals do show progress. These miniseries also must be viewed in the context of screenwriters attempting to disassociate Syrian culture from religious extremism.

In chapter 3, I analyzed *Sa-Na'ud Ba'da Qalil* in the context of fatherhood. I showed how Najeeb's denial of the political upheaval in Syria was linked to his denial of his children's problems even as they unfolded before him. The storyline was adapted from the Italian movie *Everything Is Fine*, and Hollywood produced an adaption. In the Hollywood version, one of the daughters is a lesbian, which the father initially refuses to see. Yet the father overcomes his prejudice and his daughter openly asserts her lesbian identity at the end. As mentioned earlier, women-women love is taboo in Syria, illustrated by the association between a lesbian character and terrorism in a 2010 miniseries. In this storyline, the fear that overshadows the miniseries is connected to lesbianism, as seen in the story of his daughter Mira, the last of the six children that Najeeb visits.

Mira's storyline is the first open discussion of lesbianism in Syrian television drama. When the story commences, Najeeb is in denial and believes that Mira is acting professionally in in a Beirut theater. However, viewers quickly discover that Mira makes her living doing pornographic shows and lingerie advertisements. Early scenes of Mira show her dancing, drunk, at a disco and then sleeping with Fadi, who does not respect and often strikes her. Her roommate Nadine asks her, "Are you a masochist? How do you let him do this to you?" Mira responds that they were drunk and she did not feel it.[51]

Slowly, Nadine develops an emotional and sexual attraction to Mira. When Mira returns from the disco one night, she sees Nadine, who has been trouble falling asleep and has hinted at sexual turmoil, sleeping on the couch. Mira ends her relationship with Fadi but, to Nadine's dismay, starts a friendship with a young Syrian named Yusuf, who wants to film a documentary in Sham. Nadine becomes increasingly jealous of Yusuf. When watching news of killings in Syria, Nadine upsets Mira by joking that maybe Yusuf has died. To complicate matters, Mira's former lover, Fadi, becomes aggressive and insists on reconciling. He reminds Mira that he gave her a phone, computer, and clothes. But when he accuses her of finding someone else to whom she can prostitute herself, she orders him to take his belongings and get out of her life. In the aftermath of this confrontation, Nadine comforts Mira. In another scene, Nadine gently places a blanket over Mira as she sleeps on couch and places her laptop on the table. Later, she strokes her hair and says that she was sad to see her crying. Mira gathers all the items from her closet that Fadi had given her to purge his presence from her life.

MIRA: I want to know my worth, but not with these things. You can take all these things to Fadi.

NADINE: You're taking advantage of me. You know that I love you and can't say no.

MIRA: You're my friend and love me. . . . Why are you looking at me this way?

NADINE: I don't know. Maybe I'm discovering you for the first time.

MIRA: Maybe. I hadn't even known myself. Maybe because when we met each other I hadn't even known myself.

NADINE: Me too, but in a different way. You can go after your feelings, but I can't.

MIRA: Why not?

NADINE: Because the thing I'm feeling is frightening.

MIRA: What are you feeling?[52]

Nadine leaves the room, and Mira ponders the secret Nadine is harboring. With respect to same-sex desire among women in the medieval Arab world, Sahar Amer has demonstrated the paucity of terminology for lesbianism when compared to male homosexuality. Terms that did exist referred mainly to behavior rather than to an emotional attachment or identity. Still, Amer points to more positive description of lesbians in medieval Arabic writings than in the medieval West. Indeed, lesbianism was seen as one among the multifarious kinds of sexualities that existed.[53] Al-Samman has critiqued modern Arabic culture's portrayal of female homoerotic desire as a "substitute or a prelude" to heterosexual relations. According to her, these lesbian experiences are often depicted as an escape from patriarchy or a need to satisfy desire in the case of absent husbands.[54]

Thus, this storyline, which shows Nadine struggling with her fear, serves as a transition in contemporary portrayals of nonheteronormative relationships (among women), which are now shown with more depth. Her fear and denial of her sexual attraction to Mira exist on some level as fear felt by Syrians living in denial. But the lesbian storyline is a welcome departure from the tendency that al-Samman has critiqued in Arabic literature, since Nadine's awakening to her nonheteronormative desires is not intended as a brief interlude from heterosexuality. Neither is Mira's blossoming attraction to Nadine portrayed as a mere rebound from a failed heterosexual relationship. Nadine is independent as she chooses whom to love; Mira is becoming more independent. Their love develops slowly.

Nadine tells Mira that she returned all of Fadi's things and felt that she had finally revenged him.

FIGURE 5.1 Nadine (played by Cynthia Karam) (*left*) and Mira (played by Ghida Nouri) (*right*) in *Sa-Na'ud Ba'da Qalil* (We'll Return Soon).

Courtesy of Rafi Wahbi.

MIRA: Today you had wanted to tell me something, and then you were quiet. I'd like to hear.

NADINE: I'm not sure if you're ready to hear.

MIRA: Ready?

NADINE: Can we change the subject? Have you heard from Yusuf? I'm sure he's okay. . . . Always believe what your gut is telling you.[55]

Their conversation is interrupted when Fadi knocks on their door. Nadine does not want to let him in, but he pushes his way in and makes his way to Mira. Nadine takes out a knife and tells Mira to go into the bathroom. As Nadine holds a knife, Fadi indicates his suspicion that Nadine is in love with Mira, saying, "And I saw how happy you were. You should have told me. If I knew this I wouldn't mess up your plan."[56] Nadine continues to angrily hold the knife, and he leaves, telling Mira to call him. Nadine cries in Mira's arms.

NADINE: I wanted to protect you. I couldn't take all that. My heart was beating from fear.

MIRA: There was strength that I saw for the first time. Even Fadi was scared of you.

NADINE: I would have killed him if he touched you. I couldn't imagine how he used to sleep with you. When you were with each other, I was thinking of

you. I would want you to come back. I thought of you the whole time. I lied
to myself at the beginning and said this was normal jealousy of a friend for
a friend. But over time, I discovered the lie. This was the first time I had
embarrassed myself. I'm so embarrassed. But I can't do this anymore. I'm
tired. And then when I realized all that I felt for you, Yusuf appeared. I was
upset—now you were with him.

MIRA: I don't know what to tell you.

NADINE: Please don't tell me anything. I just told you so that you can participate
in it. Sleep next to me tonight. Don't leave me alone. If you don't want to, that
won't change my love for you.[57]

Nadine puts her hand on Mira's mouth, indicating she should not speak. Mira
trembles, then leaves the room crying. The scene captures the nascent same-sex
desire and love between the women, even as Mira fears Nadine's pleasurable
gaze. Perhaps she sensed it before, but now that Nadine has openly expressed
herself, Mira feels anxious. The viewer is left to wonder if Mira leaves the room
crying in response to her own fear of transgressing boundaries. Nadine's unam-
biguous expression of same-sex desire was the first of its kind in Syrian television drama. Since it was a Syrian miniseries produced in Lebanon, Wahbi did
not face censorship with respect to social issues. However, he lamented that Syrian censors later cut many scenes related to politics.[58]

Nadine's passion and embarrassment speaks to Dina Georgis's article on
Bareed Mista3jil, which seeks to rethink Arab shame and social humiliation.
According to Georgis, shame is a resource for imagining and can be a genera-
tive resource for Arab queer becoming. Feeling shame, according to Elspeth
Probyn, activates what matters, because "whatever it is that shames you will be
something that is important to you, an essential part of yourself." Georgis shows
how as opposed to pride epistemology, *Bareed Mista3jil* storytellers do not narrate overcoming shame, just as they do not express pride in their sexualities and
gender identities. According to this perspective, shame calls for learning. Georgis cites Probyn: "In shame, our habitus becomes reordered, shaken up, admits
other possibilities. . . . Though shame is no guarantee for insight or other possibilities, it creates the conditions for us to begin to recognize how we are bound
and vulnerable to the other and what we should do about it."[59]

When Yusuf returns, Mira opens the door and embraces him. Nadine is
relieved, saying that if he had not come back she would have found him. Yusuf
brings in Abu Laila, who was wounded in a battle against the Syrian regime.
When Nadine says she will leave, Mira asks if she is upset with her. Nadine replies
that she is leaving because she is worried about getting embroiled in Yusuf's politics. Mira clarifies that she is referring to their conversation the night before,
and Nadine expresses reluctance to talk about it. As Mira removes bullets from
Abu Laila, it is clear that she has become stronger and more confident since

Nadine opened up to her. At the same time, as she nurses Abu Laila back to life, it is evident that Yusuf is not focused on her. As they are busy working on the documentary, candles are lit, and then Mira makes dinner. Then Yusuf falls asleep on the bed. Mira calls Nadine, who is staying with a friend. When Mira says that she does not just love but respects her, Nadine answers that she does not want Mira to feel sorry for her or talk to her as if she is a sexual deviant. She insists that Mira talk to her like she used to. This exchange corresponds to Afsaneh Najmabadi's argument that the modernist understanding of homosexuality blamed same-sex desire on illness, deviance.[60] Nadine, hoping for a semblance of normalcy, tries to encourage Mira's relationship with Yusuf.

Yusuf, obsessed with the documentary's last scene on the tragic suffering of Syrians in Homs, intends to return to Syria despite Mira's protests. He brings his material to Mira and asks if she trusts her roommate. She responds, "I trust her more than myself."[61] When she says she is both scared and excited to watch his documentary, he responds, "Why don't you take this opportunity to combine the feeling of excitement and fear together and experience their conflict. At one moment you approach, excited to watch the film and then fear causes you to step back, saying 'Mira, be careful! Mira be careful!' And the stronger the conflict between these two feelings, the more incredible the results. This is the difference between a person who lives and another who thinks that he is living."[62] His statement indirectly refers to Mira's own burgeoning sexual feelings for Nadine.

In another scene, Nadine expresses surprise that Mira and Yusuf have not been intimate. In the context of trying to disassociate Arab culture from religious extremism, she exclaims, "This isn't normal. He loves you and nothing has happened. And he has been here three nights. Maybe he's a religious fundamentalist."[63] In order to encourage intimacy, Mira asks Yusuf if they can take a break from working for one hour and kisses him. Later, when they are in bed together, she worried that a knock on the door is Fadi. Yusuf tells her that he wishes she had resolved her issues with Fadi before becoming involved with him. Mira apologizes, but Yusuf says he does not feel safe hiding in her room and leaves for a hotel. His discomfort is a common reaction from a man after having slept with a woman, revealing a cultural complex about the purity of a woman's body. Mira calls Nadine, who is unselfishly staying at a friend's home. Mira says that Yusuf has left and asks Nadine to return.

Returning to Mira's father, Najeeb, an imaginary woman, asks if he has ever lied to himself. This question is important, since the idea of self-delusion can be linked with Nadine's love for Mira and now Mira's struggle not to love her. Toward the end of the miniseries, as Najeeb stops by for a visit, his daughter has just come home to discover Fadi watching videos in her house. She points a gun at him and tells him to leave. Najeeb stands outside the door and hears the conversation. They discuss having had sex together and how he viewed her as a cheap sex object. Mira tells Fadi, "I had given myself to you for accessories. Why are you feeling so lost? I never loved you. It was all for appearance."[64] She kicks him out. Najeeb drops the candy intended for his daughter and aims to leave quickly. Then, when Mira finds him outside, he pretends that he had heard nothing, faints, and is admitted to the hospital. Mira calls Nadine and Nadine calls her brother, Karim. The doctors find a cancerous mass in Najeeb. Nadine gives a bag filled with Yusuf's documentary videos to Mira and hugs her. As Nadine leaves, Mira follows her with loving eyes.

The storyline of Nadine overcoming her fear and Mira struggling with fear parallels Najeeb lying to himself about his family and country, the idea of living and acting "as if." Though the story is open-ended, it reveals love between the two women, and the audience wonders whether Mira will give in to her love or continue to live in fear. In the end, the lesbian storyline is handled with sensitivity, though it could be argued that it is instrumentalized for a political message or to transform law and culture. Though the miniseries is categorized as having a neutral stance, it takes on the oppositional critique of prewar days that centered on intellectuals acting "as if," the same phenomenon examined by Lisa Wedeen in *Ambiguities of Domination* (1999). In this storyline the theme of fear runs parallel to the theme of acting "as if."

Furthermore, the storyline takes to task the notion of natural heterosexuality as we witness a nascent, burgeoning love between Nadine and Mira. Al-Samman has critiqued the "femme/butch formula," which, rather than being rooted in lesbian body politics, is firmly entrenched in heterosexual and feminist politics. According to al-Samman, this femme/butch binary must be overcome in order to overcome politicization and allow for fluidity. According to al-Samman, the idea that lesbianism is an acquired identity rather than being biologically innate takes away its credibility. She pushes for a biological and innate rather than socially constructed formula.[65] Mira and Nadine exemplify two strong and yet feminine, but not overly feminine, women who have overcome the butch/femme formula. Mira does not need a manly Nadine to substitute for the absence of other males. She not deliver comfort at a time of need. Instead, we experience a moment of self-discovery for both women. Here, desire is at the forefront of the storyline. Nadine is thoughtful rather than a stereotypical, masculine butch who preys on Mira; for example, she leaves after she declares her love, to give Mira time to reflect. Because she does not take on stereotypically male attributes, there is no need to deny the femininity of either of them either. Even the scene in which Nadine defends Mira by pointing the knife at Fadi is seen in a feminine sense in that it shows vulnerability. Mira and Nadine's story, then, goes against the idea of lesbianism as a passing stage, as al-Samman had critiqued in the cultural canon, and instead here there is a slow telling of the story.

Yet, surprisingly, the lesbian storyline is repressed at the end. All Najeeb's children face the choice of trying to solve their problems independently or visiting their dying father in the hospital. In each case, some difficulty prevents

Najeeb's children from visiting their father one last time. What hinders Mira is not her relationship with Nadine at the end. Rather, Mira's predicament arises from the fact that her brother sold Yusuf's film documentary, which he had kept in her trust (and which Mira had then kept in the trust of her brother). At the end of the miniseries, she searches for his documentary. Thus, all other children's issues directly related to storylines throughout miniseries. However, Nadine's love for Mira is submerged in the story of the film documentary and fizzles at the end into a traditional woman-woman friendship. This fizzling of the lesbian story-line reinforces the critique against the instrumentalization of nonheteronorma-tive storylines for political purposes. When this instrumentalization occurs, the nonheteronormative storyline loses significance and is submerged in the political message of the narrative.

Mashhadi's bold miniseries *Qalam Humra* (2014), directed by Hatim 'Ali, also takes on familiar themes. One of these is the refusal to wait; another is oppression by fear, as discussed in chapter 3 on the politics of fatherhood. Yet the homosexual storyline is not submerged into a heterosexual storyline as in *Sa-Na'ud B'ada Qalil*. Rather, the homosexual storyline frames the narrative. The miniseries commences with preparations for the wedding of Nada and Anas, who have known each other for just a few months as students at the Fine Arts Insti-tute. At their wedding, Anas's friend Lama shows up. Apparently, he had told her at the Fine Arts Institute that he was suffocating because of this upcoming mar-riage. She now tells him that it is a shame that he is marrying Nada just because her father is a famous director. Anas, a Kurd from Damascus and Ba'th Party member, aspires to become an actor, so this marriage was for his ambition. Nada grows jealous and the wedding is called off.

We are also introduced to Nawras at the start. Nawras's homosexuality is not in the passive, effeminate trope shown previously, though there are some stereotypical hints such as tight pants, tank tops showing skin, his dishwash-ing, his artistic talent, the fact that he shines shoes as he talks, and his habit of drawing sketches of shoes as he talks with friend at the Fine Arts Institute. Nawras is an artist, painter, and sculptor who owns an apartment that he rents out to three young men: Firas, Kemal, and Qusay. His roommate, Qusay, is a musician but has no money to pay rent and no work prospects to make money. Neither does Kemal. Nawras has no issue with this. We learn that Nawras is estranged from his family. Yet he told his friend Lina that he knows all mothers eventually forgive their children. When Lina asks why he does not let anyone close to him, he says that he does not want to have friends. She refers to him as Shaz (in Arabic used to designate queer, deviant, abject),[66] and he is surprised. It is clear that he is frustrated with his family situation and always checks his phone to see if there is a text message from his mother. He tries to call her, but she does not answer and he cries.

Nawras's resistance to normative sexual and social expectations is only hinted at in the beginning. He wants to draw a portrait of his friend, Qusay, who refuses. Nawras washes his face and sweats. In one scene we see Nawras painting a picture of a young man, and then Anas knocks at the door. They look at each other seriously and the scene ends. What happened behind the scene is evidenced only by what comes later. In the next scene Nawras has painted a picture of a man on a mirror. As his roommates return home, they think they see Anas slipping away secretly. Inside, Nawras breaks the mirror. We then see Nawras, who has just attempted suicide, on a hospital bed, being rolled by friends as Ward narrates, "You feel fear for the way you want to love. You're ruled by the customs and traditions passed down from your grandfathers."[67] Nawras's older brother, a medical doctor, tersely says that he will report that Nawras was drunk, not that he had committed suicide. He asks Qusay what his relationship is to the patient. Qusay says he is a family member, but the doctor says that he knows that is not true, since he is Nawras's brother. The brother tersely tells Qusay, "Outside the hospital, do as you wish. But here in the hospital be a man." Qusay does not understand why he is speaking to him that way and responds, "I'm more of a man than you are."[68]

Qusay wants to know why Nawras tried to commit suicide and Nawras responds, "I'm not able to be myself. I have to pretend to be optimistic for others. Why do I have to be positive? I just want to be normal, natural."[69] The older brother informs Nawras that he told their mother about his attempted suicide. Nawras responds, "It's me. I'm born like this. I tried to kill myself and reduce your scandal." Upon their return home, Qusay wants to know what is bothering Nawras. Nawras replies that he tried to commit suicide because he could not tolerate his situation anymore. Nawras tells Qusay, "Someone like you isn't scared of anything." After he finally confides to Qusay, Qusay will not look at him. "My mom won't look at me and now you won't either. I'll go."[70] Qusay no longer wants to live with Nawras, who tells his other roommate, Kemal, expecting that he, too, will be angry and leave the flat.

KEMAL: Have you attacked anyone? . . .

NAWRAS: So now I am a criminal?

KEMAL: Then it's your personal freedom.[71]

Thus, Kamal has no issue with Nawras's homosexuality, and Nawras is surprised he does not insist on leaving. Later, in a popular coffee shop hangout, Nawras tells Qusay, "You need someone like me so that you can feel free. But I don't want to live a lie. If you go to American/Europe and you meet someone like me, you would tell him you're for freedom of homosexuals for your own advantage." Then he turns to Taim, a psychologist, "You're the worst psychologist. I'm the kid that the family took from one psychologist to another for a cure. Do you remember what you told them?" He also turns to television miniseries screenwriter, Warda, after she asks him to be mindful of his manners: "I see your series. What are you writing about? I'm waiting for you to write about a real problem."[72] Al-Samman studied Huda Barakat's *Stone of Laughter* and described it was having a unique contribution, since it links Khalil's sexual identity to innate biological difference rather than behavior or psychological constructs.[73] Similarly, screenwriter Mashhadi portrays this to be the case with Nawras, who went from doctor to doctor as a young child, as his parents tried to cure him—well before a sexual awakening would have taken place.

Qusay insists that he has an open mind but that he does not feel comfortable with Nawras. "I know it isn't his fault, but it's also not my fault,"[74] he insists. One day, as Nawras paints, Qusay falls down drunk, and Nawras helps him gain strength. Gradually, Qusay and his other friends accept Nawras. When Nawras has an art exhibition, the director wants him to also exhibit in Europe and says he can get a scholarship. She also wants him to tune into his feminine side because that will get more attention and help him sell more of his work. "They will empathize with you and you will become more international,"[75] she says. He leaves the office crying, then puts oil on his paintings and starts a fire, which his friends put out. He later tells his friends that he feels like a *masakh* (monster, clown, and buffoon) and Qusay says, who doesn't feel like a *masakh*?[76] We watch the beginning of the uprising in Tunisia, and Qusay makes it clear that he is against uprisings.

Meanwhile in the larger storyline, both Ward and Taim have gotten over their fear and sleep with each other. Taim then asks Ward to marry him. A man proposing marriage after sex is a departure from previous miniseries, where premarital sex often ruined marriage prospects. Ward narrates, "Fear and desire. Desire can break fear. Fear can break desire. Fear and desire are the only thing that can make the impossible become possible."[77] Ward's narration can be compared with Yusuf's message to Mira about the conflict between fear and excitement. While the message was conveyed in the context of watching Yusuf's film documentary on Syria, it could also be viewed in the larger storyline of Mira's struggle with her fear after Nadine's confession of love. Here in this series, Ward and Taim's fear within their heterosexual union, which they struggle to overcome in order to have premarital sex, parallels Nawras' fear as he struggles to not be ashamed of who he is.

The story comes full circle at the end when Nada and Anas reconcile and marry. On the day of the wedding, Nawras sees Anas upstairs in a suit and moves away quickly. But Anas calls for him. Nawras congratulates him and Anas asks if he really means it. Nawras replies, "Of course. Don't you think I, too, want a normal life—family, house, kids?" But when Anas says it is his turn next, Nawras changes the subject and they shake hands.[78] The last scene is significant in depicting Anas's choice of a life with a wife, house, and children. When he tells Nawras he wishes him the same, Nawras changes the topic because he is set on his own path. Though subject to much censorship, the homosexual storyline is not submerged in the heterosexual storyline or dismissed as it was in *Sa-Na'ud Ba'da Qalil.*

Mashhadi recounts how a large portion of Syrian society completely refuses the positive portrayal of homosexuality, yet there is a portion of liberated youth who believe in the freedom to choose one's sexual orientation. She says, "However, the majority of viewers—whether or not they support homosexuality—accepted the character of Nawras. This can be compared to the fact that many *muwali* (pro-regime) viewers connected with the miniseries even though it took a clear oppositional stance." Mashhadi continues, "Perhaps it was the philosophical narrative thread, as well as relatable characters we associate with those we meet in everyday life, which drew viewers to the miniseries despite existential and political differences."[79]

Anas and Nawras's same-sex love story was much clearer in Yam Mashhadi's original screenplay. However, during the filming and production process, Mashhadi lamented that several key scenes were removed. Thus the final screenplay alludes only to their love story.[80] As viewers, we may infer the dynamics of their relationship due to Nawras's suicide and the small hint, which is that Anas slips quietly away. Because key scenes were cut, we do not know if he and Nawras had sex. But it appears that they did and that then Nawras tried to commit suicide. We know Nawras struggled with his sexuality. However, due to alterations during the filming process, we do not know the details. It seems, though, that Anas struggled with his sexuality, which explains why he had felt as if he was suffocating on the day of his marriage. In the end, he marries Nada and decides it is important to conform for the sake of upward mobility. Nawras will be able to remain true to himself since he has a job and salary, not to mention that he comes from a wealthy family, which allows him to escape the constraints the govern Anas's life. Nawras will be able to be open about his sexuality. All his friends know and accept him; his roommates choose to stay with him. In the end, even his mother forgives him, demonstrated by the fact that she buys all his paintings in an art exhibition.

In the article "Class and Habitus in the Formation of Gay Identities, Masculinities, and Respectability in Turkey," Haktan Ural and Fatma Umut Beşpinar study how gay men interact with masculine respectability in urban Turkey. Through an examination of twenty-four interviews based in Ankara, Ural and Bespinar, relying on Bourdieu's conception of class as "spaces of difference," manifest that gay men's self-presentation is for the most part in line with class-based social circles' expectations of masculinity. Their study adeptly shows how family-dependent gay men in the lower and traditional middle class often, through "family guy performances," manage to reconcile with hegemonic masculinity while engaging in covert same-sex desires. On the other hand, professional middle-class gay men, through their social, economic, and cultural capital, are empowered to perform what they refer to as a "sophisticated" gay identity and be a part of a gay community in some permitted areas.[81]

In *Qalam Humra*, the pressure of being ostracized is a huge fear for Anas, who was clandestine about his gay identity. Lacking financial independence and craving upward mobility, Anas would submit to a heteronormative identity and marry Nada. In line with Ural and Bespinar's research, perhaps after his marriage he would continue to engage in clandestine gay activity. Nawras, on the other hand, was financially independent and thus did not need to conform despite losing his family network. Yet one critique of Mashhadi's portrayal of Nawras's freedom from his family is that it was unclear how he attained his wealth if his family had cut him off. Sometimes in these cases financial cutting off is part of emotional blackmail—but that does not appear to be the case here. Ural and Bespinar's study, however, does not address what happens when the parents sense their son is gay and take him, like Nawras, from one psychologist to the next. He does have the financial and professional capacity to allow him to gain independence, but for him it was not an option to keep it secret. His family knew even before he himself realized. Thus, there is another configuration when the son faces expulsion from parents who already knew. Furthermore, Ural and Bespinar's article does not address the situation of Muhammad al-Amin, who was wealthy enough to stand on his own but experienced the social pressures of having an heir.

AS SEEN IN EARLIER PRE-UPRISING STORYLINES, homosexuality was often instrumentalized as a symbol of the political oppression of men, while transgender women's storylines were used to combat oppressive laws and societal norms. While post-uprising miniseries are also filled with negative images, such as a lesbian terrorist and flamboyant, drug-abusing gay man, the nonheteronormative storylines of two post-uprising miniseries, *Sa-Na'ud Ba'da Qalil* and *Qalam Humra*, depict both Nadine and Nawras as affirmative images of non-heteronormative identity. *Qalam Humra* presents a homosexual storyline of Nawras against the backdrop of rising Islamic fundamentalism that hijacked the revolution. In the same way that Nadine in *Sa-Na'ud Ba'da Qalil* is not portrayed as a stereotypical butch-lesbian, Nawras is not stereotypically extravagant and effeminate like earlier portrayals that instrumentalized oppression. This recalls Khalid Hadeed's resistance of the mandate for "epistemic closure," "treating homosexuality as one aspect among many of the symbolic ambiguity and multivalent rationality of desire and identity."[82] Like Nadine, Nawras is not predatory, and his housemates are comfortable with him, despite initial conflict. Specifically, a scene in which all the men dance shirtless together reveals no homophobia. Both storylines in *Sa-Na'ud Ba'da Qalil* and *Qalam Humra* destabilize heteronormativity and show nonheteronormative desires, practices, and gender nonconformity. The queer storylines are done with sensitivity and placed on the same level of overcoming a culture of fear. Yet *Sa-Na'ud Ba'da Qalil*, which instrumentalized the nonheteronormative storyline, ultimately submerged the storyline and once again showed the problem of allowing politics to be the driving force behind the presentation of queer storylines. Furthermore, these later, more liberal portrayals of homosexuality must be placed in the larger context of the desire to differentiate a secular collective identity from one imbued with religious fanaticism. Prior to the uprising, Eastern sexuality was constantly differentiated from Western moral corruption. I contend that the rise of Da'ish during a time of collective memory construction has made issues of sexuality easier to tackle, as it allows an imagined secular culture distinct from religious extremism.

Conclusion

In Saneh Ula Zawaj *(First Year of Marriage, 2017), Qusay, a journalist, struggles to maintain his integrity as he submits his screenplays to various directors and producers. Alongside his screenplays, he writes numerous articles in the press criticizing capitalist production companies for imposing their viewpoints on writers, who are, unfortunately, caving in to their demands. In the episode titled* Ta'dil Jazri *(A Revision Butchered to the Core), Qusay submits a screenplay. To his dismay, his uncultivated producer—who is always talking with his mouth full—wants him to write the stories of love and betrayal that are so popular in Turkish and Mexican miniseries, including a leading man who engages in countless love affairs that result in children born out of wedlock. When the script is nearly complete, the producer suggests that the leading male character should be impotent. Qusay is left wondering what new adjustments he now must make to the storyline. Qusay expresses his frustration to a friend: "The problem is that no one feels for us writers—we create a character and the producer comes in with money and cancels it. I don't know why producers do this to us. It is as if you are raising a child and someone comes and kills him."*[1]

A short, comical, and moving episode recounts once again the difficulties faced by Syrian screenwriters. While the uprising, or azmeh, is not mentioned in *Saneh Ula Zawaj*, the miniseries exposes the pressures imposed by production companies upon drama creators over superficial matters. It does not specifically explore the issue of government censorship. Yet this government censorship is masterfully portrayed in *al-Wilada min al-Khasira* (Born from the Loins, 2011), a miniseries broadcast during the first year of the uprising, in which the poet Samahar is tortured and facially deformed by Ra'oof, an evil security officer who also kills her elderly father. Later, she writes a screenplay based on her experience about a security officer who imprisons and tortures a young woman's family. However, she is devastated when the government censorship committee rejects her story, claiming that it is grossly unrealistic. The committee demands that she make adjustments, but she refuses. In the final episode, she throws her script out the window into the wind. This gesture can be interpreted as director Samer Ridwan's feelings that the adjustments imposed on his own powerful miniseries were so profound that it was as if he was tossing his work out the window.[2]

The three-season *al-Wilada min al-Khasira* shifted during its life span. At first it conveyed a clear oppositional stance; in the next season it communicated neutrality; in the final season it expressed neutrality and at times even intersected with the regime narrative. Because of this trajectory, the symbolic act of throwing the script out the window serves as a self-reflexive symbol for the situation in which Syrian screenwriters find themselves as they work to construct historical memory. By narrating these self-reflexive storylines and sketches, I have recorded the pressures of knowledge production during the azmeh. I have also provided readers with a sense of the various representative voices and points of view on the role and relevance of *musalsalat* in war-torn Syria. I have demonstrated that, while factoring in the process of remembering and misremembering along with hidden and contradictory agendas, the process of collective memory construction is a haphazard and conflicted endeavor. I've also recounted how post-uprising narratives are influenced by increased marketing and production pressures, the reality of war, the rise in nostalgia, oblivion of past oppression, the development of transnational Arab television drama, and burgeoning interest in constructing a memory of collective trauma for future generations.

Gender and Marriage Metaphors amid the Trauma of War

The efforts of Syrian drama creators to recount or forget the history of contemporary Syria have been complicated and fraught with challenges. Indeed, when the uprising began in 2011, many believed that the alleged Gulf Cooperation Council (GCC) embargo against Syrian drama would result in the death of the industry. In fact, production did initially decrease. Many screenwriters, directors, and producers complained that they were compromised by GCC demands alongside a dearth of Syrian channels. Yet this book has shown that Syrian drama has not only survived but thrived, engaging in new and innovative techniques to circumvent the censors. Due to an upsurge in random bombings, the radical growth of jihadist groups, and the increased number of government checkpoints throughout Damascus, filming for the 2013 Ramadan season was confined to calmer areas such as Tartus and Suwayda. Alternately, filming was relocated outside Syria, primarily to Lebanon, which, in turn, resulted in an increase in Syrian-Lebanese coproduction.[3]

Along with the arrival of Syrian-Lebanese coproductions and pan-Arab miniseries, I posit that a turning point with respect to gender and marriage metaphors occurred in 2013 due to the establishment of Da'ish. This leaning crystalized in 2015 with a pronounced rise in acts of terror committed by Da'ish.

Accordingly, some strands of Syrian television drama from 2015 forward sought to construct and reimagine a secular, national collective memory distinguished from Islamic fanaticism as represented by the enemy, Da'ish. I contend that from this time onward, dismantling sexual taboos in storylines became less complicated. This arose from a shift in reference points, as many Syrian drama creators differentiated an authentic Syrian culture from the extremism represented by Da'ish rather than from the culture of the West. In this context, the female body was no longer burdened by purity markers distinct from its Western counterpart. At the same time, gender, marriage, and sexuality issues were no longer used just as metaphors for political critique; in the context of war, these themes provided storylines for the reconstruction of a society devastated by war and destruction.

I have shown in this book that post-uprising miniseries contextualized within the war weave gender and marriage metaphors into five different narrative strands: the overtly oppositional, the pro-regime narrative, the politically neutral, the nostalgic, and the social for the sake of the social. What brings these diverse threads together is their focus on gender and marriage issues. In general, while the overtly oppositional and neutral political strands are not confused with pro-regime narratives, dramas employing both the nostalgic register and the social for the sake of the social can masquerade as such. This is especially true because both the nostalgic and social for the sake of the social threads offer critiques of conservative social norms that revolve around gender and marriage and disassociate themselves from the culture of Da'ish. Indeed, at times the nostalgic register and the social for the sake of the social strand intersect, given that both frequently present storylines that no longer focus on political allegory but highlight the devastating social reality in contemporary war-torn Syria. Whereas the miniseries driven by the nostalgic register long for a pre-uprising past associated with freer sexual norms, the miniseries driven by the social for the sake of the social strand resist this nostalgic turn. Instead, these miniseries portray prevailing social issues as deeply rooted and the present struggle to resolve them as continuous with the past.

Prior to the 2011 uprising, screenwriters leveled their gender and marriage metaphors against dictatorship. With the exception of the few overtly oppositional storylines, recent miniseries have shifted their target to the uprising and subsequent war that has ripped Syria apart.[4] Clearly, the trauma of war has altered the discourse in marked ways from that of pre-uprising drama. Many screenwriters have labored to generate a secular collective memory entirely dissociated from Da'ish. Yet it is important to emphasize that production pressures render the broadcasting of openly pro-uprising miniseries increasingly difficult. Indeed, even after writing a script with novelist Khaled Khalifa for the 2017 season, Haitham Haqqi, the godfather of Syrian television drama, was unable to find funding to tell the story of Aleppo from an opposition perspective.[5]

The continuation of Syrian drama and the impossibility of discrete categories can be witnessed in historical-fantasy miniseries such as *Urkadiya* (2017), which illustrates the struggle of the three kingdoms of Ashura, Urkadiya, and Samara for power, money, and women.[6] The miniseries, filmed in Tunisia and Romania, ends with three queens taking the throne after a lengthy war. The narrator portends future peace and happiness in the previously rivalrous kingdoms. While many in the press lamented the desperate situation of Syrian drama due to the "crisis," the miniseries *Urkadiya* was recognized as a sort of archetype. Despite increasing competition between Lebanese and Syrian miniseries, *Urkadiya*'s presence confirmed that Syrian drama was a powerhouse during the 2017 Ramadan season.[7]

The Advent of Web Series to Bypass Production Companies

Yet while *Urkadiya* showed the flourishing of Syrian television drama despite censorship, discussions continued about marketing difficulties facing the industry. An innovative screenwriter whose dramas construct historical archives for large audiences and future generations, Rafi Wahbi underscored the importance of a free hand unmitigated by censorship, identifying the extreme marketing challenges confronting Syrian television drama—namely, that most production companies refused to produce Syrian miniseries regardless of whether or not they dealt with current events.[8] True to his commitment to sociopolitical critique despite the challenges, the 2018 season began with Wahbi's *Bi-dun Qaid* (Undocumented), broadcast as a Syrian-Lebanese web series in mid-December of 2017 in order to bypass the restrictions of production companies as well as traditional marketing methods.[9] Wahbi's web series consists of three separate nine-episode stories that connect to each other in the narrative thread and include a final episode with the same ending for each of the three separate stories. The series also contains subtitles to increase its audience.[10] Furthermore, in order to reach larger audiences, each episode runs just three minutes instead of the standard forty, and each of the three stories is meant to be watched in any order the viewer wants, allowing for a completely new drama experience.[11] The web series includes open sex scenes and overt political stances, something not previously permissible under the auspices of production companies. Wahbi contends that his approach will start a new trend in Syrian miniseries.[12]

Wahbi's partner in creating *Bi-dun Qaid* is Lebanese writer Bassem Breish, and the show's director, Amin Dera, is also Lebanese. The series was filmed entirely in Lebanon and is considered a Lebanese production. As seen in previous chapters, many miniseries have had a Syrian writer and director but have been populated with Lebanese actors. This new web series, however, includes a cast of Syrian actors. As such, it is the first of its kind.[13] The three nine-episode stories each focus on three individuals. Wafiq (played by Wahbi) is a top

FIGURE C.1 Umm Wissam (played by Nadine Tahcin Bik) (*left*) and Wafiq (played by Rafi Wahbi) (*right*) in *Bi-dun Qaid* (Undocumented).

Courtesy of Rafi Wahbi.

mukharbarat officer who, despite a threat to his family, refuses to falsify IDs. When his son is murdered and his wife commits suicide, Wafiq escapes Syria to avoid further punishment by the regime. Karim gives private lessons and avoids politics until arrested for sheltering a friend, an anti-regime activist. The police torture Karim until he informs on where his friend is hiding. Disgusted at himself for the betrayal that leads to his friend's murder, Karim joins the fight against the regime. Finally, Reem is an irrigation engineer who refuses to sell her land to her corrupt uncle. When he threatens to hurt her young daughter, Reem flees from Syria.

The three characters' lives intersect periodically until the final episode brings them together at the Syria-Lebanon border. Reem and Karim decide to return to Dar‘a, the place where the revolution began in 2011.[14] The final scene is hopeful and conveys the possibility of new beginnings after the characters' journeys of self-discovery.[15] Throughout the miniseries the open sex scenes spurred debate about the direction of Arab drama and the new possibilities of web series. The sex scenes also garnered more criticism than even the show's explicit political discussions. Intimate kissing scenes in the bedroom between Wafiq's son and his girlfriend, played by Yara Qasem, were the first of their kind of Syrian drama. When informed in a televised interview that the web series was criticized for the "bold" sex scenes, Yara responded that she had actually filmed much more than was released. She insisted that the scenes were "perhaps provocative, but not brave."[16]

Wahbi testified to the suffering Syrians have experienced in recent years and their resistance to pretense. For this reason, the web series is open with both its political and sex scenes. By March, it already had attracted forty million YouTube views.[17] Syrian actor Muhammad Wanali echoed Wahbi in attesting to the anger aroused by the kissing scenes but emphasized that though it is kept under wraps, premarital relationships do exist in Syrian society. Like Wahbi, Wanali believes that viewers are tired of misleading and unrealistic depictions of Syria, including overt avoidance of the existence of the uprising.[18]

Social media and news programs expressed criticism about this new direction in Arab drama. Some claimed that storylines featuring premarital sex do not represent the morals, culture, and traditions of Arab society. Yet overwhelmingly, journalists around the Arab world reacted favorably to this new drama experience and believed that other web series will follow suit. According to journalist Lama Tayara, Syrian drama has scrambled to survive during the past eight years of war, experimenting with a range of approaches, from stories that were purely social and ignored the current violence to transnational Arab adaptations of foreign films or novels. These "pan-Arab" adaptations included stars from various parts of the Arab world and reached faraway audiences via various Arab satellite channels. Though popular, these miniseries were often deemed superficial. Tayara went on to write about the dominating presence of Old Damascus tales, which recycled storylines but had commercial value, while powerful, realistic miniseries such as *Sa-Na'ud B'ada Qalil*, *Halawat al-Ruh*, and *Ghadan Naltaqi* experienced similar marketing difficulties. According to Tayara, it became increasingly clear that miniseries addressing political change and current events in Syria were rejected by the majority of Arab channels. Thus Wahbi's new web series was a welcome change.[19]

Well-known Syrian drama critic Wissam Kan'an remarked that, setting aside issues of censorship, Arab channels cultivate superficial audiences who appreciate fantastically designed sets and stories about rich businessmen and -women in pretty dresses rather than realistic storylines addressing the current war. According to Kan'an, Wahbi has navigated the challenges facing Syrian drama by allowing viewers to choose their own approach to the storyline. This experimental experience not only breaks the traditional mold but also opens new routes for capturing events and tackling off-limits subjects.[20] As screenwriter Colette Bahna confirms, Arab satellite channels have refused to sponsor Syrian miniseries dealing with the uprising in the past few years, claiming that there was enough coverage on the news. Consequently, new strategies were necessary.[21] The press underscored that *Bi-dun Qaid* was the first Syrian series that allowed viewers to choose the way and order in which they wished to watch the show.[22]

As the 2018 season approached, it was evident that there would be another web series on YouTube with some important differences from *Bi-dun Qaid*. While

Bi-dun Qaid filmed in Lebanon, Iyad Shihab Ahmad's Version 4 Company produced *Doubt*, which began filming in Damascus in March 2018. Written by screenwriter Seif Hamed, directed by Merwan Barakat, and edited by Iyad Shihab Ahmad, the Syrian web series contains an English title and subtitles and would be broadcast on YouTube throughout the month of Ramadan. The revenues would come from advertisements and sponsors. Famous actors Bassam Koussa, Dima Qandaloft, Safa' Sultan, and Dana Jebr would be paid less but would help set up the web series for success, a compromise given the production ordeals facing Syrian miniseries. Each of the thirty episodes would be ten minutes. Ahmad predicted that the miniseries would critique culture, traditions, and religion but would address the government, even through symbols and metaphors, since the filming would take place in Syria.[23]

Thus it was no surprise to fans that when *Doubt* appeared at the start of Ramadan, the storyline did not mention the war or azmeh. Instead, the web series mocked the male obsession with hackneyed notions of honor and shame and mourned the lost conscience of a generation. The show begins as May and her husband, Ward, socialize with three other couples. As the other couples look on, May asks Ward to divorce her, alleging that he has had an affair with one of the other women in their company. Marital problems surface as the suspicious husbands cross-examine their wives to discover Ward's lover. Soon, it becomes clear to the viewer that May and Ward are only pretending to be at odds in order to teach their friends and coworkers a lesson, yet the marriages of the other three couples unravel due to the jealousy, suspicion, and self-doubt of the husbands as well as the duplicitous behavior of the wives. In the final episode, May and Ward summon their friends back to the villa and reveal the truth. They show how one small lie ends up revealing a great deal about their friends and coworkers, including deceit, theft, and murder. Yet poor acting, lack of character development, a disconnected storyline, and the recycling of themes related to marital betrayal prove a disappointing viewing experience.

Screenwriter Najeeb Nseir expressed excitement at the advent of this new kind of experimentation and believes that the project has great potential for further development. However, Nseir conceded that the web series fell short, given insufficient plot and scene development: "For example, in the first scene when May comes down the stairs and tells her husband to divorce her, the three couples are sitting on the couch with no movement and the scene feels artificial as everyone just stares."[24] Iyad Shihab Ahmad criticized the actors' interference with the text and the intrusion of personal political sentiments in the storyline, especially in the final episode, saying, "In Ward's final speech to his friends, when he talks of their lack of conscience and loyalty, actor Bassam Kousa appeared to be indirectly lecturing the Syrian revolutionaries and blaming them for all the death and destruction. I found this unacceptable, and I tried my best to tone it down."[25]

A Continued Crisis in Syrian Television Drama and New Directions

According to Ahmad, the refusal by most production companies to accept Syrian miniseries, whether or not the series engaged in expressing oppositional politics, precipitated a crisis in Syrian television drama. The few companies that did accept Syrian miniseries imposed their own agenda. *Shababik* (Windows), completed in 2017, was finally broadcast in the 2018 season on a Syrian drama channel. Laith Hajjo and Mamduh Hamada's sociopolitical satire *al-Waq Waq* was filmed in Tunisia and appeared, as planned, in 2018. However, *Psycho* and *Huwajes 'Abara*, filmed for the 2017 season, were rejected by Arab channels and once again not broadcast during the 2018 season. Likewise, *Hawa Asfar* was filmed and completed for the 2018 season but not purchased by any channels.[26] Ironically, *Tarjaman al-Ashwaq*, a Syrian government-sponsored miniseries, was banned due to its oppositional politics. While miniseries such as *Ra'iha al-Ruh* and *Qosmeh wa Hubb* ignored the uprising altogether, *Rozanna* took an unabashed stance in favor of the regime in its portrayal of the destruction of Aleppo and its recapture by regime forces. *Akhar Mahal Ward* (first renamed *Wujuh al-Zil*) was delayed; filming took place throughout the summer of 2018 in Lebanon since, though the production team preferred to film in Syria, that choice of location was not permitted. The miniseries was filmed in Abu Dhabi, Damascus, and Beirut over a two-year period. After completing the majority of the process in Beirut, the team returned to Syria in June to begin the second part of the filming process, but permission was again delayed. Once they did finally commence filming, they aimed for a September broadcast on OSN.[27] When the miniseries was broadcast on September 8, the name had been changed to *Kawma*.

This new wave of web series invigorated Syrian drama, according to Ahmad. Still, though, the world of Syrian drama continued to be plagued by serious marketing issues. Accordingly, from the early days of the uprising, screenwriter Inas Haqqi broadcast her short documentaries through her online production company, Under 35, on YouTube in order to capture representative voices of young people. Specifically, in 2014 she introduced a short documentary series, *Nasiha bi-Kitab* (Advice on a Book), with each season comprising no more than twelve episodes. Produced by Under 35 and Sy 24, each episode lasted several minutes and described important novels. The first two seasons (2014 and 2015) focused on Syrian and world literature, while the 2018 season focused on post-uprising Syrian novels.[28] Clearly, broadcasting via YouTube offered a solution for Haqqi as well as other drama creators. Ahmad observed, "We can now depend on ourselves rather than search for production companies. *Doubt* is the first web series of its kind that is being filmed entirely in Syria with a full Syrian cast, director, writer, and producer. I expect that this will inspire others to do the same, and in many cases, there will be absolutely no ceiling." He went on to say, "Very few

FIGURE C.2 Syrians washed ashore in *al-Waq Waq*; Maram 'Ali to the left.

Courtesy of Laith Hajjo.

FIGURE C.3 Highway billboard in Jounieh, Lebanon, announcing several Syrian and Lebanese miniseries—Ramadan 2018.

Courtesy of Jana Joubin.

are watching miniseries on the television screen anymore; all is viewed via You-Tube at one's own convenience. We call it: *video taht al-taleb* (VOD; viewing on demand)."[29]

Lebanese-Syrian joint productions were further reinvigorated in 2018 after Lebanese companies attempted to strike out on their own in 2017 and realized that they needed their Syrian counterparts. Indeed, Lebanese-Syrian joint productions were among the most popular miniseries in the Arab world during the 2018 season. For the most part these contained few, if any, references to the uprising. Mazin Taha's light comedy *Julia* exemplifies these trends. Whereas in 2017 Taha's miniseries *Karamel* featured a full Lebanese cast with an Egyptian in the leading male role, by the following year *Julia* included Syrian actor Qais al-Sheikh Najeeb in the leading male role as well as a Syrian actress in another important role. Also starring Lebanese actress Maggy bou Ghossen as the leading character, Julia, in the miniseries, *Julia* only alluded to the uprising—for example, when Julia, an actress known for becoming too immersed in her work, lands the role of a suicide bomber and her family and friends try to prevent her from accepting the role.[30] Journalist Sawsan Seidawi contended that the storyline about Julia, who continually changes her personality for the role she is playing, represents the impact of war on the human psyche. "We're all forced to wear different masks. Our current reality has forced us to do so."[31] Qais al-Sheikh Najeeb observed that because the azmeh forced many actors to leave Syria, cooperation in cross-national Arab miniseries has increased, an especially important phenomenon since some channels refuse Syrian miniseries altogether.[32]

Tango, written by actor Iyad Abu Shammat and directed by Syrian Rami Hanna, included a cast of both Syrian and Lebanese actors.[33] While Shammat's *Ghadan Naltaqi* was one of the most popular miniseries of the 2015 season, it was not distributed widely and did not receive high ratings. In 2018, however, *Tango*, based on an Argentinian miniseries, ended up being one of the most widely purchased miniseries of the season. Distributed extensively across Arab channels, it beat out *al-Haibeh: al-'Awda* in terms of popularity and ratings. Many critics in the press criticized Shammat for not focusing on the uprising, though in 2015 he was criticized for setting *Ghadan Naltaqi* during wartime.[34] Indeed, criticism became so intense that on May 24 he announced on his Facebook page that Eagle Production Company had purchased the rights of the original seventy-episode Argentinian miniseries from another production company. Though the premise of the show involved betrayal in the lives of two married couples, Shammat transformed the details to reflect Arab society. By the seventh episode Shammat had opened up the storyline to the extent that it no longer resembled the original miniseries. For example, in the original Argentinian miniseries the leading male is a wholesome romantic, while in the Syrian-Lebanese version the same character, 'Amer, who has an affair with Farah, turns out to be a criminal who launders money.[35]

Tariq (A Path), based on the Naguib Mahfouz short story "al-Sharida" (Vagabond Woman), was written by a crew of writers and stars Nadine Njeim and 'Abed Fahd. Including a cast of both Syrian and Lebanese actors, this miniseries also disregarded the uprising.[36] Despite expectations of popularity, the leading characters lacked chemistry and the show did not receive high ratings.[37] *Al-Haibeh: al-'Awda* (al-Haibeh: The Return) starred a Syrian and Lebanese cast. The series traveled back in time to 2014 and contained references to the uprising, as the characters are in the midst of a wartime arms and weapons race. The war is backgrounded when, as the first episode begins in 2014, a character returning from the airport says, "Can't you see the difficult situation in our country?"[38] The miniseries was panned for glorifying violence and, early on, sued for promoting stereotypes by depicting the inhabitants of northeast Biqa', on the Lebanese-Syrian border, as drug and arms dealers. Journalists and writers worried that this lawsuit set a dangerous precedent for censoring miniseries every time a group felt insulted.[39] Yet despite widespread criticism and a second season with lower-than-expected ratings, the miniseries incurred a loyal following. Plans for a third season were already set in motion before the end of Ramadan.[40] While *Tariq* and *al-Haibeh: al-'Awda* did not meet the same success as *Tango*, overall Syrian-Lebanese coproductions in 2018 did well and promised more cooperation in the future. Indeed, in many cases the lines between Syrian and Lebanese productions appeared blurred.[41]

Amid marketing challenges, miniseries during the 2018 season witnessed not only the dawn of web series but the emergence of films with subtitles designated for wider audiences, with many of them winning prizes at international festivals during the fall of 2018. Screenwriters began to announce on their Facebook pages that even as they continued writing drama for the upcoming season, they were also writing film scenarios.[42] Furthermore, the addition of *al-Haibeh Part One* to the Netflix collection in September and then, later, *Tango* meant that a Syrian-Lebanese miniseries could reach a worldwide audience, placing this drama on a new playing field. When *al-Haibeh Part One* originally aired in 2017, it did not have English subtitles; however, these subtitles were added once *al-Haibeh* prepared to be included in the Netflix collection. (*Al-Haibeh Part Two*, which aired during Ramadan 2018, did not include subtitles.) Indeed, previously and even now, the majority of Syrian miniseries do not include English subtitles, as these shows are clearly made for Arab audiences. This growing interest in reaching larger audiences and exposure via web series, films, or addition to the Netflix foreign serial collection would certainly continue to have an impact on Syrian television drama, marking transitions to come. Thus this book examines and uncovers a provisional period of Syrian television drama in the midst of war, announcing future change as drama creators seek to make a worldwide rather than local impact.

And yet I emphasize that during this transitional period that portends future transitions, Syrian drama has left its mark on visual culture, poignantly illustrating that gender and marriage metaphors may be woven into storylines as collective memory is constructed. As demonstrated throughout the chapters of this book, *Fawda*, a gem among Syrian miniseries, took a cultural critique of marriage and gender norms to new heights in 2018. The foremost miniseries engaging in the social for the sake of the social, *Fawda* was lauded by critic Wissam Kan'an as a deeply realistic narrative that presented "the chaotic pulse of a city burdened by war like its inhabitants."[43] As shown in previous chapters, the miniseries tells the story of Fethiyyeh's gang rape and subsequent pregnancy, revealing the depths of her suffering as she copes with guilt, self-recrimination, and nightmares. While her husband, Zeidan, is away with the war reserves, her brother-in-law, Fares, tells her that she is deceiving Zeidan by not telling him the truth. When Zeidan returns for a twenty-four-hour family visit, he tells Fethiyyeh that she is a pure flower. Feeling her husband's intense love, she slowly recounts the nightmares she has been having of a group of men attacking her. However, Zeidan becomes enraged, asks if she is hiding anything, and announces that he cannot countenance *al-ghish* (fraud and deceit). Fethiyyeh decides to curtain her confession. Instead, after Zeidan returns to the war, Fethiyyeh, unable to live a lie and afraid that Fares could reveal her secret, packs and leaves the house, heading in an unknown direction.[44]

Here, Nseir denounces the social norms that allow a woman to be seen in one instant as a pure flower, and in the next instant, tarnished.[45] He also unveils the irony of accusing a raped woman of deceit. Zeidan's subsequent readiness to discount Fethiyyeh's marriage contract and raise his brother's son as his own appears normal, and not *al-ghish*, despite uncomfortable family dynamics that arise once his brother reappears. Most problematic of all is the fact that Fethiyyeh's rape by four men is perceived by her family as treachery worthy of death. Nseir masterfully takes us into the depths of war-torn Syria to expose offensive gender and marriage norms. At the same time, he provides a glimmer of hope by showcasing moments of profound humanity. Despite the refusal of the majority of Arab channels to broadcast Syrian miniseries, *Fawda* attests not only to the survival but also to the flourishing of post-uprising Syrian television drama, which, as I have argued, is a central component of heritage preservation.

Collective Memory Construction during Instability and Turmoil

This book tells a story of Syrian drama creators struggling against the odds to build collective memory during a time of instability and turmoil. As Syria fades from the continual media rush, these artists invite us to witness the nuances, complexity, and moments of beauty in Syrian life. In 2019's *Musafat Aman*, photographer Yusuf publishes an exhibition of photos that document Syria's war in contradictory ways. For instance, near an image of a demolished building are images of intact buildings; next to hospital images of injured people are images of people enjoying life. The photographs of the destructive nature of war are shot in black-and-white, while the happy images are shot in color. When a journalist asks about these contradictions, Yusuf asserts that he is intentionally showing the coexistence of love and hate during the destruction of war.[46]

Contradictions abound in the world of miniseries themselves. Even as the market for Syrian miniseries is shrinking, the global market is expanding. At the same time, Syrian directors, writers, and editors are making vital contributions to the creation of innovative and important new work. Miniseries such as *Musafat Aman*, described above, counter the handful of miniseries such as *al-Haibeh* and *Gharabib Sud* chosen by, for example, Netflix, that overemphasize the everyday violence in Syrian and, more broadly, Arab life. Instead, the work of these Syrian drama creators rejects sensationalism, counters dominant hegemonic Western narratives and stereotypes of Syrians, and resists the numbing of the Syrian population toward their national tragedy by asserting that there is life beyond bloodshed.

As shown in Appendices C and D, the 2019 season was much like others in that it faced both cancelations and continuations of Syrian miniseries along with a flourishing of pan-Arab and Syrian-Lebanese miniseries. Some magazines sold in kiosks in Lebanon lauded the growing strength of Syrian miniseries and continued important in the Arab world, despite marketing challenges. Many articles offered detailed interviews with Syrian drama producers both during and after Ramadan.[47] Syrian editor Iyad Shihab Ahmad worked on the series *Prova* (considered Lebanese but more accurately Syrian-Lebanese) for the 2019 season before leaving Lebanon and returning to Syria after the season; he lamented that though Syrians had contributed to Lebanese drama, there was a movement to push them aside. Indeed *Prova*, written by Syrian screenwriter Yam Mashhadi and directed by Syrian director Rasha Sharbatji, involved no Syrian characters due to stipulations by the production company. According to Shihab, the leading female actress was Lebanese and the leading male character was Egyptian because the production company believed that having an Egyptian leading male would allow the miniseries to reach an Egyptian audience.

As stated earlier, the 2019 season would consolidate the trend toward Netflix, and drama creators believed there would also emerge new and competing platforms.[48] Director Rami Hanna's *al-Katib* (The Writer), a Syrian-Lebanese production, could be viewed on Netflix from the beginning of the season, while Rasha Sharbatji's *Prova* would be added to the Netflix collection in September 2019.[49] Syrian films and Syrian-Lebanese miniseries are thus reaching global audiences, a huge shift in drama, as it opens questions about the politics of production and miniseries' intended audiences, questions that did not exist when these series existed for local audiences without English subtitles. It still remains to be seen what the impact of these transitions toward global marketing will have on Syrian television drama. According to Reem Hanna, who wrote *al-Kitab*, Netflix has discovered the market of miniseries from the Arab world and wants to transport these miniseries to their platform as a new moneymaker. She continued, "Netflix as a platform for viewing does not worry me. No one watches series on television anymore and instead many watch on YouTube. Netflix is just one more way to access certain miniseries."[50] Iyad Shihab Ahmad contended, "Miniseries are now entering the age of internet, which has replaced television in importance. In the next few years, many new platforms will come forth and no one will be watching Syrian series on television or even YouTube."[51] On the other hand, Lebanese actress Takla Chamoun worried about the conditions that the world of the internet and platforms such as Netflix would impose on storylines from the Arab world.[52] Najeeb Nseir, however, expressed that he was not worried about whether Netflix would cause Syrian miniseries to cater to broader international audiences, thus producing more shallow storylines. He continued, "Netflix wants a workshop of writers to produce a series, and I believe they will want strong storylines that will be able to compete with other emerging platforms such as MBC. More platforms will ensure the continued quality of the writing."[53] Despite the cancellation of miniseries, the instability of market forces, the pushing aside of Syrian drama creators, and the new politics of production that accompany global audiences, this book has demonstrated these drama creators are committed to presenting us with stories about Syrian life—some that encourage social transformation and others that simply intend to tell a story. Many of these stories are about love. Internationally acclaimed clarinetist Kinan Azmeh dedicated a performance during the fall of 2018 to all the Syrians around the world who still managed to fall in love these past few years amid war, violence, and bloodshed, saying "that falling in love is a basic human right that no dictatorships are able to take away."[54] In this same way, amid censorship and production pressures, dislocation and personal devastation, these drama creators have struggled to continue their art and to build collective memory for future generations. They have dared to dream about social revolution and have innovated with techniques and media outlets. This is a story of their attempt to preserve their heritage for their generation, as well as others who will follow.

APPENDIX A

Miniseries for Ramadan, 2011–2018

Note: Miniseries that touch directly on the uprising are in bold.

Ramadan 2011		
Societal Issues	*Comedies*	*Biography*
• **Fawq al-Saqf (Above the Ceiling)**	• *al-Khirba* (Ruins)	• *Fi Hadret al-Ghiyab* (In the Presence of Absence)
• **al-Wilada min al-Khasira Part One (Born from the Loins)**	• *Yawmiyyat Mudir 'Am Part Two* (Memoirs of a Director-General)	
• *al-Ghufran* (Forgiveness)	• *Maraya 2011* (Mirror)	
• *al-Sarab* (Mirage)	• *Buq'at Daw' Part Eight* (Spotlight Part Eight)	
• *Ishq al-Haram* (Forbidden Love)	• *Sa'in Da'in* (Lost Trouble Makers)	
• *Suq al-Waraq* (Market of Papers)		
• *al-Mun'ataf* (The Winding)		
• *Jalasat Nisa'iyyeh* (Women's Gatherings)		
• *Sabaya Part Three* (Young Women)		
• *Ayyam al-Dirasa Part One* (Days of My Studies)		
• *Shifoon*		
• *Ta'b al-Mishwar* (Exhaustion of the Path) (broadcast after the season)		

(Continued)

Ramadan 2011 (continued)

Old Damascus	Historical	Police Thriller
• al-Za'im (The Local Leader)	• Dalila wa Zaybaq Part One	• Kashf al-Iqna' (Unrevealing the Masks)
• al-Dabbur Part Two (The Hornet)	• Tawq (Longing)	
• Rijal al-'Izz (Men of Honor)		
• Tali'a al-Fidda		
• Milh al-Hayat (Salt of Life)		

Ramadan 2012

Societal Issues	Comedy
• **al-Wilada Min al-Khasira: Sa'at al-Jamr Part Two (Born from the Loins: Time of Embers)**	• **Buq'at Daw' Part Nine (Spotlight Part Nine)**
• **Khalasat (It's Over)**	• Haret al-Tanabir (al-Tanabir Neighborhood)
• **Abu Janti Part Two**	• Zeit Kaz (Kerosene)
• al-Miftah (The Key)	• Rumantika
• Banat al-'Aileh (Girls of Good Family)	
• Raffat 'Ain (Blink of the Eye)	
• Sabaya Part Three (Young Women)	
• Awraq Banafsajiyyeh (Violet Papers)	
• Ayyam al-Dirasa Part Two (Days of My Studies)	
• Urwah 'Ariya (Naked Souls)	
• Ma Takhlas Hikayatna (Our Stories Won't End)	
• Anta Huna (You're Here)	
• al-Shabbiha (Resemblance)	
• Zunud al-Sitt (Arab Sweets) (literal meaning: Lady's Arm)	
• Ruby	

Ramadan 2012 (continued)

Old Damascus	Historical
• *Zaman al-Barghut* (Time of Flees)	• *'Omar*
• *Tahun al-Shar* (Mill of Evil)	• *al-Amimi*
• *La'nat al-Qism* (Curse of the Division)	• *Delila wa Zaybaq Part Two*
• *Masabih al-Zurq* (The Blue Lanterns)	• *Amam al-Fuqaha* (Before the Juriprudent)

Ramadan 2013

Societal Issues	Comedies	Historical
• **Ha'irat (Helpless Women)**	• ***Watan Haff (Bare Homeland)***	• *Hadath fi Dimashq (Ya Mal al-Sham)* (It Happened in Damascus: Oh, Precious Sham)
• **al-Wilada Min al-Khasira: Menbar al-Mawta Part Three (Born from the Loins: Platform of Death)**	• *Hudud Shaqiqa* (Friendly Borders)	• *Qiyamat al-Banadeq* (Rise of Rifles)
• **Sa-Na'ud Ba'da Qalil (We'll Return Soon)**	• *Maraya 2013* (Mirrors 2013)	
• **Taht Sama' al-Watan (Under the Sky of the Country)**	• *Kharza Zarqa'* (Protection from Evil Eye)	
• **Fi Qalb al-Lahib (At the Center of the Flame)**	• *Fattet Le'bet* (Game Start)	
• *Zahr al-Banafsaj* (Blossoms of Violet)	• *Ruznama* (Almanac)	
• *Sukar Wasat* (Medium Quantity of Sugar)	• *Suber Fameeli* (Super Family)	
• *Sarkhat al-Ruh* (Scream of the Soul)		
• *Awham Jamila* (Beautiful Allusions)		
• *Sabaya Part Five* (Young Women)		

(Continued)

Societal Issues	Comedies	Historical
• *Natarin* (Waiting) • *Zunud al-Sitt Part Two* • *al-'Ubur* (Crossing) Never Broadcast		

Old Damascus	Adaptations	Police Thriller
• *Tahun al-Shar Part Two* • *Zaman al-Barghut Part Two* • *Yasamin 'Atiq* (Old Jasmin) • *Qamar al-Sham* (Damascus Moon) • *Hikayat Haratna* (Tales of Our Neighborhood) • *al-Shamiyyat* (Shami Women) • *Tawq al-Banat* (Strength of Girls) (delayed 2014) • *Hammam Shami* (Damascus Bath) (delayed 2014)	• *Lo'bat al-Mawt* (Game of Death)	• *al-Tali* (Next)

Ramadan 2014

Societal Issues	Comedy
• **Qalam Humra (Lipstick)** • **al-Qurban (Sacrifice)** • **al-Hubb Kullu (All the Love)** • **Halawat al-Ruh (The Beauty of the Soul)** • **Nisa' min Hadha al-Zaman (Women of the Time)**	• **Dhoboo al-Shanati (Hurry Up and Pack!)** • **Buq'at Daw' Part Ten (Spotlight Part Ten)** • *New Look* • *Suber Family Part Two*

Societal Issues	Comedy
• *al-Khuwatem* (Rings)	
• *Sarkhat al-Ruh Part Two* (Cry of the Soul Part Two)	
• *Raqs al-Afaʻi* (Dance of Snakes)	
• *Zunud al-Sitt Part Three*	

Old Damascus	Adaptations
• *Bab al-Hara Part Six* (The Neighborhood Gate Part Six)	• *al-Ikhweh* (The Brothers)
• *Tawq al-Banat* (The Necklace of Girls)	• *Law . . .* (If . . .)
• *al-Ghurbal* (A Sifter)	
• *Khan al-Darawish*	
• *Bawwab al-Rih* (Doorkeeper of the Wind)	
• *Hamam Shami* (Shami Bathhouse)	
• *Rijal al-Hara* (Men of the Neighborhood)	

Ramadan 2015

Societal Issues	Comedy
• *Alaghat Khasa* (February–March prior to Ramadan)	• **Buqʻat Daw' Part Eleven** (Spotlight Part Eleven)
• **Shahr Zaman** (Once Upon a Month) (aired March 1 prior to Ramadan)	• *Donia 2015*
• **Harat al-Musharaqa*** (al-Musharaqa Neighborhood) (aired May 1 prior to Ramadan)	• **Fitnet Zamanha** (Sedition of Her Era)
• **al-ʻInaya Mushaddada** (Urgent Care)	• *Waʼetini ya Rafiʼi* (You Woke Me, Dear Friend)
• **Wujuh wa Amaken** (Faces and Places)	• *Fares wa Khams Awanes* (A Knight and Five Old Maids)

(Continued)

Ramadan 2015 (continued)

Societal Issues	Comedy
• **Ghadan Naltaqi** (We'll Meet Tomorrow)	• *Ahlain Jarti* (Hello My Neighbor)
• **Imra' min al-Ramad** (Woman of Ashes)	• *Fazlakeh Arabiyyeh Part One*
• **Bi-Intizar al-Yasmin** (Waiting for Jasmin)	
• **Zuruf Ghameda** (Obscure Circumstances)	
• **Dimasku**	
• *Sarkhat al-Ruh Part Three* (Scream of the Soul Part Three)	
• *24 Qirat* (24 Carat)	
• *Bukra Ahla* (Tomorrow's More Beautiful)	
• *Ma' Wara' al-Wujuh* (What's Behind the Faces) (produced but never broadcast)	
• *Khiyaneh Mu'ajeleh* (Delayed Betrayal) (never completed)	
• *al-Khataya* (Sins) (never completed)	

Old Damascus	Adaptations
• *Bab al-Hara Part Seven*	• *al-'Arrab*
• *Bint al-Shah Bandar*	• *al-'Arrab: Nadi al-Sharq* (The Godfather: Club of the East)
• *Tawq al-Banat Part Two*	• *Chello*
• *al-Hara'ir* (The Independent Ones)	
• *al-Ghurbal Part Two*	
• *Harat al-Aseel* (Neighborhood of the Noble One)	
• *Sadr al-Baz* (delayed)	

Ramadan 2016

Societal Issues	Comedy
• *Madrasat al-Hubb* (School of Love) (broadcast preseason)	• *Buq'at Daw' Part Twelve*
• *Samra* (broadcast preseason)	• *Salimoo wa Harimoo*
• *al-Nadam* (Regret)	• *Madinat Naranj* (City of *Naranj*)
• *Jarimat Shaghaf* (Crime of Passion)	• *Limozeen al-Nujum* (Limousine of the Stars)
• *Ayyamon La Tunsa* (Days Not Forgotten)	• *al-Tawarid*
• *Nabtadi Mnein al-Hikayeh?* (Where Do We Begin the Story?)	• *Bath Tajribi* (Test Broadcast)
• *Bila Ghamad* (Without Cover)	
• *Ya Reit* (I Wish)	
• *Zawal* (Vanishing)	
• *Ahmar* (Red)	
• *Domino*	
• *Mudhnabun Abriya'* (Innocent Guilty Ones)	
• *Sarakhat al-Ruh Part Four* (Scream of the Soul)	
• *Ahl al-Gharam Part Three* (delayed)	

Old Damascus	Adaptations
• *Bab al-Hara Part Eight*	• *al-'Arrab: Taht al-Hizam Part Two* (The Godfather: Under the Belt)
• *'Atr Sham* (Shami Perfume)	• *Nus Yawm* (Half a Day)
• *Khatun*	
• *Sadr al-Baz*	
• *Tawq al-Banat Part Three*	

Ramadan 2017

Societal Issues

- **Ahl al-Gharam Part Three** (People of Love Part Three)
- **Shawq**
- **al-Haibeh** (The Name of a Place, Which Literally Means Prestige)
- **Madrasat al-Hubb Part Two**
- **Mudhakarat 'Ashiqa Sabiqa** (preseason broadcast)
- **Hikm al-Hawa**
- **Gharabib Sud** (Black Crows)
- *Lestoo Jariya* (I'm Not a Slave Girl)
- *Jnan Niswan* (Craziness of Women)
- *al-Gharib* (delayed)
- **Shababeek** (Windows) (delayed)
- **Akhar Mahal Ward** (delayed)
- **Fawda** (filming delayed)

Comedy

- **Azmeh 'Ailiyyeh** (Family Crisis)
- **Buq'at Daw' Part Thirteen**
- *Shoo al-Qissa* (What's the Story?)
- *Sana Uwla Zawaj* (First Year of Marriage)
- *Banati Hayati* (My Daughters, My Life)
- *Huwajes 'Abara* (Passing Borders) (delayed)
- *Psycho* (completed but broadcast delayed)

Old Damascus

- *Bab al-Hara Part Nine*
- *Khatun Part Two*
- *'Atr Sham Part Two* (Sham Perfume)
- *Tawq al-Banat Part Four*
- *al-Khan* (The Khan)
- *Warda Shamiyyeh* (Shami Flower) (completed but not sold to networks)

Historical

- *Urkadiya*
- *Qanadil 'Ushaq* Adaptations
- *al-Raboos* (Fright) (adapted from The Grudge)

Ramadan 2018

Societal Issues	Comedy
• **Bi-dun Qaid (broadcast December 2017)**	• *al-Waq Waq*
• ***al-Haibeh: al-'Auda Part Two***	• *Yawmiyyat al-Mukhtar* **(Diaries of a Mukhtar)**
• **Fawda (Chaos)**	• *Fazlakeh 'Arabiyyeh Part Two*
• **Rozanna**	• *Qosmeh wa Hubb* (Destiny and Love)
• **Tango**	• *Julia*
• **Akhar Mahal Ward (renamed *Wajuh al-Zil*: filming and broadcast delayed) (renamed *Kawma* when broadcast on September 9)**	• *Harim al-Shawish* (Women of the Policemen)
• **Wahem (Illusion)**	
• **Shababik (Windows)**	• *Huwajes 'Abara* (Passing Borders)
	• *Psycho* (not sold and broadcast for the season; however, broadcast on Bein Drama during fall 2018)
• *al-Gharib* (The Stranger)	• *Zuwaj Safar* (Marriage to Go) (delayed)
• *Musalsal Watha'qiyya: Nasiha bi-Kitab*	
• *Doubt*	
• *Fursa Akhira* (60 episodes starting September)	
• *Tariq* (A Path)	
• *Wehdan* (Loneliness)	
• *Ra'iha al-Ruh* (Smell of the Soul)	
• *Nasiha bi-Kitab* (Advice on a Book)	
• *Hawa Asfar* (Yellow Air) (not sold and broadcast)	
• *Awlad al-Shar* (Children of Evil) (not completed)	
• *Tarjaman al-Ashwaq* (Translator of Desires) banned due to political storyline)	
• *Talqat Hubb* (Shot of Love) (not completed)	

(Continued)

Ramadan 2018 (continued)

Old Damascus	*Historical*
• *Warda Shamiyyeh*	• *Harun al-Rashid*
• *'Atr Sham Part Three*	• *al-Mahalab bin Abi Sufra*
• *Jarah al-Ward* (Wound of the Flower)	
• *Zahr al-Kabid* (Blossom of the Heart)	

APPENDIX B

Percentages of Miniseries, 2011–2018

211 Miniseries Total from 2011 to 2018	*Transnational Series Percentages*
60 miniseries on war—28.5%	Pan-Arab—12 miniseries—6% of total
151 miniseries not on war—71.5%	Syrian-Lebanese—13 miniseries—6% of total
	Syrian—186 miniseries—88% of total
Social for the sake of the social—73 miniseries in total—34.5%	Nostalgic register—49 miniseries in total—23%

60 Miniseries on War	*151 Miniseries Not on War*
Social for the sake of the social—22 miniseries—36.5%	Social for the sake of the social—51 miniseries—33.5%
Nostalgic—7 miniseries—11.5%	Old Damascus (nostalgic)—42 miniseries—28%
Opposition stance—5 miniseries—8%	History and biography—13 miniseries—8.5%
Regime propaganda—9 miniseries—15%	Comedies—34 miniseries—22.5%
Neutral—17 miniseries—29%	Adaptations—9 miniseries—6%
	Police thrillers—2 miniseries—1.5%

APPENDIX C

Miniseries for Ramadan, 2019

Note: Miniseries that touch on the uprising are in bold.

Societal Issues	Comedy
• *Ma fi* (started filming late October 2018 and broadcast January 9, 2019)	• **Kuntak**
• *al-Basha* (The Pasha)	• **Buq'at Daw' Part Fourteen**
• **Turjuman al-Ashwaq** (Interpreter of Desires)	• *Fazlakeh 'Arabiyyeh Part Three*
• **Masafat Aman** (Distance of Security) (previously called: *Ardh Mahruqa*)	• *Harakat Banat* (Cunning of Girls)
• **'An al-Hawa wa-l-Jawa** (Of Love and Passion)	• *Live* (started filming October 2018) (not broadcast)
• *'Indama Taskaikh al-Dh'ib* (started filming February 16)	• *Miraya 2019* (not broadcast)
• *Prova*	• *Sana Thania Zawaj* (not broadcast)
• *al-Haibeh: al-Hisad Part Three* (al-Hayba: The Harvest)	
• *Hawa Asfar* (Yellow Air)	
• *Ghafwat al-Qulub* (Slumber of Hearts)	
• *Khamsa wa Nusf* (Five-Thirty)	
• *Daqiqat al-Samt* (Moment of Silence)	
• *Nabadh* (Throbbing)	
• *Nas Min Waraq* (People from Paper)	
• *Ayyam al-Dirasa Part Three* (not broadcast)	
• *Bukra Ahla Part Two* (not broadcast)	
• *Awlad al-Shar* (not broadcast)	

Old Damascus	Historical
• *Bab al-Hara Part Ten*	• *Harmalek*
• *Salasal Dhahab* (Chain of Gold)	• *Maqamat al-'Ishq* (*Maqamat* of Passion) (Police Thriller)
• *'Atr al-Sham Part Four* (Perfume of Sham)	• ***al-Katib*** (The Writer)
• *Shawari' al-Sham al-'Atiqa* (Old Streets of Sham)	• *Sani' al-Ahlam* (Creator of Dreams)
• *Warda Shamiyyeh Part Two* (Shami Flower)	

APPENDIX D

Percentages of Miniseries, 2019

27 Miniseries Total 2019	*Transnational Series Percentages*
Miniseries on war—6 miniseries—22%	Pan-Arab—2 miniseries—7% of total
Miniseries not on war—21 miniseries—78%	Syrian-Lebanese—4 miniseries—15% of total
	Syrian—21 miniseries—78% of total

Miniseries on War	*Miniseries Not on War*
Neutral—5 miniseries—83%	Social for the sake of the social—11 miniseries—52%
Social for the sake of the social—1 miniseries—17%	Old Damascus (nostalgic)—5 miniseries—24%
	History—2 miniseries—9.5%
	Comedies—2 miniseries—9.5%
	Police Thrillers—1 miniseries—5%

Note: al-Katib does not really mention the uprising; however, there is a passing reference in Episode 6 when Marjaline's father asks Yunus about his parents. When Yunus says that they are both dead, Marjaline's father asks, "Because of the *ahdath*?" and Yunus responds, "They were over eighty; thus, they passed due to old age." I have thus placed this series within the category of those that touch on the war.

ACKNOWLEDGMENTS

Syrian television drama and culture has been a formative part of my research since 2000. I conducted preliminary fieldwork in Damascus in 2000 and 2001 and then intensive fieldwork between 2002 and 2008 when I lived in Sahnayah, a village north of Damascus. During this time I observed miniseries during the Ramadan season and throughout the year when shows were broadcast again. I traveled to Damascus during the summers of 2010 and 2011, but as the uprising turned to civil war, it was no longer possible for me to return. Thus, since 2014 I have traveled to Beirut every summer to conduct research on this current book on post-uprising Syrian television drama. I have also spent several transits in Paris conducting interviews with drama creators who settled there after the start of bloodshed in Syria.

The list of screenwriters, directors, actors, and producers of Syrian television drama who have generously answered my numerous questions through the years is considerable. All interviews—both informal and formal—were conducted openly in private studies, restaurants, cafés, and homes and at public gatherings, as well as via Skype and the internet. First, I thank the late poet/screenwriter Mamdouh 'Adwan and novelist/screenwriter Khaled Khalifa for first introducing me to Syrian television drama through conversations in Damascus at our home, restaurants, and the Journalist Club when I first commenced my research in 2001. Despite the current upheaval in his country, Khaled has continued to patiently answer my questions on Syrian drama. He visited Davidson during the spring of 2016 and treated me and my students to a Q&A session after a screening of his miniseries *Sirat al-Jalali* (2000) and *al-Miftah* (2012). A humble, generous, and kind human being, he was a breath of fresh air on campus that spring semester.

Screenwriter Najeeb Nseir previously met with me in Damascus and met with me regularly at Café Younes in Hamra during my visits to Beirut from 2014 through 2018. He has answered my numerous questions with patience and kindness. Television editor and producer Iyad Shihab Ahmad introduced me to numerous drama creators and throughout the years via Skype has always been there to confirm numerous facts related to Syrian television drama. Among others, he introduced me to screenwriter Reem Hanna, who since 2014 has opened her home to me for amazing gatherings with a broad range of Syrian and Lebanese drama creators whose work I follow. These informal discussions have been invaluable, and I thank her immensely. The cover design from *Bi-dun Qaid* (Undocumented) is courtesy of screenwriter Rafi Wahbi, and I can't thank him enough for his continual support. Through the years he has patiently answered my many queries on Syrian television drama.

Director Haitham Haqqi, director Laith Hajjo, and set design artist ʿItab Hreib have met with me regularly throughout the years and have generously answered my questions. Numerous other screenwriters, directors, and actors have spoken to me in person, via Skype, or by email and have patiently supported my research. In particular, I would like to thank screenwriters Hoozan ʿAkoo, Buthaina ʿAwad, Colette Bahna, Fuʾad Humayra, Yam Mashhadi, Iyad Abu Shammat, Nihad Sirees, Mazin Taha, Merwan Qawuq, and Fadi Qoshaqji; directors Ahmad Ibrahim Ahmad, Muhammad Ferdos Atassi, Rami Hanna, Inas Haqqi, and Iman Saʿid; producer Hani al-ʿAshi; actors Jihad ʿAbdo, Sawsan Arsheed, Maysoun Abu ʿAssad, Sulaf ʿAweesheq, Hossam Tahcin Bik, Fares al-Heloo, Maksim Khalil, Qais al-Sheikh Najeeb, Yara Sabri, Rafiq Sbaʿi, and Ahmad Sheikh. I am grateful to Najeeb Nseir, Haitham Haqqi, Laith Hajjo, Rafi Wahbi, Muhammad Ferdos Atassi, Khaled Khalifa, Hoozan ʿAkoo, and Yam Mashhadi for granting permission to publish Syrian drama images in this book. Without the incredible humility, kindness, and generosity of all these drama creators I could not have completed this research.

At Davidson, Nicole Snyder, associate dean of undergraduate research and creativity, Fuji Lozada, associate dean of faculty, and Verna Case, associate dean for teaching, learning, and research, have been great pillars of support. Donella Mayes, research programs assistant at the Center for Teaching and Learning, has graciously facilitated my paperwork upon receiving Faculty Research Grants for summer research. My pretenure Malcolm O. Partin research stipend allowed me to conduct fieldwork in Lebanon during the summers of 2014 and 2015. I then received a Faculty Research Grant during the summers of 2017, 2018, and 2019 to conduct fieldwork in Lebanon. These generous grants allowed me to travel to Beirut to observe the drama season firsthand, to conduct interviews, and also to gather press reviews throughout the new Ramadan season. Davidson work study funds allowed me to appoint research assistants AJ Naddaff, Nick Lobo, and Elliot Lannon to assist with the chronology included in this book and conduct library research.

Davidson College faculty travel funds allowed me to present earlier versions of my research at the Middle East Studies Association conferences in DC (2014) and Denver (2015). I presented my research "Images of Syrian Refugees in Current Syrian Television Drama" at Duke University's "From Geneva to Shatila: Arab Refugee Crisis in the 21st Century" meeting (2016) and "Mediating the Crisis: The Politics of Gender and Marriage in Post-Uprising Syrian Television Drama" at Duke University during the spring of 2018. I thank colleagues in the Middle East and Asian Studies Department at Duke for their gracious invitations as well as the incisive questions, which stimulated and inspired my research. My mentor at Columbia University, teacher-scholar Hamid Dabashi, has always been a great source of guidance and inspiration. His words of wisdom, patience, and support were invaluable throughout my book's journey to print. I thank my colleagues and friends Ellen McLarney, Malak Swed, Hanadi al-Samman, Chris Alexander, Jonathan Berkey, Vivien Dietz, Rizwan Zamir, Ellen Amster, Silvi Toska, Sara Waheed, Hanan Kholousy, Marlé Hammond, Chris Toensing, Rayed Khedher, Laurent Cohen, Hassan 'Abbas, and Samer al-Saber for conversations on Syria and our various research interests throughout the years. In particular, I have learned so much about Syrian culture from Christa Salamandra, miriam cooke, and Donatella Della Ratta. I have enjoyed following their research and have been grateful for the opportunities I have had at conferences to discuss Syrian culture and our various perspectives with each other. Students in my "Contemporary Syrian Television Drama," "Politically Critical Parodies in Syria: Past and Present," "Mediating the Conflict: Syrian Television Drama and Revolution," and "Politics of Middle Eastern Melodrama" classes allowed me to share my research and discuss with them during the lonely writing process. I am thankful for Allison Brown, who discussed my introduction with me at length and helped me fine tune my argument. My trusted colleague and friend Christine Marshall's magical and poignant feedback was invaluable as I prepared the manuscript during the final stages of writing. She generously helped me polish my prose, and I am grateful for her positive energy, kindness, patience, and support.

Chapter 2, "Sociopolitical Satire in the Multiyear Syrian Sketch Series *Buq'at Daw* (Spotlight): Artistic Resistance via Gender and Marriage Metaphors, 2001–2017," appeared in a shorter version in the *Middle East Journal* (2014). Chapter 3, "The Rise and Fall of the *Qabaday* (Tough Man): (De)constructing Fatherhood as Political Protest," appeared in an earlier version in the *Journal of Middle East Women's History* (2015). Chapter 4, "The Politics of Love and Desire in Post-Uprising Syrian and Transnational Arab Television Drama," was published in a shorter version in the *Arab Studies Journal* (2016). I thank the *Middle East Journal*, the *Journal of Middle East Women's History*, and the *Arab Studies Journal* for granting permission to publish these book chapters based on shorter versions that appeared in their journals.

At Rutgers University Press, I am indebted to Péter Berta, series editor, for believing in my project from the commencement and for his encouragement throughout the various stages of my writing process. His wisdom, patience, and guidance were invaluable in ensuring that I kept the momentum to carry this project through. I am grateful to Jasper Chang, editorial assistant at Rutgers University Press, who was patient, kind, diligent, and generous throughout the process. He made the entire process enjoyable and stress-free. Péter and Jasper's belief in my work galvanized me to work hard to present the very best version of my research and writing. I sincerely thank the anonymous peer reviewers for their incisive critique, which helped me improve my writing and strengthen my analysis. Alissa Zarro and the amazing production team at Rutgers University Press, Melody Negron from Westchester Publishing Services, and copyeditor Joseph Dahm most generously helped carry this book through the final stages of production. I alone am responsible for any shortcomings found in this book.

I thank my family for their constant encouragement. My mother, Behnaz Kordestani Joubin, an amazing pillar of support and true friend, has always believed in me, pushed me to reach my potential, and stood by me through the toughest of times. Siblings, Kathy and Cyrus, and nieces, Sophia Eugenie, Laila Alexandra, and Luna Isabelle, have brightened my life. My father, Jahan, stimulated my love of writing from early on and selflessly supported me. I know that this book would have brought him much joy, and I regret that he is no longer with us. Special thanks go to my darling daughter, Jana Soffia, who has been with me through the whole process of research and writing. She has been gracious during meetings, often keeping herself busy reading, drawing, knitting, and crocheting. She has also been patient during the late-night dinners with drama creators, way past her bedtime. Her sweet disposition, kindness, and creativity fill me with gratitude. She provided the picture of the highway billboard in Jounieh, Lebanon, for the conclusion. My thanks to her are infinite and impossible to properly express.

NOTES

INTRODUCTION

1. Ridwan Shibli, *Buq'at Daw' Part Thirteen*, Episode 6, directed by Fadi Saleem and produced by SAPI (Sama al-Fann al-Dawliyya li-l-Intaj), 2017.
2. Donatella Della Ratta, *Shooting a Revolution: Visual Media and Warfare in Syria* (London: Pluto Press, 2018), 3.
3. Della Ratta, *Shooting a Revolution*, 2.
4. Rania Abouzeid, *No Turning Back: Life, Loss, and Hope in Wartime Syria* (New York: Norton, 2018), xi.
5. Rebecca Joubin, "The Politics of Love and Desire in Post-Uprising Syrian Television Drama," *Arab Studies Journal* 24, no. 2 (Fall 2016): 149–150.
6. Adam Baczko, Gilles Dorronsoro, and Arthur Quesnay, *Syrie: Anatomie d'une Guerre Civil* (Paris: CNRS Éditions, 2016), 15–16, 21–36, 69, 98–141, 219–274.
7. Anand Gopal, "A Reporter at Large: 'Syria's Last Bastion of Freedom,'" *New Yorker*, December 10, 2018.
8. Omar Haj Kadour, "Courte Trêve/*Ariha, Province d'Idlib/Syrie*," *Le Figaro Magazine* (August 9, 2019): 10.
9. Rebecca Joubin, *The Politics of Love: Sexuality, Gender, and Marriage in Syrian Television Drama* (Lanham, MD: Lexington, 2013), 1–21.
10. Christa Salamandra, "Arab Television Drama Production in the Satellite Era," in *Soap Operas and Telenovelas in the Digital Age: Global Industries and New Alliances*, ed. Diana I. Rios and Mari Castenada (New York: Peter Lang, 2011), 275–290; Christa Salamandra, "Spotlight on the Bashar al-Asad Era: The Television Drama Outpouring," *Middle East Critique* 20, no. 2 (2011): 157–158; Najeeb Nseir and Mazin Bilal, *al-Drama al-Televizioniyya al-Suriyya: Qira'a fi Adawat Mushafaha* (Damascus: Dar al-Hisad, 1998), 5–99; Najeeb Nseir and Mazin Bilal, *al-Drama al-Tarikhiyya al-Suriyya: Hulm Nihayat al-Qarn* (Damascus: Ziyad al-Suruji, 1999), 32–54.
11. Christa Salamandra, "Through the Back Door: Syrian Television Makers between Secularism and Islamization," in *Arab Media: Power and Weakness*, ed. Kai Hafez (New York: Continuum, 2008), 252–253.
12. Marlin Dick, "The State of the Musalsal: Arab Television Drama and Comedy and the Politics of the Satellite Era," *TBS*, no. 15 (2005): 2–5; Salamandra, "Spotlight on the Bashar al-Asad Era," 157.
13. Nseir and Bilal, *al-Drama al-Televizioniyya al-Suriyya*, 5–99; Nseir and Bilal, *al-Drama al-Tarikhiyya al-Suriyya*, 32–54.
14. FilmIrsad.com, October 20, 2012; AlKhaleej.ae, October 17, 2012; al-Safir, December 9, 2012; StarTimes.com, October 30, 2012.
15. Skype interview by the author with Iyad Shihab Ahmad, February 17, 2013.

16. Rebecca Joubin, "Syrian Drama and the Politics of Dignity," *Middle East Report*, no. 268 (Fall 2013): 27.

17. The GCC—a political and economic union of Arab states along the Persian Gulf and Arabian Peninsula—comprises six members: Bahrain, Kuwait, Oman, Qatar, Saudi Arabia, and the United Arab Emirates. See Naomi Sakr, *Arab Television Today* (London: I.B. Taurus, 2007), 124–125; Naomi Sakr, "Gaps in the Market: Insights from Scholarly Work on Arab Media Economics," in Hafez, *Arab Media*, 185–198.

18. Joubin, *Politics of Love*, 407–434.

19. "Al-Drama al-Misriya al-Ramadaniya . . . al-Romansiya, al-Komediyya, wa Saitara Jara'im al-Qatl," *al-Manara*, no. 135 (June 2014): 80–83.

20. Interview by the author with Inas Haqqi, Beirut, June 20, 2014.

21. Interview by the author with Inas Haqqi, Beirut, June 20, 2014.

22. Interview by the author with Rafi Wahbi, Beirut, June 27, 2014.

23. For instance, actor Mustafa al-Khani expressed a pro-regime, nationalist stance. See "Mustafa al-Khani: Lastu Muwazzafan fi al-Dawla wala Dhabitan fi al-Jeysh wala as'a ila Tabawwo' 'Ey Manseb Rasmi wa Mawaqifi min Iqtina'ati al-Mutlaqa wa Dhamiri al-Watani," *Nasreena*, October 2014, 119–125.

24. "Bi-l Suwar: al-Sada wa Thamaniyet Nujum 'ala Khat al-Nar fi Suriyya," *al-Sada*, June 8, 2014, 124–130.

25. "Suzanne Nejm al-Din: "Ba'edh al-Fannanin al-Suriyyin Khawana wa Ba'oo al-Watan 'an Gheyr Jahel," *Alwan*, no. 1019 (January 2015): 27–29.

26. Jocelyn Hadda, "Sulafa Me'mar Na'ish Harban 'Alamiyyeh Thalitha," *Alwan*, no. 1025 (July 2015): 24–26.

27. Interview by the author with Reem Hanna, Beirut, July 3, 2015.

28. "Mo'tasam al-Nahar Laqab 'al-Jaghal' Yu'abber 'an Ra'i al-Nas," *Laha*, 2016, 96–98.

29. Interview by the author with Reem Hanna, Beirut, June 24, 2016.

30. Joshua Hirsch, *After Image: Film, Trauma, and the Holocaust* (Philadelphia: Temple University Press, 2004), 1–27.

31. Abouzeid, *No Turning Back.*

32. Interview by the author with Rafi Wahbi, Beirut, June 27, 2014.

33. Interview by the author with Rafi Wahbi, Beirut, June 27, 2014.

34. Raz Yosef, *The Politics of Loss and Trauma in Contemporary Israeli Cinema* (New York: Routledge, 2011), 26–36.

35. Telephone interview by the author with Rafi Wahbi, September 16, 2014.

36. Salamandra, "Arab Television Drama Production in the Satellite Era," 280.

37. Kamran Rastegar, *Surviving Images: Cinema, War, and Cultural Memory in the Middle East* (Oxford: Oxford University Press, 2015).

38. Interview by the author with Haitham Haqqi, Paris, January 3, 2015.

39. Interview by the author with Haitham Haqqi, Paris, July 9, 2016.

40. Hisham al-Wawi, "Musalsal *Wujuh waAmaken* Waqt Mustaqta' am Dha'e'," *al-Nahar*, July 8, 2015, 12.

41. Interview by the author with Iyad Shihab Ahmad, Beirut, June 24, 2016.

42. Interview by the author with Haitham Haqqi, Paris, August 3, 2015.

43. "Jamal Suleiman: Ba'dh al-Fannanin Kashafoo Karahiyyatahum li-Zumala'ihem," *Laha*, 2015, 94–96.

44. Interview by the author with Haitham Haqqi, Paris, January 3, 2015.

45. Interview by the author with Khaled Khalifa, Davidson, NC, February 15, 2016.

46. Interview by the author with Haitham Haqqi, Paris, August 3, 2015.

47. Interview by the author with Khaled Khalifa, Davidson, NC, February 15, 2016.

48. For examples of reviews in the press, see Rabi'a Hunaydi, "Karis Bashar wa Maksim Khalil wa 'abd al-Mun'im 'Amayri kayfa dafa'oo Thaman al-Azma al-Suriyya," *Zahrat al-Khaleej*, July 4, 2015, 196–205; "Ghadan Naltaqi Yakshef Ahwal al-Suriyyin al-Muhajirin," *Laha*, 2015, 33.

49. 'Ala' Mur'eb, "al-MTV Tushawweh Sootat al-LBCI bi-Sabab *Ghadan Naltaqi*," *al-Jaras*, July 3–10, 2015, 42–43.

50. Interview by the author with Hoozan 'Akko, Beirut, June 30, 2015; interview by the author with Najeeb Nseir, Beirut, June 29, 2015; interview by the author with Haitham Haqqi, Paris, August 3, 2015.

51. "Basha'at al-Harb Tentasser fi *Buq'at Daw'* Eleven," *al-Safir*, July 7, 2015, 13.

52. Telephone interview by the author with Rafi Wahbi, September 16, 2014.

53. Interview by the author with Hoozan 'Akko, Beirut, June 30, 2015.

54. Jamal Fayad, "Drama Ramadan lima kol hazha al-'onf," *Zahrat al-Khaleej*, July 4, 2015, 208; see also *"(Donia)* Amal 'Arafeh wa Shukran Murtaja Yahtal al-Martaba al-'Ula," *al-Jaras*, July 3, 2015, 40–41.

55. "Shukran Murtaja: Ijtaztu al-Mu'adala al-Sa'ba," *al-Safir*, July 9, 2015, 11.

56. Sami Moubayed, "What Will Post–Arab Spring Intellectuals Write About?," *Huffington Post*, December 8, 2011, www.huffington post.com/sami-moubayed/what-will-postarab -spring_b_1136621.html.

57. Lisa Wedeen, *Ambiguities of Domination: Politics, Rhetoric, and Symbols in Contemporary Syria* (Chicago: University of Chicago Press, 1999), 88–92.

58. miriam cooke, *Dissident Syria: Making Oppositional Arts Official* (Durham, NC: Duke University Press, 2007), 72–77.

59. Donatella Della Ratta, "Dramas of the Authoritarian State," *Interventions*, February 2012, www.merip.org/mero/interventions/dramas-authoritarian-state; Donatella Della Ratta, "The Whisper Strategy: How Syrian Drama Makers Shape Television Fiction in the Context of Authoritarianism and Commodification," in *Syria from Reform to Revolt, Volume 2: Culture, Society, and Religion*, ed. Christa Salamandra and Leif Stenberg (New York: Syracuse University Press, 2015), 53–76.

60. Della Ratta, *Shooting a Revolution*, 10.

61. Della Ratta, "Dramas of the Authoritarian State"; Della Ratta, "Whisper Strategy," 53–76; Della Ratta, *Shooting a Revolution*, 5–6.

62. Interview by the author with Najeeb Nseir, Beirut, June 22, 2014.

63. Yves Gonzales-Quijano, "La Révolution: Un Drame Pour la Télé Arabe! (2/2: la Syrie)," June 14, 2011, http://cpa.hypotheses.org/2796; Yves Gonzales-Quijano, "Séries en Syrie: Le Mystère de la Drama Damascène," April 30, 2013, http://cpa.hypotheses.org/4339; Yves Gonzales-Quijano, "Le Feuilleton Syrien et la Crise (Feuilletons et Géopolitique: 2/2)," December 19, 2012, http://cpa.hypotheses.org/4075.

64. Joubin, "Syrian Drama and the Politics of Dignity," 26–29; Rebecca Joubin, "Resistance amid Regime Co-optation on the Syrian Television Series *Buq'at Daw'*, 2001–2012," *Middle East Journal* 68, no. 1 (2014): 9–32.

65. Telephone interview by the author with Hazim Suleiman, September 26, 2013.

66. Interview by the author with Laith Hajjo and Iyad Shihab Ahmad, Beirut, June 21, 2017.

67. Joubin, *Politics of Love*, 8–17.

68. Lila Abu-Lughod, ed., *Remaking Women: Feminism and Modernity in the Middle East* (Princeton, NJ: Princeton University Press, 1998), 3–25.

69. Purnima Mankekar, *Screening Culture, Viewing Politics: An Ethnography of Television, Womanhood, and Nation in Postcolonial India* (Durham, NC: Duke University Press, 1999), 1–162.

70. Joubin, *Politics of Love*, 15–17.

71. Joubin, *Politics of Love*, 421–428.

72. Rassam al-Madhoom, "Hayat al-Irhabi fi *Gharabib Sud*," *al-Hayat*, no. 19802 (June 22, 2017): 18.

73. *Gharabib Sud* is the second miniseries from the Arab world to be shown on Netflix. The first was the Egyptian miniseries *Grand Hotel*, which launched on Netflix in March 2018. See "al-Modon—'Ghurabib Sud' fi Netflix," May 1, 2018, www.almodon.com /media.

74. Interview by the author with Iyad Shihab Ahmad, Beirut, June 21, 2017.

75. Jamil Khader, "The Arabic Fantastic and ISIS Terror: The Aesthetics of Antiterrorism and Its Limits," *Middle East Report*, no. 282 (Spring 2017): 32–39.

76. Beth Baron, *Egypt as a Woman: Nationalism, Gender, and Politics* (Berkeley: University of California Press, 2005), 2–3.

77. Jeffrey C. Alexander, *Trauma: A Social Theory* (Cambridge: Polity, 2012), 6.

78. Saul Friedlander, *When Memory Comes*, trans. Helen R. Lane (New York: Other Press, 2016); Alexander, *Trauma*, 10–11.

79. Paul Ricoeur, *Memory, History, Forgetting*, trans. Kathleen Blamey and David Pellauer (Chicago: University of Chicago Press, 2004), 7–9.

80. Jeffrey C. Alexander, "Toward a Theory of Cultural Trauma," in *Cultural Trauma and Collective Identity* (Berkeley: University of California Press, 2004), 18.

81. For example, *al-ʿInaya al-Mushaddada*, directed by Ahmad Ibrahim Ahmad and produced by Qabnad, fosters a regime perspective. It takes place five years into the "azmeh," a time of war crimes and profiteers and the rise of Daʿish. Yet it never mentions regime complicity. In this storyline, Zikwan, a war criminal, kidnaps people, kills them, and sells their organs. He works with his girlfriend, Nahla, and also a butcher woman. Zikwan is violent with his girlfriend; they have sex on top of money, and she enjoys it when he beats her up. "What a *qabaday* you are!" she shrieks in ecstasy (Episode 3). The story is interspersed with documentary footage of injured people entering the hospital. When Jalal, psychologically injured from the war, comes home, the good officer Refʿa washes the dirt off his body. The miniseries depicts members of the opposition, like the character Maya, as corrupt. Daʿish has a strong presence in this storyline, as members kidnap the opposition artist Sobhi, asking him to give them the names of *muwali* artists. Likewise, *Bila Ghamad*, written by ʿUthman Jaha, directed by Fahd Miri, and produced by Syriana (Diana Jabour), is situated during the uprising and offers a direct regime perspective. Similar to *al-ʿInaya al-Mushaddada*, gender and marriage are key here in representing formal opposition to the culture of Daʿish.

82. Interview by the author with Haitham Haqqi, Paris, July 9, 2016.

83. Personal correspondence by the author with Haitham Haqqi, June 4, 2017.

84. Joubin, *Politics of Love*, 295–316.

85. Lila Abu-Lughod, *Dramas of Nationhood: The Politics of Television in Egypt* (Chicago: University of Chicago Press, 2005), 14–163.

86. A key miniseries in the nostalgic register, *Shawq*, takes place against a backdrop of the kidnappings and terror of Daʿish.

87. Rebecca Joubin, "The Politics of the *Qabaday* (Tough Man) and the Changing Father Figure in Syrian Television Drama," *Journal of Middle East Women's Studies* 12, no. 1 (March 2016): 50.

88. Interview by the author with Najeeb Nseir, Beirut, June 20, 2017.

89. Najeeb Nseir and Hassan Sami Yusuf, *Fawda*, directed by Samir Husayn and produced by SAPI (2018); in this storyline, Fethiyyeh loses her home and family during a

bombardment. When Zeidan learns that she is pregnant, he is terrified of scandal and wishes to protect her from people's gossip. She angrily responds, "What people? Did these people help me when I desperately needed it?" (Episode 4). In this way, Nseir challenges stale notions of honor and shame, notions that seem especially hollow amid the wartime disintegration of family and community. As we shall see in chapter 3 and 4, Nseir will also capture the turmoil of a war-torn society further aggravated by long-standing social norms that enable two brothers to be emotionally and legally bound to the same woman. While some criticized the slowness of certain episodes, *Fawda* was considered among the most distinguished miniseries of the 2018 season. See "Jadal Hawl Musalsalat Ramadan 2018: *Sayidaty* Tarsod Nabdh al Shari' wa Muwaqi' al-Tawasul al-Ijtima'i," *Sayidaty*, no. 1944 (June 9, 2018): 123.

90. Interview by the author with Najeeb Nseir, Beirut, June 14, 2018.

91. Kevin Harris and Jillian Schedler, "What Is Activism?," *Middle East Report*, no. 281 (Winter 2016): 2–5.

92. Interview by the author with Reem Hanna, Beirut, July 3, 2019; interview by the author with Iyad Shihab Ahmad, Beirut, July 3, 2019.

93. Hanadi al-Samman, "Out of the Closet: Representations of Homosexuals and Lesbians in Modern Arabic Literature," *Journal of Arabic Literature* 39 (2008): 270.

CHAPTER 1   MEDIATING THE UPRISING

1. Salamandra, "Arab Television Drama Production in the Satellite Era," 276–279.

2. Sakr, *Arab Television Today*, 124–125; Sakr, "Gaps in the Market," 185–198.

3. Interview by the author with Najeeb Nseir, Damascus, July 23, 2010.

4. For a detailed description of this scene, see Joubin, *Politics of Love*, 36–38.

5. Interview by the author with Najeeb Nseir, Beirut, June 29, 2015.

6. Interview by the author with Najeeb Nseir, Beirut, June 22, 2016.

7. Al-Samman, "Out of the Closet," 293–296.

8. Interview by the author with Najeeb Nseir, Beirut, June 20, 2017.

9. Joubin, *Politics of Love*, 38, 407–415.

10. Interview by the author with Inas Haqqi, Beirut, June 20, 2014.

11. Interview by the author with Rafi Wahbi, Beirut, July 3, 2015.

12. Interview by the author with Khaled Khalifa, Davidson, NC, February 15, 2016.

13. Judith Butler and Athena Athanasiou, *Dispossession: The Performative in the Political* (Cambridge: Polity, 2013), 149–150.

14. Judith Butler, *Frames of War: When Is Life Grievable?* (New York: Verso Press, 2009), x–75.

15. Sune Haugbolle, *War and Memory in Lebanon* (Cambridge: Cambridge University Press, 2010), 1–28.

16. Lucia Volk, *Memorials and Martyrs in Modern Lebanon* (Bloomington: Indiana University Press, 2010), 1–114.

17. Line Khatib, *Lebanese Cinema: Imagining the Civil War and Beyond* (London: I.B. Taurus, 2008), xviii–xx, 153–179.

18. Hazim Suleiman, *Buq'at Daw' Part Nine*, Episode 2, directed by 'Amr Fahd and produced by SAPI (Suriya al-Dawliyya li-l-Intaj al-Fanni), 2012.

19. "Bassim Yakhour: Raqaba bi-Tuhmat ... al-Ghalaza," November 27, 2012, www.al-akhbar .com/node/98553.

20. Interview by the author with Fares al-Heloo, Paris, December 30, 2012.

21. Joubin, *Politics of Love*, 48, 185.

22. Telephone interview by the author with Merwan Qawuq, September 9, 2012.

23. Iyad al-Jaja, "al-Katib wa-l-Mukhrij al-Masrahi Talal Lababidi li-Dam Press: *al-Wilada min al-Khasira* Samm Ladhidh," August 29, 2012, http://dampress.net/?page=show _det&select_page=51&id=22331.

24. Skype interview by the author with Iyad Shihab Ahmad, September 12, 2012.

25. Roland Barthes, *Le Plaisir du Texte* (Paris: Éditions du Seuil, 1973), 9–41; Roland Barthes, *Le Bruissement de la Langue: Essais Critiques IV* (Paris: Éditions du Seuil, 1984), 28–46.

26. Interview by the author with Colette Bahna, Damascus, July 16, 2011.

27. "Taqrir Qanat al-Jazeera Hawl Mawqif al-Fannanin al-Suriyyin," May 16, 2011, www .youtube.com/watch?v=O8FILI23osM.

28. Mirvat Syoofi, "Musalsal *Bab al-Hara* Qabadayat min Waraq," *Nadine*, no. 1744 (June 22–29, 2014): 14–15.

29. "Akhta' *Bab al-Hara*: Abu Marzuq Tuwuffiya fi al-Juz' al-Khames wa Sharaka bi-l-'Aza' fi al-Juz' al-Sabe'," *Nadine*, July 6–12, 2015, 28. In an interview, actor Milad Yusuf stated that many critiqued *Bab al-Hara* for historical inaccuracies, but in truth it is a story not based on history and should be seen as such. See "Milad Yusuf: *Bab al-Hara* Hikaya Sha'biyya la Yumkin Tahmiluha Waznan Tarikhiyyan," *Laha*, 2015, 96–97.

30. Interview by the author with Iyad Shihab Ahmad, Beirut, June 24, 2016. See also Amin Hamada, "*Bab al-Hara* Muhakat Sakhira Zalima wa Mazluma," *al-Hayat*, posted on *Bosta*, June 15, 2016.

31. Abu-Lughod, *Dramas of Nationhood*, 160–161.

32. See "Fadhihat Nizam al-Asad 'ala Mostawa 'Ali Jiddan—Masrab al-Taswir bi-l-Kawalis," September 24, 2013.

33. See "Qissat Rawan Qadah: Khutifat Am Maraset 'Jihad al-Nikah?,'" October 1, 2013; "Rawan Qaddah Shahada 'ala Kizb al-Nizam al-Suri," October 4, 2013.

34. Numerous magazine articles summarized the important Syrian miniseries of the season. See, for example, "Aham 'Asher Musalsalat Suriyya wa Pan Arab fi Ramadan," *Zahrat al-Khaleej*, no. 1890 (June 13, 2015): 195–197.

35. Tariq al-'Abd, "Musalsalat Dha'at fi al-Zaman," *al-Safir*, July 13, 2015, 13.

36. See "Ba'dh Musalsalat MBC fi Ramadan," "Musalsalat 'ala Qanat OSN Ya Hala HD," "Baramaj wa- Musalsalat Qanat al-Imarat Abu Dhabi fi Ramadan," and "'Ala Shashat Abu Dhabi fi Ramadan," *Laha*, 2015, 102–106.

37. For some articles that spoke of the *Ramadan Rating* show, please see "Maysa' Maghribi wa al-Tawassu' 'Arabiyyan," *Zahrat al-Khaleej*, July 4, 2015, 209; "*Ramadan Rating*: Nujum al-Drama wa Sunna'uha ila al-Muwajaha," *al-Jumhuriya*, June 19, 2015, 31.

38. Interview by the author with Fu'ad Humayra, Paris, December 30, 2014.

39. For a recent article recounting the reasons for the success of Turkish drama in the Arab world, see "al-Drama al-Turkiyya wa Asbab Najahha fi al-'Alam al-'Arabi," *Achabaka*, no. 3199 (July 3, 2017): 36–37.

40. "Samer Ridwan: 'Aradhtu Nassan Muzayyafan li-l-Raqaba wa Tamma Rafdhahu fa-Kayfa law 'Aradhtu al-Asli," *al-Jaras*, July 10, 2015, 9.

41. Interview by the author with Reem Hanna, Beirut, June 23, 2014.

42. Interview by the author with Reem Hanna, Beirut, June 23, 2015.

43. Interview by the author with Reem Hanna, Beirut, July 3, 2015.

44. "Maggy bou Ghossen law Khanani 'Abd Fahd la-Taraket *24 Qarat*," *al-Jaras*, June 26—July 3, 2015, 10–17; "Musalsal 24 Qirat . . . Maggy bou Ghossen Afdhal Mumathila wa 'Abed Fahd Karizma Khathira wa Cyrine 'abd al-Nour Batala Thaniya," *Nadine*, June 29—July 5, 2015, 27; Maggy bou Ghossen: Sa'ida li'anna *24 Qirat* Wasala ila al-Martaba al-Ula," *Nadine*, July 13–19, 2015, 28–31; "'Abed Fahd Yata'arradh li-l-Khathef wa Cyrine 'abd

al-Nour Tonqizahu," *Nadine*, June 8–14, 2015, 22; "Fi 24 Qirat Ghaltata al-Shater 'Abed Fahd bi-Alfeyn," *Achabaka*, July 13–20, 2015, 34–35; "Cyrine 'abd al-Nour: 'Indama ya'tarifoon bi-Annahum Sabbabu li al-'Aza sa-Oobader li-Musalsalatihum," *Layalina*, no. 178 (July 2015): 16–25; "Mo'tamar Sahafi li-Etlaq Musalsal *24 Qirat*," *Nadine*, no. 1763 (November 2014): 30–33.

45. Interview by the author with Najeeb Nseir, Beirut, June 22, 2014.

46. Interview by the author with Najeeb Nseir, Beirut, June 29, 2015.

47. Rana Astih, "Nadine Njeym: Kafa Nifaqan wa Mujafatan li-l-Waqa'. . . "Sorry wayn 'Ayshin?," *al-Jumhuriyya*, July 10, 2015, 30; "*Chello* Muttaham bi-l-Tatbi' ma' Isra'il: Kayfa wa Limadha?," *al-Jaras*, July 10, 2015, 14–15; Ninar al-Khatib, "*Chello*: Akthar min Mujarrad Eqtibas," *al-Safir*, June 29, 2015, 13; "Madha Hadatha fi Laylat al-Million Dollar: al-Muhafaza 'ala al-Rooh al-Sharqiyya Tazid Musalsal *Chello* Ghumudhan," *Achabaka*, July 13–20, 2015, 16; "Drama Mushtaraka Takhtof al-Jamahir bi-Abtal min Kartoon," *al-Akhbar*, July 13, 2015, 22; "Shek Yaqtol Sahibahu," *al-Hayat*, July 10, 2015, 18; "Fi Liqa' Mushtarak Kashafa Mada Taqarubhuma wa-Insijamuhuma fi al-Tamthil Ma'an," *Sayidaty*, July 13, 2015, 110–116; "Yusuf al-Khal wa Nadine Nassib: Takhathayna al-Jamal wa Ada'una al-Tamthili Silahuna," *Laha*, 2015, 26; "*Chello* wa-l-Fouta al-Sohhiyeh li-Nadine Njeym wa-l-Hamam," *al-Jaras*, no. 597 (June 26–July 3, 2015): 32; "Man Yantasser: al-Hubb am al-Mal am al-Sulta," *Nadine*, June 29–July 5, 2015, 28; "Televizion al-Mustaqbal Yotleq Shabakat Baramijahu li-Shahr Ramadan," *Nadine*, June 22–27, 2015, 14; Nada 'Ammad Khalil, "Musalal *Chello*: al-Mal Yantasir 'ala al-Hubb," *Nadine*, July 6–12, 2015, 31; "Yusuf al-Khal wa Nadine Nassib: Takhathayna al-Jamal wa Ada'una al-Tamthili Silahuna," *Laha*, no. 770 (June 24, 2015): 36.

48. See, for example, "Bi-ra'i arba'a min Nujum al-'Arrab hal huwa Taqlid wa-Istinsakh," *Snob*, July 2015, 168–171; "Assi al-Hallani Fares al-'Arrab al-'Arabi," *Sawa Magazine*, no. 58 (2015), 68–69; "Jamal Suleiman: 'Lan Takoon Ma'raka wa-li-hadha 'Ufakker fi Jensiyya Ghayr al-Suriyya," *Zahrat al-Khaleej*, June 20, 2015, 178–179; "Amal Bushusha: 'Jamal Suleiman 'Arrabi wa-sa-a'mal fi al-drama al-Khalijiyya iza . . . ," *Zahrat al-Khaleej*, June 20, 2015, 180–181; Asma' Shorfi, "Jamal Suleiman Za'im fi al-Sham wa Fashel ma' 'A'ilatihi," *Nadine*, June 2–12, 2015, 30; "'Amal Bushusha: Jamal Suleiman Lamma'a Soorati wa lam Afham 'Abed Fahd," *Laha*, 2015, 26–30.

49. Michel Kallab, "Nadi al-Sharq: Dood al-Nizam al-Suri Minnu w-fi," *al-Nahar*, July 9, 2015, 8.

50. Interview by the author with Rafi Wahbi, Beirut, July 3, 2015.

51. Interview by the author with Khaled Khalifa, Davidson, NC, February 15, 2016.

52. Interview by the author with Haitham Haqqi, Paris, July 9, 2016.

53. Samer Muhammad Isma'el, "Naqd al-Drama al-Suriyya Yahtadem 'ala Facebook," *al-Safir*, July 1, 2015, 13.

54. Samer Muhammad Isma'el, "Naqd al-Drama al-Suriyya Yahtadem 'ala Facebook," *al-Safir*, July 1, 2015, 13.

55. "Sulafa Me'mar: al-Insan al-Mahzooz Huwa allazi Yatamakkan min al-Qiyam bima Yuhibbuhu," *Good Health al-Arabi*, June 2015, 11.

56. "Suzanne Nejm al-Din: "Ba'edh al-Fannanin al-Suriyyin Khawana wa Ba'oo al-Watan 'an Gheyr Jahel," *Alwan*, no. 1019 (January 2015): 27–29.

57. Ron Eyerman, "Cultural Trauma: Slavery and the Formation of African American Identity," in *Cultural Trauma and Collective Identity*, 66.

58. Eyerman, "Cultural Trauma," 67, 72–75, 82–92.

59. Ninar al-Khatib, "*Chello*: Akthar min Mujarrad Eqtibas," *al-Safir*, June 29, 2015, 13.

60. Interview by the author with Hoozan 'Akko, Beirut, June 30, 2015.

61. Skype interview by the author with Iyad Shihab Ahmad, February 17, 2013.

62. Interview by the author with Talal al-Jurdi, Beirut, July 3, 2015.

63. "Al-Musalslat al-Lubnaniyya badilan li-l-drama al-Turkiyya . . . Fa-Hal Tentehiz Hazihi al-Forsa?," *al-Bawab*, no. 1019 (July 2015): 17.

64. "Al-Muntij Marwan Haddad *Ahmad wa Kristina* Musalsal Lubnani li-l-'Adhem," *Nadine*, June 2015.

65. "Al-Shashat al-Televizioniyya fi Shahr Ramdan Tartadi Thawb al-Drama al-Lubnaniyya," *al-Hadeel Magazine*, no. 108 (June/July 2015): 78–79.

66. "Al-Shashat al-Televizioniyya," 78–79.

67. "Al-Drama al-Lubaniyya Tatatawwar wa Azmat Wujud Nusus Tastamer," *Nadine*, July 13–19, 2015, 8–11.

68. "Al-Drama al-Lubaniyya Tatatawwar," 8–11.

69. Jocelyn Hadda, "Sulafa Me'mar Na'ish Harban 'Alamiyya Thalitha," *Alwan*, no. 1025 (July 2015): 24–26.

70. "Al-Muntij Mufeed al-Rifa'i: al-Drama Tijara Tahtamel al-Ribh wa-l-Khasara," *Nadine*, June 29–July 5, 2015, 8–13.

71. "Maksim Khalil: Ra's al-Mal Yu'akes al-Fannanin wa Yatahakam bi-l-'a'mal al-Fanniya," *Achabaka*, no. 3147 (June 27–July 4, 2016): 26; "*Jarimat Shaghaf*: Yuhaqiq Nisbat Mushahada Murtafi'a," *Achabaka*, no. 3147 (June 27–July 4, 2016): 29.

72. Muhammad al-'Ezen, "al-Drama al-Suriyya Akalaha 'al-Ghool,'" *al-Akhbar*, no. 2922 (June 28, 2016): 10.

73. Interview by the author with Najeeb Nseir, Beirut, June 22, 2016.

74. Rabi' Farah, "Suqut al-Drama al-Lubnaniyya al-Mushtaraka," *al-'Arabi*, posted on *Bosta*, June 14, 2016.

75. Wissam Kan'an, "al-Mawsam al-Suri Madrub fi 'Entizar Mu'jiza," *al-Akhbar*, posted on *Bosta*, June 10, 2016; see also Fatima 'Abdallah, "Sitat Wujuh Ramadaniya al-Taqadom wa-l-Ta'athor," *al-Nahar*, June 16, 2016, 83.

76. Wissam Kan'an, "*Jarimat Shaghaf* Ihzaru al-Mushahada," *al-Akhbar*, no. 2924 (June 30, 2016), 12; see also "al-Jaghal Qusay Ha'er Wasat al-Nisa' Zakiya al-Dirani," *al-Akhbar*, no. 2915 (June 20, 2016): 11.

77. Zakiya al-Dirani, "*Jarimat al-Shaghaf*: Nadine al-Rasi bi-Kamel Anaqatiha fi al-Habess," *al-Akhbar*, in *Bosta*, June 13, 2016.

78. Rose Suleiman, "Hal Taktafi al-Drama al-Suriyya bi-Jomhuriha al-Mahali," *al-Safir*, posted in *Bosta*, June 11, 2016.

79. Interview by the author with Najeeb Nseir, Beirut, June 20, 2017.

80. Nada 'Imad Khalil, "al-Drama al-Lubnaniyya al-Fa'iza al-Akbar bi-9 Musalsalat wa-l-Misriyya Tataraja' wa-l-Khalijiyya Tatatawar wa-l-Suriyya fi Azmat al-Istinsakh," *Nadine*, no. 1901 (June 26, 2017): 14–17.

81. Wissam Kan'an, "Qanadil al-'Ashaq . . . Malhama Naqisa," *al-Akhbar*, no. 3209 (June 24, 2017): 23.

82. "Nadine Nassib Njeym Tatrok Taim Hassan fi al-Waqt al-Munasab," *Achabaka*, no. 3197 (June 12–19, 2017): 33; Hanadi 'Issa, "Nadine Nassib Njeym: Fikrat al-I'tizal Tarawadni Kathiran," *Achabaka*, no. 3198 (June 19–26, 2017): 14–16; Fadwa al-Rafa'i, "Taim Hassan wa Nadine Njeym 'Number One' bi-l-Thalatha," *Nadine*, no. 1900 (June 19–25, 2017): 6–9; Caroline Bazi, "Mona Wassef Idafat 'Awatif al-Umm al-Mithaliya ila al-Haiba," *Laha*, no. 874 (June 21, 2017): 118–119.

83. Amin Hamada, "*al-Haiba*: Ardh Dramiyya Jadida . . . wa 'Atharat," *al-Hayat*, no. 19791 (June 16, 2017): 18.

84. Interview by the author with Iyad Shihab Ahmad, Beirut, June 21, 2017.

85. Interview by the author with Najeeb Nseir, Beirut, June 20, 2017.

86. Interview by the author with Reem Hanna, Beirut, June 23, 2017.

87. Interview by the author with Iyad Shihab Ahmad, Beirut, June 21, 2017; *Shababik* would later be broadcast on OSN in September 2017.

88. Crista Salamandra, *A New Old Damascus: Authenticity and Distinction in Urban Syria* (Bloomington: Indiana University Press, 2004), 102–112.

89. *Mudhakkirat 'Ashiqa Sabiqa*, Episode 1.

90. Alexander, *Trauma*, 2–3.

91. Eyerman, "Cultural Trauma," 62–63, 69, 71–79, 94–95.

92. *Mudhakkirat 'Ashiqa Sabiqa*, Episode 5.

93. *Mudhakkirat 'Ashiqa Sabiqa*, Episode 14.

94. *Shawq*, Episode 11.

95. Interview by the author with Iyad Shihab Ahmad, Beirut, June 21, 2017.

96. Khatib, *Lebanese Cinema*, 155, 166–168.

97. Interview by the author with Reem Hanna, Beirut, June 23, 2017.

98. Interview by the author with Reem Hanna, Beirut, June 23, 2017.

99. Interview by the author with Najeeb Nseir, Beirut, June 14, 2018.

100. Adnan Zira'i, "Aba'd," *Buq'at Daw'* Part Six, Episode 10, directed by Samer al-Barqawi and produced by SAPI (Suriya al-Dawliyya li-l-Intaj al-Fanni), 2008.

101. Ziad Sarky, "Ra'yak Yahemna," *Buq'at Daw'* Part Eight, Episode 24, directed by 'Amer Fahd and produced by SAPI (Suriya al-Dawliyya li-l-Intaj al-Fanni), 2011.

102. *Buq'at Daw'* Part Eight, Episode 14.

103. Mazin Taha, "Pan-Arab," *Buq'at Daw'* Part Eleven, Episode 1, directed by Seif al-Sheikh Najeeb and produced by SAPI (Sama al-Fann al-Dawliyya li-l-Intaj), 2015.

104. *Buq'at Daw'* Part Eleven, Episode 20.

CHAPTER 2   SOCIOPOLITICAL SATIRE IN THE MULTIYEAR SYRIAN SKETCH SERIES *BUQ'AT DAW'* (SPOTLIGHT)

1. Hazim Suleiman, "Khitab Mu'athir" (A Moving Speech), *Buq'at Daw'* Part Nine (Spotlight), Episode 7, directed by 'Amer Fahd and produced by SAPI (Suriya al-Dawliyya li-l-Intaj al-Fanni), 2012.

2. See also Rebecca Joubin, "*Buq'at Daw'* (Spotlight, Part Nine): *Tanfis* (Airing), a Democratic Façade, Delayed Retribution, and Artistic Craftiness," *Syrian Studies Bulletin* 17, no. 2 (2012).

3. Telephone interview by the author with Hazim Suleiman, September 26, 2013.

4. A. I. Dawisha, "Syria Under Asad, 1970–78: The Centers of Power," *Observer Foreign News Service* 13, no. 3 (1978): 341; Alasdaire Drysdale, "The Syrian Political Elite, 1966–1976: A Spatial and Social Analysis," *Middle East Studies* 17, no. 1 (January 1981): 3; Raymond A. Hinnebusch, "Syria under the Ba'th: State Formation in a Fragmented Society," *Arab Studies Quarterly* 4, no. 3 (1982): 192–193; Raymond A. Hinnebusch, "Syria under the Ba'th: Social Ideology, Policy, and Practice," in *Social Legislation in the Contemporary Middle East*, ed. Laurence O. Michalak and Jeswald W. Salacuse (Berkeley: University of California Press, 1986), 61–68.

5. Joubin, *Politics of Love*, 25.

6. Personal correspondence by the author with Najeeb Nseir, October 17, 2012; "Zurafa' al-Drama—Nihad Qal'i," broadcast on Suriya Drama, written and directed by Elyas al-Haj, produced by Syrian Arab Television, 2011.

7. Telephone interview by the author with Rafiq Sbai'i, April 26, 2013.

8. Sami Moubayed, *Steel & Silk: Men and Women Who Shaped Syria 1900–2000* (Seattle: Cune Press, 2006), 550–576.

9. Telephone interview by the author with Hossam Tahcin Bik, November 10, 2012.

10. Jean-Marie Quéméner, *Docteur Bachar Mister Assad: Ses Secrets & Ses Mystères* (Paris: Encre d'Orient, 2011), 73–85; Carsten Wieland, *A Decade of Lost Chances: Repression and Revolution from Damascus Spring to Arab Spring* (Seattle: Cune Press, 2012), 103–107.

11. Marlin Dick, "Syria under the Spotlight: Television Satire That Is Revolutionary in Form, Reformist in Content, *Arab Media & Society* (2007): 2–4; Christa Salamandra, "Prelude to an Uprising: Syrian Fictional Television and Socio-political Critique," *Jadaliyya*, May 17, 2012, www.jadaliyya.com/pages/index/5578/prelude-to-an-uprising -fictional-television; Salamandra, "Spotlight on the Bashar al-Asad Era," 157–158.

12. Dick, "Syria under the Spotlight," 2–4.

13. Interview by the author with Haitham Haqqi, Paris, December 29, 2012.

14. Personal correspondence by the author with Laith Hajjo, October 16, 2012.

15. Interview by Mustaffa Aloosh with Colette Bahna, October 15, 2005, http://tishreen .news.sy/tishreen/public/read/52253.

16. Personal correspondence by the author with Colette Bahna, October 10, 2012.

17. Interview by the author with Colette Bahna, Damascus, July 16, 2011.

18. Personal correspondence by the author with Jihad 'Abdo, October 14, 2012.

19. Salamandra, "Spotlight on the Bashar al-Asad Era," 157–158.

20. Rafiq Sbai'i, *Thaman al-Hubb: Min al-Sira al-Dhatiyya* (Damascus: Mu'assassat al-Wahda li-l-Sahafa wa-l-Tiba'a wa-l-Nashr, 1998), 155–175.

21. "Ta'ifiyya wa Hoqd Hafez al-Asad wa Durayd Lahham . . . Qatalat al-Fannan al-Kabir Nihad Qal'i (Husni Burazan)," http://all4syria.info/Archiv/49675.

22. Joubin, *Politics of Love*, 41.

23. "Al-Fannanin al-Suriyyin Bayna al-Tamthil wa-l-Haqiqa/Durayd Lahham," April 19, 2011, www.youtube.com/watch?v=63tHOKuEt9U. See also Durayd Lahham, www .youtube.com/watch?v=sjVctki8dQ; "Al-Fannan Durayd Lahham Yo'len Anahu Didd al-Thawra," May 9, 2011, www.youtube.com/watch?v=9eHMWDvuHYs; "Enta Amalna ya Bashar—Rafiq Sbai'i mp4," YouTube, March 30, 2011.

24. Telephone interview by the author with Jihad 'Abdo, October 23, 2012.

25. Interview by the author with Fares al-Heloo, Paris, December 30, 2012.

26. Interview by the author with Samir Gharibeh, Paris, December 30, 2012.

27. Telephone interview by the author with Hazim Suleiman, September 26, 2013.

28. "Al-Jazeera Mubashar ma' Lora Abu-As'ad wa-l-Drama al-'Arabiyya," September 23, 2009, www.youtube.com/watch?v=bwNQF_t5CwY.

29. Salamandra, "Prelude to an Uprising."

30. Christa Salamandra and Leif Stenberg, "Introduction: A Legacy of Raised Expecta-tions," in Salamandra and Stenberg, *Syria from Reform to Revolt*, 1–3.

31. Christa Salamandra, "Syria's Drama Outpouring: Between Complicity and Critique," in Salamandra and Stenberg, *Syria from Reform to Revolt*, 36–52.

32. miriam cooke, *Dancing in Damascus: Creativity, Resilience, and the Syrian Revolution* (New York: Routledge, 2017), 1–59.

33. Edward Ziter, *Political Performance in Syria: From the Six-Day War to the Syrian Uprising* (New York: Palgrave Macmillan, 2015), 1–56.

34. 'Omar Hajjo, "al-Liss wa-l-Fannan," *Buq'at Daw' Part One*, Episode 11, directed by Laith Hajjo and produced by SAPI (Suriya al-Dawliyya li-l-Intaj al-Fanni), 2001.

35. Edward Ziter, "Clowns on the Revolution: The Malas Twins and Syrian Oppositional Performance," *Theatre Research International* 38, no. 2 (2013): 138.

36. Colette Bahna, *Buq'at Daw' Part One*, Episode 17.

37. Ayman Rida and Bassem Yakhour, *Buq'at Daw' Part Three*, directed by Naji al-To'meh and produced by SAPI (Suriya al-Dawliyya li-l-Intaj al-Fanni), 2003.

38. Interview by the author with Fares al-Heloo, Paris, December 30, 2012.

39. Skype interview by the author with Iyad Shihab Ahmad, September 11, 2012.

40. Lobna Haddad and Lobna Mashlah, *Buq'at Daw' Part Three*, Episode 22.

41. Interview by the author with Fares al-Heloo, Paris, December 30, 2012.

42. See YouTube clip titled "Isketch min *Buq'at Daw'* Mana' 'Ardahu: Sheikh Selteh," December 17, 2010, http://www.youtube.com/watch?v=yn2hKI6M4bg.

43. Personal correspondence by the author with Colette Bahna, November 28, 2012; also see "Qissat Inbi'ath Awal Haraka Nisa'iyya li-l-Ehaya' al-Dini: al-Akhwat al-Qubaysiyyat," October 13, 2010, www.nabd-sy.net/index.php/drasat/5911-2010-10-13-08-14-33.html.

44. "Ba'da al-Ta'arrud li-l-Mutadayyinat . . . *Buq'at Daw'* Yuthir Ghadab al-Suriyyin," October 11, 2003, www.vb.eqla3.com/showthread.php?t=120053.

45. Skype interview by the author with Iyad Shihab Ahmad, January 7, 2013.

46. Dick, "Syria under the Spotlight," 20.

47. Personal correspondence by the author with Jihad 'Abdo, October 22, 2012.

48. Joubin, *Politics of Love*, 31–32.

49. "Al-Qubaysiyyat . . . Intilaqa min Suriya ila al-Khaleej," October 12, 2008, http://alrased .net/main/articles.aspx?selected_article_no=4549; "Man la Sheikha lahu, fa-Sheik hatahu al-Shaitan ... al-Qubaysiyyat ... al-Mozlimat ... al-Mazlumat ... Zolumat!!," December 22, 2011, www.syriano.org/2011/12/%D9%85%D9%86-%D9%84%D8%A7%D8 %B4%D9.

50. Interview by the author with 'Itab Hreib, Damascus, July 16, 2011.

51. Interview by the author with Haitham Haqqi, Paris, December 29, 2012. See also Thomas Pierret, *Baas et Islam en Syrie: La Dynastie Assad Face aux Oulémas* (Paris: Presses Universitaires de France, 2011), 13–32.

52. Line Khatib, "Islamic Revival and the Promotion of Moderate Islam from Above," in *State and Islam in Baathist Syria: Confrontation or Co-optation?* (Scotland: University of Andrews for Syrian Studies, 2012), 35. Information on Hamsho's alleged money-laundering practices was gleaned from a Skype interview by the author with Iyad Shihab Ahmad, September 11, 2012.

53. Mazin Taha, *Buq'at Daw' Part Four* (Spotlight Part Four), directed by Laith Hajjo and produced by SAPI (Suriya al-Dawliyya li-l-Intaj al-Fanni), 2004.

54. Interview by the author with 'Itab Hreib, Damascus, July 16, 2011.

55. Rana Hariri, *Buq'at Daw' Part Six* (Spotlight Part Six), Episode 16, directed by Samer al-Barqawi and produced by SAPI (Suriya al-Dawliyya li-l-Intaj al-Fanni), 2008.

56. Interview by the author with 'Itab Hreib, Damascus, July 16, 2011.

57. *Buq'at Daw' Part Six*, Episode 3.

58. Skype interview by the author with Iyad Shihab Ahmad, September 11, 2012.

59. Diana al-Hazim, "'Amer Fahd Yo'len Tarikh Bada' *Buq'at Daw'* 8," March 17, 2011, www .bostah.com/news/local-news/15514-%D8%B9%D8%A7%D9%85%D8%B1.

60. Muhammad al-Ezen, "'Amer Fahd *Buq'at Daw' Nine* Yatahadeth bi-Lisan al-Shari'. . . La Yumken 'an Nakun Kharij al-Sirb," http://startimes.com/f.aspx?t=31152252.

61. Mazin Taha, "Abu Samu'il," *Buq'at Daw' Part Eight* (Spotlight Part Eight), Episode 9, directed by 'Amer Fahd and produced by SAPI (Suriya al-Dawliyya li-l-Intaj al-Fanni), 2011.

62. Mazin Taha, *Buq'at Daw' Part Eight*, Episode 12.

63. Hazim Suleiman, *Buq'at Daw' Part Eight*, Episode 18.

64. Muhammad al-Ezen, "'Amer Fahd *Buq'at Daw' Part Nine* Yatahadeth bi-Lisan al-Shari'. . . La Yumken an Nakoon Kharij al-Sirb," http://startimes.com/f.aspx?t=31152252.

65. "*Buq'at Daw' Part Nine* Jur'a fi Madhmun wa Shakl Jadid," August 12, 2012, http://tishreen.news.sy/tishreen/public/read/265334.

66. "Al-Musalsalat al-Komedya fi Mawsim 2012 . . . Bayna al-Tafawwaq 'ala Dhat wa-l-Ghuluw fi al-Tahrij," September 24, 2012, http://forum.koora.com/f.aspx?t=31395337; "Drama," July 26, 2012, www.dp-news.com/pages/opinion.aspx?opinionsubjectid=265.

67. Telephone interview by the author with Hazim Suleiman, September 26, 2013.

68. Wissam Kan'an, "al-Komediyya al-Suriyya Mawsim al-Na'y (bi-l-Nafas) ila Dubai," June 27, 2012, www.startimes2.com/f.aspx?t=30940131.

69. Telephone interview by the author with Hazim Suleiman, September 26, 2013.

70. "*Buq'at Daw' Nine* Jur'a fi Madhmun wa Shakl Jadid," August 12, 2012, http://tishreen.news.sy/tishreen/public/read/265334.

71. "Al-Musalsalat al-Komedya fi Mawsim 2012 . . . Bayna al-Tafawwaq 'ala Dhat wa-l-Ghuluw fi al-Tahrij," September 24, 2012, http://forum.koora.com/f.aspx?t=31395337; "Drama," July 26, 2012, www.dp-news.com/pages/opinion.aspx?opinionsubjectid=265.

72. Muhammad al-Ezen, "'Amer Fahd *Buq'at Daw' Nine* Yatahadeth bi-Lisan al-Shari'. . . La Yumken an Nakoon Kharij al-Sirb," http://startimes.com/f.aspx?t=31152252.

73. Telephone interview by the author with Hazim Suleiman, September 26, 2013.

74. Wissam Kan'an, "al-Komediyya al-Suriyya Mawsim al-Na'y (bi-l-Nafas) ila Dubai," June 27, 2012, www.startimes2.com/f.aspx?t=30940131.

75. Telephone interview by the author with Hazim Suleiman, September 26, 2013.

76. "Al-Juz' al-Tasi' min Musalsal *Buq'at Daw'* . . . Jur'a Televizioni Tafshal fi al-Iqtirab Jur'at al-Shari'," August 20, 2012, www.aksalser.com/?page=view_news&id=7e2cb9353925 642da.

77. Hazim Suleiman, *Buq'at Daw' Nine* (Spotlight Part 9), Episode 1, directed by 'Amr Fahd and produced by SAPI (Suriya al-Dawliyya li-l-Intaj al-Fanni), 2012.

78. Hazim Suleiman, *Buq'at Daw' Part Nine*, Episode 2.

79. Samir Suleiman, *Buq'at Daw' Part Nine*, Episode 4.

80. Mazin Taha, *Buq'at Daw' Part Nine*, Episode 15.

81. Hazim Suleiman, *Buq'at Daw' Part Nine*, Episode 4.

82. Hazim Suleiman, *Buq'at Daw' Part Nine*, Episode 13.

83. Husam Sa'ub, *Buq'at Daw' Part Nine*, Episode 20.

84. "*Buq'at Daw'* Tajawaz Irtibakahu fi al-Nuskha al-Madiya wa Isti'ad Tawazanahu," August 14, 2012, www.damaspost.com/%D8%AB%D9%82%D8%A7%D9%81%D8%A9-%D9%88; Amana Mulhem, "*Buq'at Daw' Nine* . . . Ghabat al-Raqaba wa Fadat al-Khutut al-Hamra'," August 11, 2012, www.cimadrama.com/view.aspx?id=601.

85. "Al-Juz' al-Tasi' min Musalsal *Buq'at Daw'*."

86. Shadi Naseer, "Samer Ridwan: A'mali al-Dramiyya Hikayat Haqiqiyya," November 8, 2012, www.bostah.com/art-cafe/2010-06-17-12-38-57/23092-%D9%83%D8%A7%D9%8.

87. Hazim Suleiman, *Anti wa la Ahad*, *Buq'at Daw' Part Nine*, Episode 3.

88. Interview by the author with Iyad Shihab Ahmad, September 11, 2012.

89. Joubin, "Resistance amid Regime Co-optation," 28–29.

90. Skype interview by the author with Iyad Shihab Ahmad, September 11, 2012.

91. Telephone interview by the author with Hazim Suleiman, September 26, 2013.

92. Hazim Suleiman, *Buq'at Daw' Part Nine*, Episode 3.

93. Muhammad al-Ezen, "'Amer Fahd *Buq'at Daw' Part Nine* Yatahadeth bi-Lisan al-Shari'. . . La Yumken 'an Nakun Kharij al-Sirb," http://startimes.com/f.aspx?t=31152252.

94. Skype interview by the author with Iyad Shihab Ahmad, September 11, 2012.

95. Hossam Labash, "Bassem Yakhour: al-Drama Suriyya la Yumken Muqata'ataha . . . la al-Yawm wa la al-Sanawat," August 25, 2011, www.elnashrafan.com/news/show/45324; see also "Bassem Yakhour wa Mawqifahu min Bashar wa-l-Thawra al-Suriyya," January 18, 2013, www.youtube.com/watch?v=OWCqRwzoi8E.

96. "Tafawaqat al-Drama al-Suriyya 'ala Nafsaha wa 'ala al-Zuruf wa Najahat li-Intaj 24 'Amalan Mawsim 2012, wa ha hiya To'len Isti'dadaha li-l-Dukhul fi Mu'tarak al-Mawsim al-Jadid," December 13, 2012, http://alwatan.sy/dindex.php?idn=127313; "Al-Drama al-Suriyya Tatahada al-Zuruf wa Tasta'ed le 2013," October 20, 2012, www.filmirsad.com/content/%D8%A7%D9%84%D8%AF%D8%B1%D8%A7%D.

97. Personal correspondence by the author with Mazin Taha, April 29, 2013.

98. Skype interview by the author with Iyad Shihab Ahmad, September 26, 2013.

99. "Al-Drama al-Suriyya Tasir Bayna Ghaim al-Azma," October 30, 2012, www.startimes.com/f.aspx?t=31583977; Hal Tatahawal Madina al-Sweida li-'Asimat al-Drama al-Suriyya," August 11, 2012, www.elaph.com/Web/Entertainment/2012/8/754333.html; "al-Drama al-Suriyya Tusir Bayna al-Gham al-Azma," December13, 2012, http://startimes.com/f.aspx?t=31583977.

100. Telephone interview by the author with Hazim Suleiman, September 26, 2013.

101. "Basha'at al-Harb Tentasser fi *Buq'at Daw' Part Eleven*," *al-Safir* (July 7, 2015): 13.

102. Hazim Suleiman, *Buq'at Daw' Part Ten*, Episode 13, directed by 'Amer Fahd and produced by SAPI (Sama al-Fann al-Dawliyya li-l-Intaj), 2014.

103. Hazim Suleiman, *Buq'at Daw' Part Ten*, Episode 3.

104. *Buq'at Daw' Part Eleven*, Episode 5, directed by Seif al-Sheikh Najeeb and produced by SAPI (Sama al-Fann al-Dawliyya li-l-Intaj), 2015.

105. Ma'an Sheqbani, *Buq'at Daw' Part Eleven*, Episode 19.

106. Hazim Suleiman, *Buq'at Daw' Part Ten*, Episode 19.

107. *Buq'at Daw' Part Ten*, Episode 1.

108. *Buq'at Daw' Part Ten*, Episode 2.

109. Hazim Suleiman, *Buq'at Daw' Part Ten*, Episode 10.

110. Shadi al-Saghri and Jamal Shaqir, *Buq'at Daw' Part Twelve*, Episode 1, directed by Seif al-Sheikh Najeeb and produced by SAPI (Sama al-Fann al-Dawliyya li-l-Intaj), 2016.

111. Ziyad al-'Amer, *Buq'at Daw' Part Twelve*, Episode 3, 2016.

112. *Buq'at Daw' Part Twelve*, Episode 9, 2016.

113. *Buq'at Daw' Part Ten*, Episode 8, 2014.

114. *Buq'at Daw' Part Ten*, Episode 17, 2014.

115. Ma'an Sheqbani, *Buq'at Daw' Part Eleven*, Episode 4, 2015.

116. Ma'an Sheqbani, *Buq'at Daw' Part Twelve*, Episode 14, 2016.

117. However, at the end of the 2018 Ramadan season, Wissam Kan'an wrote that a new installment of *Buq'at Daw'* was expected for the 2019 season. See Wissam Kan'an, ". . . Wa-l-Drama al-Suriyya Tashoo min 'al-Kawma'?," *al-Akhbar*, no. 3502 (June 29, 2018): 31.

118. Wissam Kan'an, "*Buq'at Daw'* Thirteen . . . Faqed al-Dhahak la Y'atihoo!," *al-Akhbar*, no. 3205 (June 20, 2017): 22.

119. Ma'an Sheqbani, *Buq'at Daw' Part Thirteen*, Episode 4, directed by Fadi Saleem and produced by SAPI (Sama al-Fann al-Dawliyya li-l-Intaj), 2017.

120. Shadi Kiwan, *Buq'at Daw' Part Thirteen*, Episode 5.

121. Ma'an Sheqbani, *Buq'at Daw' Part Thirteen*, Episode 23.

122. *Buqʻat Daw' Part Thirteen*, Episode 14.

123. Moweed al-Nablosi, *Buqʻat Daw' Part Thirteen*, Episode 4.

124. Shadi Kiwan, *Buqʻat Daw' Part Thirteen*, Episode 9.

125. cooke, *Dissident Syria*, 32–34.

126. Jawan Bahlawi, *Buqʻat Daw' Part Thirteen*, Episode 3.

127. Samer Salman, *Buqʻat Daw' Part Thirteen*, Episode 13.

128. *Buqʻat Daw' Part Thirteen*, Episode 10, Episode 20, and Episode 30.

129. Interview by the author with Iyad Shihab Ahmad, Beirut, June 21, 2017.

130. *Buqʻat Daw' Part Thirteen*, Episode 11.

131. *Buqʻat Daw' Part Thirteen*, "The Red Line," Episode 11.

132. *Buqʻat Daw' Part Fourteen*, Episode 13, directed by Seif al-Sheikh Najeeb and produced by SAPI (Sama al-Fann al-Dawliyya li-l-Intaj), 2019.

133. *Buqʻat Daw' Part Fourteen*, Episode 15, 2019.

134. *Buqʻat Daw' Part Fourteen*, Episode 20, 2019.

CHAPTER 3 THE RISE AND FALL OF THE *QABADAY* (TOUGH MAN)

1. Scott Coltrane, "Father-Child Relationships and the Status of Women: A Cross-Cultural Study," *American Journal of Sociology* 93, no. 5 (1988): 1065.

2. Charlie Lewis and Margaret O'Brien, "Constraints on Fathers: Research, Theory, and Clinical Practice," in *Reassessing Fatherhood: New Observations on Fatherhood and the Modern Family*, ed. Charlie Lewis and Margaret O'Brien (Thousand Oaks, CA: Sage, 1987), 2–5.

3. Michael Johnson, "Political Bosses and Their Gangs: *Zuʻama* and *Qabadayat* in the Sunni Muslim Quarters of Beirut," in *Patrons and Clients*, ed. Ernest Gellner and John Waterbury (London: Duckworth, 1977), 207–224; Keith David Watenpaugh, *Being Modern in the Middle East: Revolution, Nationalism, Colonialism, and the Arab Middle Class* (Princeton, NJ: Princeton University Press, 2006), 255–278.

4. Personal correspondence by the author with Najeeb Nseir, January 2, 2015.

5. Interview by the author with Haitham Haqqi, Paris, January 3, 2015.

6. Interview by the author with Fu'ad Humayra, Paris, December 30, 2014.

7. Interview by the author with Fares al-Heloo, Paris, January 2, 2015.

8. Luigi Achilli, "Becoming a Man in al-Wihdat: Masculine Performances in a Palestinian Refugee Camp in Jordan," *International Journal of Middle East Studies* 47, no. 2 (2015): 263–280.

9. Viola Shafik, *Popular Egyptian Cinema: Gender, Class, and Nation* (Cairo: American University in Cairo Press, 2007), 314.

10. Walter Armbrust, "Farid Shauqi: Tough Guy, Family Man, Cinema Star," in *Imagined Masculinities: Male Identity and Culture in the Modern Middle East*, ed. Mayy Ghassub and Emma Sinclair-Webb (London: Saqi Press, 2006), 199–226.

11. Wilson Chacko Jacob, *Working Out Egypt: Effendi Masculinity and Subject Formation in Colonial Modernity, 1870–1940* (Durham, NC: Duke University Press, 2011).

12. R. W. Connell, *Masculinities* (Berkeley: University of California Press, 2005); Todd W. Reeser, *Masculinities in Theory: An Introduction* (Oxford: Wiley-Blackwell, 2010).

13. Salwa Ismael, "Youth, Gender, and the State in Cairo: Marginalized Masculinities and Contested Spaces," in *Arab Society and Culture: An Essential Reader*, ed. Samir Khalaf and Roseanne Saad Khalaf (London: Saqi Press, 2009), 223–239.

14. Marcia Inhorn, *The New Arab Man: Emergent Masculinities, Technologies, and Islam in the Middle East* (Princeton, NJ: Princeton University Press, 2012).

15. Joubin, *Politics of Love*, 12–21.

16. Joubin, *Politics of Love*, 118–126.

17. Fadi Qoshaqji, *Laysa Saraban*, Episode 2. Qoshaqji chose not to name the country where 'Amer studied. By continually referring to "the West," he hoped for it to be clear that he was speaking about the United States or Western Europe. In this way he allowed viewers to imagine for themselves. Personal correspondence by the author with Fadi Qoshaqji, January 6, 2019.

18. Fadi Qoshaqji, *Laysa Saraban*, Episode 28.

19. Rania Ahmad Bitar, *Ashwak Na'imeh*, Episode 3.

20. Gayle Kaufman, *Superdads: How Fathers Balance Work and Family in the 21st Century* (New York: New York University Press, 2013), 5.

21. *Qulub Saqira*, Episode 14.

22. Personal correspondence by the author with Yara Sabri, April 1, 2014.

23. Personal correspondence by the author with Yara Sabri, April 1, 2014.

24. Joubin, *Politics of Love*, 136–139.

25. *Takht Sharqi*, Episode 9.

26. Interview by the author with Iyad Shihab Ahmad, Beirut, June 13, 2014.

27. Rob Palkovitz and Glen Palm, "Transitions within Fathering," *Fathering* 7, no. 1 (Winter 2009): 3–22.

28. Personal correspondence by the author with Yam Mashhadi, March 17, 2014.

29. *Takht Sharqi*, Episode 25.

30. Interview by the author with Iyad Shihab Ahmad, Beirut, June 13, 2014.

31. Interview by the author with Fares al-Heloo, Paris, December 30, 2012.

32. Telephone interview by the author with Khaled al-Khalifa, December 13, 2013.

33. *Zaman al-Khawf*, Episode 1.

34. *Zaman al-Khawf*, Episode 14.

35. *Zaman al-Khawf*, Episode 28.

36. Interview by the author with Iyad Shihab Ahmad, Damascus, July 16, 2010.

37. Interview by the author with Haitham Haqqi, Paris, December 29, 2013.

38. Interview by the author with Inas Haqqi, Beirut, June 20, 2014.

39. Interview by the author with Haitham Haqqi, Paris, December 29, 2013.

40. Joubin, *Politics of Love*, 376–396.

41. Telephone interview by the author with Najeeb Nseir, September 13, 2012.

42. "Al-Mukhrij Seif Sbai'i fi Marahel al-Akhira min Taswir Musalsal *Ta'ab al-Mishwar*," December 18, 2010, www.discover-syria.com/news/9744.

43. "Televizion Abu Dhabi Yonqedh *Ta'b al-Mishwar*," August 29, 2011, www.anazahra.com /entertainment/photo-124752/%D8%AA%D9%84%D9%81%D8.

44. *Al-Miftah*, Episode 2.

45. "Hisham Sharbatji: Tanaba'et bi-ma Yajri bi-Suriya fa-Qubeltu bi-l-Takhwin," March 22, 2012, http://arabic.cnn.com/2012/enter.celeb/3/9/Hisham.Sharbatji.Intv/index.html.

46. Personal correspondence by the author with Hisham Sharbatji, March 17, 2014.

47. Kamil Nasrawi, *Watan Haff*, directed by Muhammad Ferdos Atassi and Muhannad Qateesh and produced by Mu'assassat al-Intaj al-Idha'a wa-l-Televizioni (Syrian Radio and TV Production Organization), 2013; "Dramiat Takshef Tafasil *Watan Haff* wa al-Taswir Intalaq," April 22, 2013, www.dramiat.com; "Musalsal *Watan Haff* al-Suri fi Matla' Nissan," March 17, 2013, www.ifilmtv.ir/Default/Details/59524; "Muhannad Qateesh: '*Watan Haff*' Yatahadath 'an al-Azma al-Suriyya," April 29, 2013, www .vitopress.com/news/view/2628; "*Watan Haff*: Yataqassamahu Mukhrijan," April 29, 2013, www.anazahra.com/entertainment/tv-series/article-106173/%D9%88%D8%B7%D;

"Fayez Qazaq Yatanawal al-Azma al-Suriyya fi *Watan Haff*," May 8, 2013, www.dramiat .com; "Muhammad Ferdos Atassi Yuwassel Taswir *Watan Haff*," April 27, 2013, www .dramiat.com.

48. Salamandra, "Arab Television Drama Production in the Satellite Era," 285–288.

49. *Qalam Humra*, Episode 5.

50. Alexander, "Toward a Theory of Cultural Trauma," 7.

51. Joubin, *Politics of Love*, 367–369.

52. Interview by the author with Fu'ad Humayra, Paris, December 30, 2014.

53. Muhammad al-Ezen, "Durayd Lahham Mujaddadan Amama Camera Laith Hajjo ...Laith Yabda' Taswir *Sa-Na'ud Ba'da Qalil*," December 1, 2012, www.bostah.com/news /local-news/23322.

54. "'*Sa-Na'ud Ba'da Qalil*' ... Musalsal Suri Yarsod Harakat Nuzooh al-Suriyyin bi Lubnan," March 19, 2013, www.ahewar.org/news/s.news.asp?nid=1029903.

55. *Sa-Na'ud Ba'da Qalil*, Episode 27.

56. "Al-Azma al-Suriyya fi Musalsal *Sa-Na'ud Ba'da Qalil*," March 31, 2013, www.youtube.com /watch?v=24iiwBmF1kA.

57. "Durayd Lahham fi Musalsal '*Sa-Na'ud Ba'da Qalil*' Yatanawal al-Wade' al-Rahin fi Suriya," February 23, 2013, http://www.france24.com/ . . . /20130223; "Kinda 'Aloosh Fannana Tashkiliyya," May 23, 2013, www.dramiat.com.

58. Interview by the author with Iyad Shihab Ahmad, Beirut, June 13, 2014.

59. Diana Hazeem, "Nur Shishekly: Thalathiyya Nuzuh Lam Tata'arrad li-Qass Raqabi," August 10, 2013, http://breakingnews.sy/ar/article/22549.html; Muhammad al-Ezen, "Najdat Anzour: Thalathiyya *Nuzuh* lam Tata'arrad Li-Maqass al-Raqib . . . wa Akhar Thalathiyyat *Taht Sama' al-Watan* bi-'Anwan *Thalla min al-Awalin*," August 10, 2013, www .bostah.com.

60. Personal correspondence by the author with Nur Shishekly, March 18, 2014.

61. *Sukar Wasat*, Episode 2.

62. *Sukar Wasat*, Episode 11.

63. Personal correspondence by the author with Mazin Taha, March 18, 2014.

64. *Al-Qurban*, Episode 4.

65. *Al-Qurban*, Episode 17.

66. *Al-Qurban*, Episode 31.

67. *Al-Wilada min al-Khasira Part Three*, Episode 29.

68. Joubin, *Politics of Love*, 433–434; Rebecca Joubin, "Research Notes: Samer Fahd Ridwan's *Menbar al-Mawta* (Platform of Death), Ramadan 2013," *Syrian Studies Bulletin* 18, no. 2 (2013).

69. Samer Fahd Ridwan: Sahib *al-Wilada min al-Khasira* Mo'taqal bi-Dimashq," http://arabic .cnn.com/2013/entertainment/16/19/samer.ridwan.arrest.Syria/index.html; "La I'tiqalat li-Fannanin *Menbar al-Mawta* 'ala Hudud Lubnan," June 24, 2013, www.dramiat.com

70. Interview by the author with Rafi Wahbi, Beirut, June 27, 2014.

71. Telephone interview by the author with Rafi Wahbi, September 16, 2014.

72. *Helawat al-Ruh*, Episode 1.

73. *Helawat al-Ruh*, Episode 2.

74. Telephone interview by the author with Rafi Wahbi, September 16, 2014.

75. Interview by the author with Najeeb Nseir, Beirut, June 22, 2016.

76. Interview by the author with Iyad Shihab Ahmad, Beirut, June 24, 2016.

77. Interview by the author with Haitham Haqqi, Paris, July 9, 2016.

78. Fatima 'Abdallah, "al-Nadam al-Zaman Yatabaddal wa-l-'Insan Yadfa' al-Thaman," *al-Nahar*, June 18, 2016, 8.

79. Wissam Kan'an, "Karithat al-Kawareth Lawla 'al-Nadam'," *al-Akhar*, no. 2922 (June 28, 2016): 11; "Maram 'Ali: Li-Hadha al-Isbab Talabooni Li-l-'Amal fi Hollywood," *Laha*, no. 873 (June 14, 2017): 106–109.

80. *Mudhakirat 'Ashiqa Sabiqa*, Episode 15.

81. *Mudhakirat 'Ashiqa Sabiqa*, Episode 19.

82. "Mo'tamar Sahafi Li-'Etlaq al-Musalsal al-Tarikhi *'Bint al-Shahbandar*," *Nadine*, no. 1767 (December 2014): 38–41; Fadwa al-Rifa'i, "Al-Muntij Mufid al-Rifa'i: Ana Awal Muntij Hamala al-Drama al-Lubnaniyya li-l-'Alam al-'Arabi wa-l-'Alam," *Nadine*, no. 1774 (June 2015): 8–11; "*Bint al-Shahbandar* hal Yafooz Qusay Khawli bi-Qalb Sulafa Me'mar," *Nadine*, June 29–July 5, 2015, 28; "Tatawarat fi *Bint al-Shahbandar*," *al-Hayat*, July 11, 2015, 18; "al-Musalsal Tarikhi *Bint al-Shahbandar*: Qusay Khawli wa Qais al-Sheikh Najib Yatanafasaan 'ala Qalb Sulafa Me'mar," *Nadine*, July 2–12, 2015, 33.

83. Interview by the author with Hoozan 'Akko, Beirut, June 30, 2015.

84. E. Ann Kaplan, *Trauma Culture: The Politics of Terror and Loss in Media and Literature* (New Brunswick, NJ: Rutgers University Press, 2005), 2.

85. Interview by the author with Hoozan 'Akko, Beirut, June 30, 2015.

86. Jocelyn Hadda, "Sulafa Me'mar Na'ish Harban 'Alamiyya Thalitha," *Alwan*, no. 1025 (July 2015): 24–26.

87. *Al-Gharib*, Episode 14.

88. *Al-Gharib*, Episode 13.

89. *Al-Gharib*, Episode 29.

90. *Al-Gharib*, Episode 31.

91. *Tango*, Episode 17.

92. Interview by the author with Najeeb Nseir, Beirut, June 14, 2018.

93. *Fawda*, Episode 16.

94. *Fawda*, Episode 19.

95. Joubin, *Politics of Love*, 12–21.

96. Interview by the author with Haitham Haqqi, Paris, January 3, 2015.

97. Joubin, *Politics of Love*, 376–396.

98. Telephone interview by the author with Iyad Shihab Ahmad, May 12, 2019.

99. *Turjuman al-Ashwaq*, Episode 19.

100. *Musafat Aman*, Episode 24.

CHAPTER 4   THE POLITICS OF LOVE AND DESIRE IN POST-UPRISING SYRIAN AND TRANSNATIONAL ARAB TELEVISION DRAMA

1. Buthaina 'Awad, *Nisa' min Hadha al-Zaman*, Episode 8.

2. Evelyne Accad, *Sexuality and War: Literary Masks of the Middle East* (New York: New York University Press, 1990), 1–163.

3. Joubin, *Politics of Love*, 2–17.

4. Joubin, "Resistance amid Regime Co-optation," 12–13.

5. See "Interview with Bernard Lewis—Turkish Policy Quarterly," www.turkishpolicy.com /dosyalar/files/interview/bernard_lewis-10_4.pdf; Richard Landes, "Edward Said and the Culture of Honor and Shame: Orientalism and Our Misinterpretations of the Arab-Israeli Conflict," *Israeli Affairs* 13, no. 4 (October 2007): 844–858, www.theaugeanstables .com/ . . . /edward-said-and-the-culture-of-honor-and-shame; Edward Said, *Orientalism* (New York: Vintage, 1979).

6. Joubin, *Politics of Love*, 13–17; Joubin, "Syrian Drama and the Politics of Dignity," 26–29.

7. Razi Warda and Samer al-Mesri, *Abu Janti: Malek al-Taxi* (Abu Janti: Owner of a Taxi), directed by Zuhair Ahmad Qanoo' and produced by Bana, 2010.

8. See Lila Abu-Lughod, "Feminist Longings and Postcolonial Conditions," in Abu-Lughod, *Remaking Women*, 3–25.

9. Abu-Lughod, *Remaking Women*, 15.

10. Joubin, *Politics of Love*, 13–17.

11. Interview by the author with Merwan Qawuq, Damascus, July 8, 2010.

12. *Zaman al-Khawf*, Episode 26.

13. *Zaman al-Khawf*, Episode 19.

14. *Zaman al-Khawf*, Episode 20.

15. Interview by the author with Najeeb Nseir, Damascus, July 23, 2010.

16. Interview by the author with Najeeb Nseir, Beirut, June 22, 2016; interview by the author with Reem Hanna, Beirut, June 24, 2016.

17. "Al-Jazeera Mubashar—Sulafa Me'mar wa-l-Drama al-Suriyya," November 16, 2010, www.youtube.com/watch?v=B9rVfT.

18. Yam Mashhadi, *Takht Sharqi*, Episode 34, 2010.

19. Hassan Sami Yusuf, *al-Ghufran*, 2011.

20. A traditional Islamic marriage contract is composed of two kinds of *mahr*: the *muqaddam* is paid at the time of the signing of the marriage contract, while the *mu'akhar* is a delayed payment given to the woman upon divorce or the death of her husband.

21. Najeeb Nseir and Hassan Sami Yusuf, *al-Sarab*, Episode 10.

22. Nseir and Yusuf, *al-Sarab*, Episode 19.

23. Nseir and Yusuf, *al-Sarab*, Episode 21.

24. Interview by the author with Najeeb Nseir, Damascus, July 23, 2010.

25. Joubin, *Politics of Love*, 411–421.

26. Cathy Caruth, ed., *Trauma: Explorations in Memory* (Baltimore: Johns Hopkins University Press, 1995), 151.

27. Caruth, *Trauma*, 153.

28. Caruth, *Trauma*, 3–11, 151–157.

29. Kaplan, *Trauma Culture*, 36–37.

30. "Jessika Nassar: A'taref bi-Fadhl 'Ammar Shalaq 'Alayya," *Nadine*, June 22–19, 2014, 30–31; "Rania Yusuf: Istibdali bi-Bushra Qellat Zawj was a-'Uqadhi al-Sharika al-Muntija," *Nadine*, June 12–22, 2014, 38–39; "Amal Beshusha: Atamanna an Ansaheb min al-Fan Qabla an Ya'kol Shababi," *Alwan*, no. 1013 (July 2014): 40–42; "al-Ikhweh: Drama Suriyya bi-Nakha 'Arabiyya," *Kul al-Usra*, no. 1070 (April 15, 2014): 118–120; "Muhammad Hadaqi: al-Fannan al-Suri Musharrad," *Kul al-Usra*, no. 1080 (June 24, 2014): 116.

31. Telephone interview by the author with Buthaina 'Awad, May 23, 2014.

32. Telephone interview by the author with Ahmad Ibrahim Ahmad, May 23, 2014.

33. Buthaina 'Awad, *Nisa' min Hadha al-Zaman*, Episode 1.

34. 'Awad, *Nisa' min Hadha al-Zaman*, Episode 1.

35. Telephone interview by the author with Buthaina 'Awad, May 23, 2014.

36. Awad, *Nisa' min Hadha al-Zaman*, Episode 32.

37. Telephone interview by the author with Ahmad Ibrahim Ahmad, May 23, 2014.

38. Telephone interview by the author with Ahmad Ibrahim Ahmad, May 23, 2014.

39. 'Awad, *Nisa' min Hadha al-Zaman*, Episode 14.

40. Awad, *Nisa' min Hadha al-Zaman*, Episode 24.

41. 'Amer 'abd al-Salam, "*Nisa' min Hadha al-Zaman*, Yaqoos fi 'Alam al-Mara' al-Suri," November 25, 2013, www.elaph.com/Web/Entertainment/2013/11/851234.html.

42. Rose Suleiman, *"Nisa' min Hadha al-Zaman,* fi 'Aqm al-Azma," December 2, 2013, www .assafir.com/Article/328984.

43. Telephone interview by the author with Ahmad Ibrahim Ahmad, May 23, 2014.

44. Telephone interview by the author with Buthaina 'Awad, May 23, 2014.

45. Interview by the author with Iyad Shihab Ahmad, Beirut, June 13, 2014.

46. "Taim Hassan: Lan Arod 'ala Kalam Taliqati Dima Baya'a Hawla Khiyanati laha ma' Nisrine Tafesh," *Nadine,* no. 1743 (June 2014): 22–23.

47. Malcom Karabtiyan, "Li-Hadha al-Asbab Fashal Musalsal *al-Ikhweh,*" *al-Jars,* no. 545 (June 20, 2014): 46.

48. *"Al-Ikhweh* (Yanjah) wa Yatrah Su'alan: Hel al-Jumhur al-Arabi . . . Esbani Mughami 'Alayha?," *Achabaka,* no. 3040 (June 2014): 32–33.

49. Interview by the author with Inas Haqqi, Beirut, June 20, 2014.

50. Telephone interview by the author with Ahmad Ibrahim Ahmad, May 23, 2014.

51. Interview by the author with Khaled Khalifa, Davidson, NC, February 15, 2016.

52. Interview by the author with Najeeb Nseir, Beirut, June 14, 2014.

53. *Al-Ikhweh,* Episode 4, directed by Seif al-Din Sbai'i and Seif al-Sheikh Najeeb and produced by Clacket, 2014.

54. Interview by the author with Najeeb Nseir, Beirut, June 14, 2014.

55. Interview by the author with Najeeb Nseir, Beirut, June 14, 2014.

56. Interview by the author with Inas Haqqi, Beirut, June 20, 2014.

57. *Al-Ikhweh,* Episode 104.

58. Interview by the author with Iman Sa'id, Beirut, June 17, 2014.

59. Interview by the author with Inas Haqqi, Beirut, June 20, 2014.

60. Interview by the author with Najeeb Nseir, Beirut, June 29, 2015.

61. Interview by the author with Najeeb Nseir, Beirut, June 29, 2015.

62. Rana Astih, "Nadine Njeym: Kafa Nifaqan wa Mujafatan li-l-waqa'. . . 'Sorry wayn 'Ayshin?,'" *al-Jumhuriyya,* July 10, 2015, 30; *"Chello* Muttaham bi-l-Tatbi' ma' Isra'il: Kayfa wa Limadha?," *al-Jaras,* July 10, 2015, 14–15; Ninar al-Khatib, *"Chello:* Akthar min Mujarrad Eqtibas," *al-Safir,* June 29, 2015, 13; "Madha Hadatha fi Laylat al-Million Dollar: al-Muhafaza 'ala al-Rooh al-Sharqiyya Tazid Musalsal *Chello* Ghumudhan," *Achabaka,* July 13–20, 2015, 16; "Drama Mushtaraka Takhtof al-Jamahir bi-Abtal min Kartoon," *al-Akhbar,* July 13, 2015, 22; "Shek Yaqtol Sahibahu," *al-Hayat,* July 10, 2015, 18; "Fi Liqa' Mushtarak Kashafa Mada Taqarubhuma wa-Insijamuhuma fi al-Tamthil Ma'an," *Sayidaty,* July 13, 2015, 110–116.

63. Accad, *Sexuality and War,* 1–2.

64. Elizabeth Thompson, *Colonial Citizens: Republican Rights, Paternal Privilege, and Gender in French Syria and Lebanon* (New York: Columbia University Press, 2000), 49.

65. Baron, *Egypt as a Woman,* 40.

66. Iyad Abu Shammat, *Ghadan Naltaqi,* Episode 11.

67. Interview by the author with Reem Hanna, Beirut, June 23, 2015.

68. Hayden Bates and Rebecca Joubin, "Growing Up in Wartime: Images of Refugee Children's Education in Syrian Television Drama," *Middle East Report,* no. 278 (2016): 31–32.

69. *Ghadan Naltaqi,* Episode 11.

70. *Ghadan Naltaqi,* Episode 13.

71. *Ghadan Naltaqi,* Episode 14.

72. Interview by the author with Haitham Haqqi, Paris, July 9, 2016.

73. Interview by the author with Hoozan 'Akko, Beirut, June 30, 2015.

74. Joubin, "Syrian Drama and the Politics of Dignity," 26.

75. Interview by the author with Reem Hanna, Beirut, June 24, 2016.

76. Baron, *Egypt as a Woman*, 46–49.

77. *Bi-Intizar al-Yasmin*, Episode 30.

78. *Bi-Intizar al-Yasmin*, Episode 34.

79. "Nadine Njeym: Nejmat 'Samra' Jaljalat al-Thakira al-Ghajariya al-Mansiya," *Sawa*, no. 58 (2016): 22.

80. Telephone interview by the author with Iyad Shihab Ahmad, March 11, 2018.

81. Interview by the author with Reem Hanna, Beirut, June 24, 2016.

82. "Musalsal 'Ya Reit' Khiyana wa Hubb Jaref wa 'Iqad Nafsiya," *Nadine*, no. 1848 (June 2016): 31; "Musalsal 'Ya Reit' al-'Ilaqat Tazdad Ta'qidan Bayna Maghi wa Maksim wa Qais," *Nadine*, no. 1850 (July 2016): 65.

83. Joubin, "Syrian Drama and the Politics of Dignity," 26–29.

84. Kaplan, *Trauma Culture*, 66–93.

85. "Al-Khiyana al-Zawjiya Shi'ar Musalsalat Ramadan," *Nadine*, no. 1848 (June 2016): 62.

86. Diane Singerman, "Youth, Gender and Dignity in the Egyptian Uprising," *Journal of Middle East Women's Studies* 9, no. 3 (Fall 2013): 1, 19–22.

87. Joubin, "Syrian Drama and the Politics of Dignity," 28–29.

88. *Jarimat al-Shaghaf*, Episode 8.

89. *Jarimat al-Shaghaf*, Episode 10.

90. *Jarimat al-Shaghaf*, Episode 10.

91. *Jarimat al-Shaghaf*, Episode 23.

92. *Jarimat al-Shaghaf*, Episode 16.

93. Joubin, "Syrian Drama and the Politics of Dignity," 26–29.

94. Nada 'Imad Khalil, "Musalsal *Nus Yawm* Nadine Nassib Njeym Tajma' fi Dawr Wahed 'Eddat Shaqsiyyat," *Nadine*, no. 1849 (July 2016): 15; "Nadine Nassib Njeym: La 'Akhtafi bi-li-Tasfiq Ba'da 'Amal Najeh wa 'Ekhtar 'Adwaran Tafooq Qodorati," *Laha*, 2016, 46–58; Nada 'Imad Khalil, "Taim Hassan Tahawwala 'ila Mujrem Hareb min Wajh al-'Adala bi-Sabab Nadine Njeym," *Nadine*, no. 1850 (July 2016): 62–63.

95. "Musalsal *Nus Yawm* al-Ma'khooth min Film Original Sin," *Nadine*, no. 1848 (June 2016): 30.

96. Interview by the author with Najeeb Nseir, Beirut, June 22, 2016.

97. Interview by the author with Reem Hanna, Beirut, June 24, 2016.

98. Interview by the author with Haitham Haqqi, Paris, July 9, 2016.

99. *Nabtadi Mnein al-Hikayeh*, Episode 30.

100. Interview by the author with Laith Hajjo, Beirut, June 21, 2017.

101. Interview by the author with Najeeb Nseir, Beirut, June 20, 2017.

102. Interview by the author with Najeeb Nseir, Beirut, June 22, 2016, and June 20, 2017.

103. *Ahl al-Gharam Part Three*, Episode 11.

104. Interview by the author with Najeeb Nseir, Beirut, June 22, 2016.

105. Interview by the author with Najeeb Nseir, Beirut, June 20, 2017.

106. Interview by the author with Laith Hajjo, Beirut, June 21, 2017.

107. Interview by the author with Laith Hajjo, Beirut, June 21, 2017.

108. The French film *La Famille Ch'tite* (2018) was also inspired by *The Vow*.

109. Interview by the author with Laith Hajjo, Beirut, June 21, 2017.

110. Mehdi Zilzili, "Fath Allah 'Omar 'Lestoo Jariya' Aw al-'Aish ma' Da'ish," *al-Akhbar*, no. 3207 (June 22) 2017: 31.

111. *Lestoo Jariya*, Episode 7.

112. *Lestoo Jariya*, Episode 10.

113. Joubin, *Politics of Love*, 367–369.

114. Amin Hamada, "Farisa al-Drama: Nisrin Tafesh," *Laha*, no. 872 (June 7, 2017): 34.

115. Eyerman, "Cultural Trauma," 67.

116. Yosef, *Politics of Loss and Trauma in Contemporary Israeli Cinema*, 7.

117. "Tafa'ulakum: al-Fannana al-Lubnaniyya Daniella Rahmeh: Ta'atufat ma' al-Kha'ina fi Tango," *al-Arabiyya*, May 28, 2018. In another interview, Rahmeh continues to explain her stance against marital betrayal. She says that the fact that Farah dies in the mini-series serves as an example of the negative consequences that result from marital betrayal. For this interview, see "Ramadan 2018: Muqabala ma' Najma Musalsal Tango: Daniella Rahmeh," LBCI Lebanon, June 29, 2018.

118. "Tafa'ulakum: Batal *Tango* Bassem Moghniyyeh Yakshef Ra'yahu fi al-Khiyana wa-l-Mara' aleti Yehtarameha," *al-Arabiya*, May 29, 2018.

119. *Fawda*, Episode 8.

120. *Fawda*, Episode 28.

121. Interview by the author with Najeeb Nseir, Beirut, June 14, 2018.

122. *Fawda*, Episode 31.

123. *Fawda*, Episode 26.

124. Interview by the author with Najeeb Nseir, Beirut, June 14, 2018.

125. Joubin, *Politics of Love*, 18–19, 185–229.

126. Interview by the author with Najeeb Nseir, Beirut, June 20, 2017.

127. Interview by the author with Reem Hanna, Beirut, June 23, 2017.

128. "Tamer Ishaq: Khatun Hiya al-Batala wa 'Ibarat "Hadher ibn 'Ammi" La Tu'abber 'an Nisa' Thalika al-Waqet," *Laha*, 2016, 99.

129. *Khatun Part One*, Episode 21.

130. *Khatun Part Two*, Episode 11.

131. *Khatun Part Two*, Episode 17.

132. *Khatun Part Two*, Episode 30.

133. "Musalsal *Khatun*—Hal Yujed Juz' Thalith—al-Jawwab min Mukhrij Tamer Ishaq," You-Tube, June 25, 2017, www.youtube.com/watch?v=oRVCPCfTsl.

134. *Khatun Part Two*, Episode 10.

135. "Kinda Hanna," *Sayidity*, no. 1893 (June 17, 2017): 110–114.

136. "Milad Yusuf: al-Taqyim al-Haqigi li-Musalsal *Bab al-Hara*," *Laha*, 2016, 98–100.

137. "Bab al-Hara 8 Karitha Dramiyya bi-'Emtiyaz," *Nadine*, no. 1850 (July 2016): 26–27; "al-Azmat Tulaheq *Bab al-Hara* bi-sabab al-Khilafat ma' al-mukhrij Bassam al-Malla," *Nadine*, no. 1861 (September 19–25, 2016): 25.

138. "Musalsal *Bab al-Hara* 9: al-Mumathalin al-Judud bila Tu'ma, al-Nims Muhtal wa Abu Bedr Ghabi wa Abu Jawdat Zahaqna," *Nadine*, no. 1899 (June 12–18, 2017): 15.

139. Interview by the author with Iyad Shihab Ahmad, Beirut, June 24, 2016.

140. *Bab al-Hara Part Nine*, Episode 11.

141. "Tauqif Musalal *Bab al-Hara* al-Juz'al-'Ashar/Asbab 'Adam Wujud *Bab al-Hara* 10 fi Ramadan 2018," *Close Shots*, March 19, 2018; "Milad Yusuf Yukshef Haqiqat al-Juz' al-'Ashar min *Bab al-Hara*," *Fawshiyya*, January 10, 2018; "*Bab al-Hara* al-Juz' al-'Ashar al-Halaqa al-Ula? Tasribat *Bab al-Hara* 10 Hasriyyan," *Mustafa Alameer*, May 16, 2018.

142. *Musafat Aman*, Episode 28.

CHAPTER 5   THE POLITICS OF QUEER REPRESENTATIONS IN SYRIAN TELEVISION DRAMA PAST AND PRESENT

1. Hanadi al-Samman and Tarek El-Ariss, "Queer Affects: Introduction," *International Journal of Middle East Studies* 45 (2013): 205.

2. Al-Samman, "Out of the Closet."

3. Sahar Amer, *Crossing Borders: Love between Women in Medieval French and Arabic Literatures* (Philadelphia: University of Pennsylvania Press, 2008), 1–49, 163.

4. Joseph Massad, *Desiring Arabs* (Chicago: University of Chicago Press, 2007), 1–57. See also Rebecca Joubin, "*Zuqaq al-Midaq*: Egyptian Novel That Employs a Judgmental Colonialist Gaze in Its Portrayal of a Character Who Engages in Same-Sex Sexual Activity," in *The Global Encyclopedia of Lesbian, Gay, Bisexual, Transgender, and Queer History*, edited by Howard Chiang (Farmington Hills, MI: Charles Scribner's Sons, 2019).

5. Khalid Hadeed, "Homosexuality and Epistemic Closure in Modern Arabic Literature," *International Journal of Middle East Studies* 45 (2013): 271–291.

6. Al-Samman, "Out of the Closet," 270.

7. "Egypt—The Museum of Broadcast Communications," www.museum.tv/eotvsection .php?entrycode=egypt; interview by the author with Najeeb Nseir, Damascus, July 13, 2010.

8. Joubin, *Politics of Love*, 17–18.

9. Telephone interview by the author with Rafiq Sbai'i, April 26, 2013.

10. Hadeed, "Homosexuality and Epistemic Closure."

11. Al-Samman, "Out of the Closet," 270–310.

12. Personal correspondence by the author with Najeeb Nseir, October 14, 2012.

13. Robert Stam, *Subversive Pleasure: Bakhtin, Cultural Criticism, and Film* (Baltimore: Johns Hopkins University Press, 1989).

14. The gender masquerade of the 1960s and 1970s would come full circle in '*Awdat Ghawwar: al-Asdiqa*' (The Return of Ghawwar: Friends, 1999), which focuses on government theft and corruption in the 1990s in Syria. Here, role reversals again serve to demonstrate the nearly impossible economic situation of men. We see this in the character of Tahcin (played by Hossam Tahcin Bik), whose wife recently divorced him and left him without rights. He attempts to coerce his wife into paying him *nafaqqa* (the price that a man must pay a woman upon their divorce). See Durayd Lahham, Talal Nasr al-Din, and Ahmad al-Sayyed, '*Awdat Ghawwar: al-'Asdiqa*', directed by Merwan Barakat and director of production Jamal al-'Abd, 1999.

15. Stam, *Subversive Pleasure*, 93, 163.

16. Judith Butler, "Critically Queer," in *The Routledge Queer Studies Reader*, ed. Donald E. Hall and Annamarie Jagose (London: Routledge, 2013), 23.

17. Adania Shibli, "The Making of Bad Palestinian Mothers during the Second Intifada," in *Bad Girls of the Arab World*, ed. Nadia Yaqub and Rula Quawas (Austin: University of Texas Press, 2017), 92.

18. Joubin, "Politics of the *Qabaday*," 50–51.

19. Hadeed, "Homosexuality and Epistemic Closure."

20. Interview by the author with Iyad Shihab Ahmad, Damascus, July 16, 2010.

21. Telephone interview by the author with Reem Hanna, March 18, 2014.

22. Interview by the author with Reem Hanna, Beirut, June 23, 2014.

23. Ghassan Zakariyya, *Abna' al-Rashid: al-Amin wa-l-Ma'mun* (The Sons of al-Rashid: al-Amin and al-Ma'mun), directed by Shawqi al-Majiri and produced by Arab Telemedia Group, 2006. My current research project is titled "The Multifarious Lives of the Sixth 'Abbasid Caliph Muhammad al-Amin: Collective Memory Construction, Queer Spaces, and the Anxiety of Civilization."

24. Joubin, *Politics of Love*, 158–163.

25. *Hasiba*, Episode 7.

26. *Ashwak Na'imeh*, Episode 3.

27. *Ashwak Na'imeh*, Episode 8.

28. *Ashwak Na'imeh*, Episode 6.

29. *Ashwak Na'imeh*, Episode 19.

30. *Ashwak Na'imeh*, Episode 21.

31. *Ashwak Na'imeh*, Episode 25.

32. *Ashwak Na'imeh*, Episode 28.

33. Butler, "Critically Queer," 28.

34. Atassi and Haddad, Episode 20, "Sabi aw Bint?"

35. Joubin, *Politics of Love*, 349–351.

36. Butler, "Critically Queer," 23.

37. Butler, "Critically Queer," 28.

38. Butler, "Critically Queer," 22–23.

39. Stephen O. Murray, "Woman-Woman Love in Islamic Societies," in *Islamic Homosexualities: Culture, History, and Literature*, ed. Stephen O. Murray and Will Roscoe (New York: New York University Press, 1997), 97–102.

40. Al-Samman, "Out of the Closet," 297.

41. Diab, *Ma Malakat Aymanukum*, Episode 22.

42. Michael Allan, "Queer Couplings: Formations of Religion and Sexuality in 'Ala' al-Aswani's *'Imarat Ya'qubyan*," *International Journal of Middle East Studies* 45 (2013): 253–269.

43. Interview by the author with Reem Hanna, Beirut, June 24, 2016.

44. Interview by the author with Najeeb Nseir, Beirut, June 20, 2017.

45. *Gharabib Sud*, Episode 11.

46. *Buq'at Daw' Part Thirteen*, Episode 6.

47. *Buq'at Daw' Part Thirteen*, Episode 30.

48. *Buq'at Daw' Part Thirteen*, Episode 11.

49. Interview by the author with Najeeb Nseir, Beirut, June 14, 2018.

50. Al-Samman, "Out of the Closet," 277.

51. *Sa-Na'ud Ba'da Qalil*, Episode 3.

52. *Sa-Na'ud Ba'da Qalil*, Episode 16.

53. Amer, *Crossing Borders*, 17, 21, 48.

54. Al-Samman, "Out of the Closet," 277–278.

55. *Sa-Na'ud Ba'da Qalil*, Episode 17.

56. *Sa-Na'ud Ba'da Qalil*, Episode 17.

57. *Sa-Na'ud Ba'da Qalil*, Episode 18.

58. Personal correspondence by the author with Rafi Wahbi, July 6, 2018.

59. Dina Georgis, "Thinking Past Pride: Queer Arab Shame in *Bareed Mista3jil*," *International Journal of Middle East Studies* 45, no. 2 (2013): 245–246.

60. Afsaneh Najmabadi, "Genus of Sex or the Sexing of *Jins*," *International Journal of Middle East Studies* 45, no. 2 (2013): 212.

61. *Sa-Na'ud Ba'da Qalil*, Episode 23.

62. *Sa-Na'ud Ba'da Qalil*, Episode 24.

63. *Sa-Na'ud Ba'da Qalil*, Episode 26.

64. *Sa-Na'ud Ba'da Qalil*, Episode 29.

65. Al-Samman, "Out of the Closet," 301–302.

66. Saleem Haddad, *Guapa* (New York: Other Press, 2016), 254.

67. *Qalam Humra*, Episode 14.

68. *Qalam Humra*, Episode 14.

69. *Qalam Humra*, Episode 15.

70. *Qalam Humra*, Episode 15.

71. *Qalam Humra*, Episode 16.

72. *Qalam Humra*, Episode 17.

73. Al-Samman, "Out of the Closet," 296.

74. *Qalam Humra*, Episode 18.

75. *Qalam Humra*, Episode 24.

76. *Qalam Humra*, Episode 25.

77. *Qalam Humra*, Episode 27.

78. *Qalam Humra*, Episode 30.

79. Personal correspondence by the author with Yam Mashhadi, June 28, 2018.

80. Personal correspondence by the author with Yam Mashhadi, June 28, 2018.

81. Haktan Ural and Fatma Umut Beşpinar, "Class and Habitus in the Formation of Gay Identities, Masculinities, and Respectability in Turkey," *Journal of Middle East Women's Studies* 13, no. 2 (2017): 244–261.

82. Hadeed, "Homosexuality and Epistemic Closure," 289.

CONCLUSION

1. Episode 15. The miniseries ended with a note that there would be a second season, but it did not reappear in 2018.

2. Joubin, *Politics of Love*, 302.

3. Joubin, "Syrian Drama and the Politics of Dignity," 27. See also "al-Drama al-Suriyya Tasir Bayn Ghaim al-Azma," October 30, 2012, www.startimes.com/f.aspx?t=31583977.

4. Joubin, *Politics of Love*, 428–432.

5. Personal correspondence by the author with Haitham Haqqi, June 4, 2017.

6. Shafiq al-Asadi, "Jamal Suleiman: Urkadiya Fantaziya Tarikhiyya Tudhee' al-Hadhir," *al-Hayat*, no. 19803 (June 23, 2017): 18.

7. "Kilam al-Mutasara'oon wa Mu'araka al-Drama wa-l-Fanzat," *Zahrat al-Khaleej*, no. 1994 (June 10, 2017): 181.

8. Mawqi' Qalam Rasas, "Musalsal *Bi-dun Qaid* Drama Wafq al-Mumkin wa-l-Mutah," December 21, 2017; "*Bi-dun Qaid*: Drama al-Tabshir bi-Huriyya al-Intaj wa-l-Mushahada fi Suriya," January 5, 2018, http://manshoor.com/art/undocumented-syrian-drama-online/.

9. "*Bi-dun Qaid* Musalsal Suri 'an Waqi' Narfadh al-I'tiraf Bi," January 9, 2018, www .aljadeed.tv/arabic/entertainment/stars-news/090120184.

10. Mawqi' Qalam Rasas, "Musalsal *Bi-dun Qaid* Drama Wafq al-Mumkin wa-l-Mutah," December 21, 2017; "*Bi-dun Qaid*: Drama al-Tabshir bi-Huriyya al-Intaj wa-l-Mushahada fi Suriya," March 19, http://manshoor.com/art/undocumented-syrian-drama-online/.

11. "*Bi-dun Qaid*: Hikayat Suriyya Tas'ai li-l-Taharrur," *al-Araby*, December 2017, www .alaraby.co.uk/entertainment/2017/12/29/%D8%A8%D8%Af%D9%88%D9; "*Bi-dun Qaid*: Hikayat Suriyya Tusa'i li-l-Taharrur: Awal Musalsal Raqmi 'ala Mawqi' YouTube," December 29, 2017, www.souriyati.com/2017/12/29/92209.html.

12. Mawqi' Qalam Rasas, "Musalsal *Bi-dun Qaid* Drama Wafq al-Mumkin wa-l-Mutah," December 21, 2012.

13. Lama Tayara, "*Bi-dun Qaid* . . . Awal Musalsal Tarfihi Suri Raqmi," *al-Arab*, March 17, 2018, https://alarab.co.uk/%D8%A8%D8%AF%D9%88%D9%86-%D9%82%D9%8A%D8%A; Wissam Ken'an, "Awal Musalsal Raqmi min Ikhraji Amin Dora: al-Drama al-Suriyya Tanhad *Bi-dun Qaid*," January 5, 2018, www.al-akhbar.com/Media_Tv/242862.

14. "*Bi-dun Qaid* Yakser Routin al-Drama al-Suriyya," December 27, 2017, www.enabbaladi .net/archives/194245.

15. Wissam Kan'an, "Awal Musalsal Raqmi min Ikhraji Amin Dora: al-Drama al-Suriyya Tanhad *Bi-dun Qaid*," January 5, 2018, www.al-akhbar.com/Media_Tv/242862.

16. "Tafa'ulkum—Musalsal *Bi-dun Qaid* . . . Mushahid Jariya' wa Muwadi' Tatajawaz al-Khutut al-Hamra'," YouTube, January 7, 2018, www.youtube.com/watch?v=JRMU OActlwU.

17. Nabih Bulos, "In a New Crop of Television Dramas, Syria Confronts Its Civil War," *Los Angeles Times*, March 4, 2018.

18. "Mashahid Sakhina wa Kalimat Ibahiyya . . . . Musalsal Suri Yakhroq al-Mahzur," *Orient News*, January 1, 2018, www.youtube.com/watch?v=ZNgmC_HzvOI.

19. Lama Tayarah, "*Bi-dun Qaid* . . . Awal Musalsal Tarfihi Suri Raqmi," *al-Arab*, March 17, 2018, https://alarab.co.uk/%D8%A8%D8%AF%D9%88%D9%86-%D9%82%D9%8A%D8%A.

20. Wissam Kan'an, "Awal Musalsal Raqmi min Ikhraji Amin Dora: al-Drama al-Suriyya Tanhad *Bi-dun Qaid*," January 5, 2018, www.al-akhbar.com/Media_Tv/242862.

21. Colette Bahna, "Min Zawiyya Ukhra: Bi-dun Qaid," *al-Hurra*, January 10, 2018, https://alhurra.com/a/bedoun-qeed/413054.html.

22. "*Bi-dun Qaid* Yakser Routin al-Drama al-Suriyya," December 27, 2017, www.enabbaladi .net/archives/194245; "*Bi-dun Qaid* . . . Tariqa Jadida fi Mushahadat al-Drama," January 30, 2018, www.al-binaa.com/archives/article/182989.

23. Telephone interview by the author with Iyad Shihab Ahmad, March 11, 2018.

24. Interview by the author with Najeeb Nseir, Beirut, June 14, 2018.

25. Interview by the author with Iyad Shihab Ahmad, Beirut, July 1, 2018.

26. Telephone interview by the author with Iyad Shihab Ahmad, May 18, 2018.

27. Interview by the author with Iyad Shihab Ahmad, Beirut, June 15, 2018.

28. Personal correspondence by the author with Inas Haqqi, June 15, 2018.

29. Telephone interview by the author with Iyad Shihab Ahmad, March 11, 2018.

30. *Julia*, Episode 9.

31. Sawsan Seidawi, "Hurub min al-Waqi' ila Komediyya Khafifa: *Julia* Yuqadam Shakhsiyat Muta'addida al-Qawalib fi Itar Romansi Drami," *al-Watan*, June 19, 2018.

32. Hanadi 'Issa, "Qais al-Sheikh Najeeb Akhoodh Tajriba Jadida fi *Julia*," *Laha*, no. 925 (June 13, 2018): 90–92.

33. "Musalsal *Tango* Raqsat al-'Ishq wa-'Alam," *Nadine*, no. 1951 (June 11, 2018): 28–29.

34. Telephone interview by the author with Iyad Shihab Ahmad, May 18, 2018.

35. Interview by the author with Iyad Abu Shammat, Beirut, June 15, 2018.

36. For more on *Tariq*, see Mirvat Syufi, "Abed Fahd wa Nadine Njeym 'Abda'a fi-l-Shakhsiatayn," *Nadine*, no. 1951 (June 11, 2018): 30–31; Rabi'a Hendy, "'Abed Fahd: Lan Yanjahoo fi 'jarr Rijli' l-Harb ma' Taim Hassan," *Zahrat al-Sharq*, no. 2048 (June 23, 2018): 130–133.

37. Interview by the author with Reem Hanna, Beirut, June 15, 2018.

38. *Al-Haibeh: al-'Awda*, Episode 1.

39. Jamal Fayyad, "Fi Muqadat *al-Haibeh* . . . Hal al-Drama Haqiqiya?," *Zahrat al-Khaleej*, no. 2047 (June 16, 2018): 154; "Taim Hassan Yarod: Jahez l-Musalaha Taht al-Qanoon," *Nadine*, no. 1952 (June 18, 2018): 32; "Taim Hassan min Za'im 'Isaba Musalaha ila Rambo," *Nadine*, no. 1951 (June 11, 2018): 12–13; "Bayna Batalat al-Juz' al-Awal wa-l-Thani min *al-Haibeh*," *Nadine*, no. 1951 (June 11, 2018): 10–11; Laure Stephan, "Au Liban, La Bekaa Craint pour son 'prestige,'" *Magazine du Monde*, June 28, 2018.

40. Interview by the author with Reem Hanna, Beirut, June 15, 2018.

41. "Liqa' 'Abed Fahd ma' 'Adil Karam *Haida Haki*—al-Liqa' al-Kamil," YouTube, May 13, 2018; "Jadal Hawl Musalsal Ramadan 2018 Sayidaty Tarsod Nabdh al-Shari' wa Muwaqi' al-Tawasul al-Ijtima'i," *Sayidaty*, no. 1944 (June 9, 2018): 120–124; "al-Musalsalat

al-Ramadaniyya 'ala al-Shashat al-Lubnaniyya Qisas Gharamiyya Mutashabiha bi-Nak-ha Meksikiyya," *Achabaka*, no. 3230 (May 2018): 40–42; Hanadi 'Issa, "Bassem Moghniyyeh: *Tango* Munafess Sharess fi Ramadan," *Laha*, no. 924 (June 6, 2018): 86–89; "*Laha* Takshef Asrar al-Saha al-Faniyya," *Laha*, no. 924 (June 6, 2018): 22; Fatemah 'abd Allah, "Nihayat wa Wada'," *al-Nahar* (June 18, 2018): 8; Michel Zareeq, "al-Najah Laysa Maqsuran 'ala Ramadan," *Laha*, no. 927 (June 27, 2018): 10–12.

42. For example, Soudade Kaadan's film *The Day I Lost My Shadow* and Laith Hajjo's *The Chord*. See also *Rose* by director Rasha Sharbatji and writer Hazem Suleiman and *Damascus-Aleppo* by Bassel Khatib as well as the film *Amina*. Rami Hanna also was working on a film that he hoped would come out in the new year alongside a new mini-series he would direct that would be written by his sister, Reem Hanna.

43. Wissam Kan'an, ". . . Wa-l-Drama al-Suriyya Tashoo min 'al-Kawma?," *al-Akhbar*, 31.

44. *Fawda*, Episode 32.

45. Interview by the author with Najeeb Nseir, Beirut, June 21, 2018.

46. *Musafat Aman*, Episode 28.

47. Hanadi 'Issa, "'Abed Fahd: al-Drama Suriyya 'Adat ila 'Izzha bi-sabab Makanaha fi al-'Alam al-Arabi," *Laha*, 978 (June 19, 2019): 72–73; Hanadi 'Issa, "Mona Wassef: Oheb an Uqadam Shaqsiyya al-Mara' al-Quwiyya . . . Fahya Tardhini," *Laha*, no. 976 (June 5, 2019): 81–82; Nada 'Imad Khalil, "'Abed Fahd Mahkum bi-l-I'dam wa Stephanie Salib bi-Sha'r Qasir," *Nadine*, 1999 (May 20–26, 2019): 10; Suleiman Isfahani, "al-Musalsal Kharij al-Munafasa bi-sabab Charisma Bataloo Taim Hassan," *Nadine*, 1999 (May 20–26, 2019): 11; "Najah al-Musalsal Sababahoo al-Qissa am al-Mumathalin?," *Nadine* (May 27–June 2, 2019): 22; "Musalsal *Daqiqat al-Samt* . . . Yasalet al-Daw' 'ala al-Kharajeen 'an al-Qanun," *Nadine* (May 27–June 2, 2019): 23.

48. Interview by the author with Reem Hanna, Beirut, July 3, 2019; interview by the author with Iyad Shihab Ahmad, Beirut, 2019.

49. Telephone interview by the author with Iyad Shihab Ahmad, May 12, 2019; for an article written on *Prova*, see Nada 'Imad Khalil, "Musalsal *Prova*: Maggy bou Ghossen min 'Azifat Accordion ila Mu'allima," *Nadine*, 1999 (May 20–26, 2019): 53.

50. Interview by the author with Reem Hanna, Beirut, July 3, 2019.

51. Interview by the author with Iyad Shihab Ahmad, Beirut, July 3, 2019.

52. Interview by the author with Takla Chamoun, Beirut, July 3, 2019.

53. Interview by the author with Najeeb Nseir, Beirut, June 19, 2019.

54. Kinan Azmeh, musical performance at Davidson College, Davidson, NC, November 13, 2018.

BIBLIOGRAPHY

Abouzeid, Rania. *No Turning Back: Life, Loss, and Hope in Wartime Syria*. New York: Norton, 2018.

Abu-Lughod, Lila. *Dramas of Nationhood: The Politics of Television in Egypt*. Chicago: University of Chicago Press, 2005.

———, ed. *Remaking Women: Feminism and Modernity in the Middle East*. Princeton, NJ: Princeton University Press, 1998.

Accad, Evelyne. *Sexuality and War: Literary Masks of the Middle East*. New York: New York University Press, 1990.

Achilli, Luigi. "Becoming a Man in al-Wihdat: Masculine Performances in a Palestinian Refugee Camp in Jordan." *International Journal of Middle East Studies* 47, no. 2 (2015): 263–280.

'Adwan, Ziad. "Flying Above Bloodshed: Performative Protest in the Sacred City of Damascus." *Contention* 5, no. 1 (Spring 2017): 12–27.

Alexander, Jeffrey C. "Toward a Theory of Cultural Trauma." In *Cultural Trauma and Collective Identity*, 1–30. Berkeley: University of California Press, 2004.

———. *Trauma: A Social Theory*. Cambridge: Polity, 2012.

Allan, Michael. "Queer Couplings: Formations of Religion and Sexuality in 'Ala' al-Aswani's '*Imarat Ya'qubyan*." *International Journal of Middle East Studies* 45 (2013): 253–269.

Allen, Tim, and Jean Seaton, eds. *The Media of Conflict: War Reporting and Representations of Ethnic Violence*. London: Zed Books, 1999.

Amadiume, Ifi, and Abdullah an-Na'im, eds. *The Politics of Memory: Truth, Healing, and Social Justice*. London: Zed Books, 2000.

Amer, Sahar. *Crossing Borders: Love between Women in Medieval French and Arabic Literatures*. Philadelphia: University of Pennsylvania Press, 2008.

———. "Medieval Arab Lesbians and Lesbian-Like Women." *Journal of the History of Sexuality* 18, no. 2 (May 2009): 215–236.

Armbrust, Walter. "Farid Shauqi: Tough Guy, Family Man, Cinema Star." In *Imagined Masculinities: Male Identity and Culture in the Modern Middle East*, edited by Mayy Ghassub and Emma Sinclair-Webb, 199–226. London: Saqi, 2006.

Baron, Beth. *Egypt as a Woman: Nationalism, Gender, and Politics*. Berkeley: University of California Press, 2005.

Barthes, Roland. *Le Bruissement de la Langue: Essais Critiques IV*. Paris: Éditions du Seuil, 1984.

———. *Le Plaisir du Texte*. Paris: Éditions du Seuil, 1973.

Belhadj, Souhail. *La Syrie de Bashar al-Asad: Anatomie d'un regime autoritaire*. Paris: Éditions Belin, 2013.

Beshara, Adel, ed. *The Origins of Syrian Nationhood: Histories, Pioneers, and Identity*. London: Routledge, 2011.

Bey, Salma Mardam. *La Syrie et la France: Bilan d'une équivoque (1939–1945)*. Paris: Éditions L'Harmattan, 1994.

Bocquet, Jérôme. *La France, L'Église et le Baas (de 1918 à nos jours)*. Paris: Les Indes Savantes, 2008.

Boym, Svetlana. *The Future of Nostalgia*. New York: Basic Books, 2001.

Burgat, François, and Bruno Paoli. *Pas de Printemps Pour la Syrie: Les Clés Pour Comprendre Les Acteurs et les Défis de la Crise (2011–2013)*. Paris: Éditions La Découverte, 2013.

Butler, Judith. "Critically Queer." In *The Routledge Queer Studies Reader*, edited by Donald E. Hall and Annamarie Jagose, 18–31. London: Routledge, 2013.

———. *Frames of War: When Is Life Grievable?* New York: Verso, 2009.

Butler, Judith, and Athena Athanasiou. *Dispossession: The Performative in the Political*. Cambridge: Polity, 2013.

Caruth, Cathy, ed. *Trauma: Explorations in Memory*. Baltimore: Johns Hopkins University Press, 1995.

———. *Unclaimed Experience: Trauma, Narrative, and History*. Baltimore: Johns Hopkins University Press, 1996.

Chesnot, Christian, and Georges Malbrunot. *Les Chemins de Damas: Le Dossier Noir de la Relation Franco-Syrian*. Paris: Éditions Robert Laffont, 2014.

Cloarec, Vincent. *La France et La Question de Syrie: 1914–1918*. Paris: CNRS Éditions, 2010.

Clot, André. *Harun al-Rachid et le temps des Milles et Une Nuits*. France: Librairie Arthème Fayard, 1986.

Coltrane, Scott. "Father-Child Relationships and the Status of Women: A Cross-Cultural Study." *American Journal of Sociology* 93, no. 5 (1988): 1060–1095.

Connell, R. W. *Masculinities*. Berkeley: University of California Press, 2005.

cooke, miriam. *Dancing in Damascus: Creativity, Resilience, and the Syrian Revolution*. New York: Routledge, 2017.

———. *Dissident Syria: Making Oppositional Arts Official*. Durham, NC: Duke University Press, 2007.

———. "Tadmor's Ghosts." *Review of Middle East Studies* 47, no. 1 (Summer 2013): 28–36.

Cyrulnik, Boris. *The Whispering of Ghosts*. Translated by Susan Fairfield. New York: Other Press, 2005.

Dawisha, A. I. "Syria under Asad, 1970–78: The Centres of Power." *Observer Foreign News Service* 13, no. 3 (1978): 341.

Della Ratta, Donatella. "Dramas of the Authoritarian State." *Interventions*, February 2012. www.merip.org/mero/interventions/dramas-authoritarian-state.

———. *Shooting a Revolution: Visual Media and Warfare in Syria*. London: Pluto Press, 2018.

———. "The Whisper Strategy: How Syrian Drama Makers Shape Television Fiction in the Context of Authoritarianism and Commodification." In *Syria from Reform to Revolt, Volume 2: Culture, Society, and Religion*, edited by Christa Salamandra and Leif Stenberg, 53–76. New York: Syracuse University Press, 2015.

Dick, Marlin. "The State of the Musalsal: Arab Television Drama and Comedy and the Politics of the Satellite Era." *TBS*, no. 15 (2005): 2–5. http://tbsjournal.arabmediasociery.com/Archives/Fall05/Dick.html.

———. "Syria under the Spotlight: Television Satire That Is Revolutionary in Form, Reformist in Content." *Arab Media & Society*, October 1, 2007. www.arabmediasociety.com/syria-under-the-spotlight-television-satire-that-is-revolutionary-in-form-reformist-in-content.

Dyrsdale, Alasdaire. "The Syrian Political Elite, 1966–1976: A Spatial and Social Analysis." *Middle East Studies* 17, no. 1 (January 1981): 3–30.

El-Ariss, Tarek. "Majnun Strikes Back: Crossings of Madness and Homosexuality in Contemporary Arabic Literature." *International Journal of Middle East Studies* 45 (2013): 293–312.

Eyerman, Ron. "Cultural Trauma: Slavery and the Formation of African American Identity." In *Cultural Trauma and Collective Identity*, 60–111. Berkeley: University of California Press, 2004.

Feurstoss, Isabelle. *La Syrie et la France: Enjeux Géopolitiques et Diplomatiques*. Paris: L'Harmattan, 2013.

Friedlander, Saul. *When Memory Comes*. Translated by Helen Lane. New York: Other Press, 2016.

Geertz, Clifford. *The Interpretation of Cultures: Selected Essays*. New York: Basic Books, 1973.

Georgis, Dina. "Thinking Past Pride: Queer Arab Shame in *Bareed Mista3jil*." *International Journal of Middle East Studies* 45, no. 2 (2013): 233–251.

Gertz, Nurith, and George Khleifi. *Palestinian Cinema: Landscape, Trauma, and Memory*. Bloomington: Indiana University Press, 2008.

Gilbert, Joanne R. *Performing Marginality: Humor, Gender, and Cultural Critique*. Detroit: Wayne State University Press, 2004.

Habib, Samar. *Female Homosexuality in the Middle East: Histories and Representations*. New York: Routledge, 2009.

Haddad, Saleem. *Guapa*. New York: Other Press, 2016.

Hadeed, Khalid. "Homosexuality and Epistemic Closure in Modern Arabic Literature." *International Journal of Middle East Studies* 45 (2013): 271–291.

Harris, Kevin, and Jillian Schedler. "What Is Activism?" *Middle East Report*, no. 281 (Winter 2016): 2–5.

Hassine, Jonathan. *Les Réfugiés et Déplacés de Syrie: Une Reconstruction Nationale en Question*. Paris: L'Harmattan, 2015.

Haugbolle, Sune. "The (Little) Militia Man: Memory and Militarized Masculinity in Lebanon." *Journal of Middle East Women's Studies* 8, no. 1 (Winter 2012): 115–139.

———. *War and Memory in Lebanon*. Cambridge: Cambridge University Press, 2010.

Hinnebusch, Raymond A. "Syria under the Ba'th: Social Ideology, Policy, and Practice." In *Social Legislation in the Contemporary Middle East*, edited by Laurence O. Michalak and Jeswald W. Salacuse, 61–68. Berkeley, CA: Berkeley Institute for International Studies, 1986.

———. "Syria under the Ba'th: State Formation in a Fragmented Society." *Arab Studies Quarterly* 4, no. 3 (1982): 192–193.

Hirsch, Joshua. *After Image: Film, Trauma, and the Holocaust*. Philadelphia: Temple University Press, 2004.

Hirsch, Marianne. *Family Frames: Photography Narrative and Post Memory*. Cambridge: Harvard University Press, 1997.

Inhorn, Marcia. *The New Arab Man: Emergent Masculinities, Technologies, and Islam in the Middle East*. Princeton, NJ: Princeton University Press, 2012.

Ismael, Salwa. "Youth, Gender, and the State in Cairo: Marginalized Masculinities and Contested Spaces." In *Arab Society and Culture: An Essential Reader*, edited by Samir Khalaf and Roseanne Saad Khalaf, 223–239. London: Saqi Press, 2009.

Jacob, Wilson Chacko. *Working Out Egypt: Effendi Masculinity and Subject Formation in Colonial Modernity, 1870–1940*. Durham, NC: Duke University Press, 2011.

Johnson, Michael. "Political Bosses and Their Gangs: *Zu'ama* and *Qabadayat* in the Sunni Muslim Quarters of Beirut." In *Patrons and Clients*, edited by Ernest Gellner and John Waterbury, 207–224. London: Duckworth, 1977.

Joubin, Rebecca. "The Politics of Love and Desire in Post-Uprising Syrian Television Drama." *Arab Studies Journal* 24, no. 2 (Fall 2016): 148–174.

———. *The Politics of Love: Sexuality, Gender, and Marriage in Syrian Television Drama*. Lanham, MD: Lexington, 2013.

———. "The Politics of the *Qabaday* (Tough Man) and the Changing Father Figure in Syrian Television Drama." *Journal of Middle East Women's Studies* 12, no. 1 (2016): 50–67.

———. "Research Notes: Samer Fahd Ridwan's *Menbar al-Mawta* (Platform of Death), Ramadan 2013." *Syrian Studies Bulletin* 18, no. 2 (2013).

———. "Resistance amid Regime Co-optation on the Syrian Television Series *Buq'at Daw'*, 2001–2012." *Middle East Journal* 68, no. 1 (2014): 9–32.

———. "Syrian Drama and the Politics of Dignity." *Middle East Report*, no. 268 (2013): 26–29.

———. "*Zuqaq al-Midaq*: Egyptian Novel That Employs a Judgmental Colonialist Gaze in Its Portrayal of a Character Who Engages in Same-Sex Sexual Activity." In *The Global Encyclopedia of Lesbian, Gay, Bisexual, Transgender, and Queer History*, edited by Howard Chiang, 1753–1757. Farmington Hills, MI: Charles Scribner's Sons, 2019.

Joubin, Rebecca, and Hayden Bates. "Growing Up in Wartime: Images of Refugee Children's Education in Syrian Television Drama." *Middle East Report*, no. 278 (2016): 28–33.

Kaplan, E. Ann. *Trauma Culture: The Politics of Terror and Loss in Media and Literature*. New Brunswick, NJ: Rutgers University Press, 2005.

Kaufman, Gayle. *Superdads: How Fathers Balance Work and Family in the 21st Century*. New York: New York University Press, 2013.

Khader, Jamil. "The Arabic Fantastic and ISIS Terror: The Aesthetics of Antiterrorism and Its Limits." *Middle East Report*, no. 282 (Spring 2017): 32–39.

Khalifa, Khaled. *Pas de Couteaux dans les Cuisines de cette ville*. Translated by Rania Samara. France: Sinbad/Actes Sud, 2016.

Khatib, Line. "Islamic Revival and the Promotion of Moderate Islam from Above." In *State and Islam in Baathist Syria: Confrontation or Co-optation?*, edited by Raymond Hinnebusch, 29–57. Scotland: University of Andrews for Syrian Studies, 2012.

———. *Islamic Revivalism in Syria: The Rise and Fall of Ba'thist Secularism*. London: Routledge, 2011.

———. *Lebanese Cinema: Imagining the Civil War and Beyond*. London: I.B. Taurus, 2008.

Kuhn, Annette. *An Everyday Magic: Cinema and Cultural Memory*. London: I.B. Taurus, 2002.

LaCapra, Dominick. *Writing History: Writing Trauma*. Baltimore: Johns Hopkins University Press, 2014.

Lewis, Charlie, and Margaret O'Brien. "Constraints on Fathers: Research, Theory, and Clinical Practice." In *Reassessing Fatherhood: New Observations on Fatherhood and the Modern Family*, edited by Charlie Lewis and Margaret O'Brien, 1–19. Thousand Oaks, CA: Sage, 1987.

Majed, Ziad, *Syria: La Révolution Orpheline*. Translated by Fifi Abou Dib. Paris: Sinbad/Actes Sud, 2014.

Mankekar, Purnima. *Screening Culture, Viewing Politics: An Ethnography of Television, Womanhood, and Nation in Postcolonial India*. Durham, NC: Duke University Press, 1999.

Mansur, Muhammad. *'Ala' al-Din Kawkash: Drama Ta'sis wa-l-Taghayyor*. Damascus: Kan'an Books, 2009.

———. *al-Comedya fi al-Sinama al-'Arabi: Ru'ya Naqdiyya Tarikhiyya*. Damascus: Mu'assassa al-'Amma li-l-Cinema, 2003.

———. *Bassam al-Malla: 'Ashiw al-Bi'a al-Dimashqiyya*. Damascus: Kan'an Books, 2009.

Massad, Joseph. *Desiring Arabs*. Chicago: University of Chicago Press, 2007.

Moubayed, Sami. *Steel & Silk: Men and Women Who Shaped Syria 1900–2000*. Seattle: Cune Press, 2006.

———. "What Will Post–Arab Spring Intellectuals Write About?" *Huffington Post*, December 8, 2011.

Murray, Stephen O. "Woman-Woman Love in Islamic Societies." In *Islamic Homosexualities: Culture, History, and Literature*, edited by Stephen O. Murray and Will Roscoe, 97–102. New York: New York University Press, 1997.

Najmabadi, Afsaneh. "Genus of Sex or the Sexing of *Jins*." *International Journal of Middle East Studies* 45, no. 2 (2013): 211–231.

———. *Professing Selves: Transsexuality and Same-Sex Desire in Contemporary Iran*. Durham, NC: Duke University Press, 2014.

Nseir, Najeeb, and Mazin Bilal. *al-Drama al-Tarikhiyya al-Suriyya: Hulm Nihayat al-Qarn*. Damascus: Ziyad al-Saruji, 1999.

———. *al-Drama al-Televizioniyya al-Suriyya: Qira'a fi Adawat Mushafaha*. Damascus: Dar al-Hisad, 1998.

Olsen, Pelle Valentin. "Cruising Baghdad: Desire between Men in the 1930s Fiction of Dhu al-Nin Ayyub." *Journal of Middle East Women's Studies* 14, no. 1 (March 2018): 25–44.

Palkovitz, Rob, and Glen Palm. "Transitions within Fathering." *Fathering* 7, no. 1 (Winter 2009): 3–22.

Pierret, Thomas. *Baas et Islam en Syrie: La Dynastie Assad Face aux Oulémas*. Paris: Presses Universitaires de France, 2011.

Quéméner, Jean-Marie. *Docteur Bachar Mister Assad: Ses Secrets & Ses Mystères*. Paris: Encre d'Orient, 2011.

Rastegar, Kamran. *Surviving Images: Cinema, War, and Cultural Memory in the Middle East*. Oxford: Oxford University Press, 2015.

Reeser, Todd W. *Masculinities in Theory: An Introduction*. Oxford: Wiley-Blackwell, 2010.

Ricoeur, Paul. *Memory, History, Forgetting*. Translated by Kathleen Blamey and David Pellauer. Chicago: University of Chicago Press, 2004.

Sakr, Naomi, ed. *Arab Media and Political Renewal: Community, Legitimacy, and Public Life*. London: I.B. Taurus, 2009.

———. *Arab Television Today*. London: I.B. Taurus, 2007.

———. "Gaps in the Market: Insights from Scholarly Work on Arab Media Economics." In *Arab Media: Power and Weakness*, edited by Kai Hafez, 185–198. New York: Continuum, 2008.

Salamandra, Christa. "Arab Television Drama Production in the Satellite Era." In *Soap Operas and Telenovelas in the Digital Age: Global Industries and New Audiences*, edited by Diane I. Rios and Mari Castaneda, 275–290. New York: Lang, 2011.

———. "Creative Compromise: Syrian Television Makers between Secularism and Islamism." *Contemporary Islam* 2, no. 3 (2008): 177–189.

———. "Moustache Hairs Lost: Ramadan Television Serials and the Construction of Identity in Damascus, Syria." *Visual Anthropology* 10 (1998): 227–246.

———. *A New Old Damascus: Authenticity and Distinction in Urban Syria*. Bloomington: Indiana University Press, 2004.

———. "Prelude to an Uprising: Syrian Fictional Television and Socio-political Critique." *Jadaliyya*, May 17, 2012. www.jadaliyya.com/pages/index/5578/prelude-to-an-uprising-fictional-television.

———. "Spotlight on the Bashar al-Asad Era: The Television Drama Outpouring." *Middle East Critique* 20, no. 2 (Summer 2011): 157–158.

———. "Through the Back Door: Syrian Television Makers between Secularism and Islamization." In *Arab Media: Power and Weakness*, edited by Kai Hafez, 252–260. New York: Continuum, 2008.

Salamandra, Christa, and Leif Stenberg, eds. *Syria from Reform to Revolt, Volume 2: Culture, Society, and Religion.* New York: Syracuse University Press, 2015.

al-Samman, Hanadi. "Out of the Closet: Representations of Homosexuals and Lesbians in Modern Arabic Literature." *Journal of Arabic Literature* 39 (2008): 270–310.

al-Samman, Hanadi, and Tarek El-Ariss, "Queer Affects: Introduction." *International Journal of Middle East Studies* 45 (2013): 205–209.

Sbai'i, Rafiq. *Thaman al-Hubb: Min al-Sira al-Dhatiyya.* Damascus: Mu'assassat al-Wahda li-l-Sahafa wa-l-Tiba'a wa-l-Nashr, 1998.

Schivelbusch, Wolfgang. *The Culture of Defeat: On National Trauma, Mourning, and Recovery.* Translated by Jefferson Chase. New York: Picador, 2001.

Shafik, Viola. *Popular Egyptian Cinema: Gender, Class, and Nation.* Cairo: American University in Cairo Press, 2007.

Shibli, Adania. "The Making of Bad Palestinian Mothers during the Second Intifada." In *Bad Girls of the Arab World*, edited by Nadia Yaqub and Rula Quawas, 92–111. Austin: University of Texas Press, 2017.

Singerman, Diane. "Youth, Gender and Dignity in the Egyptian Uprising." *Journal of Middle East Women's Studies* 9, no. 3 (Fall 2013): 1–27.

Sontag, Susan. *Regarding the Pain of Others.* New York: Picador, 1993.

Stam, Robert. *Subversive Pleasure: Bakhtin, Cultural Criticism, and Film.* Baltimore: Johns Hopkins University Press, 1989.

Steward, Susan. *On Longing: Narratives of the Miniature, the Gigantic, the Souvenir, the Collection.* Durham, NC: Duke University Press, 1993.

Su, John J. *Ethics and Nostalgia in the Contemporary Novel.* Cambridge: Cambridge University Press, 2005.

Thompson, Elizabeth. *Colonial Citizens: Republican Rights, Paternal Privilege, and Gender in French Syria and Lebanon.* New York: Columbia University Press, 2000.

Ural, Haktan, and Fatma Umut Bespinar. "Class and Habitus in the Formation of Gay Identities, Masculinities, and Respectability in Turkey." *Journal of Middle East Women's Studies* 13, no. 2 (2017): 244–261.

Volk, Lucia. *Memorials and Martyrs in Modern Lebanon.* Bloomington: Indiana University Press, 2010.

Watenpaugh, Keith David. *Being Modern in the Middle East: Revolution, Nationalism, Colonialism, and the Arab Middle Class.* Princeton, NJ: Princeton University Press, 2006.

Wedeen, Lisa. *Ambiguities of Domination: Politics, Rhetoric, and Symbols in Contemporary Syria.* Chicago: University of Chicago Press, 1999.

———. "Ideology and Humor in Dark Times: Notes from Syria." *Critical Inquiry* 39 (Summer 2013): 841–873.

Wieland, Carsten. *A Decade of Lost Chances: Repression and Revolution from Damascus Spring to Arab Spring.* Seattle: Cune Press, 2012.

Yaqub, Nadia, and Rula Quawas. *Bad Girls of the Arab World.* Austin: University of Texas Press, 2017.

Yosef, Raz. *The Politics of Loss and Trauma in Contemporary Israeli Cinema.* New York: Routledge, 2011.

Yusuf, Hassan Sami. *'Atbat al-Alam.* Beirut: Alfurat, 2016.

Ziter, Edward. "Clowns on the Revolution: The Malas Twins and Syrian Oppositional Performance." *Theater Research International* 38, no. 2 (2013): 138.

———. *Political Performance in Syria: From the Six-Day War to the Syrian Uprising.* New York: Palgrave Macmillan, 2015.

FILMOGRAPHY

'Abbas, Bashar Suleiman. *Sani' al-Ahlam* (Creator of Dreams). Directed by Muhammad 'abd al-'Aziz and produced by Abu Dhabi Media, 2019.

——. *Turjuman al-Ashwaq* (Interpreter of Desires). Directed by Muhammad 'abd al-'Aziz and produced by G.E. for Television and Radio Production, 2019.

Abu Shammat, Iyad. *Ghadan Naltaqi* (We'll Meet Tomorrow). Directed by Rami Hanna and produced by Clacket and Abu Dhabi, 2015.

——. *Tango*. Directed by Rami Hanna and produced by Eagle Films, 2018.

Adwan, Mamdouh. *Jarimeh fi al-Zakira* (Crime in the Memory). Directed by Ma'mun al-Boni and produced by al-Sayar li-l-Intaj al-Fani, 1992.

'Akoo, Hoozan. *al-Haibeh*. Directed by Samer al-Barqawi and produced by Cedars Art and Sabbah, 2017.

——. *al-Haibeh: al-'Awda*. Written by Bassam al-Salka, directed by Samer al-Barqawi and produced by Sabbah, 2018.

——. *Bint al-Shah Bandar* (The Daughter of Shah Bandar). Directed by Seif al-Din Sba'i and produced by Media Revolution, 2015.

——. *Delila wa Zaybaq Part One*. Directed by Samir Hossayn and produced by al-'Aj, 2011.

——. *Delila wa Zaybaq Part Two*. Directed by Samir Hossayn and produced by al-'Aj, 2012.

'Ali, Fayezeh. *Ayyamon la Tunsa* (Days That Are Not Remembered). Directed by Ayman Zeidan and produced by Syriana, 2016.

'Amr, Fatah Allah. *Lestoo Jariya* (I'm Not a Slave). Directed by Naji al-To'meh and produced by Syriana and al-Farres Productions, 2017.

'Arafeh, Amal. *Donia (Part One)*. Directed by 'Abd al-Ghani Bilat and produced by Naqoola Abu Samah and al-Jabtoor Entertainment, 1999.

——. *Donia 2015 (Part Two)*. Directed by Zuhair Ahmad Qanoo' and produced by Golden Line, 2015.

——. *Raffat 'Ain* (Blink of the Eye). Directed by Muthana Sobh and produced by Suriya al-Dawliyya li-l-Intaj al-Fanni, 2012.

'Arbaji, George. *Imra' min al-Ramad* (Woman of Ashes). Directed by Najdat Isma'il Anzour and produced by al-Mu'assassa al-'Amma li-l-Intaj al-Televizioni, 2015.

——. *Rozanna*. Directed by 'Arif al-Tawil and produced by Syriana, 2018.

'Arsan, Ayham. *Ra'iha al-Ruh* (Smell of the Soul). Directed by Sohair Sarmini and produced by Syriana, 2018.

'Asaf, 'Ala'. *Shawari' al-Sham al-'Atiqa* (The Old Streets of Damascus). Directed by Gharwan Qahwaji and produced by G.E. for Television and Radio Production, 2019.

Atassi, Yezan, and Lobna Haddad. Episodes 19 and 20, "Sabi aw Bint?" (Boy or Girl?). *Sirat al-Hubb: Min Ajmal Qisas* (A Portrait of Love: From the Most Beautiful Stories). Directed by 'Ammar Radwan and produced by Ghazzal Production and Art Distribution, 2007.

al-'Auda, 'Adnan. *Urkadiya*. Directed by Hatim 'Ali and produced by Ebla, 2017.

———. *Ya Mal al-Sham* (Oh, Precious Sham). Directed by Bassel al-Khatib and produced by al-Mu'assassa al-'Amma li-l-Intaj al-Televizioni wa-l-Idha'i, 2013.

'Awad, Buthayna. *Nisa' min Hadha al-Zaman* (Women of the STime). Directed by Ahmad Ibrahim Ahmad and produced by Qabnad, 2014.

'Awad, Buthayna, and Ghassan al-'Uqla. *Domino*. Directed by Fadi Salim and produced by Phoenix Media Productions, 2016.

al-Aziz, Suleiman 'abd. *Bab al-Hara Part Eight* (The Neighborhood Gate). Directed by Naji al-To'meh and produced by MBC, 2016.

———. *Bab al-Hara Part Nine*. Directed by Naji al-To'meh, supervised by Bassam al-Maleh, and produced by MBC, 2017.

———. *Wahem* (Illusion). Directed by Muhammad Yassin Waqaf and produced by Syriana Art Production and Distribution, 2018.

al-'Azma, Yasser. *Maraya 2011*. Directed by Samer al-Barqawi and produced by Qabnad, 2011.

al-Baba, Hakam, and Selma Karkootli. *Ahlam Abu al-Hana* (Abu al-Hana's Dreams). Directed by Hisham al-Sharbatji and produced by Sharikat 'Ayn al-Sharq li-l-Intaj al-Fanni, 1996.

Baghdadi, Jamal. *Abna' wa Ummahat* (Sons and Mothers). Directed by Muhammad al-Shaliyan and produced by 'Arab li-l-Intaj wa-l-Tawzi' al-Fanni, 1993.

Balji, Fu'ad, *Shoo al-Qissa* (What's the Story). Directed by 'Ali Diyub and produced by Sada al-Sham, 2017.

al-Batoosh, Muhammad. *Maqamat al-'Ishq*. Directed by Ahmad Ibrahim Ahmad and produced by Abu Dhabi Media, 2019

Bayazi, Yehia, and Zeki Mardini. *Zawal* (Vanishing). Directed by Ahmad Ibrahim Ahmad and produced by al-Mu'assassa al-'Amma li-l-Intaj al-Idha'i wa-l-Televizioni, 2016.

Bitar, Rania Ahmad. *Ashwak Na'imeh* (Soft Thorns). Directed by Rasha Hisham Sharbatji and produced by al-'Aj li-l-Intaj, 2005.

Boraq, Zuhair, and Riyad Naasan Agha. *al-Tabibeh* (The Female Doctor). Directed by Muhammad Ferdos Atassi and produced by Suriya li-l-Intaj wa-l-Tawzi' al-Fanni, 1988.

al-Daqr, Ayman. *Harat al-Musharaqa*. Directed by Naji al-To'meh and produced by al-Mu'assassa al-'Amma li-l-Intaj al-Idha'i wa-l-Televizioni, 2015.

al-Dhahabi, Khayri. *Hasiba*. Directed by 'Azmi Mostaffa and produced by Mu'assassat al-Rif li- l-Intaj al-Fanni, 2006.

Diab, Hala. *Ma Malakat Aymanukum* (Those Whom Your Right Hand Possesses). Directed by Najdat Anzour and produced by Najdat Anzour Company, 2010.

———. Part 3 of "al-Samt" (Silence). *Taht Sama' al-Watan* (Under the Nation's Sky). Directed by Najdat Isma'il Anzour and produced by Syrian Radio and TV Production Organization, 2013.

———. *Shifoon*. Directed by Najdat Anzour and produced by Bana li-l-Intaj al-Fanni wa-l-Tawzi', 2011.

al-Din, Diana Kemal. *Wehdan* (Loneliness). Directed by Najdat Anzour and produced by Sama al-Fann al-Dawliyya li-l-Intaj, 2018.

al-Din, 'Imad Seif. *Fitnet Zamanha* (Sedition of Her Era). Directed by 'Imad Seif al Din and produced by Golden Line, 2015.

Drubi, Maher. *al-Mun'ataf* (The Winding). Directed by 'Abd al-Ghani Ballot and produced by al-Heyat al-'Amma li-l-Idha'a wa-l-Televizion, 2011.

Dweear, Shadi. *Romantika*. Directed by Muhanad Qotaish and produced by al-Khalijiyya, 2012.

Fares, Lin. *Gharabib Sud* (Black Crows). Directed by Hisam Qassem, 'Adel Adeeb, and Hussein Sharakat and produced by O3 and Sabbah Pictures, 2017.

Fleihan, Reema. *Qulub Saghireh* (Small Hearts). Directed by 'Ammar Radwan and produced by al-Suriya li-l-Intaj al-Fanni, 2006.

Ghazi, Fadi. *Banati Hayati* (My Daughters, My Life). Directed by Fadi Ghazi and produced by Future Cinema and TV Production, 2017.

———. *Fazlaka Arabiyyeh Part One*. Directed by Fadi Ghazi and produced by Leen Art Production, 2015.

———. *Fazlaka Arabiyyeh Part Two*. Directed by Fadi Ghazi and produced by Fadi Ghazi Art Production and Distribution, 2018.

———. *Jnan Niswan* (Women's Madness). Directed by Fadi Ghazi and produced by Shamyana, 2017.

Haider, 'Abd al-Majid, and 'Ala' 'Assaf. *al-Gharib* (The Stranger). Directed by Muhammad Zuhair Rajab and produced by Qabnad, 2018.

Hajli, Yamen, and 'Ali Wajiha. *Hawa Asfar* (Yellow Air). Directed by Ahmad Ibrahim Ahmad and produced by Cut Art Production & Distribution, 2019.

al-Halabi, Muhammad Kheir. *Qamr Sham* (Damascus Moon). Directed by Merwan Barakat and produced by Golden Line, 2013.

Hamada, Mamdouh. *al-Khirba* (Ruins). Directed by Laith Hajjo and produced by Suriya al-Dawliyya li-l-Intaj, 2011.

———. *al-Waq Waq*. Directed by Laith Hajjo and produced by Emar al-Sham, 2018.

———. *Dhoboo al-Shanati* (Hurry Up and Pack!). Directed by Laith Hajjo and produced by Sama al-Fann Production International, 2014.

Hamed, Ahmed. *Tawq al-Banat* (Necklace of Girls). Directed by Muhammad Zuhair Rajab and produced by Qabnad, 2014.

———. *Tawq al-Banat Part Two*. Directed by Iyad Nahhas and produced by Qabnad, 2015.

———. *Tawq al-Banat Part Three*. Directed by Iyad Nahhas and produced by Qabnad, 2016.

———. *Tawq al-Banat Part Four*. Directed by Muhammad Zuhair Rajab and produced by Qabnad, 2017.

———. *Tawq al-Banat Part Five*. Directed by Muhammad Zuhair Rajab and produced by Qabnad, 2018.

Hamed, Seif Rida. *Doubt*. Directed by Merwan Barakat and produced by Version, 2018.

Hanna, Amal. *Jalasat Nisa'iya* (Women's Gatherings). Directed by al-Muthana Sobh and Produced by Suriya al-Dawliyya li-l-Intaj al-Fanni, Damascus, 2011.

Hanna, Reem. *al-Katib* (The Writer). Directed by Rami Hanna and produced by Eagle Films, 2019.

———. *Lo'bat al-Mawt* (Game of Death). Directed by Laith Hajjo and Samer al-Barqawi, 2013.

———. *Rasa'il al-Hubb wa-l-Harb* (Letters of Love and War). Directed by Bassel al-Khatib and produced by Suriya al-Dawliyya li-l-Intaj al-Fanni, Damascus, 2007.

———. *24 Qirat* (24 Carat). Directed by Laith Hajjo and produced by Eagle Films, 2015.

Haydar, Khalid. *Yawmiyyat Mudir 'Amm* (Diaries of a Director General, Part Two). Directed by Zuhair Ahmad Qanoo' and produced by Syrian Art Production International, 2011.

Hinawi, Sa'di. *al-Raboos* (Fright). Directed by Iyad Nahhas and produced by Zawa li-l-Injtaj al-Fanni and Nahhas li-l-Intaj al-Fanni, 2017.

Homsi, Na'im. *Sana Uwla al-Zawaj* (First Year of Marriage). Directed by Yamen Ibrahim and produced by Landmark, 2017.

Isma'il, Hadeel. *Ghafwa al-Qulub* (The Slumber of Hearts). Directed by Rasha Kawkash and produced by G.E. for Television and Radio Production, 2019.

al-Ja'foori, Mahmud. *Kashf al-Iqna'* (Unveiling the Masks). Directed by Hassan Dawood and produced by Jeeda Films and al-Masar Art, 2011.

Jaha, ʻUthman. *Bila Ghamad* (Without Cover). Directed by Fahd Miri and produced by Syriana (Diana Jabour), 2016.

———. *Harun al-Rashid*. Directed by ʻAbd al-Bari Abu al-Kheir and produced by Golden Line, 2018.

Jermani, ʻAla. *Suq al-Waraq* (Market of Papers). Directed by Ahmad Ibrahim Ahmad and produced by General Establishment TV and Radio Production, 2011.

al-Jundi, Jihan, and Ahmad Qassar. *Kawma* (Coma). Directed by Maher Slaybi and Zuhair Ahmad Qanooʻ and produced by Ebla International Cinema and TV Production, 2018.

Kawkash, Oussama. *al-Haʼirat* (Helpless Women). Directed by Samir Hossayn and produced by Syriana, 2013.

———. *Bi-Intizar al-Yasmin* (Waiting for Jasmin). Directed by Samir Hossayn and produced by ABC li-l-Intaj al-Fanni, 2015.

———. *Fi Qalb al-Lahib* (Center of Fire). Directed by Muhammad Zuhair Rajab and produced by al-Hani li-l-Intaj wa-l-Tawziʻ al-Fanni, 2013.

al-Khaled, ʻAnood. *al-Haraʼir* (The Independent Ones). Directed by Bassel al-Khatib and produced by Syriana, 2015.

Khalifa, Khaled. *al-ʻArrab: Taht Hezam* (The Godfather: Under the Belt). Directed by Hatim ʻAli and produced by Clacket, 2016.

———. *al-Miftah* (The Key). Directed by Hisham Sharbatji and produced by al-Muʼassassa al-ʻAmma li-l-Intaj al-Idhaʻi wa-l-Televizioni, 2012.

———. *Sirat al-Jalali* (A Portrait of the Jalali Family). Directed by Haitham Haqqi and produced by Reelfilms Production, Syria, 2000.

———. *Zaman al-Khawf* (A Time of Fear). Directed by Inas Haqqi and produced by Reelfilms Production, 2007.

Kiwan, Shadi. *Azma ʻAiliyeh* (Family Crisis). Directed by Hisham Sharbatji and produced by Syriana, 2017.

Koussa, Rami. *al-Qurban* (Sacrifice). Directed by ʻAla al-Din Kawkash and produced by Syriana, 2014.

al-Maghut, Muhammad, and Durayd Lahham. *Kasak ya Watan* (Cheers to the Homeland). Directed by Khaldun al-Maleh and produced by Usra Tishrin, 1979.

———. *Wayn al-Ghalat?* (Where's the Mistake?). Directed by Khaldun al-Maleh and produced by Studio Shamra, 1979.

Marchalian, Claudia. *Ma Fi*. Directed by Rasha Sharbatji and produced by Sabbah Media Productions, 2019.

———. *Samra* (Samra). Directed by Rasha Sharbatji and produced by Sabbah Media Productions, 2016.

———. *Ya Reit* (I Wish). Directed by Filip Asmar and produced by Eagle Films, 2016.

al-Mardini, Bashar. *Qosmeh wa Hubb* (Destiny and Love). Directed by ʻAmar Soheil Tamim and produced by Shamyana Art, 2018.

Mardini, Talal. *Ayyam al-Dirasa* (Days of Our Studies). Directed by Mostafa al-Barqawi and produced by Media li-l-Sawtiyyat wa Marayyat, 2012.

———. *Khatun*. Directed by Tamer Ishaq and produced by Golden Line, 2016.

———. *Khatun Part Two*. Directed by Tamer Ishaq and produced by Golden Line, 2017.

———. *Khatun Part Three*. Directed by Tamer Ishaq and produced by Golden Line, 2018.

———. *Rijal al-ʻIzz* (Men of Honor). Directed by ʻAlaʼ al-Din Kawkash and produced by Ghazzal, 2011.

Mashhadi, Yam. *Prova*. Directed by Rasha Sharbatji and produced by Eagle Films, 2019.

———. *Qalam Humra* (Lipstick). Directed by Hatim ʻAli and produced by Ebla International for Cinema and TV Production, 2014.

———. *Takht Sharqi* (Eastern Bed). Directed by Rasha Sharbatji and produced by Sharikat al-'Aj li-l-Intaj, 2010.

Miri, Fahd. *Fursa Akhira* (Last Change). Directed by Fahd Miri and produced by Qabnad, 2018.

Mustafa, Muhannad Qateesh Hassan. *Huwajez 'Abara* (Passing Borders). Directed by Muhannad Qateesh and produced by Hatim li-l-Intaj al-Fanni, 2018.

Nasrawi, Kamil. *Watan Haff* (Bare Homeland). Directed by Muhammad Ferdos Atassi and Muhannad Qateesh and produced by Syrian Radio and TV Production Organization, 2013.

Nseir, Najeeb. *Chello.* Directed by Samer al-Barqawi and produced by Eagle films and O3 Productions, 2015.

Nseir, Najeeb, and Hassan Sami Yusuf. *al-Sarab* (Mirage). Directed by Merwan Barakat and produced by al-Jabri li-l-Intaj, 2011.

———. *Fawda* (Chaos). Directed by Samir Husayn and produced by Sama al-Fann al-Dawliyya li-l-Intaj, 2018.

———. *Nisa' Saqirat* (Little Women). Directed by Basel al-Khatib, 1999.

———. *Zaman al-'Ar* (The Time of Shame). Directed by Rasha Sharbatji and produced by Sharikat al-'Aj li-l-Intaj, 2009.

'Othman, Reem Jamil. *Hakam al-Hawa* (Love's Judgment). Directed by Muhammad Yassin Waqaf and produced by Qabnad, 2017.

Qal'i, Nihad. *Maqalib Ghawwar* (Ghawwar's Tricks). Directed by Naqoola abu Samah and produced by al-Sharikat al-Televizion Lubnan wa-l-Mashriq, 1966.

———. *Milh wa Sukkar* (Salt and Sugar). Directed by Khaldun al-Maleh and produced by Studio Shamra, 1973.

Qanoo', Zuhair Ahmad. *Shahr Zaman* (Once Upon a Month). Directed by Zuhair Ahmad Qanoo' and produced by Clacket and Syriana, 2015.

Qatlan, Khaldun. *Qanadil al-'Ushaq* (Candles of Lovers). Directed by Seif al-Din Sbai'i and produced by Sama al-Fann al-Dawliyya li-l-Intaj, 2017.

Qawuq, Merwan. *al-Khan* (The Khan). Directed by Muhammad Suleiman Ma'roof and produced by Golden Line, 2017.

———. *al-'Ush Dabbur* (The Hornet's Nest, Part One). Directed by Tamer Ishaq and produced by Golden Line, 2010.

———. *al-'Ush Dabbur* (The Hornet's Nest, Part Two). Directed by Tamer Ishaq and produced by Golden Line, 2011.

———. *'Atr al-Sham Part One* (Perfume of Sham). Directed by Muhammad Zuhair Rajab and produced by Qabnad, 2016.

———. *'Atr al-Sham Part Two* (Perfume of Sham). Directed by Muhammad Zuhair Rajab and produced by Qabnad, 2017.

———. *'Atr al-Sham Part Three* (Perfume of Sham). Directed by Muhammad Zuhair Rajab and produced by Qabnad, 2018.

———. *'Atr al-Sham Part Four* (Perfume of Sham). Directed by Muhammad Zuhair Rajab and produced by Qabnad, 2019.

———. *Bab al-Hara Part Ten.* Directed by Muhammad Zuhair Rajab and produced by Qabnad, 2019.

———. *Harat al-Aseel* (Neighborhood of the Noble One). Directed by Muhamad Ma'roof and produced by Qabnad, 2015.

———. *Haret al-Tanabir.* Directed by Fadi Saleem and produced by Golden Line, 2012.

———. *Raqs al-Afa'i* (Dance of Snakes). Directed by Kinan al-Iskandari and produced by Majmu'a al-Asail al-Dawla, 2014.

——. *Tahun al-Shar* (Mill of Evil). Directed by Naji al-To'meh and produced by Golden Line, 2012.

——. *Tahun al-Shar* (Mill of Evil, Part Two). Directed by Naji al-To'meh and produced by Golden Line, 2013.

——. *Warda Shamiyyeh* (Shami Flower). Directed by Tamer Ishaq and produced by Golden Line, 2018.

Qawuq, Merwan, and Ranim 'Awda. *Jarah al-Ward* (Wound of the Flower). Directed by Muhammad Suleiman Ma'roof and produced by Golden Line, 2018.

Qoshaqji, Fadi. *Fi Zuruf Ghamida* (Obscure Circumstances). Directed by al-Muthana Sobh and produced by Sama al-Fann al-Dawliyya li-l-Intaj, 2015.

——. *Laysa Saraban* (It's Not a Mirage). Directed by al-Muthana Sobh and produced by Suriya al-Dawliyya li-l-Intaj, Damascus, 2008.

——. *Nabtadi Mnein al-Hikayeh?* (Where Do We Begin the Story?). Directed by Seif al-Din Sbai'i and produced by Syriana, 2016.

——. *Ta'b al-Mishwar* (Exhaustion of the Journey). Directed by Seif al-Din Sbai'i and produced by Bana Productions, 2011.

——. *Urwah 'Ariya* (Naked Souls). Directed by Laith Hajjo and produced by Syriana and Clacket, 2012.

Qussar, Ahmad. *al-'Arrab: Taht al-Hizam* (The Godfather: Under the Belt). Directed by Hatim 'Ali and produced by Clacket, 2016.

Ridwan, Samer Fahd. *al-Wilada min al-Khasira* (Born from the Loins). Directed by Rasha Sharbatji and produced by Clacket, 2011.

——. *al-Wilada min al-Khasira: Menbar al-Mawta Part Three* (Born from the Loins: Platform of Death). Directed by Rasha Sharbatji, Seif al-Din Sba'i and produced by Clacket, 2013.

——. *al-Wilada min al-Khasira: Sa'at al-Jamr Part Two* (Born from the Loins: Time of Embers). Directed by Rasha Sharbatji and produced by Clacket, 2012.

——. *Daqiqat al-Samt* (Moment of Silence). Directed by Shawqi al-Majiri and produced by Cedars Art Production and Ebla, 2019.

——. *La'nat al Tin* (Curse of the Clay). Directed by Ahmad Ibrahim Ahmad and produced by Qabnad K, 2010.

Sabri, Yara, and Reema Fleihan. *Quyud al-Ruh* (Bonds of the Soul). Directed by Maher Slaybi and produced by Ferdos Production, 2010.

Sa'd al-Din, Mahmud. *al-Shabbiha* (Resemblance). Directed by Firas Dehni and produced by Alanoud Art Production, 2012.

Sa'id, Iman. *Khamsa wa Nus* (Five-Thirty). Directed by Filip Asmar and produced by Sabbah Media Productions, 2019.

——. *Musafat Aman* (Distance of Security). Directed by Laith Hajjo and produced by Emar alSham, 2019.

Saleem, Fadi. *'An al-Hawa wa-l-Jawa* (Of Love and Passion). Directed by Fadi Saleem and Produced by G.E. for Television and Radio Production, 2019.

al-Salka, Bassem. *al-Haibeh: al-Hisad* Part Three (al-Haiba: The Harvest). Directed by Samer al-Barqawi and produced by Cedars Art, 2019.

Salka, Samir. *Nus Yawm* (Half a Day). Directed by Samer al-Barqawi and produced by O3 and Sabbah Media, 2016.

Sayf, Walid. *'Omar.* Directed by Hatim 'Ali and produced by MBC and O3, 2012.

al-Sayyed, Wassim. *Ruznama* (Calendar). Directed by Wassim al-Sayyed and produced by Syria Drama, 2013.

Shahadat, Bilal, and Nadine Jaber. *Law...* (If...). Directed by Samer al-Barqawi and produced by Eagle Films, Sabbah Media, and O3 Productions, 2014.

Shaya, Farah, and Salam Kasiri. *Tariq* (A Road). Directed by Rasha Sharbatji and produced by Sabbah Media, 2018.

Shishekly, Nur. *Alaghat Khasa* (Intimate Relations). Directed by Rasha Sharbatji and produced by Online, 2015.

——. *Jarimat Shaghaf* (Crime of Passion). Directed by Waleed Naseef and produced by Media 7 Revolution, 2016.

——. *Sabaya 5* (Your Women Part Five). Directed by Mahmoud Dawawima and produced by Bana, 2013.

Shishekly, Nur, and Mazin Taha. *Madrasat al-Hubb* (School of Love). Directed by Safwan Na'mu and produced by Black2, 2016.

——. *Madrasat al-Hubb* (School of Love). Directed by Safwan Na'mu and produced by Black2, 2017.

——. *Mudhakirat 'Ashiqa Sabiqa* (Diaries of a Former Lover). Directed by Hisham Sharbatji and produced by Mars Media, 2017.

Suleiman, Hazim. *Abu Janti Part Two*. Directed by 'Anmar Radwan and produced by Ward, 2012.

——. *Hudud Shaqiqa* (Brotherly Borders). Directed by Oussama al-Hamd and produced by Ferdos, 2013.

——. *'Indama Tashaikh al-Dhi'b* (When the Wolf Grows Old). Directed by 'Amer Fahd and produced by ISEE Media Productions, 2019

——. *Shawq*. Directed by Rasha Hisham Sharbatji and produced by Emar al-Sham, 2017.

Taha, Mazin. *al-Tawarid*. Directed by Mazin al-Sa'idi and produced by Clacket, 2016.

——. *Julia*. Directed by Elie F. Habib and produced by Eagle Films, 2018.

——. *Karamel*. Directed by Elie F. Habib and produced by Eagle Films, 2017.

——. *Sukar Wasat* (Medium Quantity of Sugar). Directed by al-Muthana Sobh and produced by Sama al-Fann al-Dawliyya li-l-Intaj, 2013.

Wahbi, Rafi. *al-'Arrab: Nadi al-Sharq* (Club of the East). Directed by Hatim 'Ali and produced by Clacket, 2015.

——. *Helawat al-Ruh* (Beauty of the Soul). Directed by Shawqi al-Majiri and produced by Abu Dhabi, 2014.

——. *Sa-Na'ud Ba'da Qalil* (We'll Return Soon). Directed by Laith Hajjo and produced by Clacket, 2013.

Wahbi, Rafi, and Bassem Breish. *Bi-dun Qaid* (Undocumented). Directed by Amin Dora and produced by Spring Entertainment, 2017.

Wajih, 'Ali, and Yamen al-Hajali. *Ahmar* (Red). Directed by Jude Sa'id and produced by Sama al-Fann al-Dawliyya li-l-Intaj, 2016.

Yusuf, Hassan M. *Fi Hadrat al-Ghiyab* (In the Presence of Absence). Directed by Najdat Isma'il Anzour and produced by Firas Ibrahim productions, 2011.

——. *Milh al-Hayat* (Salt of Life). Directed by Ayman Zeidan and produced by al-Mu'assassa al-'Amma li-l-intaj al-Televizioni/RGB Productions, 2011.

Yusuf, Hassan Sami. *al-Ghufran* (Pardon). Directed by Hatim 'Ali and produced by al-'Aj, 2011.

——. *al-Nadam* (Regret). Directed by Laith Hajjo and produced by Sama al-Fann al-Dawliyya li-l-Intaj, 2016.

al-Za'im, Wafiq. *al-Za'im* (The Local Leader). Directed by Mu'min al-Malla and produced by MBC, 2011.

Zainab, Hani. *Harim al-Shawish* (Wives of the Policemen). Directed by As'ad 'Aid and Produced by Qabnad, 2018.

Zakariyya, Ghassan, and Ghazi al-Daniba. *Abna' al-Rashid: al-Amin wa-l-Ma'mun* (The Sons of al-Rashid: al-Amin and al-Ma'mun). Directed by Shawqi al-Majiri and produced by Arab Telemedia Group, 2006.

al-Zayed, Muhammad Zaid. *Zaman al-Barghut* (Time of Flies). Directed by Ahmad Ibrahim Ahmad and produced by al-Manar, 2012.

INDEX

ABOUT THE AUTHOR

REBECCA JOUBIN is associate professor and chair of Arab studies at Davidson College. She lived and conducted research in Syria for close to a decade. Her articles in English and Arabic have appeared in the *International Journal of Middle East Studies*, *Journal of Middle East Women's Studies*, *Middle East Journal*, *Arab Studies Journal*, *al-Warda*, *Hayat al-Sinama'iyya*, and *al-Mada*.